Management of New Technologies for Global Competitiveness

Management of New Technologies for Global Competitiveness

Christian N. Madu

Q

Quorum Books
Westport, Connecticut • London

Library of Congress Cataloging-in-Publication Data

Madu, Christian N. (Christian Ndubisi)
  Management of new technologies for global competitiveness /
Christian N. Madu.
        p.   cm.
  Includes index.
  ISBN 0-89930-713-2 (alk. paper)
  1. Industrial management.   2. Total quality management.
3. Technological innovations—Management.   4. Industrial management—
United States.   5. Industrial management—Japan.   I. Title.
HD31.M2815   1993
658.5'62—dc20   92-31712

British Library Cataloguing in Publication Data is available.

Library of Congress Catalog Card Number: 92-31712
ISBN: 0-89930-713-2

First published in 1993

Quorum Books, 88 Post Road West, Westport, CT 06881
An imprint of Greenwood Publishing Group, Inc.

Printed in the United States of America

The paper used in this book complies with the
Permanent Paper Standard issued by the National
Information Standards Organization (Z39.48-1984).

10 9 8 7 6 5 4 3 2 1

Contents

III. STRATEGIC MANAGEMENT

IV. KNOWLEDGE-BASED TECHNIQUES

V. PRODUCT DESIGN AND INVENTORY MANAGEMENT

Figures and Tables

Figures

Tables

Preface

Management of new technologies is a critical issue facing the corporate world today. We have in the recent times witnessed the proliferation of new technologies and, also, a shorter life cycle for these technologies. Increasingly, many executives believe that capital investment in new or advanced technologies is necessary in order to improve productivity. As the United States responds to its declining rate of growth in productivity, automation has assumed a critical role. The importance of advanced and new technologies in enhancing productivity, and in improving quality and competitiveness, is widely accepted. The pressure to manufacture high-quality products or provide high-quality services that meet the specifications and demands of consumers has led to a systemic approach to the management of technology. Many companies today rely on advanced technologies to achieve high precision, maintain tolerance, and provide high value-ended services and products.

Advanced technologies are widely applied in both the manufacturing and the service sectors, significantly influencing the quality of services delivered. For instance, many service institutions such as banks, insurance, and health care have drastically improved the quality of their services by making effective use of technology. Imagine what it would be like to conduct today's financial transactions in a bank that is not computerized. Obviously, the waiting time for a basic transaction would be high, turnout would be low, cash flow would be limited, and customer goodwill would be lost as they developed negative perceptions of the services rendered by that bank. Clearly, these factors would negatively influence the productivity, quality, and competitiveness of the bank. Technology is, therefore, instrumental in the survival of modern corporations.

Today's environment is dynamic and complex. Corporations have to be cognizant of both their operating and their external environments. Hardly a day passes without mention of the competition U.S. companies face, especially from the Japanese. Total quality management has become critical to understanding why American companies are losing their competitive edge. This book tackles this important problem through a holistic approach to the management of new technologies. It considers both manufacturing and service sectors, and looks at different aspects of process technology to determine how it can help achieve global competitiveness.

The book is divided into five *parts. Part 1*, Total Quality Management, features articles that offer pragmatic approaches to the management of quality. The role of expert systems in quality assurance is also presented. Furthermore, a distinction is made between Japanese and American production management systems, and the role of notable quality-management philosophers is described. The articles in *Part 2*, Selection and Implementation of New Technologies, demonstrate the shortcomings of cost-accounting techniques in justifying the use of new technologies. The authors identify the strategic functions of new technologies that may not be easily captured by traditional cost-accounting techniques, and provide procedures to effectively consider tactical and strategic factors in selecting such new technologies. A project-management approach to implementation and adoption of new technologies is also provided. *Part 3*, Strategic Management, demonstrates the role of top management and technology in improving organizational performance. Emphasis is on specific applications—manufacturing, health care, and information systems. *Part 4*, Knowledge-based Techniques, deals with the role of artificial intelligence and expert systems in management of new technologies. The articles in this section show how knowledge-based systems can improve the quality of decision making at different levels in the organization. Also, effective use of knowledge to meet organizational challenges is demonstrated. *Part 5*, Product Design and Inventory Management, deals with performance evaluation of specific technologies, such as flexible manufacturing systems, robotics, and computer-integrated enterprises. Procedures are provided to reduce set-up time in order to effectively manage inventory via a just-in-time system. Product design is also discussed as an emerging competitive factor.

Finally, this comprehensive approach reveals the different approaches to managing new technologies in order to achieve global competitiveness. The systemic approach of this book makes it an important reference book, useful as a basis for courses in new technology management or as a supplementary text for production and operations management classes.

Acknowledgements

I extend my sincere thanks to all the contributors in this book. Your dedication to meet the deadline and produce outstanding research work is rewarding. I hope that you will all be proud of this book. I also thank my editor, Eric Valentine, for his support, and my production editor, Nita Romer for a thorough review of this manuscript.

I especially thank Ms. Diana Ward, Editor, Lubin Letters, at Pace University, who has always been quite helpful and supportive of my research endeavors; Ms. Koula Kilaras, Secretary and Coordinator of the Accounting Department, at Pace University, for her utmost dedication to my work; and my graduate assistant, Thomas Tsai, for conducting library and computer searches for some of the chapters of this book.

Finally, but not least, I especially thank my wife, Assumpta, and our three sons, Chinedu, Chike, and Chidi, for their love and support.

Christian N. Madu

I

Total Quality Management

Chapter 1

Strategic Total Quality Management (STQM)

Christian N. Madu and Chu-hua Kuei

Recently, there has been a significant shift in the quality movement from traditional quality-assurance practice to total quality management (TQM). Total quality management is a customer-driven approach to quality, emphasizing the involvement and commitment of every employee in an organization to provide quality products and services. Customers are increasingly sophisticated, with increasingly more complex demands to be satisfied. The increase in international competition also suggests that only quality-driven companies will survive. Therefore, for a company to achieve quality, customer needs, expectations, and aspirations must be satisfied. Mercer (1991) (project director, European Council on Quality, The Conference Board, Europe) identifies key quality issues. If TQM is achieved, the company is able to improve productivity, competitiveness, and market share. Although total quality management is today's fashionable management practice, the literature has failed to indicate how to further improve quality. van Ham (secretary general, European Foundation for Quality Management) points out that "Executives who believe in only applying the existing body of knowledge are missing the point—using existing standards and systems will only give at best, an average result" (1991). In Deming's "Profound Knowledge," he points out that (1) experience teaches nothing unless studied with the aid of a theory; and (2) an example teaches nothing unless studied with the aid of a theory (1986). Therefore, our intention here is to offer a strategy for quality management.

To begin, we broadly define or clarify some of TQM concepts.

● *Quality.* Quality is seen from the perspective of the customer. Products and services must be produced to conform to customer specifications. Thus, tight specifications must be maintained, and performance standards should ensure that customer requirements are met. With TQM, the attempt is to prevent rather than detect errors.

● *Cost of Quality.* The cost of quality is based on Juran's cost-of-quality accounting system. This method shows top management the cost of not producing products or services that are "fit for use." As March (1990) notes, money is the language that top management understands. Once they see what quality costs, they listen. Juran has identified four types of costs: internal and external failure costs and prevention and appraisal costs.

● *Organizational Culture.* Organizational culture must change to embrace the new focus on customer-driven quality. A flexible, horizontal management approach can effectively implement TQM. Every employee, from top to bottom, must be committed to TQM as a business strategy. A never-ending commitment to continuous improvement must be maintained if TQM is to be achieved.

● *Process of Change*.   Change is inevitable in a "new" organization if total quality management is emphasized.   The change may include new processes to adopt more precise technologies; flexible and efficient human resource development through education, training, and retraining; shifts in communication patterns and information flow; increased power sharing through teamwork and greater responsibilities for workers; top management commitment to and participation in total quality management; a heightened understanding of customer need.   These new directions necessitate management of change in a proactive manner to achieve organizational goals and mission, and accomplish the vision set by the organization.

● *Quality Improvements*.   Quality is improved only if potential problem areas can be isolated and measures adopted to prevent rather than cure quality problems later. Obviously, quality improvement starts with clear and concise organizational objectives that are customer focused.   The process technology and human resources should target specific outcomes rather than outputs.   To effectively achieve this, customer requirements must be fully understood.   Improving quality also requires maintaining quality from suppliers.   They should not be selected simply on the basis of cost, but rather also on their ability to meet quality guidelines.

In this chapter, we introduce a new approach, Strategic Total Quality Management (STQM).   STQM can serve as an extension of TQM.

THE PHILOSOPHY OF STRATEGIC TOTAL QUALITY MANAGEMENT

Our Strategic Total Quality Management philosophy is based on developing a systemic view of quality.   This approach views quality as the driving force to ensuring the survivability and competitiveness of a company.   However, rather than view quality only from the standpoint of direct products and services, we see quality as a reflection of *overall performance*.   In other words, the performance of a company in its immediate and extended environment in all matters—even those that may not be related directly to the product—is assessed as an attribute of quality.   For example, the claim by a major fast-food chain such as McDonald's that its paper bags are "made with recycled paper" is intended to convey the message that the company is socially responsible and environmentally conscious.   The McDonald's package further states the most obvious, "Please put litter in its place."   Clearly, these messages are a response to growing concerns of consumers about degradation of the environment by manufacturers who do not care about pollution or that are not socially conscious.

Also, banks with holdings in South Africa during the divestment period of the 1980s lost a share of their business from municipal councils, major pension funds, and private individuals who disagreed with apartheid policies.   Fur manufacturers have been the target of negative campaigns and have seen a subsequent drop in sales revenue as a result of activities by animal rights groups.   Corporations like Exxon, Petroba, and Union Carbide have been involved in serious environmental accidents and have suffered from a bad reputation and a poor public image that oftentimes implies the quality of products and services are secondary.

Thus STQM integrates socially responsible and environmentally sensitive decisions into total quality management in order to improve global competitiveness.   It does this by strengthening and enhancing the company's quality objectives.   These issues have become so critical that special government agencies have been set up in the United States to deal with them.   For example, the Office of Technology Assessment (OTA), the Food and Drug Administration (FDA), and the Environmental Protection Agency (EPA) assess issues of environmental quality and socially responsible actions by manufacturers and service providers. The Technology Assessment Act enacted in 1972 and the Clean Air Act revised in 1990 show the growing concern by not only the government but also the public about these vital issues. Yet the current focus on total quality management has not really addressed these concerns.

TQM is widely applied today. The Conference Board of New York's recent report *Global Perspectives on Total Quality* includes viewpoints of top executives from thirteen countries (1991). From this report it is obvious that TQM has been embraced wholeheartedly. There is a unanimity of thought on what TQM is and how to achieve its goals: every company must adopt TQM to remain competitive. We can also deduce that if companies are to successfully implement TQM and significantly reduce product defects, quality and conformance to customer needs very soon will no longer be a competitive weapon or an instrument for survival. In fact, van Ham (1991) points out that the cellular telephone division of Motorola—the winner of the 1988 Malcolm Baldridge Quality Award—reduced its defects per million from 1,000 to 100 between 1985 and 1988; in addition, this division has a target of 4 defects per million in 1992. van Ham further notes that quality companies will soon be able to measure defects in parts per *billion*. This concept—popularly known as "six sigma"—is widely publicized and many more companies are targeting it. Obviously, when this level of quality is achieved, product defects will be almost nonexistent. This good news should be considered a warning that the era of the "quality product" as a competitive weapon is ending. When a company and its competitors all achieve zero defects and their products are all designed to customer specifications and are "fit for use," no one company has a competitive edge. Then strategies such as marketing and technological innovation will become prominent, no longer hampered by the bad publicity that comes from defects.

The customer-oriented focus and market-driven quality, as described in the literature and by individual companies, are often narrow, focusing primarily on the ability of a product or service to satisfy a customer's direct need. But they are no longer relevant, with today's increasing awareness of the environment and the need for environmental protection. Thus, to deal with these dire issues, we use STQM, which encompasses all aspects of TQM.

Dimensions of Strategic Total Quality Management

Quality is a critical aspect of the management function, no longer left entirely to the operators. But a top-management commitment is necessary to realize improvements in quality. The continuing competitiveness of U.S. corporations depends on how well quality is managed. Several strategies to quality management have been developed, especially with growing emphasis on *total* quality management.

The dimensions of Strategic Total Quality Management and their definitions are listed in Table 1.1. These dimensions have two main focuses—global issues and strategic planning—grouped accordingly.

In order to be competitive, a company must react to its strategic targets. The strategic targets identified in STQM are customers, system transformation, cultural transformation, and suppliers. All these strategic targets influence Strategic Total Quality Management. Table 1.2 presents these targets as the new management focus. A classification is also developed for STQM dimensions based on these four strategic targets and the two main focuses for the future.

Table 1.1
Dimensions of Strategic Total Quality Management
_____

o **Customer Needs**
The first objective should be to identify customer needs. Evidently, products and services are produced to satisfy some needs. The customer's needs must be identified and appropriate product designs instituted for satisfying those needs. Management should not focus completely on Wall Street and the stockholders, but also on customers, society, and the environment. Through marketing surveys, customer needs can be identified. A systematic approach such as the quality function deployment can then be used to link customer needs and a firm's strategic plan or to translate customer needs into specific designs and specifications. Daily management techniques can also be used by a firm and its suppliers to meet customers' needs.[1]

o **Capabilities and Weaknesses**
This is the process of linking our resources to the demands. We need to identify the strengths we have in terms of process technology, human resources—skilled labor and management—and also the weaknesses and how they influence our ability to satisfy the customer's needs. Internal scrutiny and environmental scan at both business and functional levels are needed for identifying a firm's strengths and weaknesses and its business opportunities and threats. For environmental scanning at the business level, Porter's five-forces model (i.e., new entrants, suppliers, rivalry, buyers, and substitutes) will be a very useful tool to apply.[2] Also, Porter's value chain model can be applied for the internal scrutiny.[3]

o **Design Specifications**
Appropriate design specifications are developed with targets and performance measures. The role of each operator is also made clear and the operators are given the necessary tools to achieve the quality goals. Performance and appraisal measures are also made obvious to those involved.

o **Appropriate Process Technology**
Appropriate process technology must be in place and should be capable of meeting the design specifications, tolerances, target levels, and product conformance requirements.

o **Management Commitment**
Top management must be committed to the goal of quality improvement. This must be clearly stated and management actions taken to ensure that quality improvement goals are achieved. Top management should also lead quality teams to ensure that the defined objectives and design specifications are achieved. Top management participation will help to deal with common causes and operators will have the incentive to deal with special causes.

o **Organizational Vision and Mission**
The organization's vision, mission and value system must be shaped around total quality management (see Table 1.2).

o **Management of Change**
Strategies to manage and cope with change should be adopted to maintain order. Change should be seen as inevitable and it should be planned for to minimize the associated risks. Organizational culture and structure must be adapted to change if the quest for continuous improvement, innovation, and creativity are to be achieved.

o **Organizational Flexibility**
Implicit in the definition of change is the fact that organizational flexibility must exist. The organization should not be static and should encourage the flow of new ideas and information to improve the management of quality. A new organizational

Table 1.1 (continued)

form is made up of clusters of working groups. Each working group is responsible for the production of a specific product. A typical group on the floor shop includes quality engineers, maintenance people, and mechanics.

○ **Multidisciplinary Background**
Management must develop multidisciplinary background through education, training, and hands-on experience. This exposure to different functional areas will help unite the functional goals to that of the organization. The cross-functional background will help management to understand the importance and the implications of quality in each functional area in achieving total quality.

○ **Teamwork**
Quality circles or quality teams must be established to share information on work-in-process. These teams should have the power to make work-related decisions. Team members should have the cross-functional background needed for effective decision making.

○ **Employee Motivation and Organizational Cultural Change**
Employees have to be motivated to do their work right the first time. In order to achieve this, organizational culture has to change to acknowledge the importance of quality and group work.

○ **Training and Retraining**
Workers need to be continuously trained and retrained on the different aspects of quality especially the cost of quality and its relationship to the survivability of the organization. They need to be frequently reminded of the importance of satisfying customer needs and specifications in order for the organization to survive.

○ **Education**
In-service training should be instituted to educate workers on the application of quality techniques such as statistical process control (SPC), robust quality designs, and quality philosophies in line with organizational quality objectives. Workers should be trained to use statistical charts and financial planning so they can position their firm in a financial grid and compare its success to that of competitors.

○ **Never-ending Philosophy**
A policy for continuous improvement must be adopted. The goal should be to continuously seek quality improvement. There is no amount of improvement that is enough. Also, everyone must participate in achieving total quality.

○ **Environmental Sensitivity**
There must be a sensitivity to the environment. How is the organization's performance influencing the environment (e.g., ozone depletion) and how are the significant interest groups reacting? Forecasting of future needs and reactions of consumers to certain operations should also be conducted. This entails environmental impact assessment.

○ **Benchmarking**
The organization should always compare itself to its competitors in the same industry and should always aim to outperform its competitors. Functional benchmarking (looking outside one's industry at best of class in a given function) should also be used to improve the organization's performance. To effectively use benchmarking, one must have a good understanding of the industry and be willing to learn from world-class competitors.

○ **Cost Analysis of Quality**
The aim of a strategic approach to quality should be to increase profitability, increase market share, and become more competitive. These goals can be achieved if top management understand that the high cost of poor-quality items diminishes profit

Table 1.1 (continued)

margins and market share. Social costs should also be considered as part of the cost of poor quality. For example, what cost is incurred through litigations when an automaker installs a braking system that fails under normal use and contributes to loss of life and destruction of properties?

o **Organizational Commitment to Employees**

The organization must show concern for its labor force and its immediate environment. Workers must feel that their jobs are secure and that they have a future in the corporation. There should be no limit to their organizational achievements. They must perceive themselves as having equal opportunity in terms of organizational aspiration. The organization should operate as a team with each member actively seeking means to improve quality.

o **Image Building and Social Responsibility**

The organization should invest in good causes. It should participate actively in its immediate environment in worthy causes, especially those of importance to the majority of workers. The organization has to show sensitivity to critical issues that are unrelated directly to work and provide self-identification to its employees and the community. Drucker notes that "raising the productivity of service work is management's first social responsibility."[4]

o **Communication Among Workers**

Effective communication among workers should be stressed and barriers that limit such communication should be broken. Top management should communicate even to the floor level and should not always expect a bottom-up approach. Top management should also solicit and hold town meetings with employees to identify problems at work before developing corrective measures.

o **Human Input in Work**

Human input should be encouraged to increase the self-esteem of workers. They should actively participate in designing their jobs and in measuring job performance. Incentive schemes should be developed to reward them accordingly.

o **Supplier Relationship**

Suppliers must maintain quality guidelines instituted by the manufacturer. Suppliers should be innovative and employ cost-cutting strategies to improve quality and satisfy due dates. In order to provide a higher quality product or service to the society, a firm must communicate and work with its suppliers in order to achieve customer needs and expectations.

o **Reduced Gap Between Top Management and Least Paid Employees**

Employees should not see the salary scheme as unfair. For example, top executives should not be rewarded with fat bonuses when layoff is lingering. Also, the gap between top executives' salary and bonuses and that of the operators should be minimized if equal devotion and dedication to the job is to be achieved.

o **Strategic Information System**

Maintain an information base system that will provide critical environmental information to management and make the information operational to all the employees of the organization.

o **Functional Strategies**

Functional strategies such as information technology, human resources, and manufacturing and marketing strategies are key ingredients for successfully implementing a strategic plan. The present focus of strategic planning on business and corporate units should be extended to include functional strategies. When a functional strategy is developed, Porter's value chain model can then be used to identify project opportunities and risks.[5]

Table 1.1 (continued)

○ **Focus on Value Strategy**

In addition to cost leadership (i.e., lower cost product provider), product and service differentiation, and innovation strategies, more and more people are interested in the "value" of products or services. Such values include fair prices for the products or services, better quality, and sales services.

○ **Redesigned Business Process**

Information and advanced manufacturing technologies are important for achieving consistent quality. The application of these technologies enables things to be done in novel and more efficient ways. Presently, many existing businesses are not fully exploiting these opportunities. Business process redesign is, therefore, necessary to integrate these new technologies. For example, Ford redesigned its invoice process after it benchmarked Mazda's invoice process. As a result, Ford has achieved drastic improvements: a reduced head count in accounts payable by 75 percent, invoices eliminated, and improved accuracy.[6] A firm should "reengineer" its business by using modern information technology to radically redesign business processes to achieve improvements in the firm's performance.[6]

○ **Redesigned Business Network**

In order to create or maintain a strategic advantage, many firms today link their computer systems with that of their customers and suppliers so that real-time responses to customer requirements are possible.

○ **Working Smarter**

Drucker identified five steps for working smarter: (1) defining the task; (2) concentrating on the task; (3) defining performance; (4) management-forming a partnership with the people who hold the jobs; and (5) continuous learning and teaching. Clearly, these steps help to focus on the job and may contribute to quality improvements.[7]

○ **Organizational Learning and Sharing**

This dimension is based on hear, see, do, and share. A firm *hears* a new concept or a new technique to improve quality. The firm *sees* it in action then, the firm applies this concept (*do*) and *shares* its experience with its suppliers and strategic alliances.

Notes:

1. Moran (1991).
2. Hax and Majluf (1991).
3. Ibid.
4. Drucker (1991).
5. Hax and Majluf (1991).
6. Economist (1990).
7. Drucker (1991).

Table 1.2
New Management Focus and Target for Strategic Total Quality Management

Strategic Target	Focus on Global Issues	Focus on Strategic Planning
Customer	* Benchmarking	* Customer needs * Never-ending philosophy of quality improvement
Company: System Transformation (see also Figure 1.2)	* Appropriate process technology * Design specifications * Management of change * Image building and social responsibility * Strategic information system management * Environmental sensitivity analysis * Redesigned business processes	* Strengths and weaknesses * Organizational mission and vision * Organizational flexibility * Teamwork * Focus on value strategy * Functional strategies * Cost analysis of quality
Company: Culture transformation	* Management commitment	* Multidisciplinary background * Employee motivation and organizational cultural change * Training and retraining * Education * Organizational commitment to employees * Communication among workers * Human input in work * Reduced gap between top management and the least paid employee * Working smarter
Supplier	* Redesigned business network * Organizational learning and sharing	* Supplier relationship * Work with supplier

Differences Among STQM, TQM, and TQA

Strategic Total Quality Management is different from both total quality management (TQM) and total quality assurance (TQA). STQM is an extension of TQM designed to prepare companies for the future—the future after six sigma. STQM identifies the limitations of present TQM literature and offers a framework to look at quality from the standpoint of overall performance. Specifically, focus is on the company's internal and external environments and how it conducts itself in these environments. The issue of social responsibility, therefore, becomes a critical factor as society confronts the complexity of environmental protection. Global corporations are becoming increasingly aware of the different demands of their operating environments and also understand that the operating cultures in these environments influence the perception of quality of their products and services. Also, differences in the political, business, economic, and social structures under which these companies operate suggest that a new outlook must be developed to manage the complex organizational and environmental worlds.

Quality as a competitive tool goes beyond the present focus on direct products or services rendered. STQM sees quality as holistic; it is customer and environment driven, with both factors considered in developing an effective quality program. For example, *Business Week* ran a cover story titled "The Greening of Detroit—A Push Is on to Make Cars More Environmentally Friendly" (Woodruff et al., 1991). This article showed that major auto manufacturers in the United States, Europe, and Japan are extensively researching alternatives to the gasoline engine. Possible new options are engines that burn methanol or natural gas, or that use solar energy, electricity, or hydrogen. The move toward these alternatives comes in the wake of the Persian Gulf war which once again reminded people in the industrialized world of the volatility of the oil market. However, the overriding pressure on manufacturers to embark on this research seems to stem from concern for the environment. While many automobile manufacturers consider this project expensive, it is one they cannot do without. New state and federal laws are being passed to limit the emission of carbon dioxide and ozone-depleting pollutants. These laws reflect customer concerns about quality of life that often are not considered when a company's concentration is only on the end product. In 1990, the U.S. Congress passed a new Clean Air Act to ensure compliance by about 100 cities to new federal air-quality standards. The state of California, where 2.2 million cars and trucks are sold annually, passed more stringent air-quality standards designed to cut auto emissions in the 1990s. New York and Massachusetts have also adopted the air-quality standards established by California, and about seven additional northeastern states are expected to follow suit. Auto manufacturers cannot ignore these growing concerns from their ultimate customers. While many auto makers view this challenge solely in terms of the direct cost involved in initiating such a massive research project, they accept it as necessary since their competition has already embarked on the same journey. For example, the new president of Honda, Nobuhiko Kawamoto, set environmental goals at the top of his priority list, saying that, "If a maker doesn't build more efficient cars, it can't survive" (Woodruff et al., 1991). He has set his Japanese and overseas employees to meet this manufacturing challenge. Yet, Japan is already targeting the environmental market. Japanese manufacturers are becoming "green giants" with efforts to develop environmentally sound products cutting across all industries (Gross, 1992). Table 1.3 identifies Japan's green technologies, and Table 1.4 lists the strategies of several Japanese companies in terms of research and product development to limit or control the emission of pollutants. Likewise, Vandermerwe and Oliffe (1990) have shown that

European corporations are responding to consumer demands for "green" goods by changing their corporate strategies and operational procedures.

Table 1.3
Japan's Green Technologies

Japan's Green Technologies

INCINERATING WASTE: Due to limited space available for landfills, powerful and low-emission incinerators have been built for solid and liquid wastes.

AUTO INDUSTRY: Automobiles are being redesigned to burn less fuel and release less carbon dioxide. These designs include the use of lighter body materials, lean-burn engines and better catalytic converters.

STEEL PLANTS: 35% of Japan's industrial waste comes from the steel industry. This is larger than any other industry. New plants are designed to recycle much more heat and waste product.

TREATING WASTE WATER: Sewage-control and sludge-treatment equipment and expertise are now being exported to other Asian countries.

ALTERNATIVE ENERGY SUPPLY: Japan has responded to global warming by becoming a leader in the development of solar and fuel cell technology. Such alternatives, offer the best solution to global warming by ceasing the production of greenhouse gas emissions.

ELIMINATION OF CARBON DIOXIDE: Both the government and electric power companies are conducting research on the use of genetically engineered micro-organisms to absorb carbon dioxide.

NEUTRALIZING FLUE GASES: Several Japanese companies are now marketing equipment to eliminate sulfur oxides and nitrous oxides from the stacks of steel and electric power plants.

Source: Adapted from Gross (1992, p.74)

The second major thrust of STQM is social responsibility. Drucker (1991) notes that "raising the productivity of service work is management's first social responsibility." Competitive companies develop strategies to retain their customers and, at the same time, attract new customers. Remember, quality efforts are not restricted to present customers but also are aimed at potential customers. In that regard, we classify customers as either *direct* or *indirect customers*, and use a case study to illustrate why productivity and quality of service to indirect customers often do not measure up, thereby, discouraging potential customers.

A commercial bank in New York maintains a payroll account for many companies that can be considered direct customers. However, employees of those companies who cash their paychecks from that bank could be considered either direct or indirect customers. Direct customers have personal accounts with the bank independent of their company's account. The bank provides selective services to those with these personal accounts and maintains special lines for them. For example, there are several special-account bank tellers, and the bank credits five dollars to the customer's account if he or she waits more than seven minutes to carry out a transaction. On the other hand, indirect customers have only one bank teller to go to, and there is no compensation for

Table 1.4
Japan's Industry Strategies for the Greening of the Environment

Industry/Company	Strategy
Steel Industry	Responsible for 25% of the carbon dioxide emission in Japan. Has slashed energy consumption per ton of steel by 20% since the mid-1970s. Plans to apply direct iron-ore smelting by 1994 with the potential of reduction in its energy use by 10 points.
Automakers (Toyota, Honda, Nissan, and Mazda)	Redesigned their cars to increase fuel efficiency and reduce the emission of carbon dioxide.
Toyota Electric Power	Introduced an electric car that achieved a driving peak of 109 mph and drove 340 miles on a single battery charge. This is the most efficient of all the electric cars produced.
Construction (Taisei Corp. and Kajima Corp.)	Developed integrated systems to sort and transport waste within office buildings and complexes.
Sanyo, Sharp and Matsushita Electric Industrial	Leaders in solar batteries.
Fuji Electric Co.	Leader in fuel cell technology.
Matsushita Battery Industrial Co.	Introduced the first mercury-free alkaline batteries in 1991. The technology has already been licensed to Rayovac Corp., the No. 3 U.S. battery producer.
Ministry of International Trade & Industry (MITI)	The Ministry is funding a project on the use of biotech to make hydrogen. Hydrogen offers the cleanest burning of all fuels.
Nippon Stell Corp.	Converts coal ash to zeolite (a mineral used in water treatment).
Japan Atomic Energy Research Institute, Chubu Electric Power Co., and Ebara Corp.	Engaged in research to convert sulphur and nitrogen oxides (major causes of acid rain) into ammonium sulfate and ammonium nitrate for use in fertilizer. The technique has already been licensed to research groups in the U.S., Poland, and Germany.
Mitsubishi Heavy Industries	Teamed with Corning Inc., U.S.A. to use chemical catalysts to remove nitrogen oxides from coal-fired power plants.
Ebara Corp.	Tapped Zurn Industries Inc., in U.S.A. to build industrial waste incinerators.
Ishikawajima-Harima Heavy Industries	Licensed nitrogen-oxides removal technology for industry and power plants to Foster Wheeler Engineer Corp., U.S. largest boilermaker.

Source: Adapted from Gross (1992, pp. 74-75)

waiting if the line is long. Apparently the bank does not care about these potential customers and tends to forget that these employees have power to get their companies to pull their company accounts from the bank. Also, a critical attribute of quality is the customer's perception. Indirect customers can hardly relate their experiences to those of direct customers, and they may perceive the bank as inefficient, dissuading them from opening a personal account there.

What is the problem with a bank offering special services to direct customers and ignoring potential direct and already indirect customers? To answer this we must understand that the direct customers in this case are the companies that employ the indirect customers of the bank. The companies suffer a decline in productivity when employees spend more than their lunch time waiting to cash their payroll checks. This decline in productivity starts a chain reaction, since many operations around the bank are interdependent. Thus action must be taken to maintain or increase productivity, possibly seeking a more efficient bank.

We can also use the Deming Chain Reaction to explain the effect of this bank's narrow-minded definition of its customers (Neave, 1990). This posits that improved quality leads to a decrease in costs because there are fewer mistakes, less rework, fewer delays and snags, and better use of time and materials. All these, in turn, improve productivity and lead to capturing a market with lower priced, better quality products and services. Thus, the company is able to stay in business and provide more jobs. The Deming Chain Reaction argues that the first social responsibility a company meets is to provide more jobs. This supports Drucker's views stated earlier (1991). Notice, also, that with more customers in the long line, the single bank teller is overworked and suffers stress. All of these factors contribute to a decline in quality and productivity by employees of the bank.

Service organizations must understand the impact of their actions on other organizations and see that their inability to improve quality and productivity affects the productivity of organizations dealing directly or indirectly with them. As a result, society suffers as productivity declines and companies are not able to provide more jobs. Note that social responsibility deals also with perceptions of the quality of services rendered by a company. Thus a company should try to be responsive to its environment and show concern for societal needs and demands.

Table 1.5 uses ten principles of quality to distinguish among TQA, TQM, and STQM. This table shows the role of STQM in improving TQM. Observe that in a company with a STQM focus, top management develops new management strategies to achieve the goals of the company. These new strategies emphasize an organizational mission and vision driven by quality. Thus, nine strategies for top management and the reasoning behind them are presented in Table 1.6.

STQM Transformation Process Overview

In today's global competitive environment, many companies must be willing to make profound changes in order to survive. These changes will be driven by a new vision, by transformation processes, by a greater willingness to work with suppliers, and by a never-ending philosophy for improvement and practice.

Top management must create long-range plans for the company. The vision—based on detailed analyses of current business realities (e.g., global issues, business groups, political and economic integrated communities), environmental challenges (e.g., preservation of the environment, growing world population, and scarcity

Table 1.5
A Contrast of Strategic Total Quality Management to Total Quality Management and Traditional Quality Assurance

Principles of Quality	Traditional Quality Assurance (TQA)	Total Quality Management (TQM)	Strategic Total Quality Management (STQM)
Definition	Product driven	Customer driven	Customer and environment driven
Priorities	Emphasis on cost and output	Emphasis on outcome and quality as the means	Organizational focus and vision driven by *overall* quality
Decisions	Short-term goals emphasized	Short-term and long-term goals emphasized	Short-term and long-term goals are environmentally sound and sensitive
Objective	Detect errors	Prevent errors	Prevent errors in products and services and maintain socially responsible decisions that are environmentally sound and sensitive
Costs	Quality increases costs	Quality reduces costs and improves productivity	Quality reduces costs, improves productivity and corporate image
Errors are due to	Special causes which result from workers' mistakes and inefficiency	Common causes which result from the failure of top management to manage effectively	Special and common causes as well as irresponsible management decisions and lack of commitment to social and environmental issues
Responsibility for quality	Inspection centers and quality control departments	Involves every member of the organization	Involves every member of the organization but requires top management to take the lead to ensure

Table 1.5 (continued)

Principles of Quality	Traditional Quality Assurance (TQA)	Total Quality Management (TQM)	Strategic Total Quality Management (STQM)
			that socially responsible decisions are made and effectively implemented
Organizational culture	Numerical targets are used and employees can be singled out for their mistakes	Continuous improvement is emphasized and team work is the approach	Never-ending philosophy of continuous improvement emphasized; employees are provided the necessary tools and skills to improve their performance and productivity
Organizational structure and information flow	Top-down and bottom-up approach; bureaucratic, restricts information flow, rigid	Horizontal approach; provides real time information, flexible	Horizontal and vertical approach; allows active participation of important stakeholder groups in making quality decisions
Decision making	Top-down approach	Team approach is used with team of employees	Team approach with teams of employees and important stakeholder groups

Table 1.6
Top Management Strategies for Quality Improvement

Top Management Strategies	**Reasoning**
Awareness	Strategic total quality management is seen as the key to global competitiveness and the long-term survivability of the firm. Top management and employees begin to see their future in the organization as dependent on the firm's survivability. They begin to adopt measures to achieve strategic total quality management goals.
Customer-demand focus	A new product strategy such as the one initiated by Aisin (a Japanese firm that twice won Japan's Quality Control Medal) must be developed. This new strategy is based on merchandise planning. Focus should be to identify the kind of merchandise that customers really want.[1]
Management philosophy/quality attitude/quality environment	Appropriate management philosophy such as the win-win philosophy, profound knowledge, long-term commitment, and continuous improvement are important in creating a quality environment and in developing a "quality" attitude.
Organizational vision	Top management develops a clear business vision that articulates the strengths, weaknesses, opportunities and threats of the organization as well as its internal and external environment. Appropriate criteria, standards, and priorities are established for achieving customer and environment-driven quality plans.
Quality/reliability vision	Quality and reliability issues are seen as inter-related and influential in determining the quality of the product and services offered by the firm. Plans are adopted to improve the quality of products or services rendered by a firm and the reliability of the process technology. Measures such as statistical operator control and statistical process control are adopted for products and services and process maintenance planning and policies are adopted for the process technology.
Organizational mission drives quality	Quality is seen as customer and environment driven. Management develops policies that will utilize quality function deployment to identify customer needs and applies the seven manage-

17

Table 1.6 (continued)

Top Management Strategies	Reasoning
	ment tools in assuring quality improvement.
Organizational message must be communicated to everyone	Top management sees the need to develop corporate quality programs. Organizational communication becomes important in assuring that organizational focus is clear and well understood by everyone in the organization. Quality improvement is seen as a continuous process and the only means to remain competitive.
Resources and commitment	Top management commits the time necessary to achieve strategic total quality management, encourages team work and develops reward systems based on quality and team achievement. Necessary resources such as continuous training of employees are provided to achieve strategic total quality management.
Organizational learning	Only organizations that learn will stay ahead. A firm must be abreast with changes in its environment. Critical information such as technological, quality, social and global trends must be obtained and thoroughly analyzed before a long-term plan can be developed.

Notes:
1. Aiki (1992).

of food), and current organizational structure, culture, and resources—must be customer and environmentally focused.

Once there is a clear vision for the future, management must answer the next question, "How do we get there?" In other words, how does the company become a new organization sensitive to the environment and caring about its customers? There must be a systemic as well as a cultural transformation with the company willing to share its experiences and work with its suppliers. In this systemic transformation process, strategic focuses are placed on the customer and the environment, with a linkage established to strategic planning and technological processes. In the cultural transformation process, the strategic focus is on both the human side of the company, and its awareness and commitment to customers and their environment. Being willing to work with suppliers is the link between supplier input and the customer and the environment.

Critical success factors (customer satisfaction and environmental sensitivity) and performance measures are used to measure improvement. If a company receives unfavorable results on certain performance measures, management can use the problem-solving techniques discussed later to improve. Likewise, if certain performance measures yield positive results, management should *still* try to find new opportunities (innovative business processes or practices, technology breakthroughs) to optimize current and future performance. There is no finish line for a customer and environmentally focused business.

Figure 1.1 presents an STQM transformation overview. The present organization assesses its changes from the perspective of customer- and environment-driven quality strategies. For example, the environment and customer impact on a traditional business leads to a system transformation and creates a greater need to work with customers and suppliers. In fact, the traditional company is unable to manage environmental and organizational complexities. Reliance on previous experience to deal with and manage change has indeed become a handicap as the organization of the future evolves. Keen (1991) notes that "In a context of constant change, experience often becomes a liability rather than an asset. The value of experience generally rests on the status quo—the less things change, the more experience is worth. The more things change, the more people have to invest in continuous self-education." Radical changes taking place today, and expected to continue way into the future, demand that a new focus be used to develop the new organization. Organizations that undergo the transformations identified in Figure 1.1 will emerge with enhanced performance and quality. Although we cannot ascertain the outcome of this transformation process, other than as an organization with a new focus, the result may lead either to more or less value for the products and services produced. When more value is realized, there is a need to optimize the opportunity and continue to innovate, developing a new and better managed organization. However, when performance falls below expectation, only continuous improvement can save the existing organization.

THE STQM TRANSFORMATION PROCESS

Deming popularized the use of the PDCA (Plan-Do-Check-Act) cycle. The PDCA cycle, also known as Deming's cycle, is a cornerstone for achieving continuous improvement in quality management (Neave, 1990). The PDCA cycle is also useful in explaining the STQM transformation process, as presented in Figure 1.2.

Figure 1.2 operationalizes the PDCA cycle by detailing the process of achieving continuous quality improvement, and by identifying when the necessary quality tools should be used. Also, the STQM transformation process sees the PDCA cycle from a strategic point of view, where *Plan* represents *strategic planning and formulation*, *Do* represents *strategy implementation on a smaller scale*, *Check* represents *evaluation and control*, and *Act* represents *strategy implementation on a full scale*. So what we have as a result of this process can well be referred to as a *strategic cycle*. As this figure shows, the strategic cycle is continuous, analogous to the loop in the PDCA cycle. The loop shows the need for always striving for the best, acquiring new information and using that information to improve on the strategic framework. We have partitioned this transformation process accordingly.

Plan: Strategy Planning and Formulation

The first phase of the STQM transformation process is planning or policy making. At this stage, the company conducts the popular strengths, weaknesses, opportunities and

Figure 1.1
STQM Transformation Process Overview

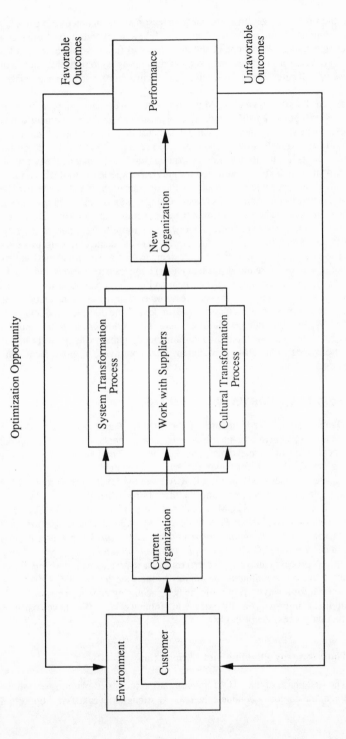

Figure 1.2
System Transformation Process

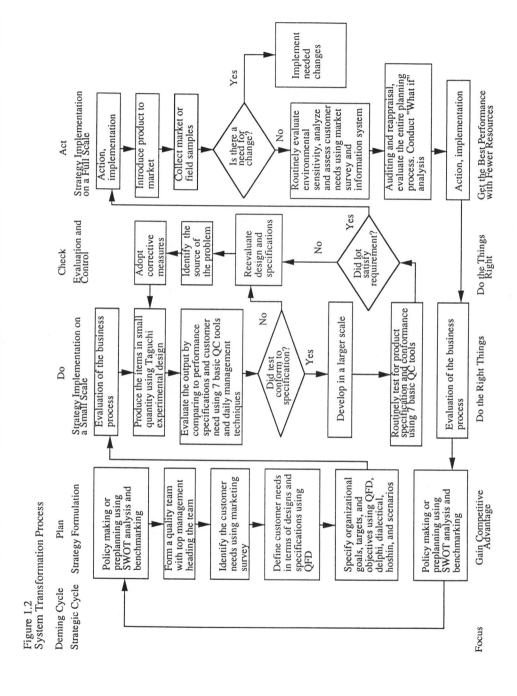

threats (SWOT) analysis. Knowledge of its strengths and weaknesses will enable it to better position itself against competitors. The company also uses benchmarking, comparing itself to the industry's best; it may, in fact, look outside the industry, using functional benchmarking to see how to exploit inroads made by others. A quality team headed by top management is formed. Top management's commitment to quality, in terms of both time and resources, will help spread the focus on quality to everyone in the organization. The team's major task is to identify customer needs. Marketing surveys can identify such needs. However, producing the products or services that satisfy these identified needs is much more complex. Customer needs must be spelled out in design specifications and requirements, and there must be a corporate goal to achieve such specifications. Increasingly, quality function deployment (QFD) is used to break down customer needs into specific targets and identify the specifications critical to establishing the customer's perception of quality products and services. Once these specifications are identified, organizational quality goals, targets, and objectives must be defined as customer and environment or market driven. In fact, QFD is again critical in specifying how such goals can be achieved. However, more traditional methods such as scenarios, Delphi, and dialectical approach can be applied. The Japanese have used Hoshin planning in such cases. This is a Japanese technique intended to steer the organization in the right direction; it deals with management and control of targets to ensure that such targets are reached. Hoshin planning is gaining popularity in the United States, often referred to as policy deployment, management by policy (MBP), or management by planning.

This stage of the strategic cycle focuses on *gaining competitive advantage*. The planning enables the company to position and compare itself to competitors, and then formulate strategies that are achievable given its strengths, weaknesses, opportunities, and threats.

Do: Strategy Implementation on a Small Scale

Once the strategies are formulated, they need to be implemented. The implementation process should consider the risks involved, with an incremental approach when they are high. For a manufacturing company, smaller quantities of the product are produced. The products are evaluated by comparing them to performance specifications and customer needs. At this point, the seven quality control tools and the daily management techniques are applied. The evaluation phase then detects if the products conform to specifications. If so, full-scale production commences. There is, however, a need to continue routine testing of the production process to ensure that product specifications are still being satisfied. The goal of this phase is to ensure that the company is *doing the right things*.

Check: Evaluation and Control

When the evaluation of the small-scale production shows nonconformance to specification, there is a need to reevaluate the design and specifications. This is an error-checking procedure intended to identify the source of the problem. Once the problem is identified, corrective measures can be applied and a sample run conducted to confirm that the problem has been solved. Notice the loop between *Do* and *Check*. Also notice that the strategic cycle requires that *Evaluation and Control* be employed when full-scale production is carried out and routine tests are conducted on the product. This particular phase ensures that the company is *doing the things right*.

Act: Strategy Implementation on a Full Scale

The *Act* phase deals with introduction of the product full scale to the market. While the product is on the market, field surveys are being conducted to detect customer perception of the product and suggestions for improvements in the product. Environmental sensitivity analyses are also conducted at this time. These analyses record responses to the product in terms of its safety and how well it satisfies environmental protection laws and meets public concerns. An on-line information system with customers and suppliers is also developed to obtain real-time information about the product. Information thus obtained can be used to assess the performance of the product and evaluate the planning process. Further sensitivity analysis can compare the performance of the product to alternative designs or modifications. The product is further compared to substitute products on the market in terms of customer reactions and perceptions. Reports from independent agencies such as consumer advocacy groups are also compared and evaluated. Strategies are devised to enhance the marketability of the product. Obviously, this auditing and reappraisal is intended to increase market share by providing high-quality products to consumers—products that are not only fit for use but also environmentally sound. In addition, the process ensures continuous improvement and benchmarking of the product, thus providing a competitive posture for the company. The *Act* phase has the objective of *getting the best product performance with fewest resources*. All measures are aimed at ensuring the continued survival of the product in the market. As seen in Figure 1.2, this framework establishes a continuous cycle open to revision when new information emerges. Thus the strategic cycle integrates future information for improving the quality of the product.

Table 1.7 is a list of management and quality control tools referred to in Figure 1.2. This table briefly defines the tools and shows their applicability in this framework.

CONCLUSION

Systemic and holistic concepts of quality are codified as Strategic Total Quality Management, as differentiated from total quality management and total quality assurance. A strategic framework is used to show the relationship of the STQM strategic cycle to the Deming cycle. STQM analyzes the internal and external performance of a company and considers the environment as a critical component in measuring performance. Quality is, therefore, customer and environmentally driven. STQM performs a continuing holistic customer- and environment- driven analysis of internal and external performance to drive defects to zero and maximize the intrinsic and extrinsic satisfaction of customers. STQM will become more important as companies achieve total quality management. Thus, this chapter also highlighted the importance of organizational social responsibility as an influence on the customer's perception of quality and, thereby, of product performance. Transformation of traditional organizations to new, consumer- and environment-driven organizations is mandatory to survival.

Finally, in the context of Porter's value-chain model, protection of the environment is a value-added activity that yields benefits in the long-run. From the perspective of social welfare maximization, the responsibility of the company is enhanced.

REFERENCES

Aiki, S. "Aisin Envisions Its Path to Success." *Quality Progress*, March 1992, pp. 83-87.

Deming, W. E. *Out of the Crisis*. Cambridge, MA: MIT Center for Advanced Engineering Study, 1986.

Drucker, P. E. "The New Productivity Challenge." *Harvard Business Review* (Nov-Dec 1991): 69-79.

Economist, June 16, 1990, p. 7.

Gitlow, H. S. *Planning for Quality, Productivity, and Competitive Position*. Homewood, IL: Dow Jones-Irwin, 1990.

Global Perspectives on Total Quality. New York, The Conference Board, 1991.

Gross, N. "The Green Giant? It May be Japan." *Business Week*, February 24, 1992, pp. 74-75.

Hax, A. C., and L. S. Majluf. *The Strategy Concept and Process—Pragmatic Approach*. Englewood Cliffs, NJ: Prentice-Hall, 1991.

Keen, P. G. W. *Shaping The Future Business Design Through Information Technology*. Cambridge, Ma: Harvard Business School Press, 1991.

March, A. "A Note on Quality: The Views of Deming, Juran, and Crosby." *Harvard Business* School 9-687-011, Rev. 2/90.

Mercer, D. "Key Quality Issues." In *Global Perspectives on Total Quality*. New York: The Conference Board, 1991, p. 11.

Moran, J. W., et. al. *Daily Management* GOAL/QPC, MA, 1991.

Neave, H. R. *The Deming Dimension*. Knoxville: SPC Press, 1990.

van Ham, K. "Setting a Total Quality Management Strategy." In *Global Perspectives on Total Quality*, New York: The Conference Board, 1991, p. 15.

Vandermerwe, S., and M. D. Oliffe. "Customers Drive Corporations Green." *Long Range Planning* 23 (6) (1990): 10-16.

Woodruff, D., T. Peterson, and K. L. Miller. "The Greening of Detroit." *Business Week*, April 8, 1991, pp. 54-60.

Table 1.7
Major Techniques in the STQM Transformation Process

Benchmarking: The practice of "learning from the best" in terms of business strategies, business operations, and business processes. The purpose of benchmarking is to improve the company quality, productivity, and competitive position.

SWOT Analysis: Before a company formulates its vision and mission, the most important internal and external factors that will affect the company's future must be identified. SWOT (Strengths, Weaknesses, Opportunities, and Threats) analysis can be used for this purpose.

Marketing Survey: A systematic approach that involves data collection and analysis of customer requirements. Popular survey methods include interviewing, library research, and questionnaires.

Quality Function Deployment: A systematic approach used to translate customer requirements into specific functional and controllable attributes for a product. This approach translates a company business plan into specific functional strategies and further breaks down into specific tasks so that everyone in the organization knows what is expected in order to achieve the company business goals.

Taguchi Design: A fractional factorial design approach used to identify the best level for the process factors so that product and service quality can be improved.

Seven Management Tools: Tools that can be used for effective tactical and operational planning: Affinity diagrams (for collecting and grouping large amount of input data such as opinions, factors, and ideas); interrelationship digraph (for identifying the logic relationships among those major group inputs); tree diagram (for further identifying possible subgroups that are associated with the major group inputs); matrix diagram (for identifying correlated relationships between any two or more items); prioritization matrices (for assigning priorities tasks, actions, and projects); process decision program chart (for developing contingency plans for any potential problem); and activity network diagram (for scheduling tasks completion times).

Seven Basic Quality Control Tools: In a continuous improvement environment every employee should know some basic tools such as fishbone or Ishikawa, or cause-and-effect diagram, flowchart, Pareto diagram, control charts, histograms, scatter diagram, and check sheets to help identify problems and root causes, understand production or service processes, and hold gains.

Daily Management Techniques: In order to better communicate customer requirements and expectations to company suppliers, daily management techniques such as baseline instrument and customer-supplier map can be used. A baseline instrument is a set of predesigned questions that help evaluate a company's capability of meeting customer requirements and expectations. The customer-supplier map is a structured approach that reflects how well a company and its suppliers match customer requirements and expectations.

Value Chain Model: A conceptual framework that classifies company business activities that add value to its products or services into two major groups: primary activities and support activities. Primary activities group include inbound logistics, operations, outbound logistics, marketing and sales, and services while support activities group include corporate infrastructure, human resource management, technology development, and procurement.

Hoshin Planning: A technique used to direct the organization in the right direction. It deals with the management and control of targets to ensure that such targets are reached.

Chapter 2

Strategies for Global Competitiveness with Information Technology

Christian N. Madu and Chu-hua Kuei

The business environment has changed significantly since the advent of information technology. Business organizations have undertaken drastic restructuring by modifying their means of communication and coordination of work activities. Information technology has made it possible for companies to operate on a real-time basis, whereby products and services are delivered to the right place at the right time. Since then, information technology has proliferated and has undergone considerable improvements. Costs have continued to decline as these new technologies have emerged. A business not supported by a network of computer systems (primary information technology) is almost destined to fail, since it will be unable to compete effectively in today's complex and dynamic environment.

Companies are not the only ones who have benefited from advances in modern information technology. Consumers and interest groups have formed strategic alliances and are now able to coordinate their activities as well as exchange ideas and thoughts through several database and network systems. For example, owners of personal computers can subscribe to a computer network and easily retrieve information on the products and corporations on line. Such information can also easily be transmitted to other users. This vast use of information technology by both consumers and companies affects the way business is run today. These consumer strategic alliances know no geographical boundaries; oftentimes, they are global in nature, especially among the industrialized nations.

While companies can reap enormous profits from the better coordination, greater product flexibility, improved quality, leaner production, and more time-based competitiveness that information technology offers, they also face the threat that can come from these consumers' strategic alliances. For example, corporations can no longer ignore consumer demands for consistent product quality, integrity and respect for the environment, or timely delivery of services.

There is, therefore, a need to develop new strategies to deal with these challenges. This chapter looks at strategic options that can enable an organization to continue focusing on customer needs. These strategies will also help the company remain competitive in this dynamic environment.

VISION

In today's strategic management literature, the word *vision* is prominent. What really is vision? *Webster's New Universal Unabridged Dictionary* (Simon & Schuster, 1979, p. 2043) offers some interesting definitions out of which we have picked two. Vision is defined as:

the ability to perceive something not actually visible as through mental acuteness or keen foresight

force or power of imagination

These definitions are pertinent in the context of strategic management. It can be said that *organizational vision* exists when there is the ability to look into the future and accurately develop a plan that will guide the company into its future. This power of imagination very well determines the survivability of the company. In fact, most successful companies have a vision. For example, Aisin Seiki Company Ltd., the first company to twice win Japan's Quality Control Medal, develops its vision every five years. According to Aiki (1991), the Aisin Seiki Co. Ltd. vision is based on three fundamental management philosophies: (1) quality first, (2) management based on vision, and (3) improvement and reinforcement of the company structure through total quality control. Formulation of a vision is necessary for an organization to plan ahead, position itself in its environment, and internally adjust to changes in that environment. Visions help to restructure and redesign an organization so it can cope with its changing environment.

Collins and Porras (1991) note that vision is an important "component of corporate success." They argue that the heightened interest in corporate vision may be a result of decentralization in many organizations. The companies became flatter as decision-making powers were decentralized. While this effort has helped stimulate innovation, has increased responsibility among workers, and has improved quality, it has also created problems. An organization's vision, mission, and goals are often lost in this flatter structure, making it difficult for management to achieve cohesiveness and strive for a common cause. However, a shared vision may help to resolve this problem. Visions focus people on the expected future environment that will lead to a "tangible image." The organization aims to achieve a mission that is well established. There is, therefore, a shared vision with expected outcomes or results.

The key issue now is how an organization can develop such a vision. As an example, we develop a vision for a hypothetical fast food chain as follows:

Values and Beliefs

1. Customer satisfaction is the primary goal of the company.
2. The customer is always right and must be treated courteously.
3. Employees should never argue with customers.
4. The company encourages and rewards good work and ideas.
5. The company encourages innovativeness.
6. The company communicates and listens to customers and employees, and shares ideas on how to improve work.
7. Every customer is a valuable customer.
8. Integrity is important to the long-term survival of the company. The company is committed to environmentally sensitive programs and must lead the industry in protecting the environment.

9. The company is committed to providing high-quality service to its customers at reasonable prices.
10. The company is committed to total quality management programs, through which it will help employees enhance their skills and performance.
11. Teamwork is encouraged, with top management commitment to improving quality.

● *Objective*: The objective of the company is to be innovative, and to introduce high-quality products and services at competitive prices.
● *Mission*: The company intends to be among the top three fast-food chains in the country in the next ten years.
● *Vivid Description*: The goal of the company is to become recognized as the best fast-food chain for providing quality products and service at low prices. The customer satisfaction level will be high, assessed from the comments and complaints filed by customers.

Many major corporations have formal vision statements. For example, Giro Sport Design, a sports bicycle manufacturer, has a well-formulated vision statement that projects where the company should be by the year 2000. It also benchmarks itself against leaders in other industries. For example, its vision statement projects that Giro Sport Design will, by the year 2000, assume the same role in the bicycle industry as Nike and Apple Computers have in athletic shoes and the computer industry, respectively.

Gooding (1990) also reports the three-stage corporate planning process used by Ford Motor Company in Europe. Ford's vision statement and corporate plans are not static, and can be revised frequently with new information. For example, on noticing that Japanese automakers had a competitive advantage on time, quality, and productivity, Ford in Europe revised its CAD/CAM strategy, a major part of its corporate plan or business vision.

Organizational vision is necessary in order to achieve quality. One of Deming's fourteen points stresses the need for constancy of purpose (1982, 1986). This requires that an organization embark on continuous improvement of its products and services.

However, having a vision and a mission statement is not enough to ensure survival. Both the vision and mission must be operational, with appropriate courses of action and strategies to steer the company in the right direction. The organization needs to undergo two major transformations—namely, changes in quality and technology.

In Chapter 1, we presented a different perception of quality as a strategic variable in achieving competitiveness. A major ingredient of the quality transformation process discussed there was the need to improve the company image by "caring" for its customers, workers, suppliers, and environment. This caring attitude, often referred to as *integrity*, may be a key factor in survival. Weiner (1992) points out that, "Integrity is not an economic or quantitative measure of performance, but an attitudinal and value-based method of doing business." While ethical issues cannot be quantitatively measured, they certainly cannot be ignored. In Chapter 1, there were several examples given as to how companies can improve their integrity. Likewise, Weiner (1992) projects that companies who "consider the needs of their employees, their customers, and society at large, companies that embody concern and affection, service and caring, honor and fairness," are the ones that will survive.

STRATEGIC VARIABLES

It is evident that quality is linked to strategic variables such as technology, time, and variety and cannot be achieved in isolation. Thus, a spectrum of these variables is discussed.

Time-based Competitiveness

An emerging strategy in achieving competitiveness is time. Stalk and Hout (1990) point out that companies are going through a transition process whereby time and choice are replacing cost as competitive weapons. The emphasis on time involves a shortening of delivery time for products and services. Ford, Toyota, and Honda all have relocated their factories closer to their customers in order to minimize manufacturing and development time. New products are being introduced into the market at a much faster rate. The just-in-time inventory philosophy is a major aspect of manufacturing competitiveness. It assures that items are at the right place at the right time, leading to an improvement in the quality of service and also to zero inventory. Thus, time-based competitiveness may help reduce cost.

Strategic Alliances

Companies either in the same industry or in different industries are forming partnerships. These partnerships add value and may offer a competitive advantage to the participating companies. For example, American Airlines, Citibank, and MCI formed a strategic alliance through which special incentives are offered to customers of participating companies on the American Airlines frequent-flyer program (Premkumar and King, 1991).

These partnerships can help to cut costs. For example, manufacturers and suppliers can share the same database for customer requirements, product specifications, and designs. This linkage provides real-time information to the parties involved and also helps improve coordination and quality. Auto parts dealers, for example, use an industry-wide network known as MEMA/Transnet to connect to their retailers (Premkumar and King, 1991).

Strategic alliances provide for organizational learning and sharing. For instance, suppliers and manufacturers can share common information to improve quality and avoid the poor quality that comes from lack of coordination between manufacturer and supplier. Both manufacturer and supplier learn at an early stage what future demands, limitations, and problems they may confront. Remedial actions are taken on a timely manner to deal with these problems before they develop.

Technological Change

There has been rapid proliferation of new technologies. Advanced technologies such as flexible manufacturing systems or computer integrated manufacturing, are often credited with the advances made by both product manufacturers and service providers when there is an improvement in quality and increased flexibility, or greater variety of products at lower costs, with more reliability. The Japanese automakers especially have taken advantage of these emerging technologies to improve quality and reduce inventory. Their concept of "lean production" exploits the opportunities presented by these new technologies to produce a variety of products that build to mass production. This approach avoids the high cost and rigidity associated with traditional means of production.

The new technologies have also influenced the cost-accounting systems used to evaluate and select these technologies. It is, therefore, inadequate to apply such selection procedures. Instead, corporations must develop technology policies that go beyond the standard return on investment or net present value principles, and see that some new technologies may add intangible values that can make the corporation viable and more competitive.

The Environmental View

Only a few years ago, manufacturers resisted environmental regulations on the premise that they increased costs and consumers were not willing to pay these added costs. Chapter 1 showed that environmental factors and social responsibility issues may, in fact, emerge as the new issues to determine competitiveness and survivability in the marketplace.

Consumer behavior now reflects an environmental consciousness and a willingness to pay extra to maintain and protect the environment. Schlossberg (1992) notes that:

A study by Infocus Environmental of Princeton, New Jersey, shows that one-third of parents have changed their shopping habits because of environmentally related information from their children, who have studied it in school. Those actions include 17% of households avoiding products they learned about from their kids, and 20% purchasing products because they learned about it from their kids.

Several interest groups have emerged to address the problem of deterioration of the environment. Nations as well as corporations are paying attention to the issues these groups are generating. As noted by Weiner (1992), world markets are interdependent, with information exchanged on a global basis. It is becoming apparent that environmental pollution and degradation of the environment respect no geographical boundaries. The actions of corporations in any nation with regard to the environment affect the entire universe. Concerns about global warming—a result of the emission of carbon dioxide into the earth's atmosphere and the subsequent destruction of the ozone layer—led to the 1992 U.N. Summit on the Environment in Rio de Janeiro, Brazil. Corporations that in the past exported their polluting facilities to poorer nations and where environmental laws are relaxed, are reevaluating such policies.

To hasten such corporate actions, interest groups are identifying major polluters and using information technology to alert people all over the world to the actions of such corporations. It is difficult, for a company to ignore the long-term impact of such negative publicity. Corporate image is a competitive weapon, and it cannot be effective if the company is perceived as socially irresponsible and insensitive to the environment.

Value-Chain Analysis

To achieve competitiveness, a company must disaggregate its business units into "strategically relevant stages" that consider the value added by the tasks involved (Hax and Majluf, 1991). The value-chain framework is helpful in diagnosing business units and comparing them against major competitors. The key is to identify the essential factors that enable a company to compete and to develop the necessary tools to effectively compete.

Porter and Miller (1985) have developed a classification system for competition in any industry. They identify five competitive forces as (1) threat of new entrants, (2) threat of substitutes, (3) bargain power of suppliers, (4) bargain power of customers, and (5) industry competitors. Porter (1986) argues that this classification, often referred to as his five-force model, is useful in systematically displaying and categorizing activities. Further uses of this model has been identified by others. Hax and Majluf (1991) point out that it can help evaluate a company's quality improvement opportunities. Stalk and Hout (1990) identify its value in terms of time savings in planning innovation activities.

A TECHNOLOGY STRATEGY

To compete effectively, business organizations must develop a technology strategy. Madu and Georgantzas (1991) and Madu (1992) present criteria to compare computer-integrated manufacturing (CIM) to traditional manufacturing systems. Specifically, they identify quality, flexibility, information processing capability, dependability, inventory levels, direct labor reduction, and cost as key factors in selecting technologies. Goldhar and Schlie (1991) note the role of CIM in helping U.S. companies to compete. They say that CIM will help reduce product-development time and life cycles, and make it possible to compete for fragmented market segments. CIM also helps develop differentiated products that appeal to consumers.

Some of the benefits of CIM are summarized below:

1. Inventory is significantly reduced if not eliminated. The philosophy of just-in-time or zero inventory becomes easier to implement.
2. It becomes easier to respond to variations in product design. A spectrum of products that are *not* standardized, as in mass production (traditional assembly line systems), can be offered.
3. Organizations can respond swiftly to their competitive environment through improved quality of products; reduced costs as a result of the reduction in wastes, scraps, reworks, and inventory; increased level of dependability; rapid response to product design and demand changes; ability to collect and disseminate timely information; and reduce the use of direct labor.
4. There is better coordination of activities since the production system is highly integrated and a technological link can be established with suppliers and dealers.

The Human and Organizational Side of Technology

As we move toward ever more advanced technologies, the labor force must be retrained. This training should not only expose workers to the technical matters surrounding the new process but also to the new focus of the organization. They have to be made aware of the importance of advanced technology in improving work methods and in remaining competitive. Employee commitment to the new process is imperative.

Advanced technology by itself adds little or no value to an organization. There must be organizational as well as employee commitment to exploit the technology to the maximum. For example, with increasing use of computer-integrated manufacturing systems, and the barrage of technical documentation that accompanies it, employees have to be capable of identifying the critical information at the right time. Once that information is identified and appropriately interpreted, there must be an organizational commitment to use the information to make better decisions. Without this capability, the organization cannot benefit from new technologies. Human resources management, therefore, will continue to be a critical factor in the survival of any organization.

We summarize the influence of information technology on human resources as follows:

1. Information technology changes the mode of communication and work processes.
2. Routine or standardized operations are replaced with skilled and multiskilled workers. A highly trained labor force is needed to manage information technology.
3. Worker motivation and satisfaction may improve since workers are no longer confined to routine operations, enjoy decision-making powers, and can contribute to improvements in their work processes.

Information technology also has an impact on the organization itself, as follows:

1. Organizational restructuring is required. This restructuring makes the organization flat. Decision-making powers are decentralized.
2. Communications are improved and the organization is able to make timely responses to its environment.
3. Introduction of new products and services is enhanced and varieties of products can be effectively introduced and marketed by the organization.
4. The organization is able to improve its productivity, quality, and competitiveness.

Today's advanced technology can, however, easily become a basic technology. Rapid proliferation of new technologies also brings rapid obsolescence of earlier technologies. Policies regarding technology should not be static; they should keep evolving. Stalk (1988) points out that "competitive advantage is a constantly moving target . . . The best competitors, the most successful ones, know how to keep moving and always stay on the cutting edge." A company must be able to evaluate potential new technologies quickly. The goal should be to remain competitive, and effective management of technology is a crucial step in achieving this. With increased focus on customer satisfaction, technology is a critical means for achieving customer satisfaction. Browning (1990) notes that a learning organization "uses technology ceaselessly to refresh its knowledge of its customers wants and to devise new ways of satisfying them." This commitment to be a learning organization requires vast resources, however. For example, Browning also points out that building a learning organization "requires new skills, clever people and capable machines." Clearly, technology and human resources must be used together for the organization to remain competitive.

Barabba and Zaltman (1991) note that "hearing the voice of the market and making constructive use of it with respect to the voice of the firm is a learning process." Essentially, the voice of the market has to be translated into facts and tasks that will lead to appropriate products or services to satisfy customer needs. This is similar to the application of quality function deployment, whereby the organization develops its strategic plans to satisfy customer needs. Thus, a learning organization must also be a caring organization. As a caring organization, its major goal is to satisfy its stock or stakeholders, its customers, and employees, and also to be socially responsible. The traditional organization, with the focus on satisfying stockholders alone, is changing to this new form, with a broad-based stakeholder group.

CONCLUSION

The strategies for global competitiveness have been identified and discussed. It has been pointed out that an organization must have a vision in order to remain competitive. Technology and human resources management are identified as key variables that enable an organization to improve its productivity, quality, and competitiveness. A critical component is the information technology, which offers both opportunities and challenges. The organization must show sensitivity to its environment via its policies, and be a learning and caring organization, since time and integrity influence competitiveness. Finally, organizations must innovate and continuously move to achieve new targets, especially in view of today's rapidly developing new technologies.

REFERENCES

Aiki, S. "Aisin Envisions its Path to Success." *Quality Progress*, March 1991, pp. 83-87.

Barabba, V. P., and G. Zaltman. *Hearing the Voice of the Market*. Boston: Harvard Business School Press, 1991.

Browning, J. "Information Technology Survey." *Economist*, June 16, 1990, pp. 5-20.

Collins, J. C., and J. I. Porras. "Organizational Vision and Visionary Organizations." *California Management Review* 34, 1 (Fall 1991): 30-51.

Deming, W. E. *Out of the Crisis*. Cambridge, MA: MIT Center for Advanced Engineering Study, 1982, 1986.

Goldhar, J. D., and T. W. Schlie. "Computer Technology and International Competition—Part 2: Managing the Factory of the Future to Achieve Competitive Advantage." *Integrated Manufacturing Systems* 2, 2 (1991): 22-30.

Gooding, G. "Exploiting IT in Business Development: Ford in Europe." In *Information Management: The Strategic Dimension*, edited by M. Earl Oxford: Clarendon Press, 1990.

Hax, A. C., and N. S. Majluf. *The Strategy Concept and Process: A Pragmatic Approach*. Englewood Cliffs, NJ: Prentice-Hall, 1991.

Madu, C. N. "A Quality Confidence Procedure for GDSS Application in Multi-criteria Decision Making." *IIE Transactions* (forthcoming, 1992).

Madu, C. N., and N. C. Georgantzas. "Strategic Thrust of Manufacturing Automation Decisions: A Conceptual Framework." *IIE Transactions* 23 (2) (1991): 138-48.

Porter, M. E. *Competition in Global Industries*. Boston: Harvard Business School, 1986.

Porter, M. E., and V. E. Millar. "How Information Gives You Competitive Advantage." *Harvard Business Review* 63 (4) (July-August, 1985): 149-61.

Premkumar, G., and William R. King. "Assessing Strategic Information Systems Planning." *Long Range Planning* 24 (5) (1991): 41-58.

Schlossberg, H. "Kids Teach Parents How to Change Their Habits." *Marketing News*, March 2, 1992, p. 8.

Stalk, G. "Time—The Next Source of Competitive Advantage." *Harvard Business Review* 66 (4) (July-August 1988): 41-51.

Stalk, G., and T. M. Hout. *Competing Against Time*. New York: Free Press, 1990.

Weiner, E. "Business in the 21st Century." *Futurist*, March-April 1992, pp. 13-17.

Chapter 3

A Comparative Analysis of Japanese and American Production Management Practices

Roy Nersesian

The United States is currently suffering from an inferiority malaise in manufacturing technology and in manufacturing managerial practices. The balance of payments deficit is a telling sign that Americans prefer Japanese-built products over their own. The rust belt of the Middle West, a wide swath of this nation dotted with abandoned factories, is more evidence that this nation is on an industrial decline. The most poignant questions deal with whether we, as a nation, can reestablish our industrial leadership in the world community.

Had the Japanese invented a new technology, a new hardware system, to manufacture goods, there would be no problem. We would have easily been able to copy it, much as the Japanese have learned to copy American and European technology. Unfortunately, the Japanese did not invent a new technology of manufacturing hardware; they adopted a new philosophy of manufacturing software, so to speak. While Americans can take some solace in the fact that the new manufacturing software—that is, the philosophical underpinnings of management practices in a manufacturing environment—was American in origin, the point is that we either have to copy it, or its essential features, or perish. Changing manufacturing hardware is easy. Changing ingrained habits and traditional approaches to the respective roles of management and labor in a factory setting is very difficult. Yet this is what is required. Our whole managerial approach to manufacturing must be turned upside down. It cannot be accomplished unless the alternative of ultimate corporate liquidation is faced squarely. As members of the human race, we have a penchant for avoiding change until our very survival is threatened. Or as Samuel Johnson said in the eighteenth century, "Nothing concentrates a man's mind so wonderfully as the prospect of being hanged in the morning."

In a nutshell, the Japanese have succeeded in tapping the brains in addition to the brawn of their work force. The rest of the world is working on the old model that workers are hired for their brawn—that is, they are hired to man a machine, do what they are told, and be measured against performance standards set by a stopwatch. That old model worked as long as there was no better model available. But now, a new managerial model is on the scene. Sufficient time has passed to show that the new model of managerial practices produces superior results. That means that the old model is no longer adequate for meeting the needs of companies. Companies that stay with the old model are operating with a competitive disadvantage. Companies that operate with a competitive disadvantage don't operate for long.

Two simple statistics demonstrate the point. One is that the Toyota work force has made about 2 million suggestions to management after management adopted the new way of managing manufacturing companies. Two million suggestions are quite a few suggestions; there have to be some fairly constructive suggestions in a pile of 2 million. One must conclude that the ability to have the work force volunteer 2 million suggestions for management consideration means that the management of Toyota has succeeded in tapping the brains, in addition to the brawn, of its work force. The second statistic of interest is the realization that, in America, the same number of workers, working under the old model of management principles, would be expected to submit suggestions numbering, perhaps, in the hundreds. Some feel that this may be a high estimate. Moreover, many of these suggestions are divorced from enhancing the productivity of the work force. They may deal with such items as installing an air-conditioning unit to cool down the work area, closing down the factory on the first day of hunting season, and increasing the level of pay for those on the second shift.

Tapping the brain power of the work force is no easy matter when management attitudes are inclined to treat the work force as a cost of doing business. A management oriented to cost minimization with labor being a cost factor does not create a working environment where the labor force is eager to submit suggestions that will increase the productivity of a factory. Making the workplace conducive to the work force associating its welfare with the overall welfare of the corporation means a change in corporate culture. A corporate culture is made up of behavior habits, among other things. A change in corporate culture means a change in behavior habits.

However, it is possible for behavior patterns to change. American corporations that have joined the ranks of world-class manufacturers—which implies that they have succeeded in penetrating the global market and can stand against the full aggressive force of Japanese competitiveness—have made the transition. Automobile assembly plants being built as either Japanese transplants or Japanese joint ventures with American automobile companies, or by American automobile manufacturers such as the Saturn plant in Tennessee, have made the transition. World-class manufacturers produce world-class goods. That is the only way they can attain status of world-class manufacturer. One of the best-kept secrets in the United States is that the quality difference between Japanese- and American-made automobiles has narrowed significantly in the last decade or so. For some models, the quality difference is negligible or nonexistent. Thus the transition can be made. Part of the inducement to make this transition is the stark realization by management and labor that *not* making the transition means the end of their collective livelihoods. Man, once he finds himself *in extremis*, can abandon the old and adopt the new with a minimum of pain.

AMERICA AS INITIATOR OF CHANGE

The United States has a long history of being a leader in both production and management practices—the hardware and software of production. In the hardware phase of production, America has been the historic leader in the adoption of machinery over labor in the making of goods. In the nineteenth century, this was known as the American system of manufacture. The European system of manufacture stood for handcraftsmanship. It was an American, Eli Whitney, who first popularized the notion of a uniformity system for the manufacture of goods with interchangeable parts. The idea actually originated in France where, in 1765, General Gribeauval stated the benefits of rationalizing French armaments with standard weapons with standard parts. From the point of view of fighting a battle, it would be advantageous if the soldiers used standard weapons whose parts were standard—that is, interchangeable. A soldier whose flintlock was broken needs only to obtain a spare flintlock, replace the old one, and continue fighting. To accomplish this quickly in the heat of a battle, the parts had to be interchangeable.

The French accomplished this feat. Thomas Jefferson, as minister to France, wrote to John Jay in 1785, "He presented me with fifty locks . . . in pieces. I put several together taking pieces at hazard . . . and they fitted in the most perfect manner. The advantages of this, when arms need repair, are evident."

Eli Whitney was a mechanical wizard who, on a visit to a friend in the south, heard his host bemoan the degree of manual effort on the part of the slaves to remove the seeds from a ball of cotton. Two weeks later, Eli Whitney had invented the cotton gin. He patented the invention and opened up a factory in the north to manufacture cotton gins. He sold only a few. The southern buyers opened up the gin, peered inside, noted the simplicity of the mechanical devise, and copied it. It was cheaper to make a cotton gin than buy one from Whitney with his patent-protected profit margin. The patent office refused to send anyone down to the wilds of the south to enforce Whitney's patent rights. Eli Whitney was eventually forced into bankruptcy.

Eli Whitney, on the comeback trail, succeeded in obtaining a contract for the manufacture of ten thousand muskets for the army. Such an order in the past would have been honored by the building of one barrel, one stock, one flintlock, one trigger mechanism, one of every part and component, and then the parts and components put together requiring some degree of filing for a proper fit. Thus, a contract of 10,000 muskets really meant 10,000 muskets of individual design because the parts of one musket would not fit another. Eli Whitney won his contract by proposing a "uniformity system that can produce interchangeable parts." In other words, Eli proposed manufacturing ten thousand barrels, stocks, flintlocks, trigger mechanisms, and so on, and then taking one of each, at random, and producing a musket. The essence of his uniformity system was that the 10,000 muskets would all be of the same design.

In 1798, Eli Whitney won the contract and became accredited with building the first factory for the purpose of producing a single product. He sought the maximum usage of labor-saving machines. He built his factory in New England alongside a waterfall where the machines were driven by belts connected to a shaft of a water mill. He promoted the idea of the specialization of labor to the making of a single part; that is, the best man for operating a machine was permanently assigned to that machine. The necessity that the parts be interchangeable meant the beginnings of gauges and other instruments for measuring various dimensions to ensure that parts were identical. This marks the beginnings of quality control in a manufacturing environment. The final product, the musket, was "assembled" from the interchangeable parts without, in theory, further filing or fitting.

As an aside, the price of slaves—which one would expect to fall since the labor content of producing a bale of cotton dropped considerably with the invention of the cotton gin—actually spiraled to new heights. The cotton gin made growing cotton so profitable that the south was literally plowed under and transformed into one huge cotton plantation. The demand for slaves rose because there was more land to cultivate and cotton to harvest. This is an often-quoted example of the impact of technology on society. There is more. Eli Whitney was responsible for the north's embarking on the factory system to become the manufacturing center of the nation. His first factory was the model for others to follow. While the south found its niche as an agricultural economy based on slaves, the north embarked on an industrial economy for the manufacture of goods. The two social consequences of technology, the cotton gin and the factory, eventually collided sixty years later in the Civil War.

So, too, the differing manufacturing software technologies of operating companies have social repercussions. There is a social impact associated with the Japanese usurping of America's historic role as leader in manufacturing technology and the management of technology. Japan is more than a rising star as an economic power. It dominates the world in manufacturing hardware and software. It is a world industrial economic power based on its adoption of quality as a driving force rather than short-term profits. It has learned to focus on market domination of entire product lines based on excellent quality at reasonable prices, not on cheap prices based on cheap labor and cheap parts. As a consequence of our belated entry into the world of quality as a feedback mechanism rather than short-term profits, the United States has had to endure the social consequences of a falling standard of living, an erosion of manufacturing technological leadership in the world, and the feeling among the young that their future is less than promising in being able to own a house and support a family. These are the social repercussions of America's rejection and Japan's adoption of the principles espoused by Deming and Juran.

The uniformity system successfully proposed by Whitney, although not entirely successfully demonstrated according to some of his detractors, was not popular among American manufacturers of that day because labor was cheaper than machine. It was the government that kept the idea of interchangeable parts alive because it insisted in its purchase of armaments that all parts be interchangeable. Moreover, the government owned armament factories; in particular, the Springfield Armory and the Harpers Ferry Armory developed and refined production techniques for the manufacture of interchangeable parts. Perhaps even more important, these armories created a reservoir of professionals knowledgeable and adept at producing interchangeable parts.

When Samuel Colt won a contract from the government to produce revolvers that stipulated interchangeable parts, he turned to the armories for personnel with the requisite technical knowledge and experience. So, too, did other nineteenth-century industrialists such as Isaac Singer, whose Elizabethport factory in 1880 was assembling 500 thousand sewing machines per year. This was the first use of the word *assembly* in the production of goods. At this volume of manufacture, it becomes imperative that parts be interchangeable. The best place to find the people with the requisite technological skills during the nineteenth century was the government armories.

THE LASTING CONTRIBUTIONS OF HENRY FORD

Henry Ford is the undisputed principal contributor to mass-production techniques—the quintessence of the American system of manufacture. Ford believed that "in mass production, there are no fitters." He refused to hire fitters in his factories. All parts had to be interchangeable. Indeed, they had to be interchangeable when one considers that the River Rouge plant was producing the unimaginable number (for the early twentieth century) of 2 million Model T cars per year. Ford was a mechanical genius, a line balancing wizard, and an efficiency expert in removing unnecessary costs from the manufacturing process.

The River Rouge plant was fully integrated. Iron ore was transformed into melted steel, which was poured directly into molds for the engine block. Ford did not understand the advantage of buying steel from a supplier for a process that required the steel to be reheated to a liquid state to be poured into molds. In his mind, the cooling and reheating of the steel was a waste, a step in the manufacture of the car that costs money but does not add value. Since the step costs money but does not add value, he eliminated it by making his own steel and pouring the newly made molten steel directly into engine molds.

This examining of every step of the process to see whether or not it adds value to the product was scrupulously followed by Taiicho Ohno, production manager at Toyota Motors. Ohno realized that every operation costs money but does not necessarily add value. Each individual step is evaluated as to what it adds to the value of the product. If it turns out that the step is not adding value, it is eliminated. For instance, there may be a sequence of steps in the manufacture of a part where the work stations between two steps may be widely separated in the plant. In examining every facet of each step in the manufacturing process, the simple movement of the part from one station to another comes under scrutiny. The movement costs money, but does it add value? The answer is that the movement is not adding value. The solution is to locate the two work stations close together to minimize the movement of the parts.

The movement of fenders to a stockroom and then to the assembly line costs money. The stockroom takes up space. People are required to stock the shelves, so to speak, and then take the fenders off the shelves and move them to the assembly line. Accounting records have to be kept. Inventory carrying costs accumulate, not only from the financing costs associated with items stored in the stockroom, but from the additional risks of damage, obsolescence, and possibly even pilferage. Moreover, a worker who makes up a lot of bad fenders may be able to "hide" his performance in a stockroom where the error of manufacture is not discovered until the fenders are delivered months later to the assembly line. All of these are costs. They are costs embedded in a stockroom that do not add value to the final product, the automobile. Since these costs are not adding value to the final product, the stockroom has to be eliminated.

The stockroom can easily be eliminated by making fenders just in time for their incorporation into the assembly of an automobile. The fenders are sent directly from the point of manufacture to the assembly line. The only in-process inventory is the fenders in transit between the point of manufacture and the point of assembly. Therefore, all costs associated with the stockroom and the personnel dedicated to double handling and accounting of the fenders, all associated inventory carrying costs, along with the opportunity for workers to make large batches of bad fenders, are eliminated.

Moreover, it has been observed that workers whose output is immediately consumed in the production of the final product become more productive. They realize that their responsibility is not to make up a batch of parts that are to be stored in a stockroom, but to make parts in sufficient number and quality to keep the entire factory running smoothly. Their expanded view of their position within a factory setting breeds a higher degree of work satisfaction, which in turn enhances their productivity.

Bearing in mind that a just-in-time manufacturing and assembly operation can be stopped by the poor performance of one individual, there can be no unimportant workers. Everyone plays a critical role in the continued operation of an entire factory because stopping the assembly line is not done by management, but by the worker downstream of the individual who just made a bad part. The thought that one's performance is critical to the performance of the whole organization, and that performance is measured by the worker next in line, actually raises the morale of the workers. Their individual performance becomes important to the operations of the entire organization, which translates to increased responsibility. The workers, sensing their increased responsibility to the good of the entire operation, raise their level of performance, enhancing their productivity and the quality of their work. Greater productivity on the part of the work force and better quality goods being shipped to market mean greater profitability for the company.

Ohno's managerial practice of examining each step in a process to see if it adds value to the product was not abandoned once he left the factory floor. Ohno, as did Ford, also examined every step in the administrative overhead of operating a plant. A work order may require four signatures. Are four signatures adding value to the product? Probably not. The subsequent action is to reduce the number of signatures—or perhaps change the system and eliminate the need for signatures altogether, as is accomplished in the Kanban system. Where did Ohno receive his inspiration for judging the value-added function of every step in the manufacturing process? He will gladly tell you: from studying Ford. And the Kanban system? That idea sprung to his mind while he watched a reorder point system in operation in a U.S. supermarket.

Ford strove for a high degree of efficiency to reduce the variable cost of manufacture. A higher degree of efficiency could be obtained if fenders were made and immediately assembled in a Model T rather than if they piled up in a stockroom awaiting assembly. Ford was unexcelled in his ability to balance all the various manufacturing lines to ensure that parts, once manufactured, were immediately assembled into the finished product. The only in-process inventory was the parts of a Model T moving on conveyor belt or other forms of conveyance between the point of manufacture and the point of assembly. Today this is called just in time (JIT). Ford never heard of this phrase. To him, just in time simply made common sense. He wanted a low-cost car, and a large integrated plant with all its manufacturing and assembly lines perfectly balanced was the way to achieve a low variable cost of production. There was virtually no inventory within the system. From the moment the iron ore entered his River Rouge plant to when a completed Model T rolled off the assembly lines was about three days. To the low variable cost of production Ford then added a low profit margin to create a low price. A low price enabled masses of people to buy a Model T Ford and put America on wheels.

Ford is the originator of both mass production and mass marketing. He realized that producing automobiles by the million meant that he had to sell automobiles by the million. His first mass market for selling his product was his own work force. To this end, in 1915 Ford doubled the workers' salaries without increasing the price of the Model T, an act that won him worldwide acclaim. This act may have been forced on him. To whom does Ford sell millions of cars if his own work force cannot afford to buy one? Ford had an answer to this question. He singlehandedly created America's blue-collar middle class.

Critics have noted that doubling the pay was also necessary to reduce turnover in Ford's factories because of the monotonous nature of assembly-line work. Perhaps so, but the thought that workers should receive sufficient pay to purchase the output of the goods they make is critical in a world that mass produces goods. That thought is still applicable.

In addition to copying Ford's production techniques, the Japanese have also copied his pricing policies. Ford always promoted the idea of a low profit margin on a per-unit basis. He made his fortune by selling millions of automobiles at low profit margin for high profit. Of course, once one purchased a Tin Lizzie and the crankshaft needed replacing, Ford was a bit more aggressive on the magnitude of the profit margin. This pricing philosophy of a low profit margin on manufactured goods has also been adopted by the Japanese.

Whereas Texas Instruments, a leader in the development of the hand calculator, priced its first calculators in the hundreds of dollars, Matsushita, a leader in the development of the VCR, priced its first VCRs to sell at a loss. The initial high profit margin that Texas Instruments enjoyed for a short period of time invited a host of competitors that eventually reduced the profit margin of the hand calculator to that of a common commodity. Matsushita, on the other hand, achieved world dominance in VCRs precisely because the price was too low for competitors to enter the market. Once the volume was built up to millions of VCRs, and with the economies of scale inherent in mass production, Matsushita eventually made its millions in profits.

Ford's ultimate compliment comes from Ohno of Toyota Motors in his ready and modest admission that all that he had done in the area of manufacturing hardware to transform a near-bankrupt Toyota Motors to the Bank of Toyota was to bring Ford's principles up to date. Actually Ohno did much more; he worked with the president of Toyota Motors, Kiichiro Toyoda, to implement Deming's principles on manufacturing management—something that did not exist on a Ford assembly line.

TAYLORISM

Edward W. Deming's work can be better understood by considering the contribution of Frederick W. Taylor, the "father of scientific management." Taylor created management as a profession by instilling the principle of planning and controlling in owners of factories. Taylor watched workers report to work with no idea of what they would be doing once they arrived at the factory. He watched them mill about until the foreman appeared and randomly selected a work force to perform some task. Taylor pushed for a more organized and planned way to assign tasks to people for a duration of time so that the workers knew what they would be doing when they awoke in the morning. This could only be done by transforming foremen, who were reacting to a situation, into managers, who would anticipate the requirements of a situation and plan their activities accordingly.

Taylor also noted that the poor wages of the day were hardly an incentive to put in a full day's work. He developed "slide rules" whereby production below a certain level was paid at the customary, rather low rate. However, once a target level of output was reached, the piece rate would begin to climb. He adjusted the slide rules such that a worker who diligently applied himself could bring home a decent wage. These rules were also set up to ensure that the manufacturer would capture a goodly share of the increased productivity as incremental profits. To set up these slide rules, Taylor introduced the stopwatch as a means of measuring the output of an individual to determine the point where the piece rate would change. He also had to have a firm handle on costs in order to set the piece rate at a level that would accomplish the twin goals of providing the workmen with a decent wage through diligent effort and providing the manufacturer with the proper incentive to endorse Taylor's ideas. Taylor made lasting contributions to cost accounting in the derivation of his slide rules.

In using a stopwatch to set the slide rules, Taylor was in a position to observe the sequence of steps in the work done by individual workers. It was a logical, if not inevitable, step for him to become interested in improving task performance by examining the nature of the work itself. He indoctrinated managers in the idea of examining the flow of work and the method of work to enable them to take steps to increase the productivity of workers without any incremental effort on their part. Control of the flow of work through a factory, planning of individual steps in the manufacturing process, and careful assignment of individuals to tasks were to become management functions. The purpose of management in the areas of planning and control of the manufacturing process, and in the assignment of the proper man to a particular task, was to increase the output of factories without any, or little, increase in the input of labor.   This enhanced the productivity of the factory and the profitability of operations.

Taylor's ideas on organizing the activities of a factory, controlling the nature of these activities, examining the manufacturing process itself to increase productivity, scheduling production over extended periods of time, and planning for the future of a company gave rise to management as a profession. Taylor's followers extended his work to foster the growth of management as a profession. These included Frank B. and Lillian M. Gilbreth, who incorporated photography in their time-motion studies. By examining each individual movement of a worker in the accomplishment of a task in great detail, they were able to change the setting of a work environment such that there would be greater output without any commensurate increase in labor input. Lillian M. Gilbreth also wrote a book entitled the *Psychology of Management*, which broke new ground in the study of management as a profession. Another one of Taylor's followers was Henry L. Gantt, who introduced his famous charts for the management (planning and control) of project and production scheduling. Several generations of management consultants and efficiency experts were spawned by the works and writings of Taylor and his followers.

All of this effort gave rise to Taylorism, whereby managers and engineers set work standards for workers. Man as a laborer or worker was considered merely as an extension of a machine. Man was hired for his brawn and was measured by his output. He was expected to blindly follow the orders of management, whose chief preserve is in doing all the thinking necessary in the running of a plant. This split in the respective purposes of management and labor became the mission statement for American management. The attitude spread around the world as the United States emerged as one of two superpowers, and as it grew to be a dominant economic power, during the twentieth century.

TAYLORISM AND QUALITY CONTROL

Taylorism also had an impact on quality control. Before Taylor and Ford, when factories were small establishments or workshops run by a master craftsman, quality control was a top management responsibility. That is to say, nothing left the shop without the master craftsman's approval. With mass production from large factories made possible by Ford, and with the time standards for measuring worker productivity inaugurated by Taylor, a worker's output was guided by production quotas or goals, or by the speed of the assembly line. Top management was more interested in counting the output of the factory than in measuring its quality. With time, top management focused its efforts on building new factories, marketing new products and expanding the market, and on finding financial mechanisms to control their industrial empires.

Quality control was relegated to the production manager. Even the production manager shunned quality control by setting up a quality control division within the production department. Controlling or monitoring the quality of the product leaving a factory became a wasteland for launching a corporate career. The quality control division was the place to assign people who were destined not to make it to the top of the organizational chart. Young managers took their cue and avoided quality control with a passion. With time, they also learned to avoid production management.

The establishment of an independent organization for quality control ended up divorcing the workers from responsibility for the quality of their work. They knew that poor quality products would be inspected out of the system. Inspectors were placed at strategic locations to sort the good from the bad. Therefore, workers could rely on the inspectors to ensure the quality of the output of their work. The idea of quality assurance—actions taken within the process to ensure the quality of the product—was certainly alive, but not well. Production managers and workers found it easier to become dependent on good quality products being established by inspecting teams sorting out the bad products. Taylorism inadvertently bred a system that separated quality output from both manager and worker responsibility.

This system placed an inspector at strategic points in the manufacture of goods. The most critical focal point for inspection was after the finished product came off the assembly line and before it was sent to the consumer. The inspector would pass or fail a product, a lot, or a shipment of a product. If the product passed the inspection, it would be shipped to the consumer. If not, a decision was made whether to rework the item or scrap it. This, of course, depended on the nature of the defect. If the product was reworked and the defect was corrected, the product was sent to the customer. If this was not economically justifiable, the product was scrapped. In the small chance that a defective product did pass through the inspection process undetected, a system of guarantees or warranties protected a customer. Thus, in theory, the system assured that customers either received, or ended up with, good quality products.

A system of inspection, rework, scrap, and guarantees or warranties was expensive. A. V. Feigenbaum (1961) has suggested that the cost may be as much as one-third or more of total manufacturing costs. However, with the whole world following American management practices in one form or another, it hardly mattered. If all manufacturing organizations were wasting one-third of their costs in the form of inspection, rework, scrap, and the exercise of warranties or guarantees, what difference did it make in terms of comparative advantage? All were in the same boat. The price of goods covered the costs of inspection, rework, scrap, and warranties that were essentially the same for all manufacturing concerns. There was no competitive disadvantage associated with Taylorism because all were practicing Taylorism. As long as every manufacturer practiced Taylorism, there was no incentive to change the system.

THE RULES OF THE GAME HAVE CHANGED

The essential problem facing American managers today is that the Japanese have changed the rules of the game. They changed the rules, not by devising a new set of their own, but by listening to what an American had to say about tapping the hidden capabilities of the work force, and in not treating workers as extensions of machines or as a cost to be minimized. Adoption of "Demingism" at the expense of "Taylorism" meant that the companies adopting Demingism could save about one-third of their manufacturing costs by eliminating much of the costs associated with inspection, rework, scrap, and warranties—that is, the costs associated with workers producing poor-quality goods. This is at the heart of Philip Crosby's assertion that quality is free (1979). Companies that switched from Taylorism to Demingism now had a competitive advantage over those that stayed with the old system. A company that suffers a competitive disadvantage must react to the situation or eventually be liquidated. That is the discipline inherent in the free market environment.

Edward W. Deming is a mathematical physicist who worked with F. W. Shewhart. Deming also worked at the Bell Systems Hawthorne works when seminal studies were being conducted on worker motivation. From Shewhart (one of the founders of the American Society of Quality Control), Deming developed certain ideas about the role of statistics in controlling processes and in improving processes. From his experience at the Hawthorne works, Deming developed ideas about worker motivation and its impact on productivity.

During World War II, Deming was part of the war effort to enhance the quality of goods produced by industries serving the Allied cause. And there were quality problems. Bombs did not explode on impact. Torpedoes made a full circle and struck the submarine that fired them. (Fortunately, there was also a quality problem in a torpedo's firing mechanism that permitted the submarine to return to port to report on the torpedo's poor performance and to have it removed from the hull.) During this time, Deming espoused changes in measuring quality and in achieving higher standards in quality. Some of these changes meant a change in certain principles of management, however. For this, he was promptly escorted to the factory door, not only by representatives of management but also of organized labor.

Deming's show, having bombed so to speak in Cleveland, was taken to Japan after the war. He was invited by the Japanese Union of Scientists and Engineers to help them improve the quality of Japanese products. At this time, "made in Japan" was a synonym for "junk." Toys were all that Japan could export and these were uniquely capable of falling apart while sitting on a shelf. The Deming show was about to bomb in Tokyo as it had in Cleveland because Deming found himself talking to engineers, not managers. He needed to talk to management because his thoughts on quality went far beyond statistical process control charts. These thoughts affected the fundamental way manufacturing companies were managed.

Fortunately for Deming, Kaori Ishikawa, a noted Japanese professor of management, became interested in Deming's philosophy of management and invited a group of former students to attend a lecture to be given by Deming. When Ishikawa made the call, he received a response from a high portion of his former students, many of whom had subsequently achieved high-level management positions. (Perhaps professors of higher learning should consider how many former students would answer their call to attend a lecture as a test of their classroom effectiveness. For many, the test would probably end up with a failing grade and a lesson in humility.) Be it as it may, Deming could now talk to management, who were not about to show him to the nearest door. Quality was a distinct and critical Japanese manufacturing problem begging for a solution.

Japan is an island nation without any natural resources. All raw materials and energy must be imported. Even half its food must be imported. Having lost a war intended to secure sources of food, energy, and raw materials for its industrialized society, Japan had little choice but to rely on its export industries to obtain the funds necessary to feed its people, to fuel its economy, and to obtain the necessary raw materials for its industries. The postwar challenge of how to pay for vital and critical imports to sustain the economy had to be addressed. Ishikawa made a call to a desperate group of men.

Although these Japanese managers were sympathetic to what Deming had to say, and perhaps even adopted some of his principles, the spread of Deming's managerial philosophy can be traced to one man. That man was Kiichiro Toyoda, president of Toyota Motors. Perhaps in understanding his problem, one can better appreciate Toyoda's decision to abandon Taylorism as a management model. The consequences of that decision on manufacturing software was to successfully challenge the supremacy of the United States as a world manufacturer of goods.

TOYOTA MOTORS AND THE ADOPTION OF DEMINGISM

Toyota Motors, as with the other Japanese automobile manufacturers, was noted for making a poor quality car. The standards were so poor that Japanese people preferred imported American-made cars, or cars made in American factories located in Japan. Some time after the war, the Japanese banned the import of American cars to help address the deficit of payments in trade with respect to the United States, and to protect its domestic car manufacturers from further loss of market share by guaranteeing a market for their products.

The irony of the situation is complete. The automobile situation in Japan in the years following World War II was a mirror image of the automobile situation in the United States during the 1970s and 1980s. During this later time, American buyers preferred Japanese-built cars over American, and cars built in Japanese transplant factories in the United States over cars built in American factories. There was now a balance of payments deficit between Japan and the United States in the Japanese favor. A partial remedy was to limit car imports into the United States through quotas to guarantee a market for American manufacturers. It is hoped that the 1990s will redress this imbalance in trade as U.S. automobile companies retool themselves both technologically and managerially by copying the highly successful Japanese model of production and production management, which is American in origin.

Back in postwar Japan, Mr. Toyoda operated a near-bankrupt automobile company selling cars in Japan to Japanese who preferred foreign-made cars. In an attempt to expand its market, Toyota Motors exported a shipment of automobiles to California. This was a rather famous shipment of cars. When a potential buyer grabbed the door handle of one of the cars in that particular shipment, it might come off in his hands. If the handle did not come off the car, the door might not open; or if it did open, the door might not close. If the buyer succeeded in finding a car where the door did what a door was supposed to do, he could relax in the front seat, but to his peril. The chances were that the seat would become unglued, as it were, and fall over backwards taking the driver with it. This shipment of Toyota cars was unfit for sale. It had to be returned to Japan or be scrapped.

Mr. Toyoda had to do something or the company would have to declare bankruptcy. He was *in extremis*. He had listened to what Deming had to say and decided that the traditional mode of American managerial practices did not fit his automobile company. He turned to Mr. Ohno and instructed him to employ the philosophy outlined by Deming in the operation of the factory. This started a twenty-year trek in the slow adaptation of the Deming principles of management in the Toyota factories.

It was a process of taking little steps one at a time. There was a five-year hiatus between giving the workers the right to push a button for a yellow light and a red light. The yellow light was an indication of trouble on the assembly line. Engineers and managers responded to a yellow light. With the red light, the workers had the right to stop the assembly line before something of poor quality could pass to the next station. But just as Alfred Sloan made small improvements in the General Motors line of products year after year and successfully challenged the unchanging Model T Ford, so did Toyota successfully challenge General Motors, Ford, and Chrysler on their own turf—the American marketplace.

Part of this story has already been told in Ohno's updating the principles of operation pioneered by Ford, which is not part of the Deming philosophy. The rest of the tale is the abandonment of Taylorism in favor of Demingism as the underpinnings of a philosophy for production management.

Taylorism and Demingism are mutually exclusive—one accepts one set of managerial principles or the other. Which is better? This was debatable when Deming was preaching his philosophy; it is a nondebatable issue today. The verdict is in: Toyota dominates world production of automobiles. General Motors, Ford, and Chrysler to varying degrees are reeling from an onslaught of Japanese imports. Analysts judge the future of these American giants by the degree and timing of their conversion from Taylor to Deming. While GM, Ford, and Chrysler have had their credit ratings reduced, their earnings crumble, their share of the market shrunk, Toyota has transformed itself from a near-bankrupt company to one that is now called the Bank of Toyota—one of the most cash-rich manufacturing companies in the world. Thus, there is no rational argument that can be made for a company to remain with Taylorism if its competition is switching to Demingism.

STATISTICAL CONTROL CHARTS

The story of Deming must start with his statistical process control charts, lessons he learned while under the tutorage of Shewhart. The underlying purpose of statistical control charts is not to sort the good from the bad but to provide information that will lead to improvement in the quality of the process or the product. Deming's management philosophy is the outgrowth of his approach to statistical control charts in the manufacturing process.

Suppose there is a process that produces something whose desired measure of some attribute is 10 (e.g., 10 inches long, 10 ounces in weight, 10 centimeters in width, or some performance measure where the desired reading is 10). Further suppose that its standard deviation, a description of the degree of the variation in the process, is 1. Therefore, from the normal probability distribution tables, the chance that the individual item will have a measurement above or below a value of 10 is equal, or 50 percent. Thus a throw of the die yielding an odd number (1, 3, 5) can simulate a measure at or above 10. Similarly, throwing the die and obtaining a value of 2, 4, or 6 will indicate that the measure of the desired attribute is at or below 10.

Just to add a little more reality to the simulation, the normal probability distribution table shows that the probability of a reading being one or more standard deviations away from the mean is roughly one in six. In this example, this means that measurements above 11 and below 9 will occur once in six observations. Moreover, the observed readings of the desired attribute will not likely be more than three standard deviations away from the mean. The normal probability table shows that the chance of measurement being more than three standard deviations from the mean is only about one chance in a thousand. Therefore, when the observed measure of the attribute is above 11, it will most likely be less than 13. Similarly, when a rating is below 9, it will most likely be greater than 7. Using these rules, one can construct a simple simulation of the normal variability in a process by rolling a die and assigning a value according to Table 3.1.

By actually performing this exercise, one can appreciate the meaning of a normal distribution and realize what is meant by what Deming calls a *stable process*. Figure 3.1 is a stable process where the measure of the attribute is 10 and the standard deviation of the process is one. It works the same way as throwing the die and observing the number, except that the mathematics behind the simulation more closely approximates a normal probability distribution. The process is stable in that one can return ten years

Table 3.1
Simulation of the Normal Variability in a Roll of a Die

Roll a Die and Note the Number	On Graph Paper, Plot a Point Between the Indicated Values
1	11-13
3	10-11
5	10-11
2	9-10
4	9-10
6	7- 9

later and see the same general pattern of variability in the results.

A PROCESS UNDER CONTROL

How can one conclude that the process is stable? There are two criteria that have to be met: the mean and the standard deviation must not change with time. Both are calculations made from the raw data. The calculation of the mean is easily understood. The calculation of the measure of variability, or the scatter in the data, is less easily understood. Nevertheless, the standard deviation is a calculation that can be made and compared to its former values to see if it is changing with time.

A more qualitative understanding can be achieved in noting that the chances of a value falling in the range of the mean plus one standard deviation, or in this example having a measurement reading between 10 and 11, is about two chances in six, or one in three (34.13 percent to be exact). The same is true for a measurement reading between 9 and 10. There is a 13.59 percent chance that the measurement reading will be between 11 and 12, which also holds for measurement readings between 8 and 9. This, of course, represents the probability of readings being between one and two standard deviations from the mean. Continuing on, the probability of readings between two and three standard deviations is 2.15 percent, or in this situation covers measurements between 12 and 13, or between 7 and 8. The chances of a measurement being more than three standard deviations from the mean is only 0.13 percent, or slightly over one chance in a thousand. A system is stable if readings within these various regions continues to occur with these probabilities as summarized below.

Criteria for a System Exhibiting Stability

1. The average or mean reading is 10.
2. The calculated standard deviation does not change. Another way to look at this is that the measurement readings at this stage of a manufacturing process of an item fall into the following probability categories:

Range of Rating	Probability of Occurrence
> 13	0.13%
12-13	2.15
11-12	13.59
10-11	34.13

The total probability of a reading being 10 or more is 50 percent. The probability distribution for a reading being 10 or less is the mirror image for having a reading of 10 or more.

Range of Rating	Probability of Occurrence
< 8	0.13%
7- 8	2.15
8- 9	13.59
9-10	34.13

Once a process is considered stable, one can construct the green band and red band on a statistical process control chart. The traditional red bank on an American process control chart is any measure of the desired attribute where the reading is more than three standard deviations away from the mean, or in this example, any reading below 8 and above 13. From the previous probability tables, the chances of that happening is roughly one chance in a thousand. In a random selection of ratings where the process is stable, a reading below 8 and above 13 occurs once in a thousand readings.

If 8 and 13 are the demarcation points between the green and red operating bands, what can one say about taking corrective action for readings below 8 and above 13? Since these measurements have only one chance in a thousand of occurring if the process is stable, then one can be 99.9 percent confident of not making a mistake in seeking a cause for such a reading and taking corrective action, when, in fact, the process is stable (mean is 10 and standard deviation is 1).

In America, a reading in the red band is a call to take corrective action—to find out what is wrong with the process for such a reading to be generated. There is only one chance in a thousand that the search will be fruitless in the sense that the process is stable, that is, operating within specifications. If a reading is not in the red band, then it is a safe conclusion that everything is under control and it is time for the supervisor to relax with a cup of coffee and a magazine. Such is not the case in Deming's mind. The supervisor, his manager, along with the workers below the supervisor should now start scrutinizing the statistical process control charts for unusual patterns.

What are some of these unusual patterns? Consider the probability of having four out of five readings between one and three standard deviations from the mean. In the example herein, what is the probability of four out of five successive items with performance between 11 and 13 or between 7 and 9? From the previous probability table, the chance of readings between 11 and 12 is 13.59 percent and the chance of readings between 12 and 13 is 2.15 percent. Therefore, the chance of having an item with a measure of the desired attribute between 11 and 13 is 15.74 percent. The chance of having two successive items each with a reading between 11 and 13 is only 2.47 percent (15.74 percent x 15.74 percent). The logic here is the same as rolling two 1s in succession with a die. The chance of rolling the first 1 is 1 chance in 6. The chance of rolling the second 1 in succession is 1/6 x 1/6 or 1 chance in 36.

Continuing on, the chance of three successive items having readings between 11 and 13 is 15.74 percent x 15.74 percent x 15.74 percent, or 0.39 percent, and the chance for four successive readings between 11 and 13 is 0.06 percent. Now the fifth reading is not between 11 and 13. The chance of that happening is 84.26 percent (100 percent - 15.74 percent). Thus the total probability of having four successive readings between 11 and 13 followed by a fifth reading that is either more than 13 or less than 11 is about 0.05 percent. However, there are five possible combinations that satisfy the criterion that four out of five readings be between 11 and 13. Only one has been examined. If *x* denotes a rating between 11 and 13 and *y* denotes a rating outside the range of 11 and 13, the probability calculated so far covers the situation *xxxxy*. The other combinations are *xxxyx, xxyxx, xyxxx, yxxxx*, or five combinations including *xxxxy*. Thus the probability of a pattern consisting of four out of five items having ratings between 11 and 13 is 0.26 percent, a rather low probability.

Because the probability of occurrence for this pattern is highly remote for a process that is stable and exhibiting the characteristics of one that is randomly distributed within the confines of a normal probability curve, then one can be 99.74 percent confident of not making a mistake in assuming that the process is out of control and, consequently, taking corrective action, when in fact the process is stable. Corrective action is an investigation of why such a pattern occurred, the identification of a real or potential cause, and the taking of some sort of remedial course of action, and a subsequent report of the investigation and its outcome.

In Deming's world of statistical process control charts, another unusual pattern would be two out of three readings between two and three standard deviations from the mean. In the example herein, this can be translated to two out of three items having measurements between 12 and 13 or between 8 and 9. The probability of one item having a rating between 12 and 13 has already been shown to be 2.15 percent. Two out of three translates to a total probability of 2.15 percent x 2.15 percent x 97.85 x 3 possible combinations, or about 0.136 percent. Again, this is a highly unlikely pattern for a stable process.

Another highly unlikely pattern is a run of eight readings on either side of the mean. Suppose an American supervisor sees the following set of ratings on successive items: 10.2, 10.4, 10.1, 10.5, 10.2, 10.1, 10.4, 10.3. Frankly, he would be elated. All the readings are in the green band and they are very close to the center of the band. In Deming's world, and therefore in Japan, this would be a cause for alarm. The probability of one item having a reading above the means is 50 percent or 1/2. The probability of two above the mean in succession is 1/2 x 1/2, or 25 percent. The probability of eight in a row, which is equivalent to flipping a coin and obtaining eight heads in a row, is 1/2 x 1/2 x 1/2 x 1/2 x 1/2 x 1/2 x 1/2 x 1/2, or 1/256 or 0.04 percent, again a highly unlikely pattern. Thus, in America, where one relaxes with a cup of coffee when the readings are in the green band, such is not the case in Japan. In Japan, the managers and the quality circle team members—that is, the workers—search the statistical process control charts for unusual patterns that would signal the need to take corrective action.

A PROCESS OUT OF CONTROL

Having identified the nature of the stable process, one can move into what is a nonstable process. Figure 3.2 shows a nonstable process where the mean is gradually increasing. The exhibit clearly shows that the mean is not only above 10, but is also gradually drifting further away.

A changing variance, or standard deviation, is another sign of a process that is no longer stable. Figure 3.3 shows a process where the mean is still 10, but that the variance, as measured by the standard deviation, is slowly increasing.

An arithmetic calculation of the standard deviation would show that it is increasing. Another way to view this is to count the number of occurrences of readings above 11 and below 9 in Figure 3.1 and do the same for Figure 3.3. Clearly the probability of readings being more than one standard deviation from the mean has changed for the worse. This is a qualitative measure of an increasing standard deviation, or in the degree of variation in the process.

Once a process is considered to be unstable, the first and foremost course of action is to restore it to a stable condition. The only use of statistical control charts at this point is to verify that the process has been brought back to a stable condition. Once in a stable condition, and if the process is not being acted upon, nothing can be done with the inherent variability within the process. That is, the inherent variation can be looked upon as the consequence of "common" causes—variation that will not go away unless the process itself is changed. Tampering with the process settings will not reduce its inherent variability. In fact, it will make it worse.

To demonstrate this point of Deming's, a simulation can be performed where the settings are continuously changed in an attempt to reduce the variability in the process. Suppose a measurement reading of an item just manufactured is 11 with an initial setting of 10 on the machine making the item. Then suppose the setting is changed to 9.5 in order to compensate for the fact that the item just produced had a reading of 11. The next item has a performance rating of 9. Now the machine setting is changed to 10.5 and the next item is produced.

The rule guiding this sequence of adjustments to the machine or the process setting to reset the machine is one-half the difference between the actual reading and the desired reading of 10 from the benchmark setting of 10 in the appropriate compensating direction. For instance, if the current reading is 8, then one-half the difference between 8 and 10 is 1. The machine or process is then reset to 11 to increase the reading of the next item to be manufactured. If the next item has a reading of 13, one-half the difference between 13 and the desired rating of 10 is 1.5. As the reading is too high, the machine is reset to 8.5 prior to the manufacture of the next item. The standard deviation remains unchanged at 1 for all these adjustments. The resetting of the machine without affecting the inherent variation of the process is called tampering, whose results are shown in Figure 3.4.

The count of those times when the measurements are above 11 and below 9 is higher in Figure 3.4 than it is in Figure 3.1. This indicates in qualitative terms that the standard deviation has increased. A calculation of the standard deviation would prove this point quantitatively. Thus tampering with a stable process does not reduce the variability of the process—in fact, it increases it. Simulations can be run to demonstrate that different rules for adjusting the machine or process settings will not reduce the inherent variability of the process. The most likely outcome is that the inherent variability of the process will increase. Deming stresses that it is important for managers to realize that they cannot reduce the variability of a process unless they change the process itself.

FIGURE 3.1 STABLE PROCESS

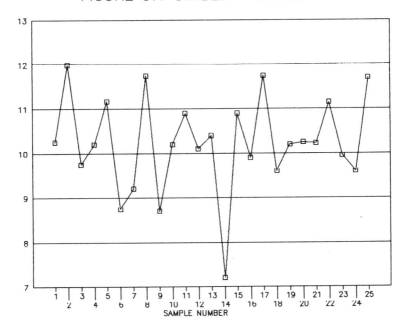

FIGURE 3.2 NONSTABLE PROCESS

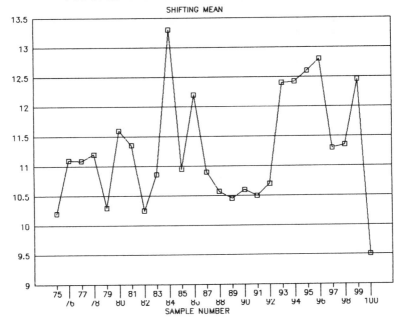

FIGURE 3.3 NONSTABLE PROCESS

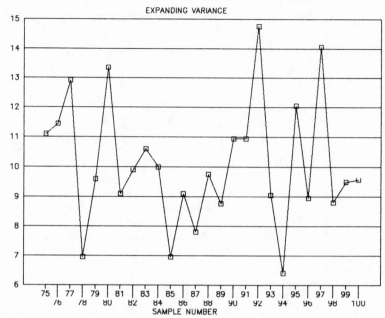

EXPANDING VARIANCE

FIGURE 3.4 STABLE PROCESS

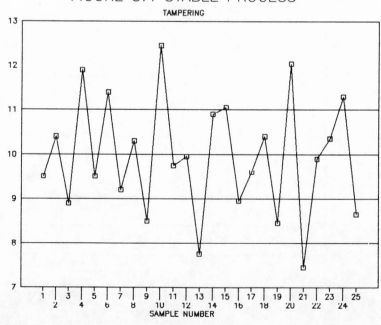

TAMPERING

THE PURPOSE OF STATISTICS AND MANAGEMENT

In Deming's world, the purpose of statistics is to examine the causes of variation in a process with the intent of taking action to reduce the variation of the process. The purpose of management is to lead an organization in the direction of never-ending and continuous improvement. In the world of Deming, there is no opportunity for a supervisor, manager, or the work force to rest on their laurels when they should be seeking ways to reduce the variation in the process.

Suppose a process consists of producing a component that involves a single shaft passing through four holes. The drilling machine is set up to drill holes with a diameter of 100 units. Its inherent variation, as measured by the standard deviation, is 0.2 units. The machine that makes the shafts can be adjusted to make shafts of different diameters, but the inherent variation (standard deviation) in the making of the shaft is also 0.2 units. The shaft must pass through four holes. If the diameter of the shaft is larger than any one of the four holes, then the shaft will not be able to turn when the component is tested. The component is then considered defective and is scrapped. On the other hand, if the difference between the diameter of any one of the four holes is greater than one unit of measure, then the spacing is too large. During the life of the component, the looseness between the shaft and the hole will lead to vibrations that will cause excessive wear. The manufacturer can expect an expense in the form of an exercise of warranty.

A third condition can arise when the spacings between the shaft and each of the four holes are all less than 0.5 units. A consumer would consider such a component to be of excellent quality. The fourth, and only remaining condition, is that the spacing between the shaft and one or more holes is in the range of 0.5 to 1.0 units. For this case, the consumer will consider the quality of the component to be good. Table 3.2 sets forth the conditions of quality.

A simulation can be run for drilling the holes and manufacturing the shafts and measuring the fit between them. This was done for five cases, or simulations, where the holes were all drilled to 100 units, but the shafts were made to different diameters. The standard deviation for both the holes and shafts was 0.2 units. For each of 1,000 components manufactured in the simulation, the spacing between the shaft and the individual four holes was measured and quality was determined in accordance with the previously described rules. The results were as shown in Table 3.3.

Table 3.2
Definition of Quality

Spacing Between the Shaft and Four Holes	Quality Description
Shaft is larger than any hole	Defective
Spacing more than 1 unit for any hole	Warranty expense
Spacing less than 0.5 units for all holes	Excellent
Spacing between 0.5-1.0 units for one or more holes	Good

Table 3.3
Managing Quality by Varying Settings

Percent Measure of Quality per Simulation					
Simulation Number	1	2	3	4	5
Diameter of Shaft in Units:	99.0	99.2	99.4	99.6	99.8
Quality Standards					
Defective (Scrapped)	0.1%	0.8%	4.9%	21.9%	50.3%
Excellent	0.0	1.1	6.1	16.7	19.5
Good	20.1	46.6	68.1	55.9	29.5
Warranty exercised	79.8	51.5	20.9	5.5	0.7

In reviewing the results, a setting of 99 in the manufacture of the shafts yields too wide a gap between the shaft and the holes leading to excessive warranty costs. A setting of 99.2 is better in that there is an appreciable drop in the number of warranties that are expected to be exercised and only a very small increase in scrappage. A setting of 99.4 and 99.6 generates an economic interplay between the cost of scrapping the components and the costs associated with the exercise of the warranties. The cost of scrapping a component is fairly quantifiable as long as the cost-accounting system can identify all labor and material costs associated with building the component up to this point. In theory, the costs associated with exercise of the warranty should be identifiable and, therefore, quantifiable. However, one would have trouble quantifying the loss of customer loyalty because of dissatisfaction engendered by the exercise of the warranty. Because loss of customer loyalty is difficult to quantify, some managers ignore such factors in analyzing the costs associated with an inferior product where there is a high probability that the warranty will be exercised. This leads to an underestimation of true costs and to possibly wrong decisions in justifying the extra costs of having an excellent quality product vis-à-vis the costs associated with guarantees and warranties stemming from average or inferior quality products.

In the world of Deming, management is intent on leading an organization in the quest of never-ending improvement through reduction of variation in the process. Suppose management focuses its attention on a shaft made with a diameter of 99.8 units. Variation in the process is reduced by taking actions that lead to a smaller value of the standard deviation, as shown in Table 3.4.

Simulation 5 is the same as before. It is used as a basis of comparison for the other simulations where the variability in the process itself has been reduced. Simulations 6 and 7 are interesting in that the simulations provide an answer to the question of whether effort is better expended in reducing the variance in the drilling of the holes or in the manufacture of the shafts. If one is restricted to improving the variability of just one part of the process, then the results of the simulation suggest that one is better off reducing the variability in the drilling of the holes rather than in the

Table 3.4
Managing Quality by Reducing Variance

Percent Measure of Quality per Simulation					
Simulation Number	5	6	7	8	9
Diameter of Shaft in Units:	99.8				
Diameter of Holes in Units:	100.0				
Standard Deviation					
of Holes:	0.2	0.2	0.1	0.1	0.05
of Shaft:	0.2	0.1	0.2	0.1	0.05
Quality Standards					
Defective (scrapped)	50.3%	50.9%	32.8%	22.1%	0.6%
Excellent	19.5	29.2	47.6	72.9	99.4
Good	29.5	19.9	19.6	5.0	0.0
Warranty exercised	0.7	0.0	0.0	0.0	0.0

manufacture of the shaft.

However, the selection of either is immaterial in the sense that Deming does not permit any rest in the reduction of variance in the process. Sooner or later, one must arrive at simulation 8, where in comparison with simulation 5, there is a substantial reduction in the number of defective components and a substantial increase in the number of excellent quality products. But there still is no resting on one's laurels. The unending commitment to reducing the variance in a process pushes a manufacturer to simulation 9 where, by single-minded determinism to reduce variation, the output of the factory has been transformed from 50 percent defective to 99.4 percent excellent quality. This has been accomplished solely by reducing the variance in the process.

Some years ago, Ford executives could not understand why transmissions built by Ford and Mazda had vastly different warranty costs. Transmissions built by both were of the same design, yet Ford had substantial warranty expenses while Mazda had virtually none. The Ford engineers took apart transmissions manufactured to the same design but in two different factories, and discovered that the variation associated with parts in the transmission built by Mazda was far less than those built by Ford. Table 3.4 illustrates this phenomenon: the lesser the degree of variation, the greater the portion with excellent quality at the sacrifice of fewer warranty claims and defects. Moreover, fewer warranty claims will probably generate greater customer loyalty, a benefit that is hard to quantify but is real in a world that shows no mercy toward manufacturers of inferior or average quality products.

In the world of Deming, having gained 99.4 percent achievement in producing products of excellent quality, can we now rest on our laurels? "Absolutely not," says

Deming. Herein lies an enormous philosophical difference between traditional American managerial values and those now prevalent in Japan.

DEMING'S FOURTEEN POINTS

Following hard on the heels of Deming's purpose of statistics to provide the information to take action to reduce variation, and the purpose of management to lead an organization in the direction of never-ending and continuous improvement (*keizen* in Japanese), is Deming's fourteen points. These points can be better understood once the statistical underpinnings of his thinking have been acknowledged. These are the points that transformed a near-bankrupt Toyota Motors into the Bank of Toyota.

1. Create Constancy of Purpose Toward Improvement of Product and Service with a Plan to Become Competitive, Stay in Business, and Provide Jobs

The Deming Chain Reaction is that building a better quality product will result in savings in cost. These savings are associated with less rework and scrap, and fewer warranty claims. The improved quality will result in more revenue as customers, satisfied with the quality of the product, become repeat customers. Repeat customers do not need the persuasion costs of advertising and marketing promotions because they intend to buy the product again.

Advertising and promotions are necessary for marginal quality products, where new customers must be drawn from the general population to replace those who are dissatisfied with the product and will not become repeat buyers. An excellent quality product is broadcast about by its satisfied consumers; word-of-mouth advertising is free—another manifestation of Crosby's claim that quality is free (1979). Interesting, word-of-mouth "disadvertising" for poor quality products is also free. It has been estimated that word-of-mouth disadvertising is four times more effective in dissuading consumers from buying a product than word-of-mouth advertising is in persuading consumers to purchase an excellent quality product. Put another way, consumers are more likely to complain about a poor quality product than praise an excellent quality product.

The enhanced revenue for a company that produces an excellent quality product comes about from increased sales both from repeat purchases of the product and from the promotional aspects of word of mouth. Revenue is further advanced by the premium that can be added to the price of the product. Surveys have shown that Americans are willing to pay up to 20 percent more for a car made in Japan than for a comparable car made in America as long as they are convinced that there is superior quality associated with the import. This premium will exist until such time as Americans feel that the Ford in their future can match the quality standards of Toyota or other Japanese car manufacturers.

The best-kept secret in America is that the quality gap between American-made and Japanese-made automobiles has already been substantially closed. This is a secret precisely because the perception among buyers is that Japanese-made automobiles still have higher quality. Whether there is a quality difference between American and Japanese automobiles is not the question; it is consumer perception that matters. The perception that Japanese cars are superior means that American car makers, whose quality is on a par with the Japanese, still have a long row to hoe before they can recapture their historic share of the market.

As consumer satisfaction enhances sales volume, the market share for the product expands. The workers benefit not only in greater job security but in more jobs being created. Thus better standards of quality mean greater job security and more jobs for workers. On the other side of the coin, not participating in the Deming revolution means greater costs in rework, scrap, and warranties, and, more important, less sales volume as the losers in the quality contest face a shrinking market share. Declining revenues and shrinking market share mean a greater risk of going out of business. That means less job security for workers and fewer jobs as the business contracts in a downward spiral to oblivion. Companies caught in the whirlpool of poor quality image, contracting sales volume, shrinking profits, and cutbacks in production, layoffs, and firings, have great difficulty reestablishing themselves in the market. The chances are that, once caught in the whirlpool, they will be sucked under. Thus it becomes clear that the constancy of purpose to never-ending improvement becomes a matter of corporate survival in a very competitive world.

Konosuke Matsushita (1989), executive director of Matsushita Electric, sums it up in words not too pleasant to hear:

> We are going to win and the industrial west is going to lose out: There's nothing much you can do about it, because the reasons for your failure are within yourselves. Your firms are built on the Taylor model; even worse, so are your heads. With your bosses doing the thinking while the workers yield the screwdrivers, you're convinced deep down that this is the right way to run a business. For you, the essence of management is getting the ideas out of the heads of the bosses into the hands of labor. We are beyond the Taylor model; business, we know, is now so complex and difficult, the survival of firms so hazardous in an environment increasingly unpredictable, competitive and fraught with danger, that their continued existence depends on the day-to-day mobilization of every ounce of intelligence.

2. Adopt the New Philosophy of a New Economic Age Where There Can no Longer be the Commonly Accepted Levels of Delays, Mistakes, Defective Material, and Defective Workmanship

The new economic age goes beyond enhancing the quality of a product on a never-ending basis. A. V. Feigenbaum states that "total quality control is an effective system for integrating the quality development, quality maintenance, and quality improvement efforts so as to enable marketing, engineering, production, and service to achieve full customer satisfaction" (1983).

In other words, quality goes far beyond the product itself. Quality includes shipping the product in time and having it arrive in good order. Quality means preparing the invoice correctly. Quality means bringing the consumer into company deliberations as to what constitutes good quality. Quality itself is defined in terms of what the consumer, or end user, thinks in terms of what is good or excellent quality from his or her perspective. The entire quality-improvement process is not driven internally by industrial engineers thinking what should be the next improvement to a product; it is driven externally by consumers interacting with industrial engineers to explain what they consider to be a quality improvement in a product.

The new economic age demands that management not go alone in the direction of never-ending improvement, but rather that management lead an organization, that includes the workers, also leaders in change. This is done by tapping worker brain power and having workers initiate change for those aspects of the process in which they are intimately involved. And no one is more involved with the operation of a machine in a factory than the worker operating the machine.

The organization of workers that best brings them into the process of initiating change is the quality control circle. These are groups of workers, often about ten individuals, responsible for a single phase of a manufacturing process. Quality control circles have not worked well in the United States when management restricts their activity to recommending an air-conditioning unit for the working comfort of the group or prevents the group from taking meaningful action to improve the quality of their product. This violates the very essence of the quality control circle. The concept of the quality control circle is doomed when management insists on maintaining its traditional Taylor rights.

The purpose of the quality control circle is to place responsibility for quality in the hands of those manufacturing the product. If the workers are to be responsible for the quality of their work, then they have to be able to make decisions that affect quality. For instance, the speed of an assembly line has a large impact on the quality of the product assembled. Lines that move too rapidly give rise to defective or inferior parts. If the workers are to be responsible for the quality of the product coming off the assembly line, then they must control the speed of that assembly line.

But this is a traditional management prerogative. It was on this point that American managers escorted Deming to the door, with directions on how best to get out of town. They could accept worker responsibility for product quality as long as management controlled the speed of the assembly line. This cannot be done; it is a contradiction in terms, an oxymoronic methodology. If workers are to be held responsible for the quality of their work, they have to control the pace of the work. If workers are to be held responsible for the quality of their goods, ultimately it is the workers who should decide whether a shipment is made to a customer. These are matters that a Taylor-inspired generation of managers could never accept.

Interestingly, U.S. labor unions joined management in ushering Deming off the premises. The concept of workers responsible for the quality of their work did not matter to them, but the consequences of such a policy did matter. They were not keen on having the labor force sympathetic to the goals of the corporation. How can there be the historic animosity between management and labor if labor associates itself with the welfare of the corporation? How can there be an old-fashioned strike under these conditions? What is left for the labor union leader to do when the union is in league with management to manufacture a superior product?

In Japan, quality control circles have been given wide responsibilities. They control the assignment of personnel to machines, set standards for preventive maintenance of those machines, and maintain quality control standards. Put another way, they control what is shipped to a customer and have usurped the management prerogatives of the factory floor supervisor.

American managers rightfully see this as an infringement of their rights: the lower-level management rung is taken by the workers. What they don't see is that there aren't many managers eager to be on that lowest rung of the management ladder. Shop floor supervisors are the most difficult management positions to fill. The Japanese production system works without the lowest-rung managers. Instead, workers supervise their own work. This gives them a feeling of control over their destiny (Theory Z). They are responsible for their own actions. They have a sense of identity with the corporation. This identity and meaning for their work intensifies their interest in the welfare of the company, increases their personal satisfaction for spending the bulk of their waking time on the shop floor, and enhances their morale and their productivity. Absentee and turnover rates plummet. A happier, or more satisfied work force is less apt to strike, since strikes are often more a matter of an unhappy work force than a dispute over the level of pay.

An excellent example of how to create a positive work environment is found in Joseph M. Juran's book *Leadership for Quality* (1989). A group of employees at a telephone company were responsible for publishing the local area directories. Publication of these directories was divided into twenty-one distinct steps, and each employee was responsible for one step. One can well imagine the ease in employing work standards and numerical goals to judge the proficiency of each employee in this twenty-one-step sequence. This is a classic Theory X workplace: the worker must be driven to produce. Unfortunately, the employees were unhappy with their work, manifesting itself in high rates of absenteeism and personnel turnover.

One day someone thought of reorganizing the entire function. Instead of one person being responsible for a single step, each person was assigned full responsibility for all twenty-one steps for a set of local area directories. In effect, one person became editor and publisher of a set of telephone books; it was his or her sole responsibility to publish the particular telephone books. That responsibility was shared with no one else, and no one supervised the employee. In effect, each employee became an independent businessperson with a mission and each had some control over his or her destiny. Theory X gave way to Theory Z.

With the work reorganized in this fashion, employees were awarded with the satisfaction of doing a complete job on their own with the company trusting them to carry out their mission. Work suddenly became meaningful. Supervisory personnel were no longer needed, nor was there need for quotas and production goals. Gone were the high absenteeism and personnel turnover rates. Productivity and personnel morale was up, costs (in the form of supervisory personnel and record keeping of performance standards and goals) were down. The story had a happy ending.

There is much for management to learn from this example. The hardest lesson is that managers must let go of their traditional mechanisms of control. They must learn to lead rather than control the workers. This is the most poignant distinguishing feature between Taylorism and Demingism.

3. Cease Dependence on Mass Inspection. Require Statistical Evidence that Quality is Being Built into the Product to Eliminate the Need for Mass Inspection

Four shift supervisors rotate regularly during the course of a day, each producing 10,000 components per shift. At the end of the shift, a random sample of 50 components is selected and tested. The nature of the process is such that one must expect a 20 percent defect rate. (A simulation was run that was equivalent to drawing 50 Beads out of a bag of 10,000 beads—8,000 white and 2,000 red. The percentage of defects was the percentage of red beads in the sample of 50.) The results of these inspections for each individual shift supervisor over a five-day period are shown in Table 3.5.

The action taken by the manager with respect to each of the shift supervisors cannot be criticized for unconventionality. It is the usual set of reactions a manager responsible for the operational performance of a factory is expected to take in trying to improve the productivity of the plant. Tom does seem to have his shift under control. Perhaps it is time for Tom to head up a seminar on how to do things right. Perhaps it

Table 3.5
Normal Management Reactions to Test Results

Percent Defect Rate in Test Sample for Each Shift Supervisor				Managerial Action
Day	Bertha	Tom	Agatha	Jim	

Day	Bertha	Tom	Agatha	Jim	
1	16%	12%	20%	24%	Give Tom the Day Award for best performance and appraise Jim privately of his results.
2	28	12	14	24	Reward Tom again with Day Award, pat Agatha on the back for improving her performance, and have a private talk with Jim and Bertha.
3	14	24	10	26	Give Agatha the Day Award and congratulate Bertha in taking care of her problem; check to see why Tom is having a bad day and give Jim a warning about the necessity of improving his performance.
4	26	18	24	22	Congratulate yourself on squaring away Tom and wonder about what to do with the others.
5	24	14	18	34	Perhaps it's time to have Tom teach the others how to improve their performance, and time to take serious remedial action against Jim for his consistently poor performance.

is too late for Jim to rectify his ways. After all, he has been successively warned about his poor performance and his performance on the last shift has been a total disaster. Jim is in danger of losing his livelihood.

Yet the sad fact is that each shift supervisor has been performing exactly the same—each producing 10,000 components of which 2,000 are defective. The shift results actually are the results of simulation of randomly selecting 50 components from a population of 10,000, with 2,000 randomly distributed defective components. Specifically, 10,000 cells are set up with 8,000 of the cells containing the number 1 and 2,000 cells containing the number 2. Fifty cells are selected randomly and the cell contents analyzed as to whether the number contained therein is 1 or 2. This is a computer version of Deming's red and white marble experiment. The manager could not differentiate between normal variance in sample results and the results of a shift supervisor's performance. In this example, the sampling distribution favored Tom at the expense of Jim, yet both were performing the same. It is the same reason why Tom may do better at a game of poker than Jim: the luck of the draw.

The sampling error can be reduced by increasing the size of the sample. However, even a sample size of 100 has a surprisingly wide variation, though considerable time and effort are expended to obtain statistically meaningful results. This effort could be better directed at having inspectors try to improve the nature of a process that has an inherent defect rate of 20 percent. However, even in Deming's world, inspection is not eliminated. It is necessary to provide the data for statistical control charts. But the purpose of the charts is not to award Tom at the expense of Jim, but to provide the statistical means whereby one can plan the next course of action to further reduce the variations inherent in the process.

4. End the Practice of Awarding Contracts to Suppliers on the Basis of Price. Depend on Meaningful Measures of Quality Along with Price. Move Toward a Single Supplier on a Long Term Relationship Based on Loyalty and Trust

Perhaps there is no greater difference in managerial practices between America and Japan than in the area of purchasing. It is almost incomprehensible that two systems can be so different (see Table 3.6)

Deming, in his book *Out of the Crisis*, states that there is always one supplier out of many that outperforms the others. This may be in the quality of the product or the nature of the service provided. There may be aspects associated with the supplier's product that are outside the specifications of the product. An analogy is a Bach violin concerto played by a high school student on a normally abused high school violin versus the same piece played by a professional violinist on a Stradivarius. Both violinists perform within specifications: all notes are played correctly and none are missed. Can one detect, in listening to the two performances, a difference in quality?

The same is true for products or components coming into a factory. There is a supplier whose product or components are better, even though there are others whose are within specifications. Select that supplier as the potential single-source supplier and begin a long-term relationship based on mutual trust and respect.

How does one accept a shipment from a supplier in Deming's world? Here is where the disciple parts with the master. The master for Deming is Shewhart. Shewhart was one of the founders of the American Society of Quality Control. That society, at least historically, has favored statistical testing of shipments so the purchaser can either accept or reject a shipment. The method is based on an agreement between purchaser and supplier as to four matters of interest:

1. What is a good shipment in terms of the percentage of defects?
2. What is a bad shipment in terms of the percentage of defects?
3. What risk is the purchaser willing to assume in accepting a bad shipment from a supplier?
4. What risk is the supplier willing to assume in the purchaser's rejecting a good shipment?

Once these matters are settled, tables that have been statistically derived can be entered to find the size, sample and test statistic, or decision point upon which to make a decision. When the shipment arrives at the purchaser's door, the purchaser draws out the requisite number of items, tests them, and calculates the defect rate. If the defect rate is above a stipulated value, the purchaser has the right to send the shipment back. If the defect rate is below the stipulated value, he is obliged to accept the shipment.

Deming's criticism of this conventional methodology is that a specified defect rate becomes legally binding, so to speak. As long as the shipment can pass the test, it must be accepted. There is no inducement to lower the defect rate; it becomes ingrained in the system. The purchaser must accept the shipment as long as the sample can pass the test.

As an alternative, Deming suggests either no inspection or 100 percent inspection. The decision as to which is strictly a matter of economics. Suppose a shipment of 1,000 components arrives and the cost of inspection is $1 per unit. If the defect rate is 1 percent and the cost of repairing a defective item is $10, then the total cost of 100 per-

Table 3.6
Purchasing: A World Apart

	UNITED STATES	JAPAN
Quantity	Large, preferably by the truckload with a largest possible discount. Store in a warehouse until needed.	Small, by the wheelbarrowful just in time for assembly in the product.
Discounts	The bigger the better.	No such thing.
Contract duration	The shorter the better.	Never-ending as long as performance is up to standards.
Number of suppliers competing	The more the better.	Single supplier usually selected from within *heiretsu*, or family of closely associated companies.
Primary criteria in selecting suppliers	Price and availability.	Reliability of delivery and quality of product.
Attitude of purchaser toward purchaser	Get the lowest price at any cost.	A deal is made for the long-term mutual benefit of both parties.
Attitude of purchaser toward supplier	Get even when the opportunity presents itself	A deal is made for the long term mutual benefit of both parties.
Market intelligence	Of great value; contracts short and new ones always needed.	No importance; deal once done is done forever.
Pricing	Intensely competitive	Administered at cost plus small profit margin.
Negotiations	End with contract signing.	Continual dialogue between supplier and purchaser.
Contracts	Legal instruments.	Usually understood without formal documentation.
Lawyers	Needed in contract writing and litigation.	Very few lawyers in Japan.

cent inspection is $1 x 1,000 units + $10 x 1 percent x 1,000 units of $1,100.

Now suppose that the incoming shipment is not inspected. Therefore, 1 percent of the output of the plant will have a defective component in it. Suppose that the output of the plant is inspected and the cost of replacing a defective part, now installed in the final product, is $150. The cost of not inspecting the incoming shipment is the defect rate of the component times the number of products times the cost of repairing the final product, or 1 percent x 1,000 units x $150 or $1,500. Thus, it is economically desirable to inspect 100 percent of the incoming shipment.

The 1 percent defect rate is merely the starting point of a long-term relationship. The objective of this long-term relationship with a single supplier is that the purchaser and supplier work together to reduce the defect rate until it is economically justified to have no inspection of incoming shipments. This breakeven defect rate *(D)* can be determined by matching the costs of no inspection with that of total inspection:

$$\$1 \times 1,000 + \$10 \times D \times 1,000 = \$150 \times D \times 1,000$$

A breakeven defect rate of 0.7 percent is the demarcation point between 0 percent and 100 percent inspection. Once the defect rate is less than 0.7 percent, incoming shipments are accepted without inspection. But eliminating inspection of incoming shipments is not the objective of lowering the defect rate below 0.7 percent. It is simply a step toward lowering the defect rate to 0.5 percent, then to 0.3 percent, and to ever lower rates until virtually defect-free products make up the incoming shipments.

Those in the six sigma crowd espouse defect rates measured in three to ten parts per million. In this virtually defect-free world, the traditional methodology of determining a good and bad shipment, and enumerating the twin risks of accepting bad shipments and rejecting good shipments, becomes irrelevant. The required sample size is so enormous that it is essentially the same as 100 percent inspection. Yet, as Deming has demonstrated economically, defects of less than ten per million is far past the point of eliminating inspections of incoming shipments.

5. Improve Constantly and Forever the System of Production and Service Using the Plan-Do-Check-Act Cycle

The Plan-Do-Check-Act (PDCA) cycle is commonly called Deming's cycle; Deming refers to it as the Shewhart's cycle in honor of the man who espoused it. The PDCA cycle is what is supposed to be done when there are no points on a statistical process control chart in the red band—that is, more than three standard deviations from the mean. The PDCA cycle is to be performed when there are no unusual patterns of points in the green band. Therefore, managers and workers are either taking corrective action because of readings in the red band or when there are unusual patterns, or they are participating in the PDCA cycle. There is no opportunity to rest on the oars when the process is stable and under control. At every waking moment, everyone is at some point in the Plan-Do-Check-Act cycle of a never-ending search for improvement in the process or product.

In short, there is no time to contemplate the origin of the universe or what is for dinner. A manager may be planning some experiment to see if a change can improve the nature of the process. But if not doing that, then he or she may be doing the test to see if the idea has merit. If not at that stage of the cycle, then the manager may be checking the results of the test. And if not there, then he or she must be acting on the results—either incorporating the new procedure into the process or abandoning it as unfruitful. Everyone must be somewhere in the cycle, since the cycle is all-inclusive when no readings are in the red band and there are no unusual patterns in the green band. Once a manager finishes the cycle, there is no choice but to start the cycle over again by planning another experiment to test a possible change that can improve the process. There is an aspect of this that seems similar to Dante's inferno: sinners are given no reprieve.

6. Institute Modern Methods of Training Including Statistical Methods and Thinking

Workers and managers alike have to be taught the meaning of the statistical control process charts, their construction and usage, and their role in reducing variation. This is just the beginning. For quality circles to function properly, workers must be taught how to bring ideas to the forefront. Brainstorming sessions can be more effective if workers are taught brainstorming techniques. The Ishikawa fishbone, or cause-and-effect diagram, is a way workers can break down the barriers that prevent them from consciously thinking about what they are doing in order to identify potential causes of variation or problems in a process.

In Japan, the very appearance of a defect is viewed as a challenge to seek its cause. Pareto diagrams have managers focus the scarce resources of an organization on a vital few, rather than the trivial many, which may be responsible for as much as 80 percent of the defects. Training is an essential part of an organization that is constantly in search of ways to do a better job. It is an inescapable responsibility of management to ensure that such training takes place.

7. Institute Modern Methods of Supervision Where the Goal is Continuous and Never-Ending Improvement

Some managers pride themselves in running their organization in a military manner. They have a penchant for formal hierarchy and chains of communication. This fits in nicely with Taylorism: managers are the officers and workers are the soldiers. Officers are expected to give orders and soldiers are expected to obey them, preferably blindly. Yet those who espouse such a model conveniently forget the relationship between the lowest ranking officer and the soldiers. It is not a managerial function when the second lieutenant gets in front of his men and signals them to move forward. That function is leadership. Leadership is the glue that binds officers to their men. Management may be the glue holding together a bureaucratic structure, but it is not the binding force on the battleground. If managers want to follow the military mode, they ought to seriously consider joining the military.

In Deming's world, leadership is exerted. Managers are expected to lead the process by which variations in quality are reduced. They are expected to lead the process of never-ending, continuous improvement. This is not a job to be delegated to others or pushed into the remotest corner of the production management department. Quality requires a leader. Mr. Toyoda of Toyota Motors leads the process, with every manager under him doing his part. The lowest rung on the management ladder—those who oversee the operations of several quality control circles, in reality the lowest rung of the middle management ladder—must learn to lead rather than direct the operations of these quality control circles. In making workers assume responsibility for their work, they have turned over to them what used to be the lowest rung of management, the shopfloor supervisor. Workers must now participate in improving the process, since they are closest to the actual manufacture of the product.

In addition to leading the workers, management must be responsible for looking outside the organization to see what other companies are doing and bring back the results to the factory floor, to the internal administrative functions of a corporation, or to any other part of the company that makes products or provides services. The most difficult aspect of the transition from management to leadership is learning how to let go of traditional mechanisms of control. The modern method of supervision hands the responsibility of performance over to those who do the performing.

8. Drive Out the Fear from the Work Force

The greatest fear of the work force is being laid off. In Japan, great care is taken to ensure workers are not laid off. Huge interlocking networks of companies, known as *heiretsu*, permit Japanese companies to shift workers from one industry to another, in contrast to the more narrowly structured western organization of independent companies. Yet Japanese managers within the *heiretsu* are not legally bound to find work for everyone employed within the *heiretsu*. Japanese management considers it its personal responsibility to look after the social welfare of its workers and managers alike.

This situation makes the Japanese worker comfortable with change. The installation of a robot is viewed as a means of deliverance from monotony, for example. As a result of the robot, the worker's job should become more interesting. The Japanese worker knows that the company will protect his job. If training is necessary to upgrade to a new status of worker, the training is made available. Japanese workers consider themselves part of an extended family.

In contrast, in the United States, installation of a robot is viewed in terms of who will lose their jobs. It is by no means clear how this fear can be driven out of the American psyche. And this is not the only fear that pervades the system. There is fear of reprisal, where workers are made cooperative through intimidation, threat of job loss, or whim of manager or supervisor. There is fear of failure, where a suggestion that does not prove workable can lead to punishment. There is fear of being the bearer of the bad news when there are poor results in a PDCA experiment. There is fear of not knowing what is going on, which leads to suspicion. There is the manager's fear of giving up control, so that workers can't assume responsibility for the goods they produce. And finally, there is fear of change, of which Niccolo Machiavelli, in 1514, wrote:

> It should be borne in mind that there is nothing more difficult to arrange, more doubtful of success, and more dangerous to carry through than initiating changes. The innovator makes enemies of all those who prospered under the old order, and only lukewarm support from those who would prosper under the new. Their support is partly from fear of their adversaries, who have the existing laws on their side, and partly because men are generally incredulous, never really trusting new things unless they have tested them by experience.

9. Break Down Organizational Barriers and Promote Teamwork

This is more easily done in Japan, where the wall between management and labor is not so well constructed as in America. In Deming-inspired factories management officers are on the factory floor and their dress is not greatly differentiated from that of workers. Their "perks" are less visible because there are less of them. Their office surroundings are functional; they park their cars in the same parking lot as the workers, and they eat in a common dining hall. A good leader can promote teamwork and, as any second lieutenant knows, retain the prerogatives of an officer. There is no need to call each other "comrade." That system, now assigned to the dustbin of history, didn't work because it preserved the hierarchy of bureaucratic command. Workers did not participate in the system; neither, for that matter, did factory managers.

What has to be changed is the concept that management is comfortably ensconced in an office far from the factory floor, communicating through memorandums with goals thought up during a round of golf. Management must have first-hand experience with what occurs on the factory floor and must be able to talk with those who are on the front lines. This common-sense type of leadership has always been part of successful companies. But the competitive advantage that comes from corralling the imagination and minds of the work force for the welfare of the corporation can no longer be ignored. The plush office is no longer the essence of a manager.

One of the great benefits the Japanese achieved by breaking down organizational barriers is what is called simultaneous or concurrent engineering. In the American system adopted by the Japanese, separate organizations represented the functions of research, development, manufacturing process design, and manufacturing. Research thought of an idea. The idea was passed on to Development. Development did not think that it was a good idea for such and such reason, and sent it back to Research. The idea was passed back and forth, until Research eventually modified its idea to be acceptable to Development. Development then did what it had to do with the idea and passed it to Manufacturing Process Design. Then the internal looping repeated itself, with Manufacturing Process Design rejecting the work done by Development, then Development modifying its work until it was acceptable to Manufacturing Process Design. The same internal loop would come into play as Manufacturing Process Design passed its work to Manufacturing.

Each of these functions was an independent bureaucracy usually well separated physically from the others. There was little communication other than the internal loop of rejection and modification. The upshot was that the time from identification of a new idea to delivery from Manufacturing was about seven years.

The Japanese inaugurated what is called simultaneous or concurrent engineering. They merged the separate and independent divisions of research, development, manufacturing process design, and manufacturing into one organization. If at all possible, the groups are placed in one building; better yet, all are on one floor of a building. Their desks are intermingled so that people in research have no choice but to become acquainted with those in development. To further encourage cross-pollination, everyone parks in the same lot, eats in the same dining hall, and shares the same recreational facilities.

Moreover, members of each functional area are not allowed to meet separately. When those in research desire to explore the possibilities of a new idea, the meeting must have representatives from development, manufacturing process design, and manufacturing. This is true for meetings of any functional area—they must have representatives from the other functions. This collaborative team of researchers, developers, design, and production engineers was expanded to include representatives of marketing plus representatives of users or consumers of the product. The upshot is that cycle time has been cut by more than half, to three or less years. Moreover, U.S.

companies that have adopted simultaneous or concurrent engineering—such as NCR, AT&T, John Deere, Ford, General Electric, Eastman Kodak, Motorola, and nearly all other world-class manufacturers—have also discovered that products developed in this environment have far fewer parts and the parts lend themselves better to manufacturing. In addition, assembly time is reduced and there are far fewer defects.

10. Eliminate Arbitrary Numerical Goals, Posters, and Slogans for the Work Force that Seek New Levels of Productivity Without Providing Methods

The manager who makes a once-a-year appearance before the troops to let them know that a 10 percent improvement in productivity will be awarded with a 1 percent bonus, only to disappear from view for another year, is anathema to Deming. Deming feels that a worthwhile manager musters some idea of how increased productivity is to be accomplished, then takes an active part in achieving this goal. Management By Objective (MBO) is not high on Deming's list of desirable management techniques. In fact, Deming feels that any manager who cannot contribute to the never-ending process of product improvement cannot, and should not, call himself a manager.

Arbitrary numerical goals divorced from reality, or posters and slogans that urge but do not tell how to enhance productivity, are not in Deming's world. Deming tells an interesting tale of being in a railroad repair facility whose walls were covered with posters urging workers on to higher levels of productivity without telling them how to accomplish these goals. Deming asked a worker for the average number of hours he spent in obtaining a part. The worker answered that he usually spent six hours a day waiting in line to obtain a part, which left him two hours a day for productive work. In Deming's world, managers ought not to think of how best to plaster the walls with posters, but how the repair facility can be reorganized to reduce waiting time. After all, shortening the waiting time by two hours per day would double the productivity of the facility without any posters at all!

11. Eliminate Work Standards and Numerical Quotas

This is the death of Taylorism. One may wonder what keeps the workers honest in Japan. Why don't they simply set the production quota at some abysmally low level so they can take a six-hour lunch break? What keeps the system honest?

The answer is the bonus system. About one-third or more of each worker's pay, is a bonus tied to the profitability of the company. In some strange way, Taylor's work standards and numerical quotas are very much alive in Japan, except that the workers set the standards. By increasing their productivity, they see larger bonus checks. The bonus checks keep the workers oriented toward what is beneficial for the company, since what is beneficial for the company is beneficial for their wallets. Restrictive work rules, indolence in fellow workers, and a punch-clock mentality all mean less pay for the workers.

The bonus system does more than focus worker attention on the best interests of the corporation. It guarantees that labor costs will fall when a company faces a deteriorating business climate. As business slows down, the amount paid in bonuses diminishes along with profitability. This gives Japanese companies more staying power during depressed business conditions because labor costs also fall. Also in Japan, the first group to have its bonuses cut is management—another factor that encourages workers to orient their thinking to the best interest of the corporation. This is not true in the United States. Labor costs remain constant though the volume of business diminishes. As a company nears negative cash flow, it cuts costs by laying off its work force.

The bonus system has been criticized in the United States because workers become accustomed to a bonus as a certain amount of money. They are not able to cope with a smaller check and become disgruntled. But the Japanese associate the bonus with the profitability of their company. They realize that smaller profits mean smaller paychecks. They also realize that smaller paychecks for all at least defers layoffs. All of this is a matter of education—acceptance is made easier for workers once they realize that management is part of the same system.

Too often in America, remuneration for top executives is so out of line with any measure of comparison that workers feel management's only real purpose is to "gut" the corporation. How can workers associate themselves with the welfare of the company when paychecks for the executives are in the millions of dollars, while, at the same time, executives are laying off blue- and white- collar employees as a cost-savings measure to enhance profitability? The mystery here is how these highly paid individuals can lay off workers without cutting their own salaries and do it with a straight face.

12. Remove Barriers that Rob Employees of Their Pride in Workmanship, Particularly Performance Appraisal Systems

In many ways, the institution of just-in-time practices on the shop floor, with quality control circles responsible for the goods being produced, does away with performance appraisal systems. Just-in-time is its own performance appraisal system. A worker who makes slipshod parts will quickly see the red light flash and the production line grind to a halt. He or she will see engineers and managers rush to the station next to his and inquire why the line was stopped—an old management prerogative taken over by the workers. The worker who stopped the line will state simply that he was handed a bad part. Since it is his responsibility to ensure the quality of what leaves his hands, he exercises his right to stop the production line. All eyes now shift to the individual who just made the defective part.

What need is there for a formal appraisal system? The worker who made the bad part has just been appraised by the worker downstream, by the engineers, by management, by the entire organization: the production line has stopped because of his poor performance. The output has been reduced, so the bonus checks have been reduced as well. In essence, the system sorts the wheat from the chaff without any shuffling of performance appraisal forms.

13 and 14. Institute a Vigorous Program of Education and Training. Create an Organizational Structure that Will Push these Points Every Day

Deming does not elaborate on the exact nature of education and training. Nor does he say much about organizational structure. These matters have been more deeply explored by Juran and others. Perhaps it is appropriate to let Mr. Matsushita (1989) conclude with his words, since they fit well with Deming's last two points:

For us, the core of management is precisely the art of mobilizing and pulling together the intellectual resources of all employees in the service of the firm. Only by drawing on the combined brainpower of all its employees can a firm face up to the turbulence and constraints of today's environment.

This is why our large companies give their employees three to four times more training than yours, this is why they foster within the firm such intensive exchange and communication. This is why they seek constantly everybody's suggestions and why they demand from the educational system increasing numbers of graduates as well as bright and well-educated generalists, because these people are the lifeblood of industry.

Your socially-minded bosses, often full of good intentions, believe their duty is to protect the people in their firms. We, on the other hand, are realists and consider it our duty to get our people to defend their firms which will pay them back a hundredfold for their dedication. By doing this we end up being more social than you.

REFERENCES

American Society for Quality Control. Proceedings of the 43rd Annual Quality Congress, 1989.

Crosby, P. B. *Quality is Free: The Art of Making Quality Certain.* New York: McGraw-Hill, 1979.

Deming, E. W. *Out of the Crisis.* Cambridge, MA: Center for Advanced Engineering Study, 1986.

Feigenbaum, A. V. *Total Quality Control.* New York: McGraw-Hill, 1983.

Juran, M. J. *Leadership for Quality.* New York: Free Press/McMillan, 1989.

Chapter 4

Quality Assurance and Expert Systems

John F. Affisco and Mahesh Chandra

As global competition increases in intensity, it is becoming more crucial than ever for companies to provide high-quality products and services to the market place. This translates into the design of new products that are easier to manufacture, faster to place in the market, and more reliable and safer to operate and maintain. The best manufacturers realize that this can be achieved only by an organization-wide focus on and commitment to quality. That is, quality should be of major concern at every point, beginning with product design, continuing through manufacture, and culminating with user support services.

Many companies have turned to information technology in their quest for improved quality. One example of this technology is expert systems, an artificial intelligence technique which, when applied to manufacturing settings, has resulted in significant quality improvements. There are two specific applications of expert systems related to quality. The first is a master machinist expert system that oversees the new $17 million flexible manufacturing system that was installed by Westinghouse Electric Corporation in General Dynamics Corporation's Fort Worth, Texas, plant. This has resulted in quality levels never less than 100 percent. The other is a system designed to diagnose defects in disk drives produced at Hewlett-Packard's Boise, Idaho, plant. Diagnosing such disk defects previously involved passing them through an environmental testing chamber and took anywhere from an afternoon to three days. The expert system built for this purpose now does the job in thirty seconds with 99 percent accuracy, and has saved more than one million dollars (Smart Factories, 1989).

Expert systems are special-purpose computer programs that use knowledge and reasoning to perform complex tasks in a specific problem domain, at a level of performance usually associated with an expert. Originally these systems were designed to replace domain experts. Today, especially in business applications, they are viewed as knowledge-based decision support systems. That is, they are systems that support managerial decisionmaking with the capability of processing knowledge in addition to quantitative data.

In this chapter we discuss the use of expert systems in quality assurance. We describe the basic concept of an expert system, give an overview of quality assurance, present a sample consultation of a simple expert system that assists in the selection of sampling plans, and present a framework for the broader use of expert systems in quality assurance.

EXPERT SYSTEMS—SOME BASIC CONCEPTS

An expert system (ES) or knowledge-based system (KBS) is a computer program that exhibits the intelligent behavior of human experts in solving difficult problems. To accomplish this, the software generally includes a knowledge base pertaining to a specific domain and an inference engine used to process that knowledge and arrive at a solution to the problem. A key feature of an ES is that it emphasizes consultation and reasoning rather than calculation.

Figure 4.1 illustrates the basic components of an expert system. The knowledge base is the repository of domain-specific knowledge that will be used to solve the problem at hand. This knowledge needs to be represented and employed in a form that can be used for reasoning. Therefore, knowledge structures are used to store knowledge and reason with it, just as data structures are used to store and deal with data. Among the most widely used of such knowledge structures are facts, rules, and frames.

Figure 4.1
Expert Systems Architecture

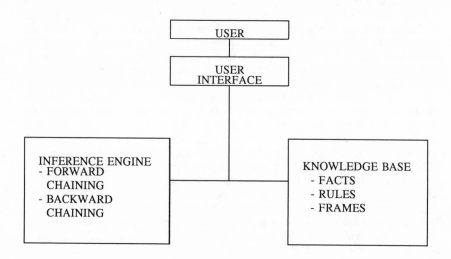

Facts are general statements of truth that may be either permanent or temporary knowledge. *Rules* are a knowledge structure of the form "if-then," where the "if" statement represents a premise and the "then" statement is a conclusion. As rules are processed, if the premise is true, then the conclusion indicates some action to be taken. That is, a rule suggests that the conclusion follows from the premise in a logical or action-oriented way. A rule is proved when the premise of the rule matches known facts. The effect of proving a rule is to confirm its conclusion. Rules allow the generation of new knowledge in the form of facts that are not originally available but can be deduced from other pieces of knowledge. These facts are generated as the conclusions of rules that have been applied.

Typical rules might be:

Rule 1: IF Inspection is Destructive THEN Sampling is Necessary.

Rule 2: IF Parts are Fatigue-Critical THEN Sampling is not Appropriate.

Depending upon which ES building tool is used, the syntax of the above rules will differ. For example, if CLIPS, an ES shell created by NASA for use in government applications, is utilized these rules will look like:

```
(defrule one                 "inspection is destructive"
(inspection destructive)
greater than
(assert (sampling is necessary)))
(defrule two                 "parts are fatigue-critical"
(parts fatigue-critical)
greater than
(assert (sampling not appropriate)))
```

Frames are a way of packaging knowledge within a well-defined structure. In many cases, it is convenient to gather in one place a number of different kinds of information about one object. Frames, which provide this capability, are composed of slots, roughly equivalent to fields in data records, in which data or characteristics associated with specific objects are stored. These frames are organized in a hierarchy similar to a material requirement planning (MRP) bill of material, which allows for sharing of knowledge through the property of inheritance. Figure 4.2 presents a simple frame representation for statistical control charts. Each rectangle represents a frame. The frames are organized in a hierarchy running from general information to more specific relations. Note that each frame has a direct relationship to its parent and that information contained in the parent's slots is inherited by the children. For example, the attribute control charts frame indicates that attribute or discrete data are required. This knowledge is inherited by both the proportion chart and the control chart frames. Therefore, both of these charts are based on discrete data. Thus, frames are especially efficient for packaging knowledge and handling the storage and retrieval of that knowledge while rules work best at making deductions. Many expert systems tasks can be effectively accomplished using either rules or frames. However, in order to capitalize on the benefits of both, some expert system building tools provide the capability to combine rules and frames.

The inference engine has the task of processing the domain knowledge contained in the knowledge base to arrive at a solution to the problem. To accomplish this, the inference engine combines facts and rules through the use of an inference process to arrive at conclusions. There are two broad inference techniques widely used by expert systems. The first is known as *forward chaining*. Forward chaining begins with known facts and the rule set and attempts to deduce new facts that may eventually lead to deduction of the goal. In forward chaining systems the inference engine cycles through the rules until one is found whose premise matches a fact. This rule is then proved or fired, and the conclusion is added to the fact base. This process continues until the implication of the conclusions reached are sufficient to provide a solution (achieve the goal) for the problem being processed. A naive example of forward chaining is given in Figure 4.3. The purpose of this consultation is to determine the correct type of control chart to be used as part of a statistical process control system for a particular item. Imagine that we have a set of rules relating to control chart selection like that shown in Figure 4.3. Further imagine that as part of the consultation the user provides the information that appears in the facts column. The facts that the item can be determined to be good or bad (go/no go) and measurement is difficult trigger the first

Figure 4.2
A Frame Representation for Statistical Control Charts

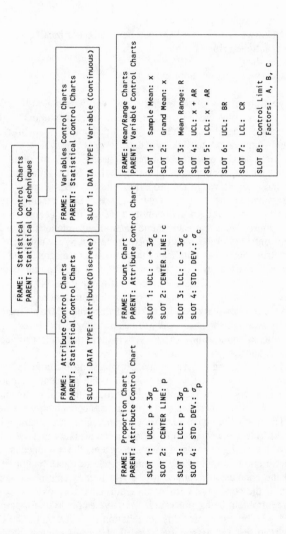

FRAME: Statistical Control Charts
PARENT: Statistical QC Techniques

FRAME: Attribute Control Charts
PARENT: Statistical Control Charts

SLOT 1: DATA TYPE: Attribute(Discrete)

FRAME: Variables Control Charts
PARENT: Statistical Control Charts

SLOT 1: DATA TYPE: Variable (Continuous)

FRAME: Proportion Chart
PARENT: Attribute Control Chart

SLOT 1: UCL: $p + 3\sigma_p$
SLOT 2: CENTER LINE: p

SLOT 3: LCL: $p - 3\sigma_p$
SLOT 4: STD. DEV.: σ_p

FRAME: Count Chart
PARENT: Attribute Control Chart

SLOT 1: UCL: $c + 3\sigma_c$
SLOT 2: CENTER LINE: c

SLOT 3: LCL: $c - 3\sigma_c$
SLOT 4: STD. DEV.: σ_c

FRAME: Mean/Range Charts
PARENT: Variable Control Charts

SLOT 1: Sample Mean: x

SLOT 2: Grand Mean: x

SLOT 3: Mean Range: R

SLOT 4: UCL: x + AR

SLOT 5: LCL: x - AR

SLOT 6: UCL: BR

SLOT 7: LCL: CR

SLOT 8: Control Limit
        Factors: A, B, C

76

Figure 4.3
Inference Processes

FORWARD CHAINING

Rules	Facts

IF: Item can be judged as good or bad ——————— Item is good or bad.
       and measurement is difficult. ———— Measurement difficult.

THEN: An attribute chart is recommended. ———

IF: Exact measurement is practical and
       exact measurement is crucial
       to quality.

THEN: Variable control charts are
       recommended.

IF: Attribute chart is recommended and ———
       (production quantities are small ———— Production Quantity Small
       or product is extremely large or ———— Product is complex.
       product is complex).

THEN: Use count (c) chart. —————

IF: Attribute chart is recommended and
       production quantities are large
       enough to achieve acceptable
       sample size.

THEN: Use proportion (p) chart.

BACKWARD CHAINING

IF: Item can be judged as good or bad ——— Item is good or bad
       and measurement is difficult. ——— Measurement difficult.

THEN: An attribute chart is recommended. ———

IF: Exact measurement is practical and
       exact measurement is crucial
       to quality.

THEN: Variable control charts are
       recommended.

IF: Attribute chart is recommended and ———
       (production quantities are small ——— Production Quantity Small.
       or product is extremely large or ——— Product is complex.
       product is complex).

THEN: Use count (c) chart. ————— Use count chart.

IF: Attribute chart is recommended and
       production quantities are large
       enough to achieve acceptable
       sample size.
THEN: Use proportion (p) chart.

rule. The conclusion that "an attribute chart is recommended" is added to the fact base. This fact in addition to the facts that the production quantity is small and the product is complex lead to the conclusion that a "count (c) chart should be used." With a larger rule base the system could assist in the specific design of the chart and offer suggestions for its use.

The second technique is known as *backward chaining*. In this technique the inference process works backward from the goal. Backward chaining inference takes the goal as a hypothesis and then seeks to prove a series of subgoals, working backward from the goal. This is done recursively until all subgoals that are required for the goal's existence are proved. An example of backward chaining is also given in Figure 4.3. The purpose of the consultation is to answer the question, When should one use a count (c) chart? Given the rule set and the user-provided facts, the inference process begins with the fact that we wish to use a count chart. From this we determine that this type of control chart is used when "production quantities are small or product is extremely large or product is complex" and an attribute chart is recommended. This information is added to the fact base. The fact that "an attribute chart is recommended" triggers the first rule, which results in the conclusion that "the item must be able to be judged as good or bad and that measurement is difficult." Modern expert system building tools not only have the capability of using both inference methods but also of specifying when in the reasoning process each should be utilized.

An expert system's user interface supports the interaction between a user and the inference engine during a consultation session. Common interfacing techniques include commands, forms, icons, menus, graphs, and their combinations. The general principle of designing a user interface is that it should match what users of the noncomputer system have been accustomed to. Two-way communication is provided by the interface; users ask the inference engine for advice and users are asked for specific data by the inference engine during consultations. In addition, a user can ask to explore the inference engine's line of reasoning after the deduced advice is presented. The ability to explain the reasoning behind a recommendation enables both naive users and experts to understand the rationale underlying a piece of advice. For a more complete introductory discussion of expert systems, see Liebowitz (1988).

EXPERT SYSTEMS BUILDING TOOLS

Software products that are used to construct expert systems are known as *expert systems building tools*. These tools are used in the development of the knowledge base, inference engine, and user interface. Early expert systems were built in the symbol-manipulation languages Lisp and Prolog. In these implementations both the knowledge base and the inference engine were programmed in the language. The inference engines of these systems were problem-dependent. That is, they were composed of reasoning processes that were peculiar to a specific problem domain. Thus, system builders, in addition to a domain-specific knowledge base, constructed their own inference engine from scratch for each application. As experience in implementing expert systems grew, researchers noted certain commonalities across problem areas and began to design inference engines whose reasoning mechanisms were independent of the problem. Thus, developers could select a tool with a standard inference engine and interface. Such ES building tools are known as *expert system shells*. Today the greatest burden in building ES is the construction of the knowledge base.

ES shells come in a wide variety of capabilities. Simple shells allow knowledge to be inserted in a specific, structured fashion. The more sophisticated tools are generally more difficult to learn, but allow the system developer a much wider choice of knowledge base representations, inference strategies, and end-user interfaces. These tools generally have been written in Lisp, but are being rewritten in languages such as C to increase speed, reduce memory requirements, and promote availability on a larger variety of computers. Presently shells are available that run on mainframes, minicomputers, and microcomputers, in addition to specially designed computers known as Lisp machines. Further, as the technology continues to improve, business implementations on personal computers are expected to increase substantially.

Table 4.1 presents a representative sample of expert system shells and their possible applications in quality assurance. They run the gamut from Kee, Knowledge Craft, and Picon which are complex, require Lisp machines to run, and cost $50,000 to $60,000; to 1st-CLASS, Guru, Personal Consultant +, and VP-Expert, which are simpler, PC based, and cost less than $5,000.

Several factors need to be considered when determining the overall usability of an expert system building tool. In addition to obvious factors such as costs and function applicability, tool choices should be guided by the size of the system to be built, how rapidly a system of the given size and complexity can be built with the tool, and the speed of operation of the tool during development and, particularly, during end use. Perhaps the most important factor, however, is the degree of satisfaction of both the developer and end user (Gevarter, 1987).

AN OVERVIEW OF QUALITY ASSURANCE

Before we can discuss the use of expert systems in quality assurance we must arrive at an acceptable definition of the concept of quality. Many such definitions exist, but perhaps the most complete and comprehensive is that offered by Deming's Triangle (1981). According to this model, quality must be measured by the interaction of three participants: (1) the product itself; (2) the user and how he uses the product, how he installs it, how he maintains it, and what he was led to expect from the product; and (3) instructions for use, training of the customer, training of the repairman, warranty, service provided for repairs, and availability of parts. Therefore, quality depends on activities involved in during the design, manufacture, and use of the product.

A more complete look at quality through these three phases of enterprise is in order. Taguchi (1985) states the core of achieving product quality is to deal with product function variation. That is, a quality product is one that will exhibit extremely small variation from its functional target values (i.e., its functional performance objectives). Variables that cause the functional characteristic of a product to deviate from its target value are called noise factors. Taguchi identifies three classes of noise factors: external factors or outer noise, manufacturing imperfection, and product deterioration or inner noise. External factors are the variables related to product use or environmental condition. Some examples are variations in the operating environment such as temperature, humidity, or supply voltage, and human errors in operating the product. Manufacturing imperfection is the variation among products manufactured with the same specifications. Included is the variation in product parameters from unit to unit that is inevitable in a manufacturing process. Thus, in Deming's parlance we speak of variations that are the result of common causes in the manufacturing process. These manufacturing variations are a measure of process capability. Product deterioration is represented by product parameters that change during usage or storage. Examples are

Table 4.1
Some Commercial Expert System Building Tools

Tool	Knowl. Struct.	Inference Engine	Quality Eng. Functions	Computers	Company
Kee	Frames	FC & BC	Diag., Mon., Real-Time Process Control	TI-Explorer Symbolics LMI	Intellicorp Mountain View, CA
Knowl. Craft	Frames	FC & BC	Design, Process Control	TI-Explorer Symbolics LMI, VAX	Carnegie Group Pittsburgh, PA
Picon	Frames	FC & BC	Industrial Automation, Real-Time Sensor Monitored Processes	TI-Explorer LMI	Lisp Machine, Inc. Andover, MA
KES	Rules	BC	Diag., Debug., Repair, Cons.	VAX, SUN IBM PC/PS2	Software Architecture and Engineering, Inc. Arlington, VA
M1	Rules	FC & BC	Diag., Debug., Repair, Cons.	IBM PC/PS2	Teknowledge, Inc. Palo Alto, CA
PC +	Frames Rules	FC & BC	Diag., Debug., Repair, Cons.	IBM PC/PS2 TI-Explorer TI-PC	Texas Instruments Austin, TX

Tool	Knowl. Struct.	Inference Engine	Quality Eng. Functions	Computers	Company
1st-CLASS	Rules	FC & BC	Diag., Debug., Repair, Cons.	IBM PC/PS2 VAX	AI Corp. Waltham, MA
ESP Advisor & ESP Frame Engine	Frames Rules	FC & BC	Diag., Debug., Repair, Design	IBM PC/PS2	Expert Systems International Philadelphia, PA
GURU	Rules	FC & BC	Diag., Debug., Repair, Cons.	IBM PC/PS2 VAX	MDBS, Inc. Lafayette, IN
VP-Expert	Frames Rules	FC & BC	Diag., Debug., Repair, Cons.	IBM PC/PS2	Paperback Software Berkeley, CA

Notes: FC = forward chaining, BC = backward chaining, Diag. = diagnosis, Debug. = debugging, Cons. = consulting (advising).

the increase in resistance of a resistor and the loss of potency of some pharmaceuticals with age or the wearing out of parts of a product owing to friction.

To reduce the impact of noise on functional characteristics of the product Taguchi offers a set of countermeasures. He systematizes these countermeasures under the heading of quality engineering. The overall aim of quality engineering is to produce products that are robust with respect to all noise factors. That is, the product's functional characteristic is not sensitive to variations in the noise factor. Quality engineering consists of a set of activities that are conducted offline and some that are conducted online.

Off-line activities are typically associated with product design and manufacturing process design. These include product system design that is concerned with the design of the basic prototype for achieving or performing a desired or required function, product parameter design by which we determine the best combination of levels of parameters of parts and components of the prototype that will allow the product to achieve the required functional performance characteristic while minimizing the effects of various noises, and product tolerance design that is concerned with determining the most economical product tolerances, which is based on a trade-off between the loss due to deviations from levels set as a result of parameter design and the cost of different grades of parts and components. Only in product design can measures be taken to minimize the impact of all three classes of noise. In terms of process design the objective of manufacturing engineering is to design and install a process capable of economically producing uniform products. Manufacturing process design consists of process system design that includes selecting processes and materials movement systems, process parameter design that deals with optimizing all process parameters to dampen the effect of all noises that may arise in the manufacturing process, and process tolerance design that deals with the removal of special causes so that the process capability may be established. During process design we may deal with potential problems that may lead to manufacturing imperfection.

On-line activities are typically concerned with the daily operation of the manufacturing process. This is what we think of as the quality control function. The Japanese viewpoint is that this is the day-to-day job of production people with an emphasis on process control. These activities include process control, which is the control of process conditions so as to maintain the process capability; quality control, which is the actual measurement of product quality to determine whether the processing has been done properly and to adjust the process if necessary; and inspection, which consists of 100 percent product inspection, the repair or discarding of defectives, and the shipment of nondefective products. Once again, only manufacturing imperfection can be ameliorated by these activities.

In contrast to Taguchi's concept of quality engineering, Deming's definition of quality suggests that an additional stage exists where countermeasures to reduce noise would prove useful. This stage is concerned with the product once it leaves the factory and is in the hands of the ultimate consumer. We suggest that this area be designated as *after-market*. After-market is concerned with training the customer to install and use the product correctly, product maintenance, warranty service, and technical service. Both external noise and deteriorating noise can be alleviated by proper use and maintenance of the product. For a more complete discussion of total quality systems, see Caplan (1980).

QUALITY ASSURANCE EXPERT SYSTEM APPLICATIONS

To understand how expert systems can assist quality assurance decision makers, it is helpful to know what tasks expert systems can perform in general. Most expert systems applications fall into a few distinct functional categories. Hayes-Roth, Waterman, and Lenat (1983) and Stefik et al. (1982) provide two similar classifications of expert tasks that we have integrated. These are presented in the first two columns of Table 4.2. The same classification scheme can be used to identify those quality assurance areas in which expert systems can play a contributing role. Some of these applications are included in column three of this table. We discuss some specific applications later in this chapter.

STANLEY—An ES for Designing Sampling Plans

STANLEY (Bates & Chandra, 1990) is an expert system designed with two goals in mind: first, to make the determination of attribute sampling plans an easier task for those who already know how to create sampling plans; second, more importantly, to create a system for use by nonexperts that completely automates the sampling plan creation process. STANLEY knowledge base contains the expertise required to use MIL-STD-105; that is, incorporated in STANLEY are the underlying concepts that gave birth to sampling documents such as MIL-STD-105. The system may be utilized to enable nonexperts to obtain an expert design of sampling plans by providing the answers to a set of simple, nontechnical questions.

STANLEY is written in CLIPS, which is an expert system shell created for government work. It is a rule-based shell that utilizes a forward chaining inference engine. STANLEY prompts the user through a series of questions arranged in sets or groups. The intent is to determine the collection of circumstances that describe the manufacturing and inspection environments present for the product being considered for attribute sampling. Facts are gathered as these questions are answered. These facts are, in turn, used to drive the inference process.

Let us look at the general flow of the system. The initial group of questions is directed at determining whether sampling should be ruled out. Referring to Figure 4.4 (Screen 1), any answer of 1 to 6 means that sampling is inappropriate; the user is so advised and processing stops. If the user's response to the first group of questions does not categorically rule out sampling, he or she is interrogated further to examine the feasibility of sampling. For example, if in the second group of questions, shown in Figure 4.5 (Screen 2), the fact "Inspection process is destructive" is deemed true, STANLEY immediately realizes the necessity to sample and therefore begins to move toward ascertaining the type of sampling that should be implemented. Should a statement such as "Volume of product is low" be chosen, then subsequent analysis must be performed to measure if sampling is even worthwhile.

When the system has finished its evaluation of the practicality of sampling, it either informs the user that sampling is inappropriate, in which case the program is terminated, or it continues defining the user environment via other categories of questions. From this point on, STANLEY is primarily attempting to choose the best plan for the string of conditions present. Some of the areas the system explores further include past training of the inspectors and level of increased record-keeping that can be tolerated. These analyses are used primarily to appraise whether a single, double, or multiple sampling plan should be used, and whether or not a switching approach is germane.

A sample consultation, typical of many that may be generated by the system, is

Table 4.2
Potential Quality Assurance Expert System Applications

Tasks	Function	QA Applications
Interpretation	The analysis of data to determine their meaning.	Failure data analysis, product return and failure analysis, statistical QC.
Prediction	Inferring likely consequences of a given situation.	Troubleshooting of quality problems, product return, and failure analysis.
Diagnosis	Inferring system malfunctions from observations.	Statistical process control.
Design	The creation of specifications for objects that satisfy a given set of requirements.	Design of product and process to produce quality items; configuration.
Planning	Designing actions. The creation of programs of action that are carried out to achieve a goal.	Establishment of reliability and maintainability levels, inspection plans, quality auditing.
Monitoring	Comparing of observations of system behavior to features that seem crucial to successful plan outcomes.	Source quality control, incoming material control, statistical process control, quality control of production.
Debugging	Prescribing remedies for system malfunctions.	Corrective actions.
Repair	Developing and executing plans to administer a prescribed remedy for a diagnosed problem.	Procedures for corrective actions.

84

Tasks	Function	QA Applications
Instruction	Diagnosing, debugging, and repairing student behavior.	Training of quality personnel.
Control	Interpreting, predicting, repairing, and monitoring system behaviors.	Process control, supplier control.
Consulting (Advising)	The recommending of certain actions or behavior in light of a given set of circumstances.	Sales, installation, service, and use.

presented in Figures 4.4 through 4.10, which are representations of the actual screens that compose STANLEY's user interface. We began with Figure 4.4 (Screen 1), which is directed at obtaining an initial evaluation of the inspection environment. In this case the user has answered "x—none of the above statements apply," and processing continued to the next screen, Figure 4.5. Here statements 8 and 10 were chosen, indicating that the volume of product is low and that inspectors have some sampling inspection training. We now proceed to the next screen, which is given in Figure 4.6 (screen 3). Here we attempt to further evaluate the level of training of the inspectors. For this consultation the user answers "18—Inspectors are capable of complex training." Based on this response, coupled with the one given on the previous screen, the system infers that the inspection crew appears to be a competent group, one that is capable of handling sampling plans of any complexity.

The next screen, Figure 4.7 (screen 4), attempts to determine what tradeoffs the user is willing to make between potentially decreasing his inspection requirements and increasing his record-keeping requirements along with possibly raising the complexity level of the process. In this case the value of "10" was given indicating that the minimal amount of inspection is desired even if it means that record-keeping requirements will be the greatest and also that complexity could potentially be very high. Figure 4.8 (screen 5) is self-explanatory. This screen asks the user to define the acceptable quality level (AQL). Here an AQL of 6.5 is chosen with an entry of "33." The final set of prompts (Figure 4.9, screen 6) seek to attain information concerning vendor quality. The screen indicates that the producer will probably deliver product with a quality level better than the 6.5 AQL that was previously chosen and that the vendor can be trusted to 100 percent inspect a rejected lot that is returned to him.

Finally, at this point all the relevant information has been processed and STANLEY displays its conclusions, as in Figure 4.10 (screen 7). The user will complement this information with additional data including the lot size and the sample size code letter, and use them in concert with MIL-STD-105 to complete the process of creating a sampling plan.

A FRAMEWORK FOR THE USE OF EXPERT SYSTEMS IN QUALITY ASSURANCE

Table 4.3 presents a framework for the use of expert systems in quality assurance. The framework is based on the quality concepts of Deming and Taguchi. Specifically, we first classify quality assurance in terms of the organizational function mainly responsible for the execution of the pertinent quality activities. Thus, the off-line system includes product design and process design, which are chiefly the responsibility of applied research and development and production engineering, respectively. We continue with the on-line system, which includes production (or operations for a service organization), which is the responsibility of production (operations) management. Finally, the after-market is concerned with the correct use of the product by the user and is generally under the purview of the technical or customer service department. Next, within each function, we list the methods or countermeasures that may be used to eliminate noise. Each of these countermeasures are explicitly implemented through a set of activities. It is these activities that may be performed more effectively when supported by well-designed expert systems. These activities and the proposed type of expert system support form the last two columns of Table 4.3. It should be noted that these entries in the table are intended to be illustrative rather than exhaustive. Further,

Figure 4.4
Screen 1—Sampling First Cut

```
*****************************************************
***                                               ***
***                                               ***
***     THE EXPERT SYSTEM FOR ATTRIBUTE SAMPLING ***
*****************************************************
*                                                   *
*                    INSTRUCTIONS                   *
*                                                   *
** GROUP 1 ****************************************  *
*                                                   *
* ENTER THE NUMBER OF EACH STATEMENT BELOW THAT     *
* REPRESENTS A TRUE STATEMENT FOR YOUR OPERATION.   *
*       ENTER AS MANY AS ARE TRUE.                  *
* PLACE A SPACE BETWEEN EACH ENTRY AND PRESS ENTER  *
*                                                   *
* 1. There is no requirement to inspect.            *
* 2. Parts are fatigue critical.                    *
* 3. parts can't be classified as simply good or bad*
*      (i.e., there are degrees of acceptability).  *
* 4. Inspectors are not capable of being trained in *
*      sampling techniques.                         *
* 5. Product is from different batch lots and lot   *
*      variations are significant.                  *
* 6. Increased record keeping is not acceptable.    *
* x. None of the above statements apply.            *
*                                                   *
*****************************************************
```

x

Figure 4.5
Screen 2—Categories of Product and Process

```
**************************************************
*                                                *
*                 INSTRUCTIONS                   *
*                                                *
** GROUP 2 ***************************************
*                                                *
* ENTER THE NUMBER OF EACH STATEMENT BELOW THAT  *
* REPRESENTS A TRUE STATEMENT FOR YOUR OPERATION.*
*          ENTER AS MANY AS ARE TRUE.            *
* PLACE A SPACE BETWEEN EACH ENTRY AND PRESS ENTER.*
*                                                *
*   7.Product has a poor quality history.        *
*   8.Volume of product is low.                  *
*   9.Inspection process is destructive.         *
*  10.Inspectors have been trained in some sampling.*
*  11.Inspection process is expensive.           *
*  12.Inspection process is time-consuming.      *
*  13.Production schedule necessitates acceleration.*
*  14.The quantity of inspectors is extremely limited*
*   x.None of the above statements apply.        *
*                                                *
**************************************************
```

8 10

Figure 4.6
Screen 3—Level of Inspectors Training

```
****************************************************************
*                                                              *
*                         INSTRUCTIONS                         *
*                                                              *
** GROUP 3 ******INSPECTOR TRAINING************************** *
*                                                              *
* ENTER THE NUMBER OF EACH STATEMENT BELOW THAT                *
* REPRESENTS A TRUE STATEMENT FOR YOUR OPERATION.              *
*             ENTER AS MANY AS ARE TRUE.                       *
* PLACE A SPACE BETWEEN EACH ENTRY AND PRESS ENTER.            *
*                                                              *
* 15.Inspectors are trained in double sampling.                *
* 16.Inspectors are trained in multiple sampling.              *
* 17.Inspectors are trained in switching techniques.*          *
* 18.Inspectors are capable of complex training.               *
*  x.None of the above statements apply.                       *
*                                                              *
****************************************************************
```

18

Figure 4.7
Screen 4—Record Keeping/Inspection Tradeoffs

```
*********************************************
*                                           *
*               INSTRUCTIONS                *
** GROUP 4 ******RECORD KEEPING *************
*                                           *
*      ENTER A NUMBER FROM 1 TO 10,         *
*  WHERE 1 REPRESENTS MINIMUM RECORD KEEPING BUT
*             MAXIMUM INSPECTION            *
*  WHERE 10 REPRESENTS MAXIMUM RECORD KEEPING BUT
*             MINIMUM INSPECTION            *
*                                           *
*********************************************

10
```

Figure 4.8
Screen 5—Desired AQL

```
*************************************************
*                  INSTRUCTIONS                 *
*                                                *
** GROUP 5 ******* DESIRED QUALITY **************
*                                                *
*   CHOOSE THE NUMBER OF THE LINE BELOW THAT     *
*   REPRESENTS THE AVERAGE PERCENT OF DEFECTS THAT *
*   YOU ARE WILLING TO ACCEPT FOR THIS PRODUCT   *
*                                                *
*          LINE NO.        %                     *
*                                                *
*             27          0.0                    *
*             28          0.65                   *
*             29          1.0                    *
*             30          1.5                    *
*             31          2.5                    *
*             32          4.0                    *
*             33          6.5                    *
*             34         10.0                    *
*                                                *
*************************************************
```

33

91

Figure 4.9
Screen 6—Capability of Vendor

```
*****************************************************
*                    INSTRUCTIONS                   *
*                                                   *
** GROUP 6 ****** PRODUCER CAPABILITY ***************
*                                                   *
* ENTER THE NUMBER OF EACH STATEMENT BELOW THAT     *
* REPRESENTS A TRUE STATEMENT FOR YOUR OPERATION.   *
*           ENTER AS MANY AS ARE TRUE.              *
* PLACE A SPACE BETWEEN EACH ENTRY AND PRESS ENTER. *
*                                                   *
* 35.Producer can be trusted to 100% inspect if     *
*      shipments are returned.                      *
* 36.Producer will probably produce at a quality    *
*      level better than the one just specified.    *
* 37.Producer will probably produce at a quality    *
*      equal to the one just specified.             *
* 38.Producer will probably produce at a quality    *
*      level worse than the one just specified.     *
*                                                   *
*****************************************************


35 36
```

Figure 4.10
Screen 7—Conclusions

```
*************************************************
*                                               *
*                   INSTRUCTIONS                 *
*                                               *
** GROUP 7 ******* CONCLUSIONS ******************
*                                               *
*  THE FOLLOWING LIST OF FACTS WERE ASCERTAINED AS *
*     A RESULT OF STATEMENTS GIVEN PREVIOUSLY.   *
*         ENTER AS MANY AS ARE TRUE.             *
*                                               *
*                                               *
*  USE THIS INFORMATION ALONG WITH THE LOT SIZE, *
*     SAMPLE SIZE CODE LETTER, AND ASSOCIATED    *
* ACCEPT/REJECT VALUES TO COMPLETE THE SAMPLING PLAN*
*                                               *
*************************************************

        MULTIPLE SAMPLING IS APPROPRIATE
        THE AQL EQUALS 6.5
        THE INSPECTION LEVEL IS II
        THE SEVERITY OF INSPECTION IS NORMAL
```

93

Table 4.3
Framework for the Use of Expert Systems in Quality Assurance

System	Organizational Function	Method	Activities	Type of ES Support
Off-line	Applied R & D (Product Design)	·System Design ·Parameter Design ·Tolerance Design	·Conceptualization ·Product Selection ·Preliminary Product Design ·Design Review ·Prototype Construction ·Testing ·Final Product Design	Consulting Design Planning
	Production Engineering (Process Design)	·System Design ·Parameter Design ·Tolerance Design	·Preliminary Process Design ·· Process Selection ·· Choice of Technology ·· Process Flow Design ·· Facility Layout ·Final Process Design	Consulting Design Planning
On-line	Production Management	·Process Control ·Quality Control ·Inspection	·Process Capability Development ·Process Controls Design ·Control Chart Selection, Design and Implementation ·Final Product Testing	Consulting Control Debugging Diagnosis Interpret. Monitoring Repair
After-market	Technical/ Customer Service	·Field Service ·Customer Relations .Training	·Installation ·Use ·Maintenance	Consulting Diagnosis Debugging Instruct. Interpret. Repair

we are aware that there are significant feedback and parallel relationships among all listed activities.

Product design activities begin with conceptualization, where ideas for new product are generated based on market information or from existing technology. Product selection restricts new products to those ideas which pass the tests of market potential, financial viability, and producibility. In many cases product selection analysis may be quite subjective in nature and based on somewhat limited information. Once a new product idea has been selected for implementation, a preliminary design is developed. During this stage the product is specified completely. As part of the process many tradeoffs between cost and product performance are considered. A preliminary set of drawings may also be completed. The preliminary design is then operationalized as a prototype. The prototype is tested in an attempt to verify market and technical performance. Several iterations through the prototyping process may be necessary. Engineering changes initiated as a result of prototype testing are then incorporated as part of the final design. During the final design phase, drawings and final specifications are developed. Design reviews are typically conducted after the preliminary design and final design stages during the design process. These formal reviews are aimed at determining whether a proposed design will perform successfully during use, can be produced at low cost, and is suitable for prompt, low-cost field maintenance. Usually the reviews are conducted by a team consisting mainly of specialists who are not directly associated with the development of the design. These specialists are generally in great demand and short supply in the organization.

Consulting, design, and planning expert systems may be used to support product design. In early phases of the procedure, consulting systems may perform the function of a repository of the history of organizational experience with new product ideas. Specific advice may be offered by the system based on experiences with similar types of products with respect to market, technology, or both market and technology. A further use of consulting systems would make scarce expertise more easily available during design reviews. Later on in the procedure design systems may be used to help produce the best possible design by assisting in developing specifications for components, determining optimal system configurations, and evolving and updating the system design based on new test data and so on. Planning expert systems may help rationalize the complete design process. An example of a product design expert system is OPTEX, which is used by Canon to aid lens designers. A more detailed explanation of the use of expert systems in design may be found in Rychener (1985).

Schroeder (1981) defines process design as encompassing a series of decisions including process selection, choice of technology, process flow analysis, and facility layout. These decisions are made in a parallel path with product design. What we learn during the product design cycle may help us improve our preliminary process design and arrive at an optimal final process design. Process selection and choice of technology are interrelated macro design decisions. Process selection determines, in a gross manner, the type of production process to be used and the appropriate span of process. This decision is intimately linked with the product design and is of a strategic nature. That is, it should be a significant part of the manufacturing strategy and the corporate strategy as a whole. Here we are concerned with whether the process will be continuous, line flow, batch, job shop, or one of the hybrids made possible by advancing technology such as flexible manufacturing systems. Choice of technology deals with the set of processes, tools, methods, procedures, and equipment that will be utilized within the process type that has been selected. Once these issues have been resolved, the focus turns to two-micro level decisions—process flow analysis and facility layout. In process flow analysis we deal with both material and information flows from input through transformation to the final product. As a result of this analysis improved methods or procedures may be discovered. Based on the type of process selected and flow patterns developed as a result of process flow analysis, a facility layout is arrived at. These micro-level decisions affect decisions in other parts of operations including scheduling, job design, inventory levels, and quality control procedures.

As is the case for product design, consulting, design, and planning expert systems can be useful in supporting process design decisions. Consulting systems can be useful in advising designers on the links among corporate strategy, manufacturing strategy, process selection, and choice of technology. Design systems may be useful in determining the combination of parameters that will minimize the chance of manufacturing imperfection. They may also help in removing special causes and setting the process capability. Planning systems, again, may help in rationalizing the complete design process. Many of these process design activities fall under the responsibility of industrial engineering. Turban (1986) provides an interesting review of potential uses of expert systems in industrial engineering. An example of a process design expert system is Manufacturing Process Planner, a system developed for internal use by Northrop Corporation that aids in the planning process for the manufacture of the approximately 20,000 parts that go into a fighter plane.

In control of quality during manufacturing consulting, control, debugging, diagnosis, interpretation, monitoring, and repair systems may prove useful. Such systems already have been successfully used in industry. For example, Photolithography Advisor is used by Hewlett-Packard to diagnose process errors during the fabrication of integrated circuits; PBA is used by FMC Corporation to monitor data and control the process for the manufacturing of phosphorous; and DEFT diagnoses defects in IBM 3380 Direct Access Storage Devices during the final test stage.

The after-market is concerned with maintaining customer satisfaction by assuring fitness for use of the product over its lifetime. As product complexity increases there tends to be a higher incidence of field problems. Juran and Gryna (1980) believe that 20 to 30 percent of problems concerning fitness for use are attributable to field factors such as inadequate operating or maintenance procedures, human error during maintenance, inaccessibility to repair, and defective spare parts. There exists here a great opportunity to reduce these problems through the use of expert systems in training and consulting capacities. Training systems can be directed both at service technicians and the user. Consulting systems can be used for the diagnosis and troubleshooting of operating problems. Many applications of this nature are already in place, including systems to diagnose steam turbine generator problems marketed by Westinghouse; a Toyota system to troubleshoot automobile engine problems; and COMPASS, a GTE-developed system for assisting switch maintenance personnel by analyzing operating data and recommending appropriate maintenance actions.

Table 4.4 lists a number of successful quality assurance related expert systems applications in addition to those previously discussed. Further, an excellent compendium of actual expert systems applications may be found in Feigenbaum, McCorduck, and Nii (1988).

CONCLUSION

This chapter has illustrated the use of expert systems in quality assurance. We discussed the basic concepts of expert systems, gave an overview of the basic concepts of quality assurance, described a fielded expert system for sample plan selection, and developed a framework for the use of expert systems in quality assurance. The framework is based on the belief that quality is a total organization responsibility and, as such, must be a predominant issue in the life of a product from design through manufacture to use. The chapter traces the activities associated with these stages and offers broad suggestions for the use of expert systems to support them. Through example we have expressed the thesis that quality engineering is a fertile field for the application of expert system technology. In addition, expert systems offer the opportunity to handle systematically routine quality problems while releasing human experts to deal with the really critical ill-structured ones that arise. Finally, we are firmly convinced that the use of expert systems in this domain not only improve quality and productivity but are essential to allow companies to remain competitive in the global economy of the nineties and beyond.

REFERENCES

Bates, R. E., and M. Chandra. "STANLEY—The Expert System for Attribute Sampling." Unpublished paper, Hofstra University, 1990.

Caplan, F. *The Quality System—A Source Book for Managers and Engineers.* Radnor, PA: Chilton, 1980.

Deming, W. E. "Management of Statistical Techniques for Quality and Productivity." New York University Faculty of Business Administration Working Paper Series, 1981.

Feigenbaum, E., P. McCorduck, and H. P. Nii. *The Rise of the Expert Company.* New York: Times Books, 1988.

Gevarter, W. B. "The Nature and Evaluation of Commercial Expert System Building Tools." *Computer* (1987): 24-41.

Hayes-Roth, F., D. A. Waterman, and D. B. Lenat. *Building Expert Systems.* Reading, MA: Addison-Wesley, 1983.

Juran, J. M., and F. M. Gryna Jr. *Quality Planning and Analysis.* New York: McGraw-Hill, 1980.

Liebowitz, J. *Introduction to Expert Systems.* Santa Cruz, CA: Mitchell Publishing, 1988.

Rychener, M. D. "Expert Systems for Engineering Design. *Expert Systems* 2 (1) (1985): 30-44.

Schroeder, R. G. *Operations Management—Decision Making in the Operations Function.* New York: McGraw-Hill, 1981.

———. "Smart Factories: America's Turn." *Business Week*, May 8, 1989, pp. 142-48.

Stefik, M., J. Aikins, R. Balzer, J. Benoit, L. Birnbaum, F. Hayes-Roth, and E. Sacerdoti. "The Organization of Expert Systems: A Tutorial." *Artificial Intelligence* 13 (2) (1982): 135-73.

Taguchi, G. "Quality Engineering in Japan." *Communications of Statistical and Theoretical Methods* 14 (11) (1985): 2785-801.

Turban, E. "Expert Systems—Another Frontier for Industrial Engineering." *Computers and Industrial Engineering* 10 (3) (1986): 227-35.

Table 4.4
Some Fielded Quality-Related Expert Systems

Expert System	Company	Application
ATREX II	Toyota*	Helps diagnose automobile engine problems.
COMPASS	GTE	Assists in telephone switch maintenance.
DASD Advisor	Boole & Babbage	Identifies DASD performance problems, analyzes their causes, recommends corrective actions, and helps in training DASD tuners.
DEFT	IBM*	Diagnoses defects in IBM 3380 DASD during final test.
Expert Probe	Unisys*	Allows workers on PC card production lines to perform quality control tasks formerly done by skilled technicians.
GEMS-TTA	AT & T	Diagnoses faults on telephone trunk lines.
GIO	Fuji Electric*	Diagnoses the presence of abnormalities inside an oil transformer.
Hoist Diagnoser	Oxko*	Isolates faults in hoisting equipment used in plating processes, and recommends repair actions.
IMP	Texas Instruments*	Troubleshoots problems with epitaxial reactors used in semiconductor fabrication.
Manufacturing Process Planner	Northrop*	Aids in the planning process for the manufacture of approximately 20,000 fighter plane parts.

Expert System	Company	Application
Mentor	Honeywell*	Helps field technicians diagnose problems in air conditioning systems.
PBA	FMC*	Acquires and monitors data to control the process of manufacturing phosphorous.
Photolithography Advisor	Hewlett Packard*	Diagnoses process errors during the fabrication of integrated circuits.
Vibration Diagnosis Expert System	General Motors*	Helps technicians diagnose auto problems associated with vibration and noise complaints.

*System for Internal Use Only.

II

Selection and Implementation of New Technologies

Chapter 5

Strategic Thrust of Manufacturing Automation Decisions: A Conceptual Framework

Christian N. Madu and Nicholas C. Georgantzas

The demand for change currently pressuring the American economy poses fundamental challenges to the traditional manufacturing policies in the United States. Increased price competition in world and domestic markets, greater uncertainty and volatility in current values and commodity prices, the availability of new information and manufacturing technology, and the greater sensitivity to product quality are all pressures on the American producer. These pressures translate into demands for labor cost moderation, flexibility, and improved productivity.

These are not features of traditional U.S. manufacturing strategies. Substantial evidence shows that American firms have been unable to adapt the production innovations that have emerged abroad (Cohen & Zysman, 1987). A sustained weakness in manufacturing capability could further endanger the technology base of the country. On the other hand, there is evidence that American factories are undergoing a significant transformation, searching for ways to meet the requirements of today's economy. A survey by the Institute of Industrial Engineers (1986), for example, found capital investment in new or automated production systems among the most frequently undertaken productivity improvement activities.

The decision process leading to automation interfaces with many internal and external factors in an organization's task environment. Although inclusion of such factors in the decision-making process may be critical, some managers and researchers still view adoption of new production technology from a microscopic perspective. More often than not, they justify automation solely on its net present value (NPV), return on investment (ROI), and return on assets (ROA), which posits a microscopic view on this vital organizational decision.

Canada (1986b) suggests that both strategic and tactical factors should be weighed, combined with financial measures. Similarly, Curtin (1984) proposes a holistic approach that integrates engineering, manufacturing, and informational factors in the economic justification of automation. Referencing a case study of Hewlett-Packard, Falter (1986) offers some guidelines for integrating economic and strategic analyses to justify investment in automation. Hayes & Garvin (1982) note that current techniques of economic justification are biased against investment on automation, and that this bias adversely affects American industry. Kaplan (1986a) posits that if discounted cash-flow criteria are established, they should include both tangible and intangible benefits. He also notes that traditional cost-accounting systems often are tied to direct labor and cannot capture the benefits of computer integrated manufacturing (CIM) (1986b). Varney et al. (1985) suggest the use of the analytic hierarchy process to justify investment decisions on FMS.

Yet much attention has been paid to excluding the intangible factors from automation decisions (Chakravarty, 1987; O'Guin, 1987; Rayner, 1986; Sullivan, 1986). The strategic thrust of automation is often identified and deemed important, however models that allow for representation of both quantitative and qualitative factors are often limited or missing. Thus, U.S. managers are forced to decide on automation by using existing cost-accounting techniques. In contrast, cost reduction is only a means to an end for their Japanese counterparts. The three dominant factors of the Japanese strategy are quality (for growth), the long term, and technology (Godet, 1987).

Short-term development can dictate corporate strategies to pursue growth, limit risk, or obtain return on investment. This preponderance of marketing and finance viewpoint dominated most U.S. firms up to the mid-1970s. At that time, U.S. managers became aware of Japan's success with its long-term strategy, followed since the 1960s. The Japanese had given themselves fifteen years to become the world leaders in automobile production and they reached that goal (Sethi, Namiki, & Swanson, 1984). The success of their strategy can largely be explained by the socio-organizational context peculiar to Japanese companies—collective discussion and concentration on corporate objectives. In addition, however, the Japanese relied on technology to upset the U.S. competitive position (Godet, 1987).

This chapter examines, from a strategic perspective, the process of adopting new technology in general, and the decision to automate in particular. To deal with the complexities involved, we have developed a conceptual framework to guide decision makers through a step-by-step process. The proposed model is supplemented by a decision support system (DSS) that includes strategic factors of both a tangible and intangible nature. The DSS is based on the analytic hierarchy process (AHP) (Saaty, 1980) and is implemented by using the Expert Choice cell (Expert Choice, 1983). An experimental analysis is conducted with a group of nine MBA students assuming the role of decision makers. The results obtained within this highly controlled experimental setting indicate that this method can greatly enhance the decision-making capability of companies contemplating automation.

RESEARCH BACKGROUND

In general, technology is a determining factor for the future of any company. It is not a question of using portfolio analysis matrices to come up with a strategy for technology but, rather, of defining a strategy through technology. More specifically, the strategic thrust of manufacturing automation must be increasingly recognized. Automation—or, alternatively, the automatic operation and control of equipment, processes, and operations systems independent of direct human action—leads to intangible benefits that no conventional justification approach can measure.

O'Guin (1987), for example, notes that information-based technologies such as flexible manufacturing systems save time and money through activity integration. Integration leads to improved system performance by eliminating redundant activities. Coupled with the intangible benefit of customer perception of quality improvements, these results suggest the need for automation. However, any attempt to justify investment in such automation under the assumptions of constant cash-flow, sales, and market share are misleading (Mason, 1969; Randhawa & Bedworth, 1985).

Chakravarty (1987) points to the importance of "second order" effects in evaluating automation. Such factors include throughput time, in-process inventory, materials handling, and consistency of quality. Accounting and financial performance measures such as return on investment place too much emphasis on "first order" effects (direct labor reduction). Thus, Chakravarty and Shtub (1987) propose model formulations that consider some of these "second order" effects.

Being more explicit, Sullivan (1986) suggests three such models: the linear additive model, expert system development, and the analytic hierarchy process. The decision support system developed by Monahan and Smunt (1987) evaluates the conversion from conventional batch manufacturing to flexible automated manufacturing. Meredith (1987) addresses the integration of organizational components with the critical role of human resources in automation strategies.

Madu (1988) studies the effects of automation on organizational change and identifies certain factors that can lead to successful implementation of automation. Randhawa and Bedworth (1985) identify criteria that can be used to compare conventional and flexible manufacturing systems. Goldhar and Jelinek (1985) note that both organizational and management practices must change to adapt to the changing nature of the factory. They also give a detailed analysis of the differences between traditional technology and computer integrated manufacturing (CIM).

Chakravarty (1987) identifies four empirical levels of technology from which different manufacturing configurations have emerged. As Blois (1986) notes, there are few (if any) fully CIM systems in the world. Thus, automation can be achieved at different levels and organizational decisions are not necessarily binary. That is, in order to define a strategy through technology, the decision need not be whether "to automate" or "not to automate," but rather on what level the automation is to be pursued.

A substantial segment of the literature on automation recognizes its strategic thrust. The affiliated issue of strategic factors is a relatively new but fast-growing area of research. Particular issues of *Industrial Engineering* (1987) and *Interfaces* (1987), the IIE productivity survey (1986), and the literature reviews by Canada (1986a) and Wallace and Thuesen (1987) support the claim that technology is a determining factor for the future of any company.

Technologies do not last forever and follow certain life cycles. Thus emergent technologies can be distinguished as those capable of modifying competitive posture. Once they become key technologies, the company that controls them acquires a competitive edge. As key technologies mature, they become basic technologies. Also, the phases of introduction, growth, and maturity are not intrinsically bound to given technology but reflect the use made of them by manufacturers. Thus, currently automation is a key technology in automobile and electronics assemblies, is only now emerging in job-shop environments, and is basic technology in continuous oil and sugar refineries.

We call for a formal approach to the process of new technology adoption in general, and the decision to automate in particular, within a strategic point of view. A conceptual framework is developed, and a decision support system is built and implemented through the use of a decision package (Expert Choice, 1983).

Mintzberg et al. (1976), and more recently Nutt (1984), show that managers do not formally and explicitly diagnose strategic decision situations. Indeed, the most popular behavior model to legitimize the return to basics and stick to knitting (Peters & Waterman, 1982) is "logical incrementalism" (Quinn, 1980). This same model was called "the science of muddling though" (Lindblom, 1959) many years back, and it can still be used by managers who assume that their companies will remain immune to technological change. Through the formal approach developed in this chapter, decision makers who do not cling to the dogma of the past will be able to consider most of the important factors that influence the process of technology adoption. This approach may also lead to productivity improvements and a better competitive position for the organization. Thus by using this approach, decision makers should be able to reduce the risk and uncertainty involved in aiming for a certain level of automation.

THE FRAMEWORK

Manufacturing automation is traditionally considered to have the objectives of increased flexibility, decreased costs, or improved quality. It can also be a strategy to, in the long run, reduce uncertainties affecting an organization's operations core. The framework presented here is comprehensive, taking a holistic or systemic view of manufacturing automation decisions. Moreover, this conceptualization of the decision-making process shows the need for, and creates the context within which, an AHP-driven DSS is developed and presented in the next section.

The proposed conceptual model can be divided into steps that constitute the total process of decision making, implementation, and control for manufacturing automation, as shown in Figure 5.1. The first step is to define and state specific objectives with respect to manufacturing automation. These have to be achievable, compatible with overall organizational goals, and realistic. Such objectives are formulated by those members of the organization who influence or are influenced by such objectives. These members may be internal (e.g., direct organizational members), or external (consultants or staff, special interest groups). Radford (1980) refers to this group as the "active" participants. The term signifies that these people can influence or are influenced by the organizational decision-making process. With respect to manufacturing automation decisions, active participants may include members of functional departments, labor unions, technical staff, or consultants. All have a stake in automation decisions.

The next step in the framework is idea generation. Participants independently generate alternatives on how manufacturing objectives can be achieved. A typical manufacturing objective may be to improve total productivity. This, in turn, enhances the firm's competitive position through low cost and increased market share. However, participants must also identify those factors that will enable the organization to achieve this objective. While this phase of decision making resembles brainstorming, it is an important step toward integrating content (what) with process (how). Some of the factors are identified in Figure 5.1.

Obviously, several alternatives and factors may be identified at this stage, and a diversity of views is represented. However, some factors may not be significant in achieving the overall objective, and a way to filter out the insignificant factors is required. Since there are bound to be conflicts in what participants perceive as important to achieving total productivity, a leader should resolve these conflicts. The decision makers can apply several strategies to control the process and identify and eliminate the insignificant factors.

Some of the known decision-making models and how they can be applied at this stage of conflict resolution are identified in Table 5.1. The objective is to build organization-wide commitment to the chosen factors while simultaneously evolving the desired objectives. Hartman et al. (1986) show how some of the process models in Table 5.1 can be used in information-processing strategies.

Next, the factors identified as significant have to be analyzed, with various de-

Figure 5.1
A Model of Manufacturing Automation Decision-Making, Implementation and Control

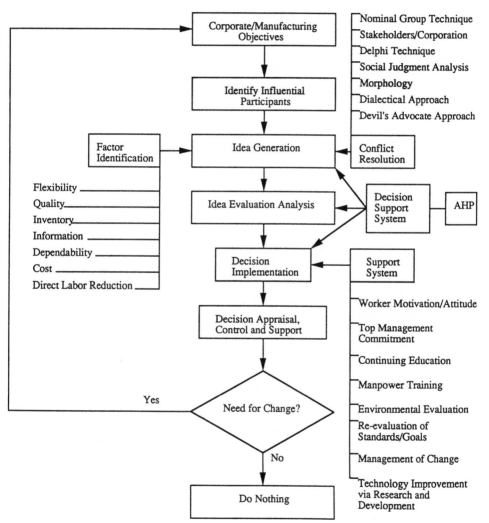

Table 5.1
Decision Making Strategies for Conflict Resolution in the Idea Generation Phase

Nominal Group Technique	Automation decisions are made in an uncertain environment. "Nominal" groups operate in a structured environment where discussions are strictly controlled. In this phase of idea generation, lists of problems and solutions that may influence automation decisions are generated. Group members make decisions on the significance of each of the identified factors by using ratings.[1]
Stakeholder analysis/cooptation	Manufacturing automation decision making framework requires the use of "active participants" in the idea generation phase. These participants all have a stake in the decision reached. This innovative approach that includes the stakeholders in the decision making process also serves as a means of managing change. Recommendations made by these groups are used by the decision maker in arriving at decisions on significant factors.[2,3]
Scenarios	The environmental factors that may affect automation decisions are identified. The most probable conditions are also stated and used as a basis for making the final decision.[4]
Delphi	The influence of environmental uncertainties on automation decisions can be best managed through the use of external experts. The inclusion of staff/consultants in the framework serves this purpose. The judgment of these experts on probable events and responses, and their innovativeness, can be used as a basis for selecting the influential factors in automation decision making.[5,6]
Social Judgment Analysis	The participants use different judgment processes to identify influential factors. The group members study the logic behind these judgments and, through consensus, identify the significant factors.[7]
Morphology	The complex factors identified have to be integrated into the overall decision making process. The decision maker acts on these to arrive at a decision.[8]
Dialectical Approach	The participants are organized into two groups that have opposing viewpoints. This leads to thesis and anti-thesis. The participants as a whole consider all these viewpoints before reaching a synthesis. Through dialectical approach, decision makers are more likely to have considered all the facts, possibilities, and viewpoints.[9,10]
Devil's Advocate Approach	The recommended factors or courses of action may be critiqued by the decision maker or any recommended person or small group. The aim is to identify the weaknesses with that course of action and problems that may lead to the failure

Table 5.1 (continued)

of the manufacturing automation decision making process if that course of action is followed. This also provides cognitive conflict for the decision maker.[11,12]

Notes:

1. Betton and Gear (1984).
2. Nutt (1977).
3. Nutt (1982).
4. Quade and Boucher (1968).
5. Dalky et al. (1972).
6. Delbeck and Van de Ven (1971).
7. Chakravarty and Shtub (1987).
8. Zwicky (1968).
9. Cosier and Aplin (1980).
10. Mason and Mitroff (1981).
11. Dalky et al. (1972).
12. Schwenk (1985).

grees of importance attached to each factor with respect to achieving manufacturing objectives. Additionally, some factors may not be quantifiable and yet may be important for achieving the manufacturing objectives. Thus, an analytical model that considers both quantitative and qualitative factors in decision making will significantly enhance the process.

The inability of conventional justification methods to consider the intangible and nonquantifiable factors makes them inappropriate for most strategic decision-making processes. However, decision support systems and multicriteria models can enhance the decision-making processes, making them a better alternative. The analytic hierarchy process presented here aids the automation decision-making process.

At this step of idea analysis, the relative level of automation required is determined and implementation follows. However, the successful result of such a decision depends on the quality of the underlying support systems. Some support system elements are listed in Figure 5.1. An automation alternative such as computer integrated manufacturing, for example, requires training and education so that workers can adapt to the new system. Through training and education, organizational and manufacturing goals and objectives become clearer. Worker participation at some level of the decision-making process may also enhance the quality of work life and may lead to increased productivity. Top management's commitment and sufficient resources are also required for an automation decision to be the correct one (Deming, 1985).

The final step in the framework consists of continuous review and appraisal of the entire process. Standards used to evaluate how well the objectives are being satisfied may also be reevaluated at this point and new standards may be set. Throughout the appraisal, the level of automation implemented may be upgraded to accommodate changing manufacturing and/or organizational needs, goals, and objectives.

Our framework provides a formal automation decision-making process in a step-by-step approach. Furthermore, using existing decision-making models offers decision support at all stages of this complex process. The support systems outlined in Figure 5.1 should enhance the potential success of the decisions when implemented. The factors, support systems, and models shown in Figure 5.1 and Table 5.1 are not exhaustive, but they offer some guidelines for making automation decisions. Factors can be added or excluded as deemed necessary; how this is done is discussed in the following section.

THE DECISION SUPPORT SYSTEM (DSS)

In order to validate the decision-making framework proposed in this study, we built a decision support system. The building block was the expert system cell called Expert Choice. The methodology underlying Expert Choice is the analytic hierarchy process (AHP), developed by Saaty (1980). In defining the AHP, Saaty states: "The analytic hierarchy process (AHP) is a multi-criteria decision method that uses hierarchic or network structures to represent a decision problem and then develops priorities for the alternatives based on the decision makers' judgments throughout the system" (p. 157).

The AHP uses a nine-point scale to depict judgments or preferences for one factor over the other. These judgments are based on experience, intuition, or data. Participants reach a decision by applying their judgments in a systematic manner, and the hierarchical structure helps organize the factors that go into that decision-making process. The structure's highest level is the *goal*. It then branches downward to the intermediate level of *factors* or *criteria*. At the bottom of the structure are listed the decision *alternatives*. Figure 5.2 shows the network diagram for the automation decision-making process.

Thus, the AHP starts by breaking down a complex problem into a hierarchy, with each level consisting of a few manageable elements and each element in turn, broken down into another set of elements. The process continues down to the most specific elements of the problem, typically the specific decision alternatives being considered. Structuring any decision situation this way helps to deal with the complexity and identify the major components of the situation. There is no single general hierarchical structure, and one of the major attributes of the AHP is its flexibility: decision makers construct a hierarchy to fit their idiosyncratic needs (Saaty, 1980).

Subsequently, the AHP model conducts a comparison of each pair of criteria with respect to the overall goal. A measurement methodology establishes priorities among the elements within each stratum of the hierarchy, then evaluates each set of elements with respect to elements in a higher stratum. This provides the framework for the data collection and analysis that constitute the analytic hierarchy process (Saaty, 1980). Structurally, the hierarchy is a series of pair-comparison matrices, and the participants are asked to evaluate the off-diagonal relationship in one-half of each matrix, while reciprocals are in the transposed positions.

With regard to the manufacturing automation decision, there is a comparison of flexibility and cost of production with respect to productivity improvement. This comparison goes on until all cells in the upper part of the matrix above the diagonal are filled with judgments. Unitary values are assigned to the diagonal cells to show the comparison of a factor to itself. Once the matrix is completed, the decision alternatives are compared with respect to the established criteria.

Another feature of the AHP is its consistency ratio, which can capture inconsistencies in judgments. It is generally assumed that decision makers behave rationally; that is, one who prefers factor *A* to *B* and factor *B* to *C*, is expected to prefer factor *A* to *C*. However, since rational behavior is not always conscious, the AHP can identify inconsistent judgments and, if desired, make adjustments to achieve consistency. At this point, it should be emphasized that consistency does not guarantee a better decision. Nevertheless, quality decisions imply consistent judgments (Harker & Vargas, 1987).

The AHP has been applied in a variety of decision-making situations (Madu, 1988a; Saaty, 1976, 1977, 1980, 1981). A recent survey by Zahedi (1986) points out the different areas where the AHP has been applied. Belton and Gear (1984) have questioned the theoretical basis of the AHP, but Harker and Vargas (1987) provide support in response to the criticisms. Their study confirms the validity of the AHP and its use as a decision-making tool.

Experimental Design

The corporate and/or manufacturing objectives, and identification of factors by influential participants to include in the decision-making process, led to the first idea generation module of the decision support system (DSS), as shown in Figure 5.1. Within this module, questions were posed and answers were recorded in order to eliminate duplication.

The second, idea analysis, module of the DSS was performed with the aid of the Expert Choice cell (Expert Choice, 1983). This module helped the students who assumed the role of managers and business or technology planners to improve their understanding of the automation decision-making process.

The third, evaluation, module of the DSS was executed on the basis of the consistency ratio featured in the AHP. This ratio, which can capture any inconsistency in judgments, was used to evaluate the final decisions reached by the participants, prior to implementation.

For the sake of simplicity, and in order not to overload the process, only two levels of automation were considered: CIM level automation versus traditional (job shop) manufacturing. In a real-life setting, it may be necessary to compare conventional production to different levels of automation.

A set of data obtained within a highly controlled experimental setting illustrates the model's use. Nine MBA students participated in this experiment. They were selected on the basis of four criteria:

1. Positive indication for participation,
2. Commitment to complete the experiment,
3. Prior exposure to computer-integrated manufacturing (CIM) in a graduate P/OM course,
4. Prior experience in a manufacturing environment.

Before they assumed their decision-making roles, the subjects were exposed to differences between traditional manufacturing and computer-integrated flexible manufacturing automation along the lines of Goldhar and Jelinek (1985). Additionally, they were given a lecture on the use of AHP.

During this preliminary training, there were several discussions to clarify the differences between conventional manufacturing and CIM, and the use of the AHP scales and techniques. These discussions were closely monitored so that group members did not voice preferences on any of the factors involved.

Experimental Analysis

It was made clear to the participants that they had to generate the factors for the decision-making process as outlined in the framework. Table 5.2 lists some criteria to be considered in deciding whether to automate. This list is not exhaustive but includes criteria suggested by Goldhar and Jelinek (1985). Thus, the subjects were well informed in the automation decision-making process. Incidentally, the group had an average score of 573 on the GMAT and a graduate GPA of 3.702. The small size of the group encouraged active discussion sessions.

Figure 5.2
Hierarchical Network Strucure of the Manufacturing Automation Decision-Making Process

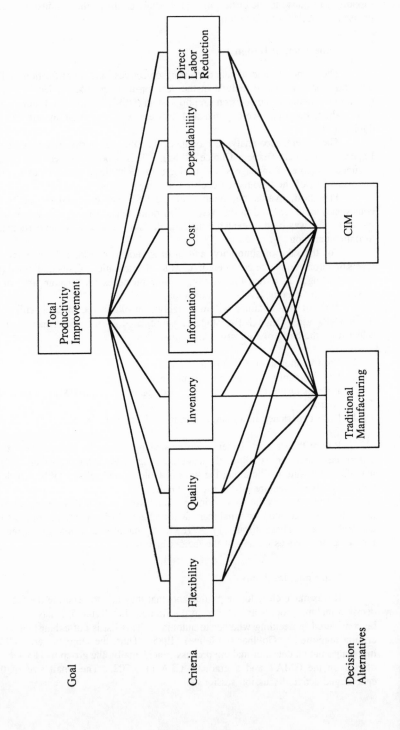

Table 5.2
Significant Factors in Automation Decision

FLEXIBILITY (FLEX)

Ability to adapt to variability in materials and process condition
Responsiveness to surges in demand
Ability to handle complex product designs
Ability to integrate new technology

QUALITY

Product performance
Customer perception of quality to type of technology
Improved relationship with customers
Improved organizational relationship between functional departments
Aesthetic value of product

INFORMATION CAPABILITIES (INFO)

Ease of obtaining information including floor information (i.e., potential bottlenecks)
Transmission and processing of information
Timeliness, accuracy, and precision of information

DIRECT LABOR REDUCTION (DLR)

COST
Cost of automation
Cost of training
Cost of hiring and screening personnel

INVENTORY (INVENT)

Set-up cost reduction
Work-in-process due inventory
Material reduction
Other waste reduction

DEPENDABILITY (DEP)

Reliability of production process
Ease of maintenance
Ease of scheduling and control
Safety conditions

Subsequently, each subject made a judgment on each pair of the criteria or alternatives under consideration. To avoid group effect or domination by any single member of the team, each subject was given a card on which his or her judgment was recorded for each pair of alternatives or criteria. The geometric mean of the group judgment was computed for each pair of alternatives or criteria. (The use of the geometric mean is discussed in the Expert Choice manual [Expert Choice, 1983]). These averages were inputed into an IBMPC application of Expert Choice to generate the results discussed below. The team regrouped if any inconsistencies were detected and the process was repeated until a consistent judgment was obtained.

Expert Choice organizes the various elements of a decision situation into an upside-down tree. The tree is upside down because it branches downward from the stated goal. Intermediate levels represent the factors or criteria of the situation. At the bottom of the tree are the leafnodes, which represent the decision alternatives of choice (Expert Choice, 1983).

Results

The geometric mean of the judgments was computed to the nearest integer for all entries presented in Table 5.3. Saaty (1987) shows that the derived scale from these comparisons is insensitive to small changes in the values of pair-wise comparisons. The result of the initial judgment of the group gave an inconsistency ratio of 0.126; consistency exists when the ratio is less than 0.1. Inconsistency is expected when a group is not homogeneous. World views and perceptions are likely to vary, reflecting group members' different experiences.

The group was informed that its preference on cost to direct labor reduction was the most inconsistent result. However, members were not informed on the particular value that would make their judgment consistent, although this value is supplied by the Expert Choice cell.

Consistency is not a guarantee for quality decisions, however this approach improves the decision-making process because it leads to rigorous discussion. The discussion sessions increase the depth of understanding for the issues and, in turn, improve the quality of each member's judgment. After two trials the group was unable to resolve this inconsistency, achieving an inconsistency ratio of 0.111. The second time, the judgment of the group as to flexibility and quality was inconsistent. The group met for a third time and rigorous discussion took place once more. This third session's judgments produced an inconsistency ratio of 0.063, a value that implied the group was now consistent in its decision.

Although the decision-making process was time consuming, some lessons were learned:

1. The discussion sessions steadily reduced of the inconsistency ratio.
2. The discussions expanded the group's understanding of the problem and the underlying methodology.
3. The need for an outside leader became apparent, as someone to monitor and control the decision-making process. This facilitator saves time by directing the discussion and moving the group toward achieving consistency, if desired.

The results of the second and third sessions, and the final tally for the decision alternative leafnodes, are presented in Tables 5.4, 5.5, and 5.6, respectively. In the final

Table 5.3
Judgments with Respect to Goal

	A	B	C	D	E	F	G
A : FLEX		(7.0)	5.0	3.0	3.0	9.0	1.0
B : QUALITY			7.0	3.0	5.0	9.0	5.0
C : COST				(5.0)	(4.0)	5.0	(5.0)
D : DEPEN					1.0	3.0	(5.0)
E : INVENT						3.0	(5.0)
F : DLR							(9.0)

Criteria	Priority Index
FLEX	0.155
QUALITY	0.443
COST	0.039
DEPEN	0.080
INVENT	0.068
DLR	0.021
INFO	0.195

INCONSISTENCY RATIO = 0.126

Note: With respect to goal the following judgment is most inconsistent: C and F. Consistency will be improved if this judgment is 1.9

Table 5.4
Goal: Total Productivity Improvement

	A	B	C	D	E	F	G
A : FLEX		>7.0<	5.0	3.0	3.0	9.0	1.0
B : QUALITY			7.0	3.0	5.0	9.0	5.0
C : COST				5.0	4.0	2.0	5.0
D : DEPEN					1.0	3.0	5.0
E : INVENT						3.0	5.0
F : DLR							9.0
G : INFO							

Criteria	Priority Index
FLEX	0.282
QUALITY	0.310
COST	0.032
DEPEN	0.078
INVENT	0.068
DLR	0.022
INFO	0.247
INCONSISTENCY RATIO = 0.111	

Note: With respect to goal the following judgment is most inconsistent: A and B. Consistency will be improved if this judgment is 2.9

Table 5.5
Judgments with Respect to Goal

	A	B	C	D	E	F	G
A : FLEX		1.0	5.0	3.0	3.0	9.0	1.0
B : QUALITY			7.0	3.0	5.0	9.0	2.0
C : COST				2.4	(4.0)	2.0	(5.0)
D : DEPEN					1.0	3.0	(5.0)
E : INVENT						3.0	(5.0)
F : DLR							(9.0)
G : INFO							

Criteria	Priority Index
FLEX	0.228
QUALITY	0.298
COST	0.055
DEPEN	0.063
INVENT	0.084
DLR	0.025
INFO	0.247
INCONSISTENCY RATIO = 0.063	

Table 5.6
Total Productivity Improvement Tally for Leaf Nodes

QUALITY	=	0.298			
			CIM	=	0.249
			TRAD	=	0.050
INFO	=	0.247			
			CIM	=	0.206
			TRAD	=	0.041
FLEX	=	0.228			
			CIM	=	0.200
			TRAD	=	0.029
INVENT	=	0.084			
			CIM	=	0.047
			TRAD	=	0.016
DEPEN	=	0.063			
			CIM	=	0.047
			TRAD	=	0.016
COST	=	0.055			
			TRAD	=	0.050
			CIM	=	0.006
DLR	=	0.025			
			CIM	=	0.022
			TRAD	=	0.003

Total Productivity Improvement
Leaf Nodes Sorted by Priority

CIM	0.804
TRAD	0.196
TOTAL	1.000

table, the leafnode results illustrate that, in order to achieve a total productivity improvement, the group must assign the highest priorities to quality, information and flexibility, respectively; namely, in Table 5.6, quality gets a priority index of 0.298; information, a priority index of 0.247; and flexibility a priority index of 0.228. The remaining criteria are assigned relatively lower priority values in the decision making process.

The participants also believed that computer-integrated manufacturing will outperform traditional manufacturing in achieving total productivity improvement. In all the criteria except cost, the participants expected CIM to perform better than conventional manufacturing. With a priority index of 0.804, shown in Table 5.6, the group decided to implement the CIM level of automation.

CONCLUSION

The purpose here has been to introduce a conceptual framework that can assist managers in making automation decisions within a strategic perspective. The proposed model offers a step-by-step approach to the automation decision-making process. It also integrates some of the well-known decision-making models of conflict resolution and idea analysis. An illustrative example analyzes the decision-making process of a group of MBA students assuming the role of business planners. A decision support system with the Expert Choice cell as its core supports the process.

We do not in any way attempt to generate an ultimate solution to the strategic problem of deciding whether or how much to automate. Our purpose is simply to show how existing models can be integrated into and applied to the process of automation decision making. The experiment is used for illustrative purposes only; since group members were not randomly selected, their behavior does not represent the behavior of all MBA students. This is not a major limitation, however, because automation-related decisions are influenced by environmental and situation specific factors that may differ widely from one manufacturer to another.

Our second limitation is with respect to the nature of the industry under consideration. The group members in this study had diverse work experience and does not necessarily represent a particular industry. In practice, decision makers will be more homogeneous, probably experts on a particular industry. In the electronics industry, for example, which is characterized by a comparatively low direct-labor content (Rayner, 1986), DLR may not be a critical factor in an automation decision.

There are advantages in using small groups of decision makers:

1. Small groups are easier to control,
2. Inconsistency in decision making is reduced,
3. It takes less time to reach a decision,
4. Larger groups may include inactive members.

Thus, considering the above limitations, this experiment should be viewed as an illustration of automation decision making within the proposed framework and using the Expert Choice cell. The framework remains to be applied in a real-life manufacturing situation.

To conclude, the automation decision-making process is often subjective. A decision maker acts based on his or her experience, world view, cognitive feelings, and perceptions; more often than not, these are elements difficult to isolate. Thus, a satisfiable, rather than an optimal, solution consciously reached through a formal decision process, may be preferred with respect to the strategic issue of manufacturing automation.

REFERENCES

Belton, V., and T. Gear. "On a Short-Coming of Saaty's Method of Analytic Hierarchies." *Omega* 11 (3) (1984): 228-30.

———. "The Legitimacy of Rank Reversal—A Comment." *Omega* 13 (3) (1985): 143-44.

Blois, K. J. "Manufacturing Technology as a Competitive Weapon." *Long Range Planning* 19 (4) (1986): 63-70.

Canada J. R. "Annotated Bibliography of Computer-Integrated Manufacturing Systems." *Engineering Economist* 31 (2) (1986a).

———. "Non-Traditional Method for Evaluating CIM Opportunities Assigns Weights to Intangibles." *Industrial Engineering* 18 (3) (1986b): 66-71.

Chakravarty, A. K. "Dimensions of Manufacturing Automation." *International Journal of Production Research* 25 (9) (1987): 1339-54.

Chakravarty, A. K., and A. Shtub. "Capacity, Cost and Scheduling Analysis for a Multiproduct Flexible Manufacturing Cell." *International Journal of Production Research* 25 (7) (1987): 1143-56.

Cohen, S. S., and J. Zysman. *Manufacturing Matters: The Myth of the Post-Industrial Economy.* New York: Basic Books, 1987.

Cosier, R. A., and J. C. Aplin. "A Critical Review of Dialectical Inquiry as a Tool in Strategic Planning." *Strategic Management Journal* 1 (4) (1980): 343-56.

Curtin, F. T. "Planning and Justifying Factory Automation Systems." *Production Engineering* 31 (5) (1984): 46-51.

Dalky, N. C., D. L. Rourke, R. Lewis, and D. Snyder. *Studies in the Quality of Life.* Lexington, MA: Lexington Books, 1972.

Delbecq, A. L., and A. H. Van de Ven. "A Group Process Model for Problem Identification and Program Planning." *Journal of Applied Behavioral Science.* 7 (4) (1971): 28-36.

Delbecq, A. L., A. H. Van de Ven, and D. Gustafon. *Group Techniques for Program Planning.* Glenview, IL: Scott Foresman, 1975.

Deming, W. E. "Transformation of Western Style of Management." *Interfaces* 15 (3) (1985): 6-11.

Expert Choice. McLean, VA: Decision Support Software, Inc., 1983.

Falter, B. "CAM Economic Justification—A Case Study in the Electronics Industry." Proceedings of the International Industrial Engineering Conference, Dallas, *IIE* (1986): 518-25.

Godet, M. *Scenarios and Strategic Management.* London: Butterworths, 1987.

Goldhar, J. D., and M. Jelinek. "Computer Integrated Flexible Manufacturing: Organizational, Economic and Strategic Implications." *Interfaces* 15 (3) (1985): 94-105.

Harker, P. T., and L. G. Vargas. "The Theory of Ratio Scale Estimation: Saaty's Analytic Hierarchy Process." *Management Science* 33 (11) (1987): 1383-403.

Hartman, S. J., M. C. White, and M. D. Crino. "Environmental Volatility, System Adaptation, Planning Requirements, and Information Processing Strategies." *Decision Sciences* 17 (4) (1986): 454-74.

Hayes, R. H., and R. Garvin. "Managing As If Tomorrow Mattered." *Harvard Business Review* 60 (3) (May/June 1982): 71-79.

Industrial Engineering 19 (11) (1987).

Interfaces 17 (6) (1987).

Kaplan R. S., "Must CIM be Justified by Faith Alone?" *Harvard Business Review* 64 (2) (March/April 1986a): 87-95.

———. "Accounting Lag: The Obsolescence of Cost Accounting Systems." *California Management Review* 28 (2) (1986b): 178-99.

Lindblom, C. E. "The Science of 'Muddling Through.'" *Public Administration Review* 19 (Spring 1959): 79-88.

Madu, C. N. "An Economic Decision Model for Technology Transfer." *Engineering Management International* 5 (1) (1988a): 53-62.

———. "A Systems Approach to Manufacturing Automation Decision Making." *Proceedings of the Decision Sciences Institute Annual Meeting*, (1988) 1315-1316.

Mason, R. O. "A Dialectical Approach to Strategic Planning." *Management Science* 15 (8) (1969): B403-14.

Mason, R. O., and I. I. Mitroff. *Challenging Strategic Planning Assumptions.* New York: John Wiley, 1981.

Meredith, J. R. "Implementing New Manufacturing Technologies: Managerial Lessons over the FMS Life Cycle." *Interfaces* 17 (6) (1987): 51-62.

Mintzberg, H., D. Rainghani, and A. Theoret. "The Structure of Unstructured Decision Processes." *Administrative Science Quarterly* 21 (2) (1976): 246-75.

Monahan, G. E., and T. L. Smunt. "A Multilevel Decision Support System for the Financial Justification of Automated Flexible Manufacturing." *Interfaces* 17 (6) (1987): 29-40.

Nutt, P. C. "The Merits of Using Experts or Consumers as Members of Planning Groups: A Field Experiment in Health Planning." *Academy of Management Journal* 19 (1977): 378-94.

———. "Hybrid Planning Methods." *Academy of Management Review* 7 (1982): 442-54.

———. "Types of Organizational Decision Processes." *Administrative Science Quarterly* 29 (3) (1984): 414-50.

O'Guin, M. C. "Information Age Calls for New Methods of Financial Analysis in Implementing Technologies." *Industrial Engineering* 19 (11) (1987): 28-34.

Peters, T. J., and R. H. Waterman, Jr. *In Search of Excellence.* New York: Harper & Row, 1982.

Quade, E. S., and W. I. Boucher. *Systems Analysis and Policy Planning.* New York: America Elsevier, 1968.

Quinn, J. B. *Strategies for Change—Logical Incrementalism.* Homewood, IL: Richard D. Irwin, 1980.

Radford, K. J. *Strategic Planning: An Analytical Approach.* Reston, VA: Reston, 1980.

Randhawa, S. U., and D. Bedworth. "Factors Identified for Use in Comparing Conventional and Flexible Manufacturing Systems." *Industrial Engineering* 17 (6) (1985): 40-44.

Rayner, B. C. P. "The Market for CIM Starts to Take Shape." *Electronic Business,* October 1, 1986, pp. 89-95.

Rohrbaugh, J. "Improving the Quality of Group Judgment: Social Judgment Analysis and the Nominal Group Technique." *Organizational Behavior and Human Performance* 28 (1983): 272-88.

Saaty, T. L. "The Sudan Transport Study." *Interfaces* 8 (1) (1977): 37-57.

———. *The Analytic Hierarchy Process.* New York: McGraw-Hill, 1980.

———. "Rank Generation, Preservation, and Reversal in the Analytic Hierarchy Process." *Decision Sciences* 18 (2) (1987): 157-77.

Saaty, T. L., and J. M. Alexander. *Thinking with Models.* Elmsford, NY: Pergamon Press, 1981.

Saaty, T. L., and M. Khouja. "A Measure of World Influence." *Journal of Peace Science* 2 (1) (1976): 31-47.

Schwenk, C. R. "Giving the Devil Its Due." *Wharton Annual* (1985): 104-108.

Sethi, S. P., Namiki, N., and C. L. Swanson. *The False Promise of the Japanese Miracle.* Marshfield, MA; Pitman Publishing, 1984.

Sullivan, W. G. "Models IEs Can Use to Include Strategic, On-monetary Factors in Automation Decisions." *Industrial Engineering* 18 (3) (1986): 42-50.

"Summary of the Sixth Annual Productivity Survey." *Productivity Today* (1986).

Varney, M. S., W. G. Sullivan, and J. K. Cochran. "Justification of Flexible Manufacturing Systems with the Analytic Hierarchy Process." *Proceedings of the Annual International Industrial Engineering Conference* (1985): 181-90.

Wallace, W. J., and G. J. Thuesen. "Annotated Bibliography on Investment in Flexible Automation." *Engineering Economist* 32 (3) (Spring 1987).

Zahedi, F. "The Analytic Hierarchy Process—A Survey of the Method and its Applications." *Interfaces* 16 (1986): 96-108.
Zwicky, F. *Discovery, Invention, Research Through the Morphological Approach.* New York: Macmillan, 1968.

Chapter 6

A Strategic Decision Model for the Selection of Advanced Technology

Chinho Lin, Chu-hua Kuei, John Aheto, Christian N. Madu

Organizational decision making is increasingly complex in today's competitive environment, yet there is a need to make accurate, timely, and informed decisions in order to compete effectively. Specifically, organizations are often confronted with four major problems:

1. How to respond swiftly to market and technological changes.
2. How to achieve flexibility in product designs, changes in demand, and variability in materials and process conditions.
3. How to improve product performance, relationships with customers and suppliers, relationships between the different functional departments, customer perceptions of the quality of the product, and the aesthetic value of the product.
4. How to effectively utilize new information to improve both the performance of the product and organizational effectiveness.

Automation—rather, new technology—is viewed by many as the best way to address these problems. Automation, as referred to in this chapter, can be grouped into four basic functions (Freeman, 1983):

1. Factory layout and design automation
2. Manufacturing automation and engineering data handling
3. Machine and design automation
4. Office automation

Categories 1, 2, and 3 can be further divided into two classes (Gaither, 1990):
• Automated system that includes machine attachments, numerically controlled (NC) machines, robots, automated quality control inspection, automatic identification systems, and automated process control.
• Automated production system that includes automated flow lines, automated assembly systems, flexible manufacturing systems (FMS), automated storage and retrieval systems (AS/RS), computer-aided design systems (CAD), computer-aided manufacturing systems (CAM), and computer-integrated manufacturing (CIM).

New technology is the key to survival for many companies in today's highly competitive environment (Madu & Georgantzas, 1991). Many automation technologies spread across activities from factory operations to marketing and service. If these technologies are properly selected and used, they can enhance operational efficiency, thereby, helping achieve a better competitive posture. However, almost all automation technologies are expensive and hence their selection should be carefully evaluated considering all relevant tangible (e.g., cost) and intangible factors (e.g., market response) as well as the limited resources (budget) of the company.

Noori (1990) suggested that the problems encountered in the selection of new technology include the following: (1) technical factors, dealing with the appropriateness of the new technology; (2) structural factors, dealing with reporting relationships, information and control systems, and reward systems; (3) behavioral-political processes, dealing with decision-making systems, conflict management, and power processes; and (4) strategic factors, dealing with management values, financial resources, and the competitive environment. The present literature has focused mostly on technical and strategic factors. It is our contention that the taxonomy created by Noori is extensive and covers the basic problems faced in the adoption of new technologies. In this chapter, we adopt a systems approach for a conceptual framework as well as pragmatic models to assist in making this important decision.

RESEARCH BACKGROUND

Arbel and Seidmann (1984), Choobineh (1986), and Wabalickis (1987) evaluate different FMS projects. Notably, Arbel and Seidmann use the analytic hierarchy process (AHP) in the performance evaluation of FMS and illustrate its effectiveness with a real-life case study. Sullivan (1986) and Randhawa and Bedworth (1985) compare an FMS to conventional manufacturing systems. Roper-Lowe and Shorp (1990) discuss a decision process on a computer operating system. Kaplan (1986) discusses the issues involved in measuring the cost of computer-integrated manufacturing (CIM); Muralichar et al. (1990) illustrate the selection process for the proper information systems. Madu and Georgantzas (1991) provide a conceptual framework to examine the adoption and selection of new technology. A decision support system based on the analytic hierarchy process (AHP) was developed and used to implement the selection of new technologies. In a recent paper, Madu (1991) applied a quality confidence procedure to AHP and used a group of business executives to illustrate how selection of new technologies can be made.

Although many of these research papers have identified the problems of cost-accounting techniques in justifying new technologies, and thereby in adopting new technologies, they do not discuss how the limited resources of a company can be allocated effectively to these new technologies. In this chapter, we maintain the systemic view adopted in these papers, but expand it to include allocation of company resources to different, mutually dependent technologies. This is necessary so companies may achieve the synergy resulting from the interdependencies among technologies.

There are many traditional decision-making techniques, such as net present value, internal rate of return, and cost-benefit ratios, that can be used to evaluate the priorities of a company's investment projects. However, these approaches consider only quantitative factors, failing to recognize the many important qualitative factors such as competitive advantage and social issues. These factors are discussed here and in Chapter 5. We choose the analytic hierarchy process (AHP) (Saaty, 1980) as our analysis tool since it effectively considers these factors, as demonstrated by the several studies on the topic. The AHP assists decision makers in evaluating multiple-attribute alternatives when subjective assessments of qualitative factors are integrated with quantitative factors.

We also consider the mutual dependence of various automation technologies considered for adoption. This implies that synergistic benefits may be derived by simultaneously adopting technologies that are interdependent. For example, implementation of FMS often benefits from computer-aided design (CAD) and computer-aided process planning (CAPP). Therefore, a linear programming model is presented here to show how to allocate limited resources to these automation technologies while considering their interdependence.

A GLOBAL OR HOLISTIC APPROACH TO THE ADOPTION OF AUTOMATION TECHNOLOGIES

Identification of the Company's Activities and Associated Technologies

The primary activities of a company include the physical creation of products, distribution of the products to customers, and after-sales support. These activities add value to the products or services rendered and can be classified as follows (Porter & Miller, 1985):

1. Inbound logistics—activities that guarantee the supply of materials for the company.
2. Operations—activities that directly increase the value of materials or work in process.
3. Outbound logistics—activities that guarantee supplies will arrive for customers on time.
4. Marketing and sales—activities that take place between items 2 and 3. Such activities include promotional efforts.
5. Service—activities involving customer support services such as after-sales support.

In order to guarantee that these activities satisfy a required tolerance level, the following support activities are necessary:

1. Company infrastructure activities—including general management, legal and accounting services, and quality management.
2. Human resources management—these activities involving education, training, recruiting, and hiring.
3. Technology development—activities to reduce variations in the manufacturing process.
4. Procurement—activities that involve purchases of raw materials.

Evidently, these activities can take advantage of new technologies. Table 6.1, for example, presents the nine activities listed above and uses a hypothetical example to describe the relationships between these activities and some of the current automation technologies shown to directly or indirectly improve operational efficiency.

Table 6.1 reflects a fundamental step in adopting new technologies. This step involves a team of knowledgeable experts or, rather, stakeholders. The team collects relevant internal and external information from diverse sources, such as an expressed need for automation to enhance performance or a manager's recommendation of an automation technology; or data from vendors about different technologies and the technologies adopted by competitors.

Table 6.1
The Relationships Among Activities and Automation Technologies

	1	2	3	4	5	6	7	8	9
FMS	I*	D**		I		I	I		
AS/RS	D	D				I	I		
CAD		I		I		I	I	D	
CAPP		D				I	I	I	
LAN		I		D	D	I	I		
TC				D		I	I		

Notes: 1. Inbound logistics; 2. Operations; 3. Outbound logistics; 4. Marketing and sales; 5. Services; 6. Firm infrastructure; 7. Humane resource management; 8. Technology development; 9. Procurement. FMS: flexible manufacturing system; AS/RS: automated storage and retrieval system; CAD: computer-aided design; CAPP: computer-aided process planning; LAN: local area network; TC: teleconference. *D: Directly contribution; **I: Indirect contribution

Identification of Objective and Criteria

A critical step in the adoption of new technologies is the identification of appropriate objectives. Sullivan (1986), for example, classifies the objectives of an FMS as "global benefits" and "global costs." In the former, advantage factors such as quality, flexibility, and shop floor information are considered; while in the latter, pitfall factors such as operating risk, required technical support, and present worth of costs are considered. Randhawa and Bedworth (1985) use "improved productivity of the organization" as an objective and consider three primary factors—economic, technical, and social issues—in measuring the attained level of this objective. Arbel and Seidmann (1984) propose "benefit aspects," which consist of cost reduction, production flexibility, and market response to evaluate the different projects of FMSs. Madu and Georgantzas (1991) identify seven technology dimensions after an extensive review of the literature: flexibility, quality, dependability, inventory management, information processing, direct labor reduction, and cost. Although maintaining a company's competitiveness is implicit in these papers, Goldhar and Jelinek (1985), Porter and Miller (1985), and Diaz (1986) show that competitive advantage should be the basic concern when introducing new information technologies. Therefore, it should be explicitly considered as the company's objective in adopting new technologies. In our study, the objective is to enhance the competitive posture of a company. Automation technologies may create barriers in entering new markets, change the basis of competition, and change the balance of power in supplier-buyer relationships.

Noori (1990) and Cash et al. (1988) also note two sets of trends, those influencing the market and those affecting manufacturing. Market trends include a shorter product life cycle, increased new product or process introductions, fragmented markets, unexpected competitors, and demand uncertainty; manufacturing trends include product and process simplification, a need to reduce inventories, pressures to improve quality, changing original equipment manufacturer (OEM)-supplier relationships, smaller plants, and smaller production lot sizes. Based on these trends, competitive factors should include quality, complexity adjustment, variety adjustment, uncertainty management, supply or distribution extension ability, time management, and information management. These seven factors are considered the means of enhancing the competitive posture of a company.

Quality. High quality is a major competitive weapon. The ongoing focus on total quality management and continuous improvement reflect the overriding importance of quality. Quality is, in fact, the most important factor in achieving customer satisfaction. It is the main reason why Japanese cars and electronic equipment are popular today. Quality is also directly linked to productivity, as shown in Deming's Chain Reaction. This link also explains why quality is instrumental in achieving global competitiveness.

Complexity Adjustment. To deal with its complex environment, a company could be a "focused firm." A focused firm deals with a narrow range of parts, products, and/or processes. Typically, this type of company has fewer employees; moreover, one or two competitive priorities are enough to survive.

Variety Adjustment. A company with high variety adjustment can produce a variety of parts, models, or products without increasing cost. This involves the issue of flexibility.

Uncertainty Management. An automation operation system can help managers manage the uncertainty characteristic of switching from one product, action, or policy to another in a very short time. Again, this involves flexibility.

Supply or Distribution Extension Ability. Automation communication techniques can link a company with its outbound customers and inbound suppliers.

Time Management. To effectively respond to customer orders or a changing market, managers have to consider time management as one of the basic weapons of the 1990s.

Information Management. A good information management system should include a traditional management reporting system, communication system, decision support system, executive information system, and expert system. It should also be capable of producing accurate information on a real-time basis for complex problems.

Ranking of automation activities. The analytic hierarchy process (AHP) is used to rank several automation technologies on the basis of these seven criteria. Here is a hypothetical example to illustrate how AHP can be used to obtain the priorities for the following technologies:

A1. FMS (Flexible manufacturing system)
A2. AS/RS (Automated storage and retrieval system)
A3. CAD (Computer aided design)
A4. CAPP (Computer aided process planning)
A5. LAN (Local area network)
A6. TC (Teleconferencing)

The seven criteria with respect to the goal of enhancing competitive posture are:

C1. Quality competition
C2. Complexity adjustment
C3. Variety adjustment
C4. Uncertainty management
C5. Supply-distribution extension ability
C6. Time management

C7. Information management

Henceforth, we use the notations introduced for both automation technologies and criteria.

The decision hierarchy of objective, criteria, and automation alternatives is shown in Figure 6.1. The input data of the analysis matrices are shown in Table 6.2. These data, though hypothetical, represent the sequence of decision making that follows the approach discussed here.

Table 6.2a, for example, shows the comparison of two criteria at a time regarding their relative importance in achieving the overall goal or objective, which we define as enhancing the competitive posture of the company. The AHP uses a nine-point scale defined as follows: 1—equal importance; 3—moderate importance; 5—strong importance; 7—very strong importance; 9—extreme importance. The even numbers 2,4,6 and 8 are for compromise, and reciprocals show inverse comparisons. For example, a comparison of C1 to C5 shows an assignment of a scale of 5. This implies that the decision maker thinks C1 has strong importance over C5 in enhancing competitive posture. Similar interpretations can be derived for all other comparisons presented in the cells of Table 6.2a.

The other comparison tables can be interpreted similarly. Notice, however, that Tables 6.2b to 6.2h represent comparisons of the six automation technologies (A1 to A6) to each of the seven criteria identified as C1 to C7. A process known as synthesization is used by AHP to analyze these tables to get a priority matrix. The priority matrix, given as matrix A, is generated using Expert Choice, a special computer software for AHP. This matrix ranks the six automation technologies in terms of relative importance when all criteria are simultaneously compared. It is apparent from the matrix that this decision maker views CAPP and FMS as the most significant automation technologies in terms of enhancing competitive posture. The priority indices for these two are 0.214 and 0.201, respectively. Similarly, AS/RS has the least importance, with a priority index of 0.085.

Figure 6.1
Decision Hierarchy of Objective, Criteria, and Alternatives

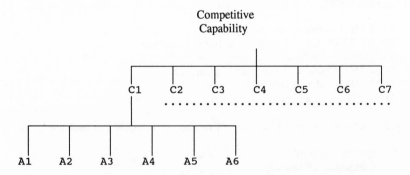

Table 6.2
The Input Data of the Analysis Matrices

6.2a: Criterion vs. Criterion with Respect to Goal

	C1	C2	C3	C4	C5	C6	C7
C1	1	4	3	2	5	2	2
C2		1	1/2	1	2	1	1
C3			1	1	2	1/2	1/2
C4				1	2	1/3	1
C5					1	1	1/2
C6						1	1
C7							1

6.2b Alternative vs. Alternative with Respect to C1

	A1	A2	A3	A4	A5	A6
A1	1	2	1/2	1/3	6	7
A2		1	1/2	1/3	3	4
A3			1	1/2	6	7
A4				1	6	7
A5					1	2
A6						1

6.2c Alternative vs. Alternative with Respect to C2

	A1	A2	A3	A4	A5	A6
A1	1	2	1/2	1/3	2	3
A2		1	1/3	1/4	2	2
A3			1	1	4	5
A4				1	5	6
A5					1	2
A6						1

6.2d Alternative vs. Alternative with Respect to C3

	A1	A2	A3	A4	A5	A6
A1	1	5	3	4	6	7
A2		1	1/2	1/3	2	2
A3			1	2	4	4
A4				1	5	5
A5					1	2
A6						1

Table 6.2 (continued)

6.2e Alternative vs. Alternative with Respect to C4

	A1	A2	A3	A4	A5	A6
A1	1	5	4	3	6	7
A2		1	1/3	1/2	2	2
A3			1	2	3	4
A4				1	3	4
A5					1	2
A6						1

6.2f Alternative vs. Alternative with Respect to C5

	A1	A2	A3	A4	A5	A6
A1	1	2	1	1	1/4	1/5
A2		1	1/2	1/3	1/5	1/6
A3			1	1	1/6	1/7
A4				1	1/6	1/7
A5					1	1/2
A6						1

6.2g Alternative vs. Alternative with Respect to C6

	A1	A2	A3	A4	A5	A6
A1	1	2	1	1	1/4	1/5
A2		1	2	1/2	1/6	1/7
A3			1	1	1/4	1/5
A4				1	1/4	1/5
A5					1	2
A6						1

6.2h Alternative vs. Alternative with Respect to C7

	A1	A2	A3	A4	A5	A6
A1	1	2	1	1	1/5	1/6
A2		1	2	1/3	1/6	1/7
A3			1	1	1/5	1/6
A4				1	1/6	1/6
A5					1	2
A6						1

The overall eigenvector priorities for these six automation alternatives are presented as matrix A.

$$
A = \begin{vmatrix}
\text{FMS} & = & .201 \\
\text{AS/RS} & = & .085 \\
\text{CAD} & = & .174 \\
\text{CAPP} & = & .214 \\
\text{LAN} & = & .171 \\
\text{TC} & = & .156
\end{vmatrix}
$$

Establishment of Interdependence Matrix

After priorities for those six automation alternatives are found, many literatures, notably Madu et al. [1991], are concerned about how to interpret the results and prepare recommendations. However, these priority weights are obtained from a "company level" point of view. In today's internationally competitive environment, we need to adjust the priority weights to reflect the following two factors: (1) the interdependent relationships among automation alternatives; and (2) the strategic impact of automation alternatives in the industry. In other words, we have to consider the nature of automation alternatives at an industry level. To do this, we propose a simple method to adjust the original priority weights (OPW). The method—matrix diagram—is motivated by the quality function deployment and is one of seven new management planning tools pervasive in the field of total quality management.

Our method begins with a matrix that lists the six automation alternatives on the left and top of the square.

	FMS	AS/RS	CAD	CAPP	LAN	TC
FMS						
AS/RS						
CAD						
CAPP						
LAN						
TC						

Once the matrix is established, a group of experts discusses and identifies the interdependence between any two technologies, with 1 being a strong interdependent relationship, 0.2 being a somewhat interdependent relationship, 0.1 being a little interdependent relationship, and "blank" being no interdependent relationship. For example:

	FMS	AS/RS	CAD	CAPP	LAN	TC
FMS	1	.2	.2	.1	.2	
AS/RS	.2	1		.2		
CAD	.2		1	.1	.1	
CAPP	.1	.2	.1	1	.2	
LAN	.2		.1	.2	1	
TC						1

Obviously, each technology has strong dependence on itself, therefore, all the diagonal entries take 1. However, each technology has different degrees of interdependence relationships with other technologies. For example, according to the experts, FMS has some interdependence with AS/RS, CAD, and LAN; has little interdependence with CAPP; and has no interdependence with TC.

Next, the total interdependence weight (TIW) of each technology is computed as the sum of numerical values for one particular technology. For example, the TIW of FMS is 1.7 (1+.2+.2+.1+.2). Following the same process, we can compute TIW for the other automation technologies as follows:

AS/RS	1.4
CAD	1.4
CAPP	1.6
LAN	1.5
TC	1

This exercise helps management understand the interdependence among automation technologies. Certain automation technologies such as FMS have significant internal impact on existing automation technologies and also on future applications of other technologies. FMS tends to have a higher TIW, thus management will tend to spend more time planning this type of automation. On the contrary, if a company adopts a TC, which has a lower TIW, it has only to find a good quality product at reasonable price and with good after-sales service. Management doesn't have to worry about developments of future automation technologies because TC has no interdependence with other automation technologies.

Perception of Levels of Strategic Impact in the Industry

If a company is going to adopt a new automation technology, it does so because that technology may improve productivity and provide consistent quality. In addition, the company may gain or maintain its competitive edge. However, certain technology, though it can offer competitive advantage at the beginning, may become a competitive necessity over time. Automated teller machines (ATMs), airline reservation systems, and electronic data interchange (EDI) are classic examples. Thus, the interdependence relationship matrix can be enhanced by considering the strategic impact of new technology in a particular industry. Strategic impact can be classified in three levels: (1) competitive advantage; (2) competitive necessity; and (3) no strategic impact. Again, we can use numerical values to represent these three levels of impact.

Competitive advantage—1.5
Competitive necessity—1.2
No strategic impact—1

This idea is similar to the sales point in the quality function deployment.

The Delphi technique becomes quite useful at this stage. Levels of strategic impact (SI) for each technology are shown in the following matrix.

	FMS	AS/RS	CAD	CAPP	LAN	TC	TIW	SI
FMS	1	.2	.2	.1	.2		1.7	1.5
AS/RS	.2	1		.2			1.4	1
CAD	.2		1	.1	.1		1.4	1.2
CAPP	.1	.2	.1	1	.2		1.6	1.2
LAN	.2		.1	.2	1		1.5	1.2
TC						1	1	1

Adjusted weight (AW) can be computed by multiplying TIW and SI for each technology alternative:

	FMS	AS/RS	CAD	CAPP	LAN	TC	TIW	SI	AW
FMS	1	.2	.2	.1	.2		1.7	1.5	2.55
AS/RS	.2	1		.2			1.4	1	1.4
CAD	.2		1	.1	.1		1.4	1.2	1.68
CAPP	.1	.2	.1	1	.2		1.6	1.2	1.92
LAN	.2		.1	.2	1		1.5	1.2	1.8
TC						1	1	1	1

New Adjusted Priority Weights

For convenience, we list the original priority weight (OPW) for each automation alternative in the last column of the matrix.

	FMS	AS/RS	CAD	CAPP	LAN	TC	TIW	SI	AW	OPW
FMS	1	.2	.2	.1	.2		1.7	1.5	2.55	.201
AS/RS	.2	1		.2			1.4	1	1.4	.085
CAD	.2		1	.1	.1		1.4	1.2	1.68	.174
CAPP	.1	.2	.1	1	.2		1.6	1.2	1.92	.214
LAN	.2		.1	.2	1		1.5	1.2	1.8	.171
TC						1	1	1	1	.156

The new adjusted priority weight (NAPW) for each technology is then defined as the product of the original priority weight and the AW (NAPW=AWxOPW). For example, the new adjusted priority weight for FMS is 0.51 (0.201x2.55).

	FMS	AS/RS	CAD	CAPP	LAN	TC	TIW	SI	AW	OPW	NAPW
FMS	1	.2	.2	.1	.2		1.7	1.5	2.55	.201	.51
AS/RS	.2	1		.2			1.4	1	1.4	.085	.12
CAD	.2		1	.1	.1		1.4	1.2	1.68	.174	.29
CAPP	.1	2	.1	1	.2		1.6	1.2	1.92	.214	.41
LAN	.2		.1	.2	1		1.5	1.2	1.8	.171	.31
TC						1	1	1	1	.156	.156

Originally, when decision makers use AHP alone, CAPP has the highest rank. However, when they consider internal interdependent relationships and strategic impact in the industry, FMS becomes Number 1.

Formulation of a Linear Programming Model

A linear programming (LP) technique is used to assist decision makers in allocating company money to automation technology. Suppose the estimated expenses required by each technology are as following:

Alternatives	Expenses ($ millions)
FMS	30
AS/RS	20
CAD	28
CAPP	30
LAN	25
TC	22

Furthermore, suppose the available budget is $100 million. By using linear programming, this budget can be allocated by importance of each automation alternative. According to Saaty and Alexander (1981), the linear programming formulation can be obtained as follows:

Max $Z = 0.51 W_1 + 0.12 W_2 + 0.29 W_3 + 0.41 W_4 + 0.31 W_5 + 0.156 W_6$
subject to

$$0 <= W_1 <= .30$$
$$0 <= W_2 <= .20$$
$$0 <= W_3 <= .28$$
$$0 <= W_4 <= .30$$
$$0 <= W_5 <= .25$$

$$0 <= W_6 <= .22$$
$$W_1 + W_2 + W_3 + W_4 + W_5 + W_6 = 1$$

where the coefficients of the objective function are obtained from the vector C, and the upper bound of the first six constraints is the ratio of the expense required by each alternative to the total available budget. The W_i represents the ratio of budget allocated to the six alternatives.

Solving this linear programming problem, we obtain:

$$W_1 = 0.30$$
$$W_2 = 0.00$$
$$W_3 = 0.15$$
$$W_4 = 0.30$$
$$W_5 = 0.25$$
$$W_6 = 0.00$$

Thus the allocation of budget is as follows:

Alternatives	Allocation of Budget for each Alternative ($ millions)
FMS	30
AS/RS	0
CAD	15
CAPP	30
LAN	25
TC	0

Clearly, this result shows that AS/RS and TC should not receive any allocations. Also, they may not significantly enhance competitive posture. On the other hand, FMS, CAPP, and LAN receive the full amount while CAD gets partial fulfillment. These are the technologies that should be adopted to achieve the company's goal.

Notice that this problem presents a special case of linear programming. The different, mutually dependent technologies considered here receive allocations in a nonincreasing order of their contributions to the objective function. FMS, which has the highest contribution of 0.51 to the objective function, receives the full allocation of $30 million. The next highest contribution is 0.41 for CAPP, and since there is $70 million left, CAPP is fully funded to the tune of $30 million. LAN has a contribution coefficient of 0.31 and demands $25 million; since the balance of $40 million is larger than $25 million, LAN is also fully funded. Now there is only $15 million left and the next highest contribution coefficient is CAD; CAD, therefore, gets the balance of $15 million. AS/RS and TC are not funded since there is no money left. This allocation process is known as a *greedy heuristic*. In fact, these results are derived without having to actually implement the linear programming. However, LP may be used to verify these results.

CONCLUSION

The systems approach proposed here, integrates different quantitative techniques into a project plan for adopting new automation technologies. Its characteristics are:

1. Inclusion of all factors related to the competitiveness of the company.

2. Consideration of dependent relationships in terms of output and input among the different automation technologies.
3. Consideration of economic as well as noneconomic factors in important decisions on adopting new technologies.
4. Consideration of the strategic significance of each automation technology based on an automation strategy assessment of competitors.
5. Consideration of budget allocation in making the automation technology decision.

This approach enhances the quality of decisions on automation with a <u>focused</u> objective on enhancing competitiveness. It also extends beyond the simple ranking of critical factors, as done in many other studies. Rather, the effectiveness of adopting various related technologies is considered.

Our framework is based on use of AHP as a decision tool. Multiple decision makers can participate in this process and help achieve the goals of the company. We must emphasize however, that unlike the purely quantitative model, this approach provides only quality decisions and may not offer an optimal decision, since subjective factors are involved. Nevertheless, decisions are rarely optimal, as they are influenced by many factors not easily controlled. This approach offers systematic guidance to the decision maker, via its systemic consideration of factors.

REFERENCES

Arbel, A. A., and Seidmann, A. "Performance Evaluation of FMSs," *IEEE* SMC-14 (4) (1984): 606-17.

Bossert, J. L. *Quality Function Deployment: A Practitioner's Approach.* New York: Marcel Dekker, 1991.

Cash, J. I., F. W. Ma Farlan, J. L. Mckenney, and M. R. Vitale. *Corporate Information Systems Management,* Homewood, IL: Dow Jones-Irwin, 1988.

Choobineh, F. "Justification of Flexible Manufacturing Systems." Proceedings of the 1986 *International Computers in Engineering* Conference, pp. 269-279.

Diaz, A. E. "The Software Portfolio: Priority Assignment Tool Provides Basis for Resource Allocation." *Industrial Engineering* (18) (3) (March 1986): 58-65.

Expert Choice. McLean, VA: Decision Support System Inc., 1983.

Freeman, C. R. "Automation and Telecommunications—the Key to Improved Productivity." In *Automation Technology for Management and Productivity Advancements Through CAP/CAM and Engineering Data Handling,* edited by P.C.C. Wang, Englewood Cliffs, NJ: Prentice-Hall, 1983.

Gairther, N. *Production and Operation Management.* Chicago: Dryden Press, 1990.

Goldhar, J. D., and M. Jelinek. "Computer Integrated Flexible Manufacturing: Organizational, Economic, and Strategic Implications." *Interfaces* 15 (3) (1985): 94-105.

Kaplan, R. S. "Must CIM be Justified by Faith Alone." *Harvard Business Review* 64 (2) (March-April 1986): 87-95.

Madu C. N. "A Quality Confidence Procedure for GDSS Application in Multicriteria Decision Analysis." *IIE Transactions* (forthcoming).

Madu, C. N., Kuei, C. H., and A. N. Madu. "Setting Priorities for the IT Industry in Taiwan—A Delphi Study." *Long Range Planning* 24 (5) (1991): 105-18.

Madu, C. N., and N. C. Georgantzas. "Strategic Thrust of Manufacturing Automation Decisions: A Conceptual Framework." *IIE Transactions* 23 (2) (1991): 138-48.

Muralichar, K., R. Anthanam, and R. L. Wilson. "Using the Analytic Hierarchy Process for Information System Project Selection." *Information and Management* 18 (2) (1990): 87-95.

Noori, H. "Managing the Dynamics of New Technology." Englewood Cliffs, NJ: Prentice-Hall, 1990.

Porter, M., and V. E. Miller. "How Information Gives You Competitive Advantage." *Harvard Business Review* 63 (4) (July-August 1985): 149-60.

Randhawa, S. U., and D. P. E. Bedworth. "Factors Identified for Use in Comparing Conventional & Flexible Manufacturing Systems." *Industrial Engineering* (17) (6) (June 1985): 40-85.

Roper-Lowe, G. C., and J. A. Shorp. "The Analytic Hierarchy Process and its Application to an Information Technology Decision." *Journal of the Operational Research Society* 41 (1) (1990): 49-59.

Saaty, T. L. "The Sudan Transport Study." *Interfaces* 8 (1) (1977): 37-57.

———. "The Analytic Hierarchy Process." New York: McGraw-Hill, 1980.

———. "Rank Generation, Preservation, and Reversal in the Analytic Hierarchy Decision Process." *Decision Sciences* 18 (2) (1987): 157-77.

———. "How to Make a Decision: The AHP." *European Journal of Operational Research* 48 (1) (1990a): 2-8.

———. "Eigenvector and Logarithmic Lest Squares." *European Journal of Operational Research* 48 (1) (1990b): 156-60.

Saaty, T. L., and J. M. Alexander. *Thinking With Models*, Oxford, England: Pergamon Press, 1981.

Saaty, T. L., and M. Khouja. "A Measure of World Influence." *Journal Peace Science* 2 (1) (1976): 31-47.

Saaty, T. L., and P. C. Rogers. "Higher Education in the United States (1985-2000)." *Socio-Economic Planning Science* 10 (1976): 251-63.

Saaty, T. L., and R. S. Mariano. "Rationing Energy to Industries: Priorities and Input-Output Dependence." *Energy Systems and Policy* 8 (1979): 85-111.

Vargas, L. G. "An Overview of the AHP and Its Applications." *European Journal of Operational Research* 48 (1) (1990): 2-8.

Sullivan, W. G. "Models IEs Can Use to Include Strategic, Non-Monetary Factors in Automation Decisions." *Industrial Engineering* 42 (March 1986): 42-50.

Wabalickis, R. N. "Justification of FMS with AHP." *Journal of Manufacturing Systems* 7 (3) (1987): 175-82.

Chapter 7

A New Look at Strategic
Capital Budgeting Decisions

Rudolph A. Jacob and Christian N. Madu

Vigorous global competition and technological advances over the last decade and a half have forced American managers to take a new look at how strategic capital budgeting decisions are made. The last decade has witnessed significant competitive gains by East Asian companies, primarily Japan, which had the ability to automate its plants through flexible manufacturing systems (FMS), computer-aided design and computer-aided manufacturing (CAD/CAM), and office automation (OA). Western companies now realize that fundamental changes must be made in the way strategic capital budgeting decisions are evaluated if they are to meet the challenges of global competition.

Strategic capital budgeting decisions play a vital role in determining a company's success or failure. They chart the destiny of a company for several years into the future and, perhaps more than anything else, determine future success. Undoubtedly the theoretical—and to a lesser extent, the practical—sophistication in this area has grown tremendously over the last two decades. From a theoretical perspective, the variety of techniques to incorporate risk into the capital budgeting process has grown by leaps and bounds. Also, the theoretical underpinnings of reasons companies choose projects to maximize shareholder wealth are well formulated. Most studies suggest that, from a practical point, more companies than ever are using sophisticated capital budgeting techniques. However, executives often reveal that these sophisticated capital budgeting tools are used only when the problems are specific, well defined, and/or well structured.

Most will agree that budgeting decisions must consider the company's strategic objectives, formal and informal organizational structure, information systems, and evaluation, reward, and punishment structure. Most will also agree that the emphasis today is sometimes misplaced, frequently isolated from strategic objectives and goals. This chapter presents a new strategic capital budgeting framework that formally links the resource allocation process with company objectives and mission, using cognitive mapping and the analytic hierarchy process (AHP). It is time for management to move forward and incorporate the enriched decision analysis paradigm that has developed in the last fifteen years.

Several subjective elements characterize a strategic capital budgeting problem. Factors such as quality improvement, political risks, short-term versus long-term goals, and manufacturing technology cannot be reduced to simple discounted cash-flow models. Our proposed framework not only gives explicit and formal consideration to both financial and nonfinancial factors but also considers the link between these factors and the overall strategic plan. This integration requires that the capital budgeting team include representatives from finance, marketing, manufacturing, engineering, and research and development, as well as support personnel from management information systems. This team must use a three-stage approach if resource allocation is to be integrated with company goals and mission. First, through the use of cognitive digraphs, the team decides the objectives and the strategies or resource allocation decisions that can accomplish these objectives. Second, again using cognitive maps, the team determines the criteria for each resource allocation strategy and evaluates all projects based on these criteria. The significant point at this stage is that appropriate weights are given to the various strategies and criteria. Third, through use of the analytic hierarchy process (AHP), the results of the first two stages are combined and integrated into the company's objectives based on their relative weights or priorities.

COGNITIVE MAPPING

Cognitive mapping was introduced in the Management Science/Operations Research (MS/OR) literature as a technique to facilitate the complex decision-making process. Because of ill structure, myopia, and lack of commitment characteristic of present-day capital budgeting practices (Pinches, 1982), a cognitive mapping approach can enhance making capital budget decisions.

Cognitive mapping, as advocated by Eden (1988), is based on *The Psychology of Personal Constructs,* a theory elaborated by Kelly (1955). Its basic tenet is what Kelly refers to as *constructive alternativism.* This principle posits that reality does not manifest itself to us but, rather, is subject to as many alternative interpretations as we can imagine. Moreover, in giving meaning to a particular event, constructs are related to each other within the explicit framework of a person's construct system, and the interconnectedness of these various constructs is assumed to be hierarchic in nature. Thus, whenever a person chooses a desired course of action, the implication of this action relative to other possible actions is based on the hierarchic organization of his constructs. As Eden, in applying cognitive maps to many OR situations, notes, the aim of cognitive maps is:

> To guide careful problem construction whereby each member of the team can gently "change their mind" and do so creatively. By seeing others' concepts in the context of their own concepts the meaning of them changes, this process coupled with sensitively managed social dynamics leads to new insights (team elaboration) created by the synergy stimulated by the team map. (1988, p. 8)

The hypothetical cognitive map in Figure 7.1 may be viewed as the consensus of a strategic planning team consisting of people from production, finance, marketing, engineering, and research and development. These views emerge after general meeting sessions, when the significance and relationship of several variables are assessed. In the map, a block of text represents a construct; the construct numbers are arbitrary, but may be used to indicate the different workshop sessions that produce the concepts. Each construct has two poles: the first part represents the "presented" pole; the second, separated by ". . .", read loosely as "rather than," represents the psychological contrast (opposite). For example, construct 26 notes that the company must "search for new foreign markets" rather than "for existing markets." The link between constructs is indicated by arrows, which read loosely as "leads to." For example, constructs 14 and

Figure 7.1.
A Cognitive Map for Strategic Capital Budgeting Decisions*

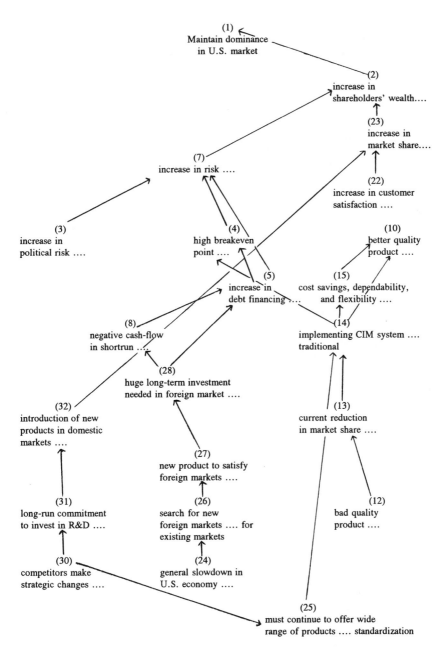

*Numbers on the map are arbitrary, used to indicate the different sessions that produced the different constructs.

15, can be construed as the idea that "implementing a CIM system" would lead to "cost savings, dependability, and flexibility" in the production process. And concepts 24 and 26 suggest that a "general slowdown in the economy" may lead to a "search for new foreign markets." Thus, an arrow extending out of a construct reveals a consequence and an arrow moving into a construct gives an explanation. In essence, each arrow gives explanatory meaning to one construct and consequential meaning to another.

Figure 7.1 further suggests that the company's mission is to maintain dominance in the marketplace, and this can be accomplished by increasing shareholder wealth.

Since the model contains enough of each person's construct of reality, it can be used as a powerful negotiating device. Under the guidance of a facilitator, the model can help members of the planning committee negotiate a consensus for action. Moreover, even though this modeling approach appears to broaden the issue—and we think this a desirable characteristic given the complexity of capital budgeting decisions—it actually identifies the links between important interrelated concepts.

The accuracy of the map depends upon how good a "listener" each participant is. Nevertheless, the cardinal purpose at this stage is not to solve the problem but to serve as a reflective device for the team members and as a focal point for group discussions. In fact, the hierarchical nature of goals, values, and criteria may be explored further by asking team members which constructs have no proffered consequences (the most hierarchical) and which are subordinate. This step, of course, is vital when using the AHP, where pair-comparison matrices and weights have to be determined for goals, strategies, and criteria.

The maps can be very large, as they represent the aggregation of constructs for individual members of the strategic planning team over numerous sessions. Since the maps reveal a host of interconnected statements (consequences and explanations), special computer software can be used to dissect the map as follows (Eden, 1988):

1. Locate the final consequences (outcome) and the explanations that lead to them,
2. Find key words that surface in various constructs,
3. Find parts of the model that are not related to other parts,
4. Search for different parts that may lead to similar outcomes,
5. Search for those constructs with the most supporting ratiocination.

Since team members are really involved in the planning process, there is likely a level of commitment higher than when traditional methods are used. Moreover, this map can become a routine part of the team members' memories, providing a framework for subsequent monitoring, control, and appraisal.

THE AHP MODEL

In order to validate the decision-making framework proposed in this chapter, we use a decision support system based on the analytic hierarchy process (AHP).

Figure 7.2 presents the AHP modeling framework for strategic capital budgeting decisions. The focus of the hierarchy is on the company's mission, as developed during strategic planning sessions. Here, the objectives are to maximize shareholder wealth, market share, and quality product. Strategies that can achieve these objectives are the introduction of a new product (NP), implementation of computer-integrated manufacturing system (CIM), and sale of the product in a new foreign market (FM). These are some of the strategies included in the cognitive map. Pair comparisons of these objectives in relation to the mission are determined by the planning committee.

Figure 7.2
AHP Model for Strategic Capital Budgeting Decision

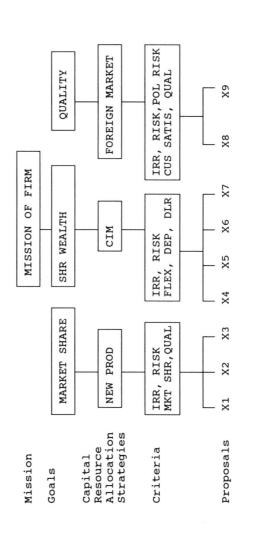

Cognitive digraphs, which help identify the variables (strategies) for achieving the mission, aid in assigning weights or determining priorities. Next, the significance of capital budgeting strategies in achieving these objectives is assessed by team members. By combining the results of these two analyses, they can then determine the priority of different capital budgeting strategies.

   The next stage of the modeling process is shown in Figure 7.3. This stage involves development of criteria to aid in the evaluation of different strategies. The criteria may include qualitative variables such as customer satisfaction, political risk, and flexibility. One of the cardinal advantages of using an AHP framework is that explicit consideration can be given to qualitative variables. Too often managers ignore significant qualitative variables because they are difficult, if not *impossible* to monetize.

Figure 7.3
Significant Criteria to Evaluate Strategies

New Product

IRR or PI
Risk
Customer satisfaction
Market share
Quality
Serviceability

Foreign Market

IRR or PI
Operating and financial risk
Political risk
Customer satisfaction
Adaptability of work force
Quality
Serviceability

CIM

IRR
Risk
Flexibility
Dependability
Quality
Set up cost reduction
Direct labor reduction
Defective rate reduction

Note also in Figures 7.3 and 7.2 that different criteria may be used to evaluate different strategies. For example, while political risk may be an important factor if entering a virgin foreign market, it is irrelevant in a domestic expansion. Also, flexibility in a CIM system may save time and money by integrating activities. The AHP framework can handle both qualitative and quantitative variables; all projects are evaluated using their respective criteria. For example, CIM projects are evaluated using the eight criteria given in Figure 7.3. The results are then tallied to ascertain the overall significance of each CIM proposal. This procedure, of course, has to be done for all projects within a given strategy. It can also be used to handle contingent projects, such as when the introduction of a new product will involve CIM. A simple approach is to treat both these projects as one, with appropriate criteria and weights derived.

The final step in the AHP framework relates the different strategies to the company's mission. This is done by multiplying the weights already assigned to the capital budgeting strategies by the various capital proposal scores as described earlier. This final step provides the articulation between the mission and goals and the capital budgeting strategies.

Too often, strategic capital budgeting decisions are made without explicit reference to the company's mission. As Liberatore (1987) notes, "a major drawback of many R & D project selection processes is that this top-level input is never clearly revealed to, or understood by, R & D during the planning cycle. The results can be unclear priorities and constant revision of the project investment portfolio." The potential benefits to be gained by using a decision support system such as AHP and the cognitive digraphs may include the following:

1. Better decisions
2. Increase commitment from all areas of the company
3. Better communication and teamwork
4. Quicker decisions
5. Explicit consideration of qualitative variables
6. Improved allocation of corporate resources
7. Cost savings
8. Examination of more scenarios and strategies
9. Involvement of all key players

It is unlikely that a single company can reap all the benefits of our proposed model. However, realizing even only some of these benefits will not only enhance the strategic capital budgeting process but improve competitiveness.

A specific illustration is now given to show the various steps involved in applying the AHP to a strategic capital budgeting proposal.

APPLICATION TO CAPITAL BUDGETING

The first step in applying the AHP model is to determine the priorities or weights of various objectives for achieving the company's mission. As shown in Figure 7.2, these objectives are maximization of shareholder wealth, better quality product, and increased market share. These judgments, as stated earlier, are based on experience, intuition, or financial information.

Figure 7.4, shows comparisons of each pair of objectives with respect to company mission—for example, a comparison of shareholder wealth and product quality. This comparison continues until all cells in the matrix above the diagonal are filled with judgments. Unitary values are assigned to diagonal cells to show comparison of a factor to itself; the cells below the diagonal represent the reciprocals of the preferences already depicted. Weights are then computed for the three objectives, also shown in Figure 7.4. The weights assigned to shareholder wealth, market share, and quality are .671, .234, and .094, respectively.

As shown in Figure 7.2, strategies to achieve stated objectives are (1) introduction of a new product; (2) implementation of CIM to improve quality and productivity; and (3) sale of products in previously untested foreign markets. These are some of the strategies apparent in the cognitive map. Over time, these strategies tend to remain the same even as the mission changes but their significance varies. Budget constraints, increased competition in the marketplace, and changes in organizational climate are some variables that may occasion shift.

Comparison of three capital resource allocation strategies can now be made with respect to the different objectives of improving market share, measuring shareholder wealth, and improving the quality of the product. For example, the strategy to implement a CIM system may be more important in producing an excellent quality product than introducing a new product to the marketplace. On the other hand, the goal of maximizing shareholder wealth may be better achieved by introducing a new product rather by implementing a CIM system.

Figure 7.4
Comparison Matrix and Weights of Goals

	Market Share	Shareholder Wealth	Quality
Market Share	1	5	5
Shareholder Wealth	1/5	1	4
Quality	1/5	1/4	1
Weights	.671	.234	.094

Figure 7.5 shows the comparison matrices and hypothetical weights of three capital allocation strategies with respect to three different goals. Since the company has three goals, three matrices are required.

The priorities of different strategies must now be calculated, as shown in Figure 7.6. The values are determined by multiplying the weights attached to the business objectives in Figure 7.4 by the weights determined in Figure 7.5 for prioritizing the capital allocation strategies. Figure 7.6 reveals that introduction of a new product is the best strategy to accomplish the company's mission.

Figure 7.5
Comparison Matrices and Weights of Resource Allocation Strategies

Goal: Market Share

	New Product	CIM	Foreign Market
New Product	1	4	8
CIM	1/4	1	6
Foreign Market	1/8	1/6	1
Weights	.678	.258	.063

Figure 7.5 (continued)

Goal: Shareholder Wealth

	New Product	CIM	Foreign Market
New Product	1	3	3
CIM	1/3	1	4
Foreign Market	6	1/4	1
Weights	.639	.273	.086

Goal: Quality

	New Product	CIM	Foreign Market
New Product	1	3	3
CIM	1/3	1	2
Foreign Market	1/3	1/2	1
Weights	.587	.251	.159

Figure 7.6
Resource Allocation Strategy Weights

	New Product	CIM	Foreign Market
Market Share	(.671) (.678)	(.671) (.258)	(.671) (.063)
Shareholder Wealth	(.234) (.639)	(.234) (.273)	(.234) (.086)
Quality	(.094) (.587)	(.094) (.251)	(.094) (.159)
Weights	.658984	.260594	.077343

     To simplify the analysis, let us focus on the strategy to improve productivity by implementing a CIM system. Figure 7.3 reveals some of the criteria to evaluate projects of this nature. Notice that some of the criteria, such as IRR and Risk, are typical for the capital budgeting model. There are also some unusual criteria, such as customer satisfaction, reliability of the production process, and flexibility in handling complex product designs. These factors also suggest that the strategic planning team ought to include people from all departments—production, marketing, and so on.

     A comparison matrix of all the criteria with respect to the CIM strategy is done first. Next, a comparison matrix must also be done for all projects with respect to each criterion for evaluating the projects. For example, if ten criteria are used to evaluate the projects, there would be ten matrices. Project rankings can now be determined as a weighted average of the criteria weights, and the weights assigned to individual projects with respect to the different criteria.

Last, the priority index of the CIM strategy, as shown in Figure 7.6, is multiplied by the various project weights. As discussed earlier, Figure 7.6 reflects the priorities of various strategies. Thus, whichever project is chosen, there is direct link to the company's goals and mission.

CONCLUSION

A review of the capital budgeting literature reveals that enormous progress has been made over the last two decades, in both capital budgeting theory and practice. However, it is safe to say that much attention has been on solutions to structured problems. Very little attention has been paid to articulation of strategic capital budgeting decisions with the organization's goals and mission.

This chapter addresses this matter by using cognitive digraphs and the AHP. Cognitive maps guide the careful construction of problems and also serve as a powerful negotiating device, enabling someone to view a particular concept in the context of others. Cognitive maps can also be used to develop comparison matrices for the AHP framework. The AHP model breaks down the capital budgeting process into a series of hierarchical layers, thereby linking project selection with organizational goals and mission.

REFERENCES

Belton, V., and T. Gear. "On a Short-coming of Saaty's Method of Analytic Hierarchies." *Omega* 11 (3) (1984): 228-30.

Eden, C. "Cognitive Mapping." *European Journal of Operations Research* 36 (1) (1988): 1-13.

Eden, C., and C. Huxham. "Action Oriented Strategic Management." *Journal of Operations Research Society* 39 (10) (1988): 889-99.

Harker, P. T., and L. G. Vargas. "The Theory of Ratio Scale Estimation: Saaty's Analytic Hierarchy Process." *Management Science* 33 (11) (1987): 1383-403.

Kelly, G. A. *The Psychology of Personal Constructs,* Vols. I & II. New York: Norton (1955).

Liberatore, M. J. "An Extension of the Analytic Hierarchy Process for Industrial R & D Project Selection and Resource Allocation." *IEEE Transactions* EM-34 (1) (February 1987): 12-18.

Madu, C. N., and N. C. Georgantzas. "Strategic Thrust of Manufacturing Decisions: A Conceptual Framework." *IIE Transactions* 23 (2) (June 1991): 138-48.

Pinches, G. "Myopia, Capital Budgeting and Decision Making." *Financial Management* 11 (3) (Autumn 1982): 6-19.

Saaty, T. L. *The Analytic Hierarchy Process.* New York: McGraw-Hill, 1980.

Chapter 8

A Quality Confidence Procedure for GDSS Application in Multicriteria Decision Making

Christian N. Madu

This chapter develops a general procedure for improving the quality of group decision making. The procedure helps identify those stakeholders whose opinions may significantly deviate from that of the group. Notably, I show how to identify outliers and also how to use the coefficient of variability (CV) as a measure of the "degree of disagreement." *Outliers* as used here represent stakeholders whose opinions differ remarkably from that of the group.

Recommendations are given for making effective use of outliers and CV to improve the quality of group decision making. These concepts are illustrated using a case study demonstrating the following: (1) outliers may be meritorious; (2) negative effects of dominant decisions may be avoided if team members participate and accept such decisions; (3) compromise can be a last resort in conflict resolution; and (4) graphical and tabular displays can improve the quality of group decisions. The chapter focuses on knowledge acquisition, influence, and rethinking as the means for improving the quality of decisions. The application of management-by-exception is stressed when outliers are identified. This procedure is demonstrated through the use of a case study and application of the analytic hierarchy process (AHP).

Belton (1986) compares multicriteria decision-making models and concludes that the analytic hierarchy process (AHP) and simple multiattribute value functions are the most effective. AHP has been applied in justifying flexible manufacturing systems (Arbel & Seidmann, 1984; Madu & Georgantzas, 1991), and in other areas where value and social judgment have to be considered, such as facility location analysis, work scheduling, planning, capital budgeting, and inter- or intratechnology transfers. To consider the several factors that influence decisions, it is necessary to include both those who influence and those who are influenced by the decisions made (i.e., stakeholders). For example, in the decision to automate a production facility, assembly-line workers may be one of the stakeholders, since they have to work with the new technology. Although inclusion of people with different views and opinions compounds the decision making, benefits abound. Therefore, it is of utmost importance that stakeholders be used in ill-structured and dynamic decision making. The quality of such decisions depends on how well can the different opinions be understood.

The ability of the AHP to measure consistency in judgments makes it a preferred method in decision making. Many other multicriteria models do not have this feature (Keeney & Raiffa, 1976).

Saaty (1987) defines AHP as "a multicriteria decision model that uses hierarchic or network structure to represent a decision problem and then develop priorities for the alternatives based on the decision maker's judgments throughout the system." Belton and Gear (1984, 1985) point out some limitations of AHP, however Harker and Vargas (1987) show that the AHP is a useful technique in multicriteria decision making.

In his article, Dyer (1990) was very critical of the AHP, especially in regard to rank reversal. This concept implies that ranks determined for alternatives through the AHP may change with the addition of a new alternative for comparison. Dyer argues that the problem can be remedied if the AHP borrows from multiattribute utility theory and expresses weights using an interval rather than a ratio scale. In follow-up articles by Saaty (1990) and Harker and Vargas (1990), the authors argue that the theoretical axiomatic conditions of AHP have been completely misunderstood, and that AHP should not be seen as an extension of utility theory, but rather that it is a new body of research. Irrespective of these debates, AHP is seen by many as an important decision tool and continues to be widely used. In this chapter, a case study illustrates how the AHP can be applied in decision making. Consequently, the chapter shows the potential for disagreements in group decision making and proposes a pragmatic approach to resolving such conflicts through use of a quality confidence procedure.

CASE STUDY

The study consisted of thirty executives who participate in manufacturing automation decisions in their respective organizations. The task was to decide whether to adopt an advanced manufacturing system such as computer-integrated manufacturing (CIM) or stay with a more traditional manufacturing approach (i.e., assembly line). The subjects were presented with seven factors (criteria) often cited in the literature as influential in making the transition from traditional to computer- integrated manufacturing (Goldhar & Jelinek, 1985; Madu & Georgantzas, 1991). These factors are flexibility, quality, inventory management, information processing, cost, dependability, and direct labor reduction. Table 8.1 defines these criteria. Although the criteria are self-explanatory, they were discussed fully and a reading assignment was given (Goldhar and Jelinek, 1985). Furthermore, a reading assignment on the methodology of this experiment, the analytic hierarchy process, was also given. It was made clear that several subcriteria may be derived from the criteria. In addition, it was imparted that the organizational objective was to improve total productivity and enhance competitiveness.

Lectures pertained to effective use of the nine-point scale and comparison of factors. This nine-point scale was as follows: 1—Equal; 3—Moderate; 5—Strong; 7—Very Strong; 9—Extreme; 2, 4, 6 and 8 were compromise; and reciprocals were for inverse comparisons. A questionnaire was administered through which participants assigned weights to pairs factors (see Table 8.2). Calculations for the numerical assignments and estimates are given in Table 8.3.

For example, a possible assignment might be to compare flexibility to quality in order to assess their relative importance in improving total productivity. Further comparison might be to compare traditional manufacturing to CIM on the basis of one of these criteria. What is the relative importance of these technologies in terms of flexibility or quality? An assignment of 7 would show very strong preference of flexibility over quality in improving total productivity.

In this case study, the weights were made anonymously, even though each assignment was preceded by detailed discussions of the pair being compared. Discussion

Table 8.1
Significant Factors in the Automation Decision

Flexibility (FLEX)	*Cost*
Ability to adapt to variability in materials and process condition	Cost of automation
Responsiveness to surges in demand	Cost of training
Ability to handle complex product designs	Cost of hiring and screening personnel
Ability to integrate new technology	
Quality	*Inventory (INVENT)*
Product performance	Setup cost reduction
Customer perception of quality to type of technology	Work-in-process due inventory
Improved relationship with customers	Material reduction
Improved organizational relationship between functional departments	Other waste reduction
Aesthetic value of product	
Information capabilities (INFO)	*Dependability (DEP)*
Ease of obtaining information including floor information (i.e., potential bottlenecks)	Reliability of production process
Transmission and processing of information	Ease of maintenance
Timeliness, accuracy, and precision of information	Ease of scheduling and control
	Safety conditions
Direct Labor Reduction (DLR)	

Source: Adopted from C. N. Madu and N. C. Georgantzas, "Strategic Thrust of Manufacturing Automation Decisions: A Conceptual Framework, *IIE Transactions*, 23 (2) (1991): 138-48.

Table 8.2
GDSS Questionnaire

Procedure:

1. Evaluate Table 8.1. Are there factors that you think should be included in this list? If so, please identify such factors and provide some definitions for them as done in Table 8.1.

2. Using the nine-point scale (see p. 150), please assign weights in a pairwise form.

Factors	1	2	3	4	5	6	7
1. Flexibility							
2. Quality							
3. Inventory							
4. Information							
5. Cost							
6. Dependability							
7. Direct Labor Reduction							

3. For each Factor, compare the traditional Manufacturing system to Computer Integrated Manufacturing System on a pairwise form.

Factor 1

	TRAD	CIM
TRAD		
CIM		

Factor 2

	TRAD	CIM
TRAD		
CIM		

Factor 3

	TRAD	CIM
TRAD		
CIM		

Factor 4

	TRAD	CIM
TRAD		
CIM		

Factor 5

	TRAD	CIM
TRAD		
CIM		

Factor 6

	TRAD	CIM
TRAD		
CIM		

Factor 7

	TRAD	CIM
TRAD		
CIM		

Table 8.3
Calculations for Study

Procedure for the Use of AHP

Define a_{ij} as the numerical assignment made by a decision maker in comparing factor i to factor j. Since the AHP involves a comparison of two factors, the matrix that contains the weight assignments must be a square matrix. Let A represent that matrix and its size as n. AHP uses a process known as *synthesization*. The procedure is as follows:

1. If group decisions are made, the geometric mean of the a_{ij} for all the participants is used as the group's numerical assignment when factor i is compared to factor j. The popular scale is the nine-point one defined in the paper.

2. The weight assignments in each of the column j are added to obtain the column total. Thus, let S_{ij} represent the total of each column, then

$$S_j = \sum_{i=1}^{n} a_{ij} . \qquad (1)$$

3. Each element in matrix A is then divided by its column total. Let V_{ij} be the result of that division. Then,

$$V_{ij} = \frac{a_{ij}}{S_j} . \qquad (2)$$

The resulting matrix is referred to as a *normalized pairwise comparison* matrix.

4. Estimate the relative priorities of each factor by computing the average of the normalized weights in each of the i rows. Let p_i represent the relative priority of factor i. Then,

$$p_i = \sum_{j=1}^{n} \frac{V_{ij}}{n} , \qquad (3)$$

where i is fixed. Also, $\sum p_i = 1 \forall i$.

Consistency Ratio Estimation

To compute the consistency ratio, the following steps are taken.

1. Each of the columns in comparison matrix A is multiplied by the relative priorities corresponding to that column and added to obtain an $n \times 1$ matrix called B. Note that $i = j$, since we have a square matrix. Thus, this new matrix can be expressed as

$$B = \begin{array}{c} b_1 \\ b_2 \\ . \\ . \\ . \\ b_n \end{array} = \begin{array}{c} p_1 a_{11} + p_2 a_{12} + \ldots + p_n a_{1n} \\ p_1 a_{21} + p_2 a_{22} + \ldots + p_n a_{2n} \\ . \quad . \quad \ldots \quad . \\ . \quad . \quad \ldots \quad . \\ . \quad . \quad \ldots \quad . \\ p_n a_{n1} + p_n a_{n2} + \ldots + p_n a_{nn} \end{array} \qquad (4)$$

The consistency index (CI) is then computed as:

153

Table 8.3 (continued)

$$CI = \frac{\lambda_{max} - n}{n - 1}, where\ \lambda_{max} = \sum_{i=1}^{n} \frac{b_i}{P_i} \tag{5}$$

Finally, the consistency ratio (CR) is obtained as CR = CI/RI, where RI is a random index. The RI represents the consistency index of a randomly generated comparison matrix. It is also a function of the number of elements that are being compared. A table of the RI is presented in Saaty (1980). For example, when $n = 3$, RI = 0.58, and when $n = 5$, RI = 1.12. A CR of 0.1 or more implies inconsistency in judgment.

Computing the Confidence Limits

From equation 3, let p_{ki} represent the priority index of stakeholder k to factor i. Thus, the arithmetic mean for each factor i can be expressed as:

$$\bar{p}_{ki} = \frac{\sum_{k=1}^{m} p_{ki}}{m}, \forall_i; i = 1,2,........,n \tag{6}$$

where m represents the number of stakeholders. Consequently, the standard error of proportions is expressed as:

$$\bar{S}_{\bar{p}_{ki}} = \sqrt{\bar{p}_{ki} \frac{(1 - \bar{p}_{ki})}{m}}; \forall i \tag{7}$$

The confidence limits are expressed as:

$$\bar{p}_{ki} \pm t_{\alpha,m-1} \bar{S}_{\bar{p}_{ki}}; \forall i \tag{8}$$

where $m-1$ is the degrees of freedom. When $m \to \infty$, $t_{\alpha,m-1}$ approaches the z-score of the normal distribution, α is the level of significance or the maximum probability of the Type I error.

---

was among group members only; a facilitator guided the discussion and collected the assignments. The assignments were anonymous to avoid any effect of groupthink.

Of the thirty questionnaires distributed only seventeen met the standard for inclusion in the study. The other thirteen were either incomplete or not returned.

METHOD OF ANALYSIS

Analysis followed the "synthesization process" briefly discussed in Table 8.3.

First, the Expert Choice (1983) program was used to compute the priority indices of each respondent for each of the criteria. Next, the geometric mean of the original assignments was computed and then the program was used to compute priority indices for each of the seven criteria; these are the group's priority indices. The higher the priority index, the more important the factor (criterion). The priorities generated for each set of criteria or decision alternatives added up to 1.

In order of preference, the criteria were dependability (0.167), information processing (0.156), quality (0.151), cost (0.139), flexibility (0.132), direct labor reduction (0.132), and inventory management (0.123). In addition, the group's priority index for CIM was 0.585 and for traditional manufacturing was 0.415 . This indicated the group's general perception that total productivity and competitiveness can be improved through adoption of CIM, and also that dependability and information processing may make the highest contribution toward achieving total productivity. Furthermore, a consistency less than 0.1 was obtained; this finding, highlighted the group's rationality in decision making. Table 8.4 shows the actual priority indices for each of the seventeen respondents as well as the group's priority indices for each of the seven criteria.

Consistency does not imply that a quality decision has been made, however, all quality decisions must be consistent. Measuring quality is difficult in the context of decision making: there is no way of determining whether a quality decision has been made until it is implemented. A *quality decision* is a decision that leads to attainment of an organizational goal. However, techniques like the multicriteria decision-making model can enhance the quality of group decisions by involving important stakeholders in the process. People are more likely to work toward organizational goals if they are part of the decision-making process. In addition, the quality of decisions is improved if opposing viewpoints are seriously considered. In fact, the procedure derives its strength from considering each participant's views and understanding why some people hold extreme views. Thus, it is best to avoid using consistency as the only criterion for measuring the quality of group decisions.

Coefficient of Variation

Table 8.5 presents the arithmetic means and standard deviations for the priority index from the group on each of the seven criteria. Based on this information, the coefficient of variation (CV) is computed as the ratio of standard deviation to mean. The CV is used in this context to measure the "degree of disagreement" among respondents. For example, a high CV shows a high degree of disagreement on the importance of each criterion. However, this assessment is made in comparison to the CV of other criteria. Table 8.5, for example, shows much higher CV values for flexibility, quality, and direct labor reduction. In fact, for the latter, the CV is 98 percent. For the other criteria, the CVs are relatively lower, and the least CV is obtained for dependability at 42 percent.

The CV identifies the sources of disagreement among participants, especially on criteria that show high variability. This may be useful when several scenarios or criteria are being considered, and it is not possible to evaluate every one. In such cases, criteria with considerably higher CVs should be analyzed.

QUALITY CONFIDENCE MEASURES

This procedure includes two major assumptions; (1) that it is a random sample,

Table 8.4
Priority Indices of the 17 Respondents

	Flexibility	Quality	Inventory	INFO	Cost	DEP	DLR
1	0.302	0.043	0.052	0.312	0.04	0.167	0.085
2	0.049	0.276	0.031	0.061	0.297	0.221	0.068
3	0.188	0.269	0.1	0.119	0.103	0.172	0.49
4	0.029	0.063	0.048	0.088	0.165	0.209	0.397
5	0.286	0.105	0.049	0.303	0.084	0.127	0.046
6	0.223	0.044	0.065	0.248	0.027	0.206	0.188
7	0.308	0.197	0.214	0.111	0.075	0.069	0.026
8	0.322	0.188	0.146	0.105	0.092	0.081	0.066
9	0.035	0.11	0.184	0.065	0.197	0.159	0.25
10	0.182	0.262	0.089	0.105	0.133	0.133	0.094
11	0.085	0.034	0.189	0.152	0.185	0.134	0.22
12	0.487	0.245	0.067	0.084	0.035	0.056	0.025
13	0.067	0.033	0.123	0.122	0.117	0.194	0.043
14	0.028	0.046	0.047	0.098	0.185	0.22	0.375
15	0.037	0.347	0.054	0.258	0.215	0.05	0.041
16	0.182	0.262	0.089	0.105	0.133	0.133	0.094
17	0.297	0.219	0.194	0.064	0.113	0.071	0.042

and (2) that priorities assigned by the stakeholders are normally distributed. A random sample may be achieved if the stakeholder approach is followed in decision making; in other words, the probability of including every stakeholder on the team is known. In this case study, it was assumed that the group represents all the significant interests normally in a typical organization. This assumption derives further cogency from the fact that these executives possessed a wide range of experience in manufacturing.

For the assumption of normality, the Kolmogorov-Smirnoff test was conducted on the priority indices obtained for the stakeholders (see Table 8.5). This test shows, at significance levels of both 0.01 and 0.05, that the priority index follows the normal distribution. With larger groups, the central-limit theorem may be invoked to use normal distribution. In addition, when the group is small and includes the entire population, the random sampling assumption is moot.

The standard error of proportions was computed for each criterion and a 95 percent confidence interval established. Obviously, the choice in level of significance depends on the decision maker and may be influenced by his or her risk aversion. With the confidence interval established, it behooves the decision maker to evaluate how individual priorities fall within the confidence limits. Figure 8.1 is a graphic display of each respondent's priority assignments on three of the seven criteria. These graphs show that all priority assignments for inventory, information processing, dependability, and

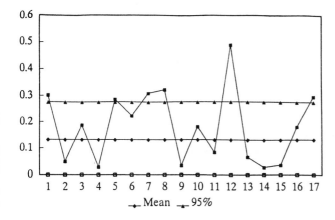

Figure 8.1a
Quality Confidence Limits for
Flexibility

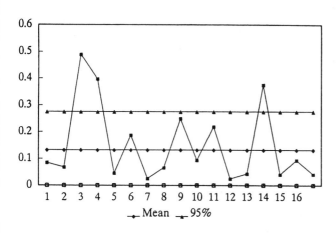

Figure 8.1b
Quality Confidence Limits for
Direct Labor Reduction

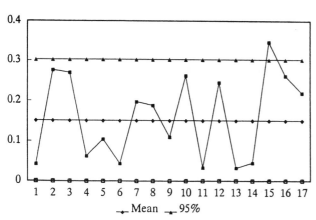

Figure 8.1c
Quality Confidence Limits for
Quality

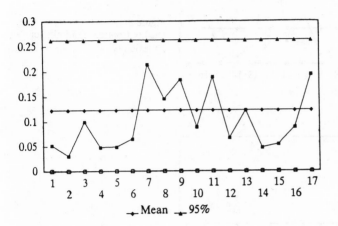

Figure 8.1d
Quality Confidence Limits for
Inventory

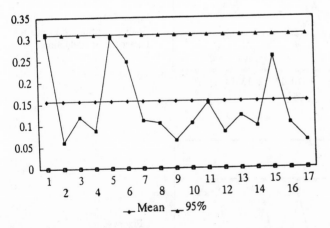

Figure 8.1e
Quality Confidence Limits for
Information

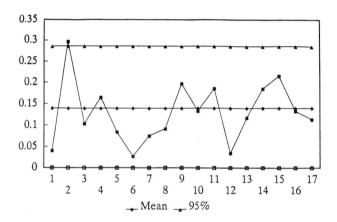

Figure 8.1g
Quality Confidence Limits for
Cost

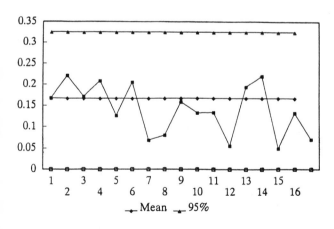

Figure 8.1f
Quality Confidence Limits for
Dependability

Table 8.5
Priority Indices of the Criteria

Criteria	Priority Index	Standard Error	Arithmetic Mean	Standard Deviation	CV (%)
FLEX	0.132	0.082096	0.183	0.137	74.86
QUALITY	0.151	0.086840	0.161	0.106	65.80
INVENTORY	0.123	0.079658	0.102	0.061	59.80
INFO	0.156	0.088005	0.141	0.084	59.60
COST	0.139	0.083904	0.129	0.072	55.80
DEPEND	0.167	0.090460	0.141	0.059	41.80
LABOR	0.132	0.082096	0.15	0.147	98.00

Table 8.6
Kolmogorov-Smirnoff Test for Normality

CRITERIA	D Max Statistic
FLEX	0.1746
QUALITY	0.1754
INVENTORY	0.1904
INFO	0.2964
COST	0.0968
DEPEND	0.1404
LABOR	0.2662

Notes:
H_0: Priorities generated follow the normal distribution.
H_1: Priorities do not follow the normal distribution.
$D_{.05,\,n=17} = 0.318$
$D_{.01,\,n=17} = 0.392$

cost fall within the established confidence limits (see Figures 8.1d-g). Notice also that these four graphs have a considerably lower coefficient of variation, showing that the "degree of disagreement" was low, attributable to chance variation.

Conversely, outliers are observed for quality, flexibility, and direct labor reduction. For example, for flexibility, stakeholders 1, 7, 8, 12, and 17 seemed to assign priorities above the upper limit of the confidence interval, while stakeholder 5 was slightly above that upper limit (see Figure 8.1a). Similarly, stakeholders 3, 4, and 14 were significantly above the upper limit for direct labor reduction (see Figure 8.1b) and stakeholder 15 was above the upper limit for quality (see Figure 8.1c). Thus, while consistency may have been achieved, the source of these wide variations should be further analyzed.

To improve the quality of decisions, the presence of outliers must be explained. For example, it is necessary to understand what factors influence the stakeholder decisions. Outliers should be managed to foster a better understanding of the problem. Perhaps they have privileged information or new information not yet available to the group. By getting them to explain their position, the group is able to make a more informed decision: group members can then consider different views that previously may have been ignored, which may lead to rethinking the problem. The presence of outliers may also reflect either misinformation or a lack of understanding. This process helps clarify issues.

Thus, this procedure identifies stakeholders outside of the confidence limits. The confidence limits establish an interval rather than a point estimate regarding priority indices. Without a formal approach, it is not always easy to identify those who deviate *significantly*. Clearly, some deviations can be observed when the group priority index is compared to the stakeholders' respective indices. However, some may fall within the tolerance levels set by the decision maker, thus, these deviations may not be significant to the decision maker.

By identifying the outliers, there can be more debate on the factors involved. It is possible that, through such discussions, the three processes of acquiring knowledge acquisition, influencing others, and rethinking original decisions may occur concurrently. Furthermore, this approach helps stakeholders think critically about the problem before they make an assignment. They know that their assignments will not be diluted by the group average; rather, each assignment is compared to a tolerance level established by the decision maker. Different management techniques can be applied to generate more thought on the problem, such as devil's advocate, dialectic approach, and nominal group technique.

The potential consequences of this process are (1) the outlier may be compelled, through debates and discussions, to change his or her assignment; 2) the group may accept the outlier as providing vital information not taken into consideration in their weight assignments. In both cases, new weight assignments have to be generated and new priority indices computed. If the first consequence occurs, the stakeholder's new priority index will shift toward the group's index. If the second consequence is the result, priority index shifts closer to the outlier.

It is also possible that the outlier disagrees with the group and that the group at the same time disagrees with the outlier's premises. Then compromise may be achieved by using the group's original priority index. Note that the outlier is also used in computing the group's priority index.

Investigating the sources of outliers involves several iterations. Graphic and/or tabular displays may show group members where they stand with respect to both the group's priority index and the tolerance levels established. The aim is not to achieve conformity in group decision making—in fact, this procedure construes conflict as positive and instrumental—but rather to make that conflict productive and meaningful.

Implementation of Decisions

The final decisions are based on consensus. Group decision support systems

(GDSS) such as the AHP are useful in obtaining this consensus. Owing to the methodology here, the following features of effective group decision making emerge:

1. *Consistent judgment is made.* This is a guide to the rationality of the decision maker. There are no guarantees on the quality of the decisions, as this cannot always be predetermined, however the quality of the decision is expected to improve as participants think through the problems.

2. *Conflict is effectively managed.* This avoids adopting a dominant decision without input from all group members. The outliers help team members rethink their premises and presuppositions.

3. *Anonymity is maintained in weighting the factors.* This avoids groupthink while allowing for knowledge acquisition and influencing to take place. Also, by identifying outliers, there is reduced possibility for groupthink. Each member becomes cautious in assigning weights and tries to make them reflect his or her own feelings about the problem.

4. *Inquiry systems can be integrated into the process.* Systems such as cognitive mapping, dialectic approach, brainstorming, devil's advocate, and nominal group technique, can help elicit different opinions and psychological attributes of the team members.

Implementation of group decisions is enhanced when members actively participate in the decision-making process. The repeated iterations of the arguments, coupled with tabular and graphic displays, discussions, and debates, and establishment of confidence limits on the group's decisions, are self-controlling. They help identify potential problems, which can be resolved at each stage of the process. The quality of the final decision is greatly enhanced, and there is, therefore, a high probability of implementing the right decision.

CONCLUSION

This chapter has shown how GDSS can be used effectively. Upon establishing confidence limits on the group consensus, outliers are subjected to further analysis. Though potentially meritorious, outliers need to be understood in order that quality of decision making can improve. In addition, use of the coefficient of variability to measure the "degree of disagreement" among stakeholders, was discussed. The CV may also be useful in analyzing the group judgments when a large number of criteria are involved.

Furthermore, the chapter has shown that GDSS may be an effective tool for resolving conflicts. The outlier may suggest that a dominant decision is best, however allowing team members to engage in a meaningful information exchange can only enhance the acceptance of this decision. This approach achieves consistency as a means to quality of decisions. Upon identifying variations from the consensus, outliers become the focus of debate and further discussion directed toward achieving a team consensus. In addition, this technique avoids groupthink by maintaining the anonymity of decision makers.

REFERENCES

Arbel, A., and A. Seidmann. "Performance Evaluation of Flexible Manufacturing Systems." *IEEE Transactions on SMC*, SMC-14 (1984): 118-29.

Belton, V. "A Comparison of the Analytic Hierarchy Process and a Simple Multi-Attribute Value Function." *European Journal of Operational Research* 26 (1) (1986): 7-21.

Belton, V., and T. Gear. "On a Short-coming of Saaty's Method of Analytic Hierarchies." *OMEGA* 12 (1984): 228-30.

―――. "The Legitimacy of Rank Reversal—A Comment." *OMEGA* 13 (1985): 143-44.

Dyer, J. S. "Remarks on the Analytic Hierarchy Process." *Management Science* 36 (1990): 249-58.

Expert Choice. McLean, VA: Decision Support Software Inc., 1983.

Goldhar, J. D., and M. Jelinek. "Computer Integrated Manufacturing: Organizational, Economic, and Strategic Implications." *Interfaces*, 15 (3) (1985): 94-105.

Harker, P. T., and L. G. Vargas. "The Theory of Ratio Scale Estimation: Saaty's Analytic Hierarchy Process." *Management Science* 33 (1987): 1383-403.

―――. "Reply to 'Remarks on the Analytic Hierarchy Process'" by J. S. Dyer. *Management Science* 36 (1990): 269-75.

Keeney, R. L., and H. Raiffa, "Decision With Multiple Objectives: Preferences and Values Tradeoffs." New York: John Wiley, 1976.

Madu, C. N., and N. C. Georgantzas. "Strategic Thrust of Manufacturing Automation Decisions: A Conceptual Framework." *IIE Transactions* 23 (2) (1991): 138-48.

Saaty, T. L. *The Analytic Hierarchy Process* New York: McGraw-Hill, 1980.

―――. "Rank Generation, Preservation, and Reversal in the Analytic Hierarchy Decision Process." *Decision Sciences* 18 (1987): 157-77.

―――. "An Exposition of the AHP in Reply to the Paper 'Remarks on the Analytic Hierarchy Process.'" *Management Science* 36 (1990): 259-68.

Chapter 9

Project Management in the Adoption and Implementation of New Technologies

Adedeji B. Badiru

Project management is the process of managing, allocating, and timing resources to achieve a given goal in an efficient and expedient manner (Badiru 1991). The objectives that constitute that goal may be expressed in terms of time, cost, or technical result, often realized as a consequence of new technologies. But to achieve these objectives, proven management approaches must be employed. No matter how excellent a technology is, it requires human actions to adopt, implement, and manage. This is where project management comes in. Its techniques are used widely in many industries, including construction, banking, marketing, health care, sales, transportation, R&D, academia, law, public service, and manufacturing (Badiru, 1988). Adoption and implementation of new technologies constitute suitable areas for use of project management techniques.

This chapter discusses how project management techniques can be applied in adopting and implementing new technologies.

THE IMPORTANCE OF NEW TECHNOLOGY

New manufacturing and service technologies have attracted attention in recent years, as a result of the high rate at which productivity-improvement technologies have been emerging from R&D institutions. But the fast pace of developing these new technologies has created implementation and management problems for many companies. Murrin (1989) stresses the need to expedite implementation of new manufacturing technology. The depressed state of technology implementation was also addressed by a board of industrialists working under the auspices of the National Research Council (1984). The group states:

> The most critical problem faced by too many U.S. industrial executives today is the steady decline in their companies' competitiveness at home and abroad, and the resultant loss in market share. A major reason for the decline has been the gradual emergence of a technology gap in manufacturing. It has not been a single identifiable event, but a slow erosion of the technological foundation of manufacturing. The keys to regaining competitiveness in most U.S. manufacturing industries are quality, productivity, and responsiveness in bringing new products to the market. A primary technology for attaining these attributes, across industries, is computer-integrated manufacturing.

New technology can be successfully implemented only if it is viewed as a system whose various components must be evaluated within an integrated managerial framework. Such a framework is the focus of project management.

Critical to successful implementation is the matter of accurately assessing new technologies. A multitude of new technologies have emerged in recent years. Group technology, cellular manufacturing, artificial intelligence, and so on have received much attention in the literature. But much more research remains to be done regarding their implementation. For instance, it is important to consider the peculiar characteristics of each new technology before establishing adoption and implementation strategies. Even the justification for adopting a new technology usually is a combination of factors rather than a single advantage to be gained from the technology (Badiru et al., 1991).

The important characteristics or attributes of a new technology include productivity improvement, improved product quality, production cost savings, flexibility, reliability, and safety. There must be an integrated evaluation performed for each proposed technology to ensure that adoption is justified both economically and technically. The scope of and goals for the proposed technology must be established at the beginning (Allmendinger, 1985). This entails comparing departmental objectives with overall organizational goals in the following areas. These factors necessitate the adoption of new technologies to achieve global competitiveness.

1. *Market position.* This analysis covers items such as the market cost of the proposed product, an assessment of competition, and evaluation of market share.

2. *Growth potential.* This evaluation addresses short- and long- range expectations, future competitiveness, and capability, and prevailing size and strength of the competition.

3. *Contribution to customers.* A prospective technology is evaluated in terms of direct and indirect benefits provided to the customer. These may include product price versus value, product quality, product reliability, and customer service.

4. *Profitability.* An analysis of how the technology contributes to profitability should consider past performance of the technology, incremental benefits of the new technology versus conventional technology, and value added by the new technology.

5. *Cash flow and cost analysis.* The conventional financial analysis with proper modifications covers fixed and sunk costs, cost of obsolescence, maintenance requirements, recurring costs, installation cost, space requirement cost, capital investment requirements, return on investment, tax implications, cost of capital, and cost of concurrent projects.

6. *Resource utilization.* The utilization of resources (manpower and equipment) in the pre- and post-technology phases is assessed based on material input and output flow, high value of equipment versus productivity improvement, required inputs for the technology, expected output, and utilization of technical and nontechnical personnel.

7. *Risk exposure.* Uncertainty is a reality in technology adoption efforts. Uncertainty needs to be assessed for the initial investment, return on investment, payback period, and volatility of the technology.

8. *Effectiveness of product.* The product of the new technology is evaluated for functionality, durability, and aesthetics.

9. *Organizational productivity.* An analysis of how the technology will contribute to organizational productivity can be verified by studying the shop throughput, delivery times, scrap rate, personnel idle time, learning rate, and design-to-production cycle.

Project management brings these elements together, with a view toward achieving organizational goals.

THE NATURE OF A PROJECT

In general, the life cycle of a project consists of conceptualization, definition, development, tracking and reporting, control, and termination, as explained below:

1. *Project conceptualization.* A need for the proposed technology is identified, defined, and justified.

2. *Project definition.* The purpose of the project is defined and clarified. A mission statement is the major output of this stage.

3. *Project development.* The operational aspects of initiating the technology project are begun in accordance with specified goals. This phase may cover a series of functions including planning, organizing, resource allocation, and scheduling.

4. *Project tracking and reporting.* The diagnostic process is begun to check whether or not project results conform to plans and specifications.

5. *Project control.* Necessary actions are taken to correct unacceptable deviations from expected performance. (The next section discusses project monitoring, tracking, and control in more detail.)

6. *Project termination.* The phase-out stage of the project, executed with full commitment.

Projects commonly drag on needlessly for months or even years. To avoid this, a terminal activity should be specified during the project definition phase. An example of a terminal activity is submission of a final report, "power on" of new equipment, or a signed release order. Conclusion of such an activity should be viewed as completion of the project. Follow-up activities may be necessary in certain cases, but those activities constitute a function outside the project itself. If a project is not terminated when appropriate, the motivation for it will wane and subsequent activities may become counter productive. This is particularly true for technology-based projects where fear of the unknown and resistance to change are already major obstacles.

PROJECT MANAGEMENT AND CONTROL

Figure 9.1 summarizes the major steps in the project management process. These steps are critical for successful management of a project.

Schedule, cost, and performance are the operating characteristics of a project. These same factors are also the basis for project control (see Figure 9.2). Project control is the process of reducing the deviation between actual performance and planned performance. Thus, to control a project, the manager must be able to measure performance with regard to schedule, performance, and cost.

Traditional procedures for measuring the progress of a project, evaluating performance, and taking control actions are not adequate for technology management, where events are more dynamic. For instance, some control problems that arise are:

Schedule Problems	Performance Problems	Cost Problems
Delay of critical activities	Poor quality	Inadequate budget activities
Unreliable time	Poor functionality	Effects of inflation
Poor mobility	Maintenance problems	Poor cost-reporting estimates
Poor precedence	Increase in scope of project	Technical problems
Change of due dates	Lack of training	High overhead cost relationships
	Lack of clear objectives	High labor cost

Figure 9.1
Project Management Steps

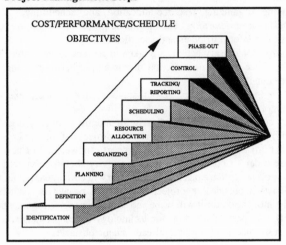

Figure 9.2
Elements of Project Control

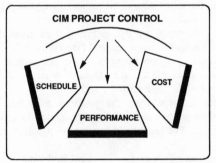

Each of these control elements are described.

Schedule Control

The Gantt charts developed in the scheduling phase of a project can serve as the yardstick for measuring progress. Project status should be monitored frequently. Symbols can be used to mark actual activity positions on the chart, while a record is also maintained of the difference between expected activities and actual ones. The more milestones or control points there are in the project, the better the monitoring function. Thus, problems can be identified and controlled, with information conveyed to appropriate personnel, before they assume unmanageable magnitude.

Corrective actions that can be taken for scheduling problems include:

Expediting
Eliminating marginal activities
Combining related activities
Revising milestones
Adjusting time estimates

Performance Control

Most performance problems do not surface until after the project is completed, making performance control very difficult. However, every effort should be made to measure interim factors, sometimes indicated by time and cost deviations. So, when schedule and cost problems exist, also analyze how those problems may affect performance. Since performance requirements usually relate to performance of the end products, controlling these performance problems may necessitate altering project specifications.

Cost Control

Numerous accounting and reporting systems have been developed over the years for monitoring and controlling project costs. The level of interest in this topic is an indication of its importance. In any discussion of cost control there are several key issues that must be addressed:

1. Better estimation of time, resources, and cost
2. Clear communication of project requirements, constraints, and available resources
3. Better coordination of project functions
4. Timely reporting of project requirements: time, materials, labor, budget.

These key issues are instrumental in order to control costs and trim down project cost. If time and resources are not efficiently utilized, cost will skyrocket and the project will become exceedingly expensive.

THE PLANNING PROCESS

Planning is the process of establishing a course of action within the prevailing operating environment to achieve an established goal. In the adoption and development of new technologies, planning is needed to:

1. Minimize the effects of technology uncertainties
2. Clarify technology goals and objectives
3. Provide the basis for evaluating progress on a project
4. Establish measures of technology performance
5. Determine personnel responsibilities

To effectively plan, we must understand the goals and the scope of the new technology. Essentially, how will this new technology contribute in achieving the organization's missions and goals given its strengths and weaknesses.

Technology Overview

The overview specifies the goals and scope of the new technology as well as its relevance to the organization's mission. The major milestones, with a description of the significance of each, should be documented. In addition, the overview should establish the organizational structure to be used for the project.

Technology Goal

A combination of objectives, the technology goal is a detailed description of the overall goal of the proposed technology. Each objective is detailed with respect to its impact on the project goal. Major actions to ensure achievement of those objectives are also identified.

Strategic Planning

The long-range purpose of the new technology is defined (Cleland, 1990) and its useful life specified. A frequent problem with technology is extended life beyond its usefulness. If a feasible technological life is defined during the planning stage, it will be less traumatic to replace the technology at the appropriate time.

Technology Policy

The technology policy refers to the general guidelines for personnel actions and managerial decision making relating to adoption and implementation of the new technology. The technology policy indicates how the project will be executed. For example, the chain of command and flow of information are established in the policy. Accordingly, a lack of policy lays fertile ground for incoherent implementation and conflicting interpretations.

Technology Procedures

Technology procedures are the detailed methods of complying with established technology policies. A policy, for example, may stipulate that approval of the project manager must be obtained for all purchases. The procedure then specifies how that approval should be obtained—oral or written.

Technology Resources

Project goals and objectives are accomplished by applying resources to functional requirements. Resources, in the context of project management, are generally made up of people and equipment, which typically are in short supply. The people needed for a particular task may be committed to other projects; a crucial piece of equipment may be under the control of an uncooperative department.

The resources required for adoption and implementation of the new technology are defined. Available resources are identified along with resources to be acquired. The time frame for availability is also specified. Issues such as personnel recruiting and technical training must be addressed early in the project.

Technology Budget

Technology cannot be acquired without an adequate budget. Some of the cost aspects that will influence technology budgeting are fixed cost, operating cost, maintenance cost, direct and indirect costs, overhead cost, and salvage value.

Clearly, the technological factors itemized above will influence the optimal technology for an organization. Such technology should be capable of meeting the organization's goals.

Operating Characteristics

Specifications for the operation of the technology should be developed, answering such questions as: What inputs will be required by the technology? What outputs are expected? What is the scope of the technology? How will its performance be measured and evaluated? Is the operating environment suitable for the technology's physical configuration? What maintenance is needed and how will the maintenance be performed? What infrastructure is required to support the technology?

Cost-Benefit Analysis

The bottom line in any technology implementation is a matter of profit, benefit, and/or performance. There should be an analysis of the expenditure required to implement the technology versus its benefits. Can existing technology satisfy needs more economically? Even if future needs dictate acquisition of the new technology, economic decisions should consider prevailing circumstances. Figure 9.3 shows the relationship between technology cost and benefit.

Technology Performance Measures

Performance standards should be established for any proposed new technology. Standards are the yardstick against which adoption and implementation progress can be compared. In addition, the methods by which performance is analyzed should be defined

Figure 9.3
Cost/Benefit Analysis of Technology

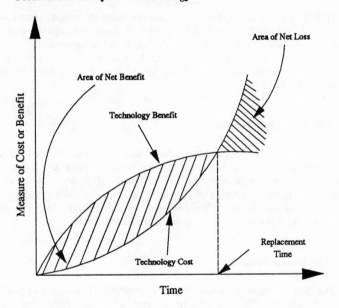

to avoid ambiguities in tracking and reporting.

Technology Organization

Technology organization involves organizing the technology personnel with respect to required duties, assigned responsibilities, and desired interactions. The organizational structure serves as the coordination model for the technology implementation project.

Technology Work Breakdown Structure

The technology implementation project can be broken down into major functional clusters. This facilitates a more efficient and logical analysis of the elements and activities involved in adoption and implementation. A work breakdown structure (WBS) shows the hierarchy of major tasks, permitting implementation of "divide and conquer" concepts. Overall project planning and control are substantially improved when WBS is used. For instance, a large project may be broken down into smaller subprojects, which may, in turn, be broken down into task groups. Individual components of a WBS are referred to as WBS elements, and the hierarchy of each is designated by a level identifier. Elements at the same level of subdivision are said to be of the same WBS level. Descending levels provide increasingly detailed definition of project tasks. The complexity of a project and degree of control desired determine the number of levels in the WBS.

Potential Technology Problems

Implementing new technologies is prone to new and unforeseen problems, so contingency plans must be established. Preparation must include handling unexpected problems such as technical failures, software bugs, personnel problems, technological changes, equipment failures, human error, data deficiency, and decision uncertainties.

Potential Acquisition

Technology acquisition deals with the process of actually procuring and implementing the new technology. Acquisition may involve both physical and intangible assets. The process normally covers the following:

1. *Hardware.* Analysis of hardware needs is the physical component of technology acquisition. Questions should be asked regarding size, weight, safety features, space requirement, and ergonomics.

2. *Software.* Analysis of software requirements encompasses the program code, user interface, and operating characteristics of computer software that supports the proposed technology.

3. *Site selection and installation.* There needs to be a suitable and accessible location for the physical components of the new technology. The surrounding infrastructure should support the proposed new technology.

TECHNOLOGY CONVERSION STRATEGIES

Implementation of a new technology can be effected in one of several ways—some are more suitable than others for certain technologies. The most common technology conversion strategies are:

•*Parallel Conversion*. The existing technology and the new technology operate concurrently, until there is confidence that the new technology is satisfactory.

•*Direct Conversion*. The old technology is removed and the new technology takes over. This is recommended only when both technologies cannot operate simultaneously owing to incompatibility or cost.

•*Phased Conversion*. Modules of the new technology are gradually introduced, using either direct or parallel conversion.

•*Pilot Conversion*. The new technology is fully implemented on a pilot basis, in a selected department. Figure 9.4 graphically shows the technology conversion options.

The new technology should be evaluated only after it has reached a steady-state performance level. This helps avoid any bias that may be present at transition, owing to personnel anxiety, lack of experience, or resistance to change. The new system should be evaluated for the following:

Quality and productivity
Sensitivity to data errors
Utilization level
Response time
Effectiveness

TECHNOLOGY IMPLEMENTATION STRATEGIES—THE TRIPLE C MODEL

The successful conversion to a new technology requires a coordinated approach that utilizes conventional project planning and control techniques as well as other management strategies. Intricate organizational and human factors come into play, so a successful technology implementation project depends on good communication, cooperation, and coordination. As such, the Triple C model facilitates the systematic planning, organizing, scheduling, and control of such a project (Badiru, 1988). It addresses the following functions of project management:

Communication
Cooperation
Coordination

Technology Communication

Many new technologies have just emerged from research laboratories. There are apprehensions and controversies regarding the potential impact, and implementing these new technologies may generate concerns both within and outside the organization. Sometimes there are uncertainties about the impact the proposed technology will have. A frequent concern is loss of jobs. Proper communication, however, can help educate all concerned. Be sure all who will be affected by the project are informed early on as to:

1. The nature, scope, and impact of the project
2. What resources are available for the project
3. Who is in charge
4. Why the project is needed
5. What the direct and indirect benefits will be
6. What personnel contribution will be needed
7. Who will be affected if the project fails
8. What the scope of the project is

Wide communication is a vital factor in securing support for the project. Make a concerted effort to inform everyone involved. Moreover, keep the communication channel open throughout the project. In addition to in-house communication, consult external sources when appropriate. Figure 9.5 is an example of communication responsibility matrix.

Technology Cooperation

Not only must people be informed but their cooperation must be sought. Signing off on a project is not assurance of full cooperation. In effect, the new technology must be sold to both management and employees. A structured approach helps identify and explain the following items to personnel:

1. What cooperative efforts are needed
2. What time frame is involved
3. How critical cooperation is to the project
4. The organizational benefits of cooperation
5. The implication of lack of cooperation

The project management approach to technology adoption and implementation can help resolve conflicts, because it provides an account of the following:

1. What is expected from the new technology
2. How the new technology is similar to existing technologies
3. How the proposed technology is different from existing technologies
4. Availability of technical personnel to support the new technology
5. Management support for the new technology
6. Where and when the new technology will be used
7. Who will use the new technology

Technology Coordination

Manpower Needs. Personnel needs for implementing a new technology are usually difficult to quantify, owing to variables in application objectives, personnel competence, lack of precedent, and technological constraints. Requests for personnel should be based on the practicality of the project. This helps secure credibility and support for the effort. The question of training should also be analyzed. Many new technologies suffer from a lack of skilled manpower, thus organizing an implementation project group may not be simple.

Figure 9.4
Technology Conversion Strategies

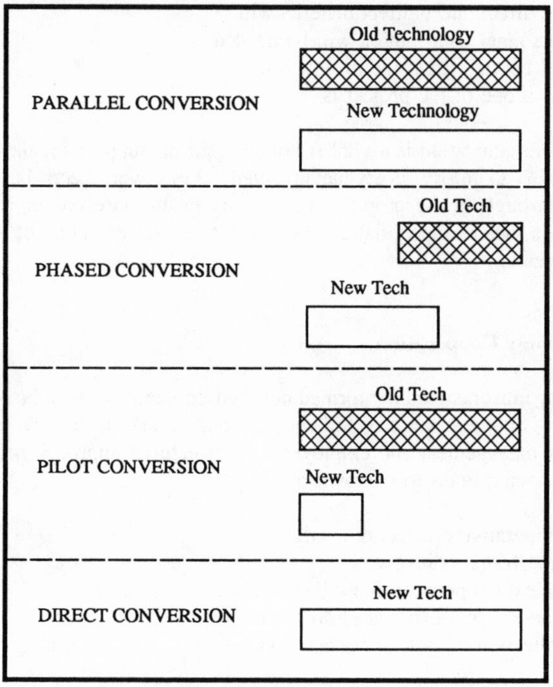

PARALLEL CONVERSION

Old Technology

New Technology

PHASED CONVERSION

Old Tech

New Tech

PILOT CONVERSION

Old Tech

New Tech

DIRECT CONVERSION

New Tech

Figure 9.5
A Communication Matrix

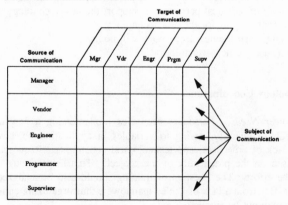

Equipment Requirements. Make a list of the physical equipment that will be needed to support the technology—both equipment already available and that to be obtained. This will help management evaluate organizational capability to implement the new technology. Detailed equipment documentation contributes significantly to winning the cooperation of management and employees.

Time Requirements. Owing to a lack of precedent, it may be difficult to draw up accurate schedules for implementation. When seeking cooperation from others, propose a conservative schedule. Also, the dynamism of new technology makes estimating times even more difficult. Setting a precarious terminal date for the project completion may provide the grounds for criticism if the deadline is not met. Time allowances should be made for technology conversion. One strategy is to present time requirements in terms of a series of milestones.

Having initiated the communication and cooperation actions, next step is to coordinate the efforts of the project team. Coordination facilitates project efforts. A Functional Responsibility Matrix can be very helpful at this stage, consisting of columns showing individual or functional departments and rows of required actions. Cells within the matrix are filled with relationship codes that indicate who is responsible for what. Shown in Figure 9.6, the matrix helps to avoid overlooking critical function requirements and responsibilities. The matrix should indicate the following:

1. Who is to do what
2. Who is responsible for which results
3. What personnel interfaces are involved
4. Who is to inform whom of what
5. Whose approval is needed for what
6. What support is needed from whom for what functions

MANAGING A TECHNOLOGY TRANSFER

The transfer of technology can be achieved in different ways. Project management provides the means for ensuring a proper transfer of technology. Three technology transfer modes are presented here to illustrate basic strategies for getting a technological product from point *A* (technology source) to point *B* (technology sink). A conceptual integrated model of the interaction between the technology source and sink is presented in Figure 9.7. The nature and operational details of the transfer modes are outlined below:

Transfer of Complete Technological Products

A fully developed product is transferred from a source to a target. Very little product development is carried out at the receiving point, however information about operation of the product is fed back to the source so that necessary product enhancements can be pursued. The technology recipient generates product information, which facilitates further improvement at the technology source.

Transfer of Technology Procedures and Guidelines

Procedures (e.g., blueprints) and guidelines are transferred from a source to a

Figure 9.6
Functional Responsibility Chart

Responsibilities	Management	Engineer	Technician	Project Manager	Technical Writer	Plant Manager	Training Dept.
1. Problem Definition						R	
2. Personnel Assignment	C			C		R	
3. Project Initiation				R		A	
4. Technology Prototype	C	R	R	I		S	
5. Full Technology	C	R	R	I		S	
6. Technology Verification	R	R	R	C	I	C	
7. Technology Validation	R	R	R	R	I	C	
8. Technology Integration	R	R	R	R	I	A	
9. Technology Maintenance	R	R	R	C	I	A	
10. Documentation	C	C	C	C	R	A	I

Codes:

R = Responsible   I = Inform
A = Approve   S = Support
C = Consult

Person/Department

Figure 9.7
Technology Transfer Model

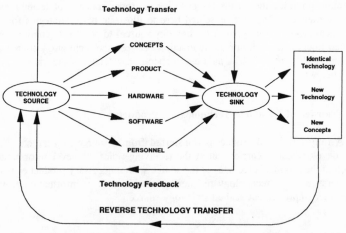

Source: Badiru (1991).

target. The technology blueprints are implemented locally to generate the desired services and products. Use of local raw materials and labor is encouraged for local production. Under this mode, implementation of the technology can generate new operating procedures, which can be fed back to enhance the original technology. With this symbiotic, loop arrangement, both the transferring and the receiving organizations derive benefits.

Transfer of Technology Concepts, Theories, and Ideas

The basic concepts, theories, and ideas behind a given technology are transferred and then enhanced, modified, or customized within local constraints to generate new technological products. The local modifications and enhancements have the potential to generate an identical technology, a new related technology, or a new set of technology concepts, theories, and ideas. These products can then be transferred back to the original source. Figure 9.8 shows a typical cycle for local adaptation and modification of technology.

TECHNOLOGY SYSTEMS INTEGRATION

With increasing shortages of resources, there will be more emphasis on sharing of physical equipment, facilities, technical information, or ideas. Technology integration is a major effort today, facilitating the sharing of limited resources. It also helps coordinate diverse technical and managerial efforts to enhance organizational functions, reduce cost, improve productivity, and increase the utilization of resources.

Technology integration ensures that performance goals are satisfied with minimum expenditure of time and resources. It may require the adjustment of functions to permit such sharing of resources, development of new policies to accommodate product integration, or realignment of managerial responsibilities. Integration can affect both hardware and software components of an organization.

Important factors in considering technology integration are:

1. Unique characteristics of each component in the technologies
2. Relative priorities of each component in the technologies
3. How components of the technologies complement one another
4. Physical and data interfaces
5. Internal and external factors
6. How performance of the integrated system will be measured

The Matrix Organization

The matrix organization is a popular project structure that facilitates resource sharing and system integration. Sometimes called a multiple-boss organization, it is particularly suitable for technology implementation, permitting both vertical and horizontal flows of information. Technology implementation projects require integration of specialized skills from different functional areas. In a matrix organization, individual projects share physical resources as well as managerial skills. An example of a matrix organization model is shown in Figure 9.9.

Figure 9.8
Project Technology Transfer Loop

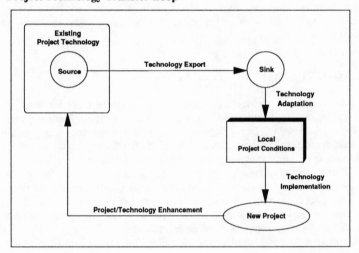

Source: Badiru (1991).

Figure 9.9
Matrix Organization

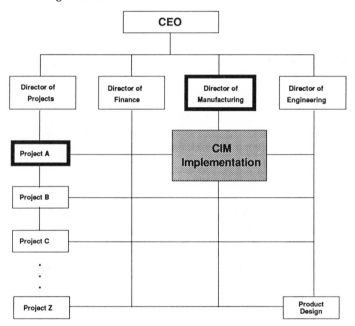

Source: Badiru (1991).

The matrix organization is suitable when there is multiple managerial accountability for a job function. Typically there are two chains of command—the horizontal and vertical chains deal with functional and project lines. The project line in the matrix is usually of a temporary nature, while the functional line is more permanent. The matrix organization can be dynamic, or static, depending on the project scenario. The matrix organization has several advantages, including the following:

1. Consolidation of objectives. The objectives of the task at hand are jointly shared and pursued by multiple departments.
2. Efficient utilization of resources. The allocation of resources is more streamlined. Manpower and equipment can be shared among departments to improve utilization levels.
3. Better flow of information. Since departments are cooperating rather than competing, there is a better flow of information.
4. Interfunctional contacts. The joint responsibility for projects creates an atmosphere of compatibility and lateral interaction.

CONCLUSION

The concepts of project management can help in planning for the adoption and implementation of new manufacturing technology. Project management techniques have been quite successful in conventional one-of-a-kind projects, and they are now being effective in other areas. Technology managers, engineers, and analysts should take advantage of these management tools.

REFERENCES

Allmendinger, G. "Management Goals for Manufacturing Technology." *Manufacturing Engineering* (95) (5) (1985): 83-84.

Badiru, A. B. *Project Management in Manufacturing and High Technology Operations.* New York: John Wiley, 1988.

———. "Strategic Planning for Automated Manufacturing." In *Justification Methods for Computer Integrated Manufacturing Systems*, edited by H. R. Parsaei, T. L. Ward, and W. Karwowski. Amsterdam, Netherlands: Elsevier Science Publishers, 1990, pp. 17-39.

———. *Project Management Tools for Engineering and Management Professionals.* Norcross, GA: Industrial Engineering & Management Press, 1991.

Badiru, A. B., B. L. Foote, and J. Chetupuzha. "A Multiattribute Speadsheet Model for Manufacturing Technology Justification." Conference on Computers and Industrial Engineering, Orlando, March 1991, *Computers & Industrial Engineering* 21 (1-4): 1991.

Cleland, D. I. *Project Management: Strategic Design and Implementation.* New York: TAB Books, 1990.

Murrin, T. "Commerce Deputy: U.S. Isn't Automating Quick Enough." *Industrial Engineering* 21 (10) (October 1989): 7.

National Research Council, Committee on the CAD/CAM Interface, Manufacturing Studies Board, *Computer Integration of Engineering Design and Production: A National Opportunity.* Washington, DC: National Academy Press, 1984, p. 1.

Chapter 10

Licensing: An Intangible but Strategic Source of Revenue

Vasanthakumar Bhat

The sale of intellectual property is becoming a major source of revenue. In 1990, the semiconductor industry was stunned when it discovered that a little-known inventor named Gilbert P. Hyatt had been awarded the patent for the basic microprocessor. Analysts predict that this patent could cost the semiconductor industry millions of dollars (Wall Street Journal, August 1990). In 1989, the Japanese patent office awarded Texas Instruments a patent for its basic integrated circuit—after twenty-nine years. The potential income from this patent is estimated to range from $200 million to $800 million a year (Wall Street Journal, 1989). Robert W. Kearns was awarded $6.3 million in a suit against Ford Motor Company over electronically controlled intermittent windshield wipers (Wall Street Journal, July 1990). It is estimated that Honeywell will collect $300 million in back royalties for its patents on autofocus technology—it recently collected $127.5 million from Minolta (Business Week, 1992).

Advances in communications technology, sky-high research and development costs, vast new markets in former Eastern Bloc countries, rapidly changing technology, and rising international competition are increasingly forcing business leaders to reconsider their international business strategies. Few companies have the wherewithal to enter every foreign market and develop all their technological inventiveness. In this environment, licensing represents a major business alternative to entering foreign markets, along with exports, joint ventures, and wholly owned subsidiaries. However, licensing has both advantages and disadvantages for both the licensor and the licensee. *Licensing* involves the sale of a technology by its owner to another party. This sale of technology may involve patents, trademarks, copyrights, industrial designs, and know-how or combination of these. A *patent* gives its owners the right to exploit, use, or sell an invention for a specified number of years in a particular geographic area. To be patentable, the know-how should be new and useful. A *trademark* provides exclusive right to its owners to distinguish its products from those of its competitors. It is a visual symbol expressed through words or illustration or combination of these. A *copyright* provides exclusive rights to its owners for an original work, authorship represented as a tangible medium of expression. *Know-how* consists of trade secrets, manufacturing processes, and industrial techniques with limited access. It can also be a process or management technique to make a product or service more valuable.

Technology is usually passed along to a licensee through equipment, training, scientists and technologists, and literature. There are two parties in every licensing transaction: the licensor and the licensee. In this chapter, I present licensing from the perspective of both parties.

LICENSING FROM THE LICENSOR'S PERSPECTIVE

From the licensor's viewpoint, the licensing decision goes through the following steps:

1. Identify technologies for licensing,
2. Organize for licensing
3. Identify potential licensees
4. Formulate a licensing kit
5. Promote and advertise
6. Decide on pricing
7. Negotiate and finalize the licensing agreement
8. Manage the technology process

Identify Technologies for Licensing

The decision whether to use licensing to enter a foreign market is significantly influenced by several factors, including host-country policies and circumstances relevant to each company and its technology. Since several countries have strong capital bases of their own, companies are using licensing as one major way to reach foreign markets. For many small companies, licensing may be the only way to earn substantial income from markets they could not enter on their own. For large companies, licensing provides a low-risk, low-investment strategy to enter a market that is hard to penetrate. A variety of factors influence the decision regarding strategies to enter a foreign market. Legal considerations such as tariffs, taxes, antitrust laws, local content laws, product liability laws, patent laws, market structure, government regulations regarding expatriation of profits, and political restrictions are some. Shipping costs, capital requirements, raw material, and labor availability can also influence a licensing decision. In addition to earning royalty and fee income, licensing may provide a company with certain tax benefits. Sometimes it may be the only way to reach a foreign market that otherwise is closed to imports. Licensing, in addition to reducing risk of expropriation of manufacturing assets by a foreign government, lessens start up and commercialization risks. It also provides opportunities for future expansion, either through joint venture or fully owned subsidiaries.

However, licensing is not without drawbacks. It usually generates a smaller percentage of profits on gross sales in comparison to exports and joint ventures. Once licensing agreements expire, the licensee may end up as a future competitor of the licensor. The licensor has least control over licensee; consequently, the licensee may produce shoddy products that can ruin the licensor's reputation. In addition, the licensee may call upon the licensor for all kinds of technical help, for which the licensee may not be adequately compensated. A company may also inadvertently agree to transfer technology not yet perfected for commercial exploitation.

So a company must evaluate costs and benefits before it decides on licensing. Table 10.1, presents the advantages and disadvantages of licensing from the licensor's perspective. Before a company licenses its technology, it should ensure that significant current and future products do not depend on that technology. In addition, it should

Table 10.1
Advantages and Disadvantages of Licensing—from the Licensor's Perspective

Advantages	Disadvantages
Uses low-risk strategy to enter a foreign market	Offers low profit potential
Generates revenue	Opens licensee up to become a future competitor
Affords opportunity to learn about licensor's foreign markets	Has possibility that licensee may not meet expectations
Requires very small investment	Can give rise to disputes
Avoids antitrust problems	Involves foreign exchange and legal risks
Preserves foreign markets	Loses option for future entry into the market
Is extremely suited for small markets	Carries administrative burden
Makes it possible to enter markets not otherwise possible	Suggests licensee may demand lenient terms for renewal
Helps to sell equipment, raw materials, products, services, and so on	Offers limited profit potential in some foreign countries
Enables company to overcome local legislation	Provides licensee with access to commercially perfected future technology
Utilizes low-cost labor	Suggests possible surrender of trade-secrets, copyrights, and intellectual properties.
Creates backup supply source	
Discourages competitors from finding ways to design around licensor's patents	
Adapts products to favorable foreign market	

ensure that its competitive position is not jeopardized as a result of the licensing. The company should consider the degree of control it wishes to impose on its technology, a major customer's entry into a foreign market, product life cycle, research intensity, technological turnover, and so on. The company should also make sure that it will not want to invest in the target market in the future.

Organize for Licensing

Once a company identifies technologies for possible licensing, it must set up an organization to perform the licensing function. Top management support is a must for successful licensing. In addition, the company must appoint an individual to act as licensing manager. In addition to being the company representative for licensing and defining the strategy, he or she should coordinate with departments such as research and development, engineering, project management, and manufacturing. The same person should handle licensing of products as well as process know-how. The company should also prepare a list of know-hows, products, processes, trademarks, and so forth that it wishes to license. These can be selected based on their value to the buyer, ease of transferability, and effort required by the company to transfer them to a licensee. Some products may have to be modified to meet requirements of a particular market.

Identify Potential Licensees

Markets for product and process licenses are small. Licensing involves considerable negotiations and decision making. Therefore, identification of potential licensees is very different from a search for consumer or industrial product markets. The purpose of this step is to identify potential licensees, decide the best way to market the technology to them, and find out about the competition.

Selecting the right partner is the name of the game. Regional and country directories, yellow pages, banks, trade fairs, international chambers of commerce, and trade and industry publications are good starting places; the *Kompass, Bottin International, Nordisk Handelskalendar, Japan Trade Directory, Thomas Register of Manufacturers*, and *The World Aviation Directory* are such publications. If a company has a branch office in a particular country, then the representative in that country could identify potential licensees there. Another strategy is to compile a list of likely prospects for know-hows based on their possible use. Government agencies and trade attachés are other often overlooked sources of information.

Engineering contractors and consultants are excellent conduits for reaching potential customers for technical know-how, however these contractors and consultants should not be selected for each region on an exclusive basis. In addition, the company should always maintain good communications with potential licensees to gain experience of know-how sales. A company should also review the competitive position of its technology vis-à-vis its competitors. Usually, technologies with lower capital costs have the edge on technologies with higher capital costs, irrespective of operating costs. If operating costs are higher than product prices, then it will be hard to sell the know-how in a country where unrestricted imports are allowed. Labor-saving technologies may not be attractive to a licensee in a low-wage country, therefore the competitive analysis of know-hows should consider local factors, conditions, and policy issues.

Formulate Licensing Kit

A critical step in the licensing decision process, the licensing kit can determine the success of any licensing effort. The company needs to decide what information to provide to its potential buyers. If too much information is offered, the company may inadvertently give away the know-how; if too little is given, a potential buyer may not fully appreciate its commercial utility. Usually, a company tailors its information package to a specific inquiry. At the introductory level, the information package contains recent annual reports; a brief description of the technology along with block diagrams indicating raw materials, labor and utility, technical and economic benefits of the technology, and unique features of the know-how; and an outline of the technical, business, and legal conditions.

Promote and Advertise

Technical brochures and articles in trade and technical journals are two ways of promoting a company's technology. Trade shows can also be used to publicize the availability of technology for licensing and to develop initial contacts. Technology transfer consultants, financial institutions, existing distributors, major customers, and past contacts can also be conduits for promotions and reaching potential customers.

Decide Pricing

In spite of burgeoning literature in technology transfer, according to a report by United Nations Industrial Development Organization (UNIDO) "there exists no standard method for determining a fair price for a technology" (Bidault, 1989). Since there are not many customers for technology, its price is determined primarily by bargaining between the licensor and licensee. Price is one of the major sources of conflict between a licensor and licensee. Since the value of a technology depends on the licensee's perception, it is hard to draw a demand curve for know-how. Though marginal cost of supplying a technology to a licensee is usually negligible, it is hard to formulate a supply curve.

The price is a major determinant in the licensee's selection of a know-how, so a licensor can use any of a variety of creative approaches. Basically, there are two forms of revenue: variable and fixed. Royalties are one of the most common forms of variable revenue. They are calculated as a percentage of sales, savings, profits, fixed sum per units sold, or otherwise. Since sales are easy to compute and also account for inflation, royalties are frequently based on sales. The royalty payment is dependent on sales or profit, so using royalties as a price places most risk on the licensor. If the licensee fails to achieve projected sales or profits, the licensor does not receive adequate compensation for the technology. Therefore, capability of a licensee is a critical factor in royalty payments for technical know-how. To offset this, sometimes the licensor will demand a minimum royalty payment each year, irrespective of sales. The licensor may also lose royalty income if patents underlying the license are challenged and declared invalid.

Since payment is spread over years, and depends on success of the know-how, the licensee usually prefers a royalty arrangement. Variable royalty payments provide the licensee with access to the technology at a very low or zero up-front fee. In addition, the licensee prefers payments based on profits rather than sales, since he or she has to pay royalties only if profits are made. Sometimes, the royalty percentage may vary, depending on the volume of sales. This way the licensor motivates the licensee to improve performance. Also, the licensor may propose a maximum limit on royalties to make the license more saleable.

A lump-sum payment involves a fixed amount of money paid in one lump sum or in installments at the initial stage of transfer of know-how. The advantages for the licensor of the lump-sum payment is that the company is certain about the amount and the risk is completely borne by the licensee. In addition, a lump-sum payment reduces the likelihood of dispute about unpaid amounts. Lump-sum payments also eliminate future uncertainty about payments should the patents underlying the license be declared invalid. From the point of view of the licensee, a fixed payment is a powerful motivator to increase profits and eliminates need to disclose confidential information to the licensor. However, the lump-sum amount may be quite large.

Cross-licensing involves an exchange of know-how considered to be equivalent in value. Cross-licensing is popular in the electronic and pharmaceutical industries. It is arranged between companies with similar technical competence, so that each obtains access to new developments. It is in lieu of royalty income.

The cost to develop a technology may not reflect the true value of the technology—the profit potential of the technology may be enormous. The price of a technology depends on its commercial potential, its patent protection, rights accorded to the licensee, availability of similar technology, and several other factors. The costs of development, past and future costs of patent protection, materials and labor costs of technical assistance, costs of indemnification, and industry practices determine the price of the technology. Remuneration for technology includes front-end payments, disclosure fees, option fees before the agreement is signed, engineering, technical assistance, consulting and other fees during implementation, and running royalties—the lump-sum payment after agreement is reached.

There are basically two empirical studies relating to technology pricing (Chapter 4 of Bidault, 1989). The first, conducted by UNIDO, focuses on sharing profits between licensor and licensee. UNIDO estimates that the percentage allocated to a licensor varies from 25 to 50 percent of total profits. Root and Contractor (1981) use a multiple-regression analysis to arrive at price. They identify the variables that determine remuneration: total transfer costs, total technical costs, agreement life, remaining patent life, trademark, export license, R&D expenditure by supplier firm in 1976, recipient's plant scale as a ratio of supplier's typical plant, degree of supplier competition, and adaption of technology for recipient. Bidault (1989) argues that price is linked to company strategies, and proposes that technology pricing be based on technology payments (which includes lump sum and front-end payments, royalties, technical assistance fees, training fees, technical compensation, and so on), technology transfer costs (technical, legal, marketing, traveling, and other costs), licensor's share in the total profit, and strategy. According to BIC (1988), some companies charge upward of 25 percent of licensee profits as licensing fees. Others fix their prices from 10 to 50 percent of the incremental profit a licensee can obtain from the know-how above the next best investment. However, licensing executives consider a variety of factors, including quality of technology, type of license, licensor's and licensee's costs, strength of patents, competitive conditions, expected profitability, and licensee contributions. Companies also try to be fair in determining price.

Negotiate and Finalize Licensing Agreement

Effective negotiation and finalization of licensing agreements require meticulous planning. Like every other function, planning for licensing starts with a definition of objectives. The licensor's objectives should relate to income, control of technology, sale of items other than know-how, and tax planning.

When a firm receives an inquiry, the first step is to collect information about the client's market potential, technological capability, financial condition, government regulations, foreign exchange restrictions, and so on. The next step is to plan a response. Take care to ensure that no confidential information is disclosed. The general tactic is to provide no more information than required by a potential licensee to evaluate technology. The response should include a brief introduction to the company, recent financial reports, a brief description of the technology, the competitive advantages of the technology and its superiority to the competitor's technology, energy and raw material requirements, and financial and commercial terms. Provide as much nonconfidential information as possible so as to generate interest in the technology.

With a view toward preventing disclosure of sensitive information, the potential licensee may be asked to sign a secrecy agreement. Another strategy is to ask for a substantial sum of money to evaluate the technology and return it without having made an analysis of its composition, or reverse engineering. The licensor may ask a consultant trusted by both parties to carry out such economic and technical evaluation on behalf of the potential licensee, without disclosing details about know-how.

The personnel responsible for the technology should receive top management's commitment to license the technology, to allocate adequate resources to transfer the technology to the licensee, and what compensation can be expected.

Choosing the proper licensee is essential for any licensing activity to be financially and technically successful. Therefore, every effort should be made to ensure that the licensee is qualified. There should be sufficient infrastructure, including availability of raw materials and competent personnel to support the technology transfer. There should be an adequate market to make the licensing commercially viable. The licensor should have financial strength to survive should the project fail. In addition, the licensee should have a distribution and service network to serve the customers. The licensee should be trustworthy and compatible. Management competence should also be critically evaluated. Obviously, a company selling competing products should be avoided, since it may be trying to lock up the technology. In addition, companies overextended with other projects should be avoided because they will not be able to fully exploit the technology.

Negotiation topics should include financial terms, commercial terms, exclusivity, services that will be provided by the licensor, and obligations of the licensor and licensee. Obviously, both parties should ensure that the licensing agreement conforms to the laws of both nations, if international.

In consultation with a licensee, the licensor should prepare the license business plan. This plan forces both licensor and licensee to critically evaluate economic, regulatory, and business issues that might otherwise be overlooked. A business plan should consider details about the property being licensed, current and potential uses of intellectual property to be licensed, financial aspects of the license, payments, and so on.

Manage Technology Transfer Process

To be successful, licensing must generate profits for the licensee. The licensor should prepare a detailed plan for implementation, formulate a technology transfer plan, review engineering and process designs and provide supervision and technical assistance for startup. The licensor should also conduct an operational audit to ensure that errors in technology transfer are not repeated in subsequent technology-transfer endeavors.

LICENSING FROM THE LICENSEE'S PERSPECTIVE

The import of technology is one of the major factors that catapulted Japan to technological superiority. Japanese firms entered into approximately 42,000 contracts in the period from 1951 through March 1984 (Abegglen & Stalk, 1985). These contracts included some of the best technologies, selected after thorough study of competing technologies, including licenses for DuPont's nylon patent, ICI's Terylene, Bell Laboratory's transistor technology, RCA's color television, and Corning's TV glass tubes. The Japanese paid a mere $17 billion over a period of more than twenty years for technologies that built modern Japan. The Japanese experience, therefore, indicates that licensing can significantly improve a company's competitive position.

A company has three methods to acquire new technology: develop it internally, buy it fully developed, or license it. Developing technology inhouse strengthens a company in future R&D and provides totally proprietary know-how; buying fully developed technology from outside reduces a company's risk and development time; licensing provides a quick entry, requires little finance, and offers time to train and adjust to the new technology. A company may opt for licensing with a view to settling a patent dispute. In short, licensing is an excellent way of supplementing inhouse R&D. Table 10.2 lists the advantages and disadvantages of licensing from the licensee's perspective.

A company that needs to acquire know-how through licensing goes through the following steps:

1. Technology identification
2. Technology appraisal
3. Relationship management

Technology Identification

Rapid technological developments and sky-high production costs are making the search for new products, technologies, and ideas a continuous activity. To conduct a concentrated search for new technology, top management must define its product, process, and commercial properties. One of the critical problems in looking for new technology is identifying the technology sources. Searching the technical literature, keeping in contact with licensing professionals, developing a formal system of technology forecasting, visiting and renewing personal contacts with scientists, going to trade shows and trade association meetings, and directly approaching companies in the industry are some methods of identifying technology sources.

There are several ways to gain access to external technologies. Under a master licensing agreement, an inventor who does not have resources or facilities conducts research and development for a fee and a fraction of any revenue his or her work may generate. Another approach is a grant-back arrangement, whereby the licensor has rights to any technological improvements made by the licensee. Two companies can swap rights to their respective technologies thorough cross-licensing, as well. Using consultants, providing grants to develop new technologies, taking equity investments in small technology-oriented firms, entering into cooperative research agreements, and

Table 10.2
Advantages and Disadvantages of Licensing—from the Licensee's Perspective

Advantages	Disadvantages
Can settle patent dispute	Takes long time to identify potential licensor
Can reduce R & D expenses	Requires license fees
Can have access to know-how	Has moderately high cost
Can supplement the licensee's research and development	Offers technology that may not be different market
Offers access to famous trademark	Has stringent conditions imposed by licensor
Can reduce development time	Is usually hard to improve licensed technology in comparison to technology developed inhouse
Is a quick way to diversify	Suggests that licensor may be using licensee to test-market its product
Is easy to adapt supply to demand in different markets	Has not-invented-here syndrome that may impede implementation

forming competitive alliances are other approaches to develop technology externally.

Technology Appraisal

Every licensor extols the virtues of its products and technologies, therefore one of the critical problems is evaluating the licensor and its technologies. The evaluation should include financial, engineering, research and development, marketing, and licensor factors.

Financial aspects play a significant role in the selection of a licensor. High capital costs generally increase the risk of a technology, so variable costs and internal rates of return are financial factors used in the evaluation of technology. The minimum capacity of the manufacturing facility, raw material requirements, energy consumption, environmental effects, and familiarity with the production processes are engineering considerations. Patent status, likelihood of patent being declared invalid, research and development costs required to adapt technology, and time requirements for adaption are research and development factors. Marketing factors include marketing and distribution channel requirements, new sales force requirements, after-sales service considerations, spare parts delivery aspects, and money needed for promotion. Licensor factors touch on general abilities and technology transfer capabilities. Worldwide leadership, extensive product lines, and experience in the region are among the licensor's general capabilities;

previous experience in technology transfer, commercial and operating experience, and availability of competent personnel are technology transfer capabilities.

Relationship Management

With a view to smoothing the technology transfer process, the licensee should appoint one person to coordinate all activities on behalf of the licensee. The licensee should ensure that technology transfer arrangements are according to agreement. Specialists should be involved early on to absorb technical know-how promptly. There should also be channels of communication with the licensor. Periodic monitoring can ensure that technology transfer is realized according to the plan.

Every licensing agreement should include provisions relating to territory, field of use, know-how, payment terms, and confidentiality. Some clauses provide particular protections.

The *quality control* clause deals with the level of quality, workmanship, content, and design of products the licensor requires from the licensee. These provisions include standards, time and methods of inspection, exact design of packaging, monitoring of production, quality tests, and reporting requirements. With a view to not infringing upon a licensee's business decision, the licensor should provide technical assistance to implement the best quality practices. If the licensee fails to adhere to them, then the licensee should be punished, usually termination of the agreement or liquidated damages.

The *most favored license* clause protects a licensee from being at a competitive disadvantage with respect to later licensees. The clause provides a choice to receive more beneficial terms than those offered to subsequent licensees. The *abatement of infringement* clause forces licensee or licensor to take action when a third party infringes on a licensed patent. If this happens, the licensor should take action if the agreement so stipulates. If the licensor does not take action, the agreement may allow the licensee to not make any payments. If, according to the agreement, it is the licensee who should take action, then the agreement may stipulate termination of licensing rights and all other benefits. Sometimes, the agreement may stipulate conversion of exclusive licenses to nonexclusive ones.

Every licensing agreement must contain a normal termination date. The agreement may also include clauses relating to termination when the licensee does not make payments or declares bankruptcy. Likewise, the licensing agreement may contain clauses relating to warranties, disclaimers, third party indemnification, tort and liability indemnification, sublicensing, advertising, and choice of law. There should also be a clause relating to nontransferability and nonassignability of the agreement.

To sum up, every licensing agreement must contain, not necessarily in the order given, clauses relating to (see Hearn, 1986, UNCTC, 1987):

    Description of parties
    Territory
    Scope of license
    Licensor's undertaking
    Licensee's undertaking
    Best efforts clause
    Most-favored licensee
    Correct trademark use
    Description of technical assistance

Payment and royalty
Accounts and record maintenance
Warranties and undertakings
Infringement by third parties
Quality control
Improvements to know-how and research and development
Supplies
Confidentiality and protection of trademarks
Duration
Bankruptcy or default
Prior termination and its effects
Responsibility for taxes
Dispute resolution or arbitration.

CONCLUSION

Licensing intellectual property is a multibillion dollar business today. Honeywell, Texas Instruments, GE, Motorola, Pfizer, and several other companies conduct periodic reviews to reap maximum benefit from their technologies. In this chapter, I have provided a brief evaluation of factors to be considered in licensing in and licensing out. BIC (1988) provides comprehensive details on current industry practices. Bidault (1989) presents an extensive review on technology pricing. Watkins (1990) offers a systematic procedure for licensing in and out. For legal aspects of technology licensing, we see Sobel (1990).

REFERENCES

Abegglen, J. C., and G. Stalk Jr. *Kaisha, The Japanese Corporation.* New York: Basic Books, 1985.

BIC, *International Licensing Management*, Business International Corporation, New York, 1988.

Bidault, F. *Technology Pricing.* New York: St. Martin's, 1989.

Business Week. March 16, 1992, p. 48.

Hearn, P. *The Business of Industrial Licensing*, 2nd edition. Hants, England: Gower Publishing Company Ltd., 1986.

Root, F., and F. Contractor. "Negotiating Compensation in International Licensing Agreement." *Sloan Management Review* (Winter 1981): 23-32.

Sobel, R. G. *Technology Licensing and Litigation.* Patents, Copyrights, Trademarks, and Literary Property Course Handbook Series, no. 287. New York: Practicing Law Institute, 1990.

UNCTC (United Nations Centre on Transnational Corporations). *License Agreements in Developing Countries.* New York: United Nations, 1987.

Wall Street Journal. November 22, 1989, p. A3.

———. July 16, 1990, p. B2, B6.

———. August 30, 1990, p. B1.

Watkins, W. M. *Business Aspects of Technology Transfer.* Park Ridge, NY: Noyes Publications, 1990.

Chapter 11

Strategic Cost Analysis
as a Global Competitive Weapon

Rudolph A. Jacob

Increasing attention is being given to the use of some new managerial accounting concepts in addressing company strategic issues. One of these concepts is strategic cost analysis, which is the focus of this chapter. I demonstrate how strategic cost analysis, when combined with the newly enriched paradigm of activity costing (accounting), can help companies achieve global competitiveness.

IRRELEVANCE OF TRADITIONAL COSTING

In recent times, numerous academics and practitioners have begun to question the usefulness of traditional managerial costing systems. Their arguments range from the irrelevance of traditional costing techniques in a flexible manufacturing environment to almost complete exclusion of meaningful cost data for marketing, distribution, and customer service functions. For example, Johnson and Kaplan (1987) note:

> Corporate management accounting systems are inadequate for today's environment. In this time of rapid technological change, vigorous global and domestic competition, and enormously expanding information processing capabilities, management accounting systems are not providing useful, timely information for the process control, product costing, and performance evaluation activities of managers.

Shank and Govindarajan (1989), disturbed by the lack of strategic relevance of managerial accounting, call on managerial accountants and accounting educators to "begin actively presenting cost analysis in the broader strategic context."

In another article, Cooper and Kaplan (1988), commenting on the obsession of companies to maximize short-term profits, assert:

> One message comes through overwhelmingly in our experiences with the three firms, and with the many others we talked and worked with. Almost all product-related decisions—introduction, pricing, and discontinuance—are long term. Management accounting thinking (and teaching) during the past half-century has concentrated on information for making short-run incremental decisions based on variable, incremental, or relevant costs. It has missed the most important aspect of product decisions.

Others (e.g., Kelly, 1988) have even claimed that "cost accounting is wrenching

American business. If we are going to remain competitive, we've got to change [our costing systems]."

The irrelevance of traditional cost-accounting techniques comes out loud and clear from the above literature. It is obvious that managerial accountants are not providing the data necessary for strategy formulation and implementation. These outcries, and the lack of competitiveness of American businesses in a global marketplace, have hastened the advent of strategic cost analysis.

WHAT IS STRATEGIC COST ANALYSIS?

Traditional cost analysis focuses primarily on the determination and control of cost and, to a lesser extent, the choice between or among financial alternatives (e.g., resource allocation problems). However, according to Shank and Govindarajan (1989), strategic cost analysis is "cost analysis in a broader context, where the strategic elements become more conscious, explicit, and formal." These authors further note that business management is a continuous cycling process of formulating strategies; communicating strategies throughout the organization; and developing, implementing and monitoring strategies. In all these areas, accounting plays a vital role. For example, accounting reports are one of the major vehicles for communicating financial information throughout the organization. Through budgets and performance evaluation systems, success is monitored. However, these reports must embrace a strategic context where the link between business functions (i.e., research and development, product design, manufacturing, marketing, distribution, and customer service) are not only explicitly recognized but exploited.

MAJOR STEPS IN STRATEGIC COST ANALYSIS

According to Porter (1985), strategic cost analysis involves the following steps:

1. Define the company value chain and assign costs and assets to value activities.
2. Examine and understand the cost drivers (what causes costs) that regulate each value activity.
3. Examine the possibilities to build sustainable competitive advantage, either through controlling cost drivers or by reconfiguring the value chain.

Each of these steps is fundamental to strategic cost analysis. The *value chain* is the sequence of total business functions or activities in which value is added to a product or service. Value to customers is "built up" by aggregating the value (costs) of these activities. These activities (building blocks) should be isolated if:

1. There is high product diversity.
2. There is high volume diversity, such as range of batch sizes.
3. The costs of activities are significant relative to total operating costs.
4. Activities are performed by competitors in different ways (for example, how customers are serviced after they have purchased a car may differ from company to company).
5. Differentiation in activities can lead to a competitive edge.

Identifying the factors that cause a change in cost of any cost object (for example, a product or a marketing function) is critical to controlling costs and the resulting pricing decisions. These factors are what Porter (1985) calls "cost drivers." He contends that there are multiple cost drivers that explain variations in costs of any activity: economies of scale, learning, pattern of capacity utilization, link to the value chain, link with suppliers, link with channels, interrelationships with other business units, level of vertical integration, timing, discretional policies, location, and institutional factors. These drivers are the cause of costs, and resources are consumed by them.

A competitive advantage can be developed and sustained once a company identifies its value chain and the cost drivers that determine the value of the activities on that value chain. This can be done by controlling and manipulating the drivers better than your competitors or by reconfiguring the activities of the value chain.

The system of accounting that allows the above-mentioned functions—to perform real strategic cost and profitability analysis—is activity-based costing (ABC).

ACTIVITY-BASED ACCOUNTING SYSTEMS

According to Horngren and Foster (1991, p. 150), "activity-based accounting [or activity-based costing or activity accounting] is a system that focuses on activities as the fundamental cost objects and uses the costs of these activities as building blocks for compiling the costs of other cost objects." The fundamental idea behind activity-based accounting can be summoned by a simple question: If one has a system that can report on those significant activities the company engages in, wouldn't the company be in a better position to understand cost and, thus, better able to control and manipulate it?

Figure 11.1 illustrates how overall business functions can be divided into departments and activities. Panel C, for example, shows how product costs are "built up" from the costs of specific activities. Full product costs can also be "built up" by summing the costs of all relevant activities of various business functions—that is research and development, product design, manufacturing, marketing, distribution, and customer service. According to Horngren and Foster (1991, p. 150), Figure 11.1 "shows how cost objects become even more finely granulated, from a particular business function to departments to activities—if that is what managers want."

WHO NEEDS ACTIVITY-BASED ACCOUNTING?

Demands for activity-based accounting have been researched and explored by several authors (Cooper, 1988; Kaplan, 1989; Horngren and Foster, 1991). According to Cooper, "Specifically implementing an ABC is advisable if the existing cost system were designed when measurement costs were high, competition was weak, and product diversity was low. But now measurement costs are low, competition is fierce, and product diversity is high."

Kaplan (1989) suggests that ABC is most beneficial when significant overhead costs are not easily assigned to individual products, where there is a variety or diversity of products, and where demands on overhead resources shared by individual products are not proportional to the volume of units.

Horngren and Foster (1991) reinforce the points made by Cooper and Kaplan by noting that "cost accounting systems exist to provide information to help executives in performing their cost management duties."

Figure 11.1
Overview of Business Functions, Departments, and Activities

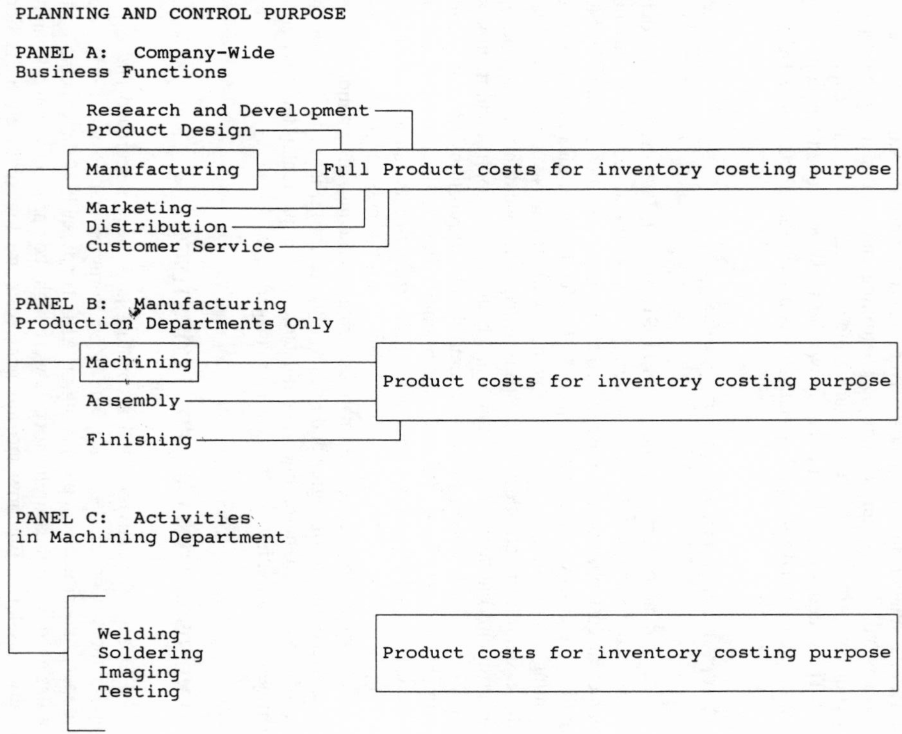

PLANNING AND CONTROL PURPOSE

PANEL A: Company-Wide
Business Functions

Research and Development
Product Design

Manufacturing

Marketing
Distribution
Customer Service

Full Product costs for inventory costing purpose

PANEL B: Manufacturing
Production Departments Only

Machining

Assembly

Finishing

Product costs for inventory costing purpose

PANEL C: Activities
in Machining Department

Welding
Soldering
Imaging
Testing

Product costs for inventory costing purpose

ACTIVITY-BASED COSTING—AN ILLUSTRATION

As the name implies, activity-based costing uses activities as the primary cost objects. Our example focuses on the manufacture of two different types of lamps, and shows how activity-based costing can provide a better understanding of a cost structure. The example also reveals how a conventional cost-accounting system, quite typical of some companies, falls short of highlighting significant differences in the underlying cost structures of these two lamps.

The example produces two types of light fixtures—lamp A and lamp B. The costs of producing these light fixtures are determined in the traditional cost-accounting mode by summing three categories of manufacturing costs: direct materials, direct labor, and manufacturing overhead. Manufacturing overhead is allocated based on direct labor hours, even though direct labor cost is relatively insignificant.

Increased domestic and global competition has resulted in dwindling profit margins over the last three years. Company profit margins have continued to drop in spite of recent installation of a computer-integrated manufacturing system and employment of a competitive selling price policy. Personnel from engineering, marketing, and designing are perplexed at the huge disparity in overhead charges, even though their operations remain fairly constant. They express mistrust in the costing system and, thus, severely question the usefulness of data produced by this system for decision making. Managers from these different departments want a full explanation of their costs and what is "driving" them. They are cognizant of the fact that, if they are to remain competitive, they have to control costs. And to control costs requires understanding the cost drivers. Managers in marketing also believe that high-volume products are "overcosted" while low-volume lines, which require proportionally more setup costs because of their complexity and diversity, are "undercosted."

Because of heightened mistrust in the current cost-accounting system and increased competition in the marketplace, the company decides to implement an activity-based costing system. A team, comprising personnel from engineering, manufacturing, and accounting, studies the problem and determines the various activity areas and their respective cost drivers. Engineering and manufacturing personnel play a significant role in determining the activity areas and the cost drivers. These activity areas and their cost drivers show how informative an activity-based costing system can be.

Activity Areas

The two fixtures require a number of molding, sonic welding, plating, replating, painting, assembling, and testing operations. Parts are also machine and manually installed. Below are the activity areas.

1. *Material handling.* Parts for building the lamps are assembled in partitioned boxes.
2. *Start station.* Instructions for the installation of various parts are programmed in the computer.
3. *Machine molding.* Some parts are assembled and molded by robotic equipment.
4. *Manual molding.* Because of the delicacy of some molding operations, skilled labor has to manually mold gaskets and housing in the assembling operation.
5. *Sonic welding.* Various lens and plates are welded.
6. *Aluminizing and painting.* The aluminizing and painting operation gives the

lamps a reflective surface.
7. *Testing and inspection.* The lamps are tested and inspected to ensure that their components are securely attached before they are ready for packing and shipping.

The activity areas, cost drivers, and indirect costs are as follows:

Activity Area	Cost Drivers Used to Apply Indirect Cost	Indirect Cost Burden Rate
Material handling	Number of parts	$2 per part
Start station	Number of lamps	$5 per lamp
Machine molding	Number of parts	$0.25 per part
Manual molding	Number of parts	$6 per part
Sonic welding	Number of parts	$0.50 per part
Aluminizing and painting	Square footage	$0.70 per sq.in.
Testing and inspection	Hours of test time	$20 per hour

The material handling activity rate is determined as follows:

$$\frac{\text{Budgeted material handling costs}}{\text{Budgeted amount of parts for the period}} = \$2 \text{ per part}$$

The other burden rates are determined in similar fashion. For example, the testing and inspecting activity rate is calculated as:

$$\frac{\text{Budgeted testing and inspection costs}}{\text{Number of test hours}} = \$20 \text{ per hour}$$

Each time a light fixture enters the material handling activity, $2 is charged for every part it consumes. As the fixture moves along the different activities, product cost is builtup.

Figure 11.2 shows the product costs of the two light fixtures.
A study of the buildup of costs by activities provides the following insights:

It is quite clear that light fixture A places a heavier demand on company resources than light fixture B. Consider differences in resource consumption of the following activity areas:

	Light Fixture A	Light Fixture B
Material handling	15 parts	10 parts
Machine molding	60 parts	40 parts
Manual molding	20 parts	10 parts
Testing and inspection	5 hours	2 hours

This vast variability in resource consumption would not have been highlighted in a traditional product cost system, where the independent variable used to apply indirect manufacturing costs is either direct labor hours or machine hours.

Activity-based costing reveals that the cost of light fixture A can be lowered by reducing the number of material handling parts, the number of parts that are machine and

Figure 11.2
Cost of Light Fixtures A and B

	Light Fixture A	Light Fixture B
Direct materials	$40	$35
Direct labor	30	32
Prime costs	70	67
Indirect manufacturing costs		
Material handling (A, 15 parts x $2);		
(B, 10 parts x $2)	30	20
Start station (A, 1 lamp x $5);		
(B, 1 lamp x $5)	5	5
Machine molding (A, 60 parts x $0.25);		
(B, 40 parts x $0.25)	15	10
Manual molding (A, 20 parts x $6);		
(B, 10 parts x $6)	120	60
Welding (A, 10 parts x $0.50);		
(B, 10 parts x $0.50)	5	5
Aluminizing and painting (A, 10 sq.in. x $ 0.70);		
(B, 20 sq.in. x $0.70)	7	14
Testing and inspection (A, 5 hrs x $20);		
(B, 2 hours x $20)	100	40
Total indirect manufacturing costs	282	154
Total product costs	$352	$221

manually molded, and the number of hours required to quality test this product.

Figure 11.2 signals product designers and process engineers to improve the manufacturing capability of the firm. As Cooper and Turney (1990, p. 291) point out, "another way to take advantage of activity-based system has emerged. In some firms, management has decided that the fastest way to improve profitability is to reduce product costs through improved design and more efficient processes. These firms are characterized by products with relatively short life cycles; thus, the firms quickly reap benefits if new products can be manufactured more efficiently."

All of the bases used to apply indirect costs were nonfinancial: parts, hours, square footage, and so on. These costs also should be used if an effective performance evaluation system is desired. For example, a supervisor in the testing and inspection area can be rewarded for a reasonable reduction in testing time. In the manual molding activity area, a supervisor may be given a bonus if he or she can achieve a rate reduction of 15 percent in the manual molding operation. In general, the implication of physical cost drivers in controlling costs is more readily understood by production people.

It is quite evident that an activity-based costing system, when compared with a conventional costing system, is likely to use multiple, as opposed to single, indirect cost pools; burden rates are more likely to be cost drivers; and cost drivers are more likely to be personified by nonfinancial variables.

CROSS-SUBSIDIZATION OF PRODUCTS

Good strategic cost analysis requires that costs in the entire value chain, from design to distribution, be traced to individual products (Shank & Govindarajan, 1989). This obviously requires that common costs, whether they may be "upstream" or "downstream," be traced to individual products and allocated based on the necessary cost drivers that reflect the individual product's resource consumption. Traditionally, allocation schemes, which may ignore relevant cost drivers, can systematically lead to products being miscosted and, ultimately, over- or underpriced. In highly competitive markets where price is the chief competitive weapon, overcosting can draw more diligent competitors into this overpriced (overcosted) market, thus placing the company at a competitive disadvantage both in the short and long run.

To eschew this problem, cost drivers—whether they may be number of setups, number of component parts, number of testing hours, or number of inspections—should be carefully selected in the allocation of common costs.

Figure 11.3 gives an example of how a high-volume standard product was overcosted relative to a low-volume complex product.

The indirect manufacturing costs consist primarily of the indirect labor incurred in setup costs, and the product design and quality testing functions. Let's assume the $2,000 are equally divided among these three areas and, because of the complexity of product B, twice as many production setups are required to produce B relative to A. Let's also assume that, because of the many moving parts in B, B requires twice as many quality testing hours as A.

Panel A of Figure 11.3 is a classic example of product cross-subsidization. Both products are insignificantly different with respect to their direct materials and direct labor content. However, since no attempt is made to identify the cost drivers responsible for the disparate consumption of the indirect manufacturing resources, both products are allocated the same indirect manufacturing costs based on equal usage of machine hours.

In Panel B, efforts are made to directly trace the indirect manufacturing costs to their cost drivers. Since the number of production setups is responsible for the incurrence of setup costs, and since B, because of its complexity, requires twice as many setups as A, B was allocated twice the setup costs of A. Again, the cost driver that leads to product design and quality testing costs is labor hours. Since B consumes twice as many labor hours applicable to the design and quality testing functions, B is allocated twice as many of these costs as A.

It is quite evident in this example that A is subsidizing B. Note in Panel A that the difference in manufacturing costs is only $100. However, in Panel B, the difference after reallocation of indirect manufacturing costs based on their respective cost drivers is now $1,764. This is a significant amount—an amount that obviously would influence the prices and profitability of these products. Ultimately, this type of cross-subsidization can lead to a misallocation of resources and an eventual loss of competitive posture in the marketplace.

TARGET COSTING

It is hard to talk about strategic cost analysis without mentioning target costing. Target costing was pioneered by the Japanese, and it is widely used in assembly-oriented industries such as automobiles, semiconductors, household appliances, and precision machinery.

Figure 11.3
Cross-Subsidization of Products

	Standard Product A	Complex Product B
Panel A: Misallocation of Indirect Manufacturing Costs		
Direct material	$1,000	$1,100
Direct labor	2,000	2,000
Indirect manufacturing costs (A, 100 machine hours x $40; B, 100 machine hours x $40)	4,000	4,000
Total manufacturing costs	$7,000	$7,100
Panel B: Proper Allocation of Indirect Manufacturing Costs		
Direct materials	$1,000	$1,100
Direct labor	2,000	2,000
Indirect manufacturing costs:		
Setup cost (based on number of setups)	1,334	2,666
Product design and quality testing cost (based on labor hours)	1,334	2,666
	$5,668	$8,432

According to Sakurai (1990, p. 48), target costing is "a cost management tool for reducing the overall cost of a product over its entire life cycle. It requires extensive interactions among the production, engineering, R&D, marketing and accounting departments." Target costing develops cost data by working backwards from market prices and subtracting a standard target profit percentage based on return on sales (ROS). This "allowable" cost, as it is called in Japan, now establishes a cost-reduction target for engineers, encouraging them to reduce costs by improving designs, value engineering activities, and, perhaps, tradeoffs in functionality. In essence, the cardinal aim of target costing is to reduce costs at the upstream stages of production.

Activity-based costing systems can provide invaluable information to the company that wants to use a target-costing approach to strategic cost analysis and profitability. It focuses on the value added and nonvalue added activities that determine the cost of a product. Here, the interrelationships of upstream costs, manufacturing costs, and downstream costs can be studied. Tradeoffs can then be made, using techniques such as value engineering, until a target cost is obtained that will lead to competitive pricing and long-term profitability.

CONCLUSION

Suffice it to say that global competitiveness can be achieved only if optimal resource allocation decisions are made within the company. As shown, this competitive edge can be attained only by having an accounting information system that reports both financial and nonfinancial information for all business functions.

Strategic cost analysis, which is the use of cost data in strategic planning, is a powerful competitive weapon. When combined with activity-based costing—a necessary foundation for insightful strategic cost analysis—strategic cost analysis can direct managers to take strategic initiatives in product designing, product cost, customer service, pricing, and automation.

Traditional cost analysis can lead to cross-subsidization of costs, and this can be evil in a globally competitive marketplace. This distortion in costs in many cases results when companies choose inappropriate strategies. Invariably it leads to inappropriate allocations of resources to low-volume, complex products that, because of cross-subsidies, do not bear their fair share of indirect costs. This problem is widespread in American industry and should be addressed. American companies should embrace this newly enriched paradigm of strategic cost analysis if they want to be competitive in a global, dynamic economy.

REFERENCES

Cooper, R. "The Rise of Activity-Based Costing—Part One: What is an Activity-Based System?" *Journal of Cost Management* (Summer 1988): 45-54.

———. "The Rise of Activity-Based Costing—Part Two: When Do I Need An Activity-Based Costing System?" *Journal of Cost Management* (Fall 1988): 41-48.

Cooper, R., and P. Turney. "Internally Focused Activity-Based Cost Systems." In *Measures for Manufacturing Excellence*, edited by R. S. Kaplan. Boston: Harvard Business School Press, 1990, pp. 291-305.

Cooper, R., and R. S. Kaplan. "How Cost Accounting Distorts Product Costs". *Management Accounting* 69 (10) (April 1988): 20-27.

Horngren, C. T., and G. Foster. *Cost Accounting—A Managerial Emphasis*, 7th edition, Englewood Cliffs, N J: Prentice-Hall, Inc., 1991.

Johnson, H. T., and R. S. Kaplan. *Relevance Lost. The Rise and Fall Of Management Accounting*. Boston: Harvard Business School Press, 1987.

Kaplan, R. "Introduction to Activity-Based Costing." NAA Conference, Global Solutions to Global Problems II, March 30-31, 1989, Boston, MA.

Kelly, K. "That Old Time Accounting Isn't Good Enough Anymore." *Business Week*, June 6, 1988, P. 112.

Porter, M. E. *Competitive Advantage*. New York: Free Press, 1985.

Sakurai, M. "The Influence of Factory Automation on Management Accounting Practices: A Study of Japanese Companies." In *Measures for Manufacturing Excellence*, edited by R. S. Kaplan. Boston: Harvard Business School Press, 1990.

Shank, J. K., and V. Govindarajan. *Strategic Cost Analysis—The Evolution from Managerial to Strategic Accounting*. Homewood, IL: Richard D. Irwin, 1989.

III

Strategic Management

Chapter 12

Synchronous Production Innovation and Performance in Manufacturing*

Nicholas C. Georgantzas and Jack Shapiro

Changes in environmental complexity and turbulence leave manufacturing companies no choice but to innovate. Global demographics, economics, and advances in information systems demand both administrative and technical innovations (Drucker, 1989). Human resource requirements are changing from manual labor and clerical workers to knowledge workers. Knowledge is becoming the new capital—a premier source of wealth that resists the militant command-and-control administrative systems of the past (Zeleny, 1991).

Production innovations attract researchers and practitioners because of the U.S. decline in national competitiveness. Since the early 1970s, U.S. companies have faced international competition not only from Japanese cars but also from Brazilian shoes, German and Japanese machine tools, and Japanese electronics. Our imbalance of trade, which has turned this country into a debtor nation, explains the surge of interest in manufacturing (Collins, Hage, & Hull, 1988). Yet balancing trade is something that all nations, even the poorest can do; the real challenge is balancing it with high and rising incomes. This is how Cohen and Zysman (1988, 1987) define national competitiveness.

Economists who associate national competitiveness with short-term profitability propose to discipline our companies, and thereby lower their value-added cost to compete in global markets (Hirsch, Friedman, & Koza, 1990). Yet emphasis on short-term production efficiency is dangerous compared to aims at long-term profitability through production innovations (Hayes & Abernathy, 1980; Hayes & Wheelwright, 1984).

American companies are responding to global competition through production innovations, but systematic data suggest that the difficulties outbalance the advances (Ettlie, 1988; Georgantzas, 1988; Shapiro & Cosenza, 1987; Schonberger, 1986). Allen Bradley, Apple, Black & Decker, Cypress Semiconductor, IBM, and Texas Instruments are some examples. It may not yet be possible to judge whether there is new life in American industry, or whether the successes are valiant but isolated. Jaikumar's verdict is:

> the battle is on and the United States is losing badly. It may even lose the war if it doesn't figure out how better to use the new technology of automation for competitive advantage.

---

*A Fordham University Faculty of Business Research Grant, and CUNY's Center for Management partly supported this research.

This does not mean investing in more equipment; in today's environment, it is how the equipment is used that it is important (1986, p. 70).

Drawing upon a diverse sample from the organizational innovation literature, this chapter incorporates administrative and technical innovation techniques, and examines the proximity of their effects on manufacturing performance. A few studies incorporate administrative and technical innovations, production performance, and their relationships (Collins et al., 1988; Ettlie & Rubenstein, 1980). Combining administrative and technical perspectives allows examining complementary as well as conflicting effects of production innovation on manufacturing performance. Depending on a company specific situation, administrative and technical innovation techniques, performance improvements, and their relationships may yield alternative or complementary forms of synchronous production innovation, each with direct manufacturing policy implications.

Perceptions of thirty-five plant managers provide the data for deriving the proximity among production innovations and manufacturing performance improvements. The results show how administrative along with technical innovations can improve performance independently, but without synchronous innovation, their independent effects may be negligible. Neither can a company improve its performance significantly through emphasis only on either administrative or technical innovations. These results support the necessity of adopting a fine-grained approach to production innovation research and practice. To understand the synergistic effects of synchronous production innovation on manufacturing performance, production managers and researchers should scrutinize the effects of administrative innovation when predicting the effects of technical innovation, and vice versa.

The following section gives a brief account of organizational innovation studies supporting the simultaneous planned adoption of administrative and technical innovations. Subsequently, the chapter outlines the methods for deriving proximity among production innovations and performance improvements. Lastly, the discussion explores practical implications of synchronous production innovation in light of the results and suggests future research extensions.

SYNCHRONOUS PRODUCTION INNOVATION

Available data show that it takes approximately 40 percent more work, and as much as 50 percent more engineering time, to design a new car here than in Japan (Clark & Fujimoto, 1987). The reason for these differences is not yet clear. One postulate is that engineering work in the United States is too segmented, specialized, and sequential. The Japanese emphasize interdependence of product-process design and marketing, and use teams of engineers and manufacturing personnel to address development problems across functions, before the final product and process design (Kochan, 1988).

Conversely, our organizational innovation researchers and practitioners focus on product development, and thereby neglect production processes (Kochan, 1988). Also, American companies concentrate on incremental as opposed to radical innovation; the latter is rare (Damanpour, 1991). Consequently, we know little about the effects of administrative and technical innovation on performance, especially when dealing with significant departures from current practice (Gerwin, 1988). This lack of knowledge is most relevant to manufacturing.

Organizational researchers examine the effects of innovation on performance from administrative and technical perspectives. Proponents of the administrative perspective focus on the effects of social relations on the amount, rate, and permanence of innovation (Damanpour, 1991; Ettlie, 1986; Hage, 1986; Hull & Hage, 1982; Kimberly & Evanisko, 1981; Landau, 1982; Solberg, et al., 1985). In a review of the organizational innovation literature, Tornatsky et al. (1983) conclude that most production innovations take the form of administrative changes.

Proponents of the technical perspective look at the combined effects of market forces and manufacturing processes—for example computer-integrated manufacturing (CIM)—on the type—for example, product versus process—and on the rate of innovation within companies (Abernathy & Townsend, 1975; Hayden 1986; Utterback, 1971; Utterback & Abernathy, 1975). Abernathy and Wayne (1974) show how highly specialized as opposed to flexible manufacturing constrains future technical choices. There has been a technical school in organizational sociology (Perrow, 1967; Woodward, 1965), but little organizational research in technical innovation.

The dynamic model of Utterback and Abernathy (1975) explains how production technology affects a company rate of innovation through product and process changes in strategic business units. Among the causes of production innovation are market demand, production technology, and a company growth objectives. In this model, product and process innovations exhibit distinct curvilinear behavior patterns. Specifically, product innovation is high in early stages of a company's life, but later declines at an accelerating rate. Initially low, process innovations increase dramatically once product markets begin to mature and production technologies become understood. Over time, both process and product innovations taper off sharply because of stable or declining demand, diseconomies of scale, or inflexible production technology.

Sahal (1981) also focuses on the effects of production technology on production innovation. He argues that extant production technology depends on production process uncertainty. Mature products decrease production uncertainty because companies become familiar with production technology and find ways to improve it—this is the *progress principle* (Dutton & Thomas, 1984, p. 235). Over time, the scale of production increases and so does its complexity. To cope with production complexity, companies adopt new technologies, but large production systems can block production innovation.

Researchers generally treat administrative and technical innovation separately or emphasize the distinctions between the two (Daft, 1978). Yet administrative and technical innovations may be interdependent in effect if not by design (Scott, 1987). Kimberly (1981) points to synergistic effects of administrative and technical innovation—the adoption of one type of innovation enables the subsequent adoption of another. The data of Fennell (1984) support the synergistic-effects hypothesis, but also call for research to disentangle the complexity of these effects. Both researchers and practitioners should try to understand exactly how administrative along with technical innovations affect organizational performance (Collins et al., 1988).

The prevailing prescription for American companies is to plan for and adopt administrative and technical change simultaneously (Cohen & Zysman, 1988; Gerwin, 1988; Kochan, 1988). For example, Ettlie (1988) argues that synchronous innovation can simultaneously change production processing, design, and control technologies while administrative changes can systematically renew outdated policies, organizational structures, and practices. Ettlie defines synchronous innovation as "the planned, simultaneous adoption of congruent technological and administrative innovations. These two types of innovations work together to create a synergistic effect on performance" (1988, p. 2).

Adopting administrative or technical innovations entails the generation, development, and implementation of new ideas, systems, products, or services in organizations (Damanpour, 1991). Administrative innovations include adoption of internally generated or purchased administrative programs, processes, and techniques new to the adopting organization, such as autonomous work groups, broader job descriptions, and contingent compensation schemes. Technical—or technological— innovations include adoption of internally generated or purchased devices, production processing systems, and techniques new to the adopting organization, such as robots, flexible manufacturing systems (FMS), and computer-integrated manufacturing (CIM).

Knowing how administrative and technical innovations affect manufacturing performance should help production managers improve performance. Managers may adopt either administrative or technical innovations, depending on how they perceive the effects of innovation on manufacturing performance. Alternatively, aiming at the synergistic effects of the simultaneous adoption of administrative and technical innovations on performance improvements, managers can plan for "synchronous" production innovation. Important for manufacturing, their proximity perceptions of production innovations and performance improvements may affect production managers' adoption choices of administrative and technical innovations.

METHODS

Sample

A structured questionnaire targeted 600 plant managers randomly selected from the Trinet Establishment Database, Dialog File 531. A team of graduate business students with experience in manufacturing helped calibrate the questionnaire and establish its external validity. Thirty-five plant managers returned completed questionnaires, yielding a response rate of 5.83 percent. Admittedly, this rate is considerably lower than the response rates of comparable populations (Gaedeke & Tootelian, 1976). However, the responses of plant managers who respectfully declined to participate in the study "due to the proprietary nature of the information requested" might explain why.

Slightly biased in favor of mature companies, most manufacturing plants in Table 12.1 employed from 100 to 1,000 people. All respondents held middle or top management positions, and most of them had a college or higher degree. Generally, individual responses bare a probability of response or functional bias. With carefully targeted plant managers, however, this probability should be low.

Variables

The respondents rated each company relative emphasis on sixteen administrative and twelve technical production innovations. The study incorporates these innovations because both Ettlie (1988) and Schonberger (1986) provide many examples of companies that achieve substantial performance improvements by adopting these innovations. The respondents also rated each company relative performance along thirty manufacturing improvements that, again, Ettlie (1988), Schonberger (1986), and other colleagues associate with simultaneous adoption of several among the twenty-eight administrative and technical production innovations.

Nine-point Likert-type scales captured the perceptions of production managers of the twenty-eight production innovations and the proximity of their effects on the thirty performance improvements. Nine-point scales are capable of capturing people's percep-

TABLE 12.1 Sample characteristics [a]

		Sample [b] (n=35)
1.	Primary business category	
	Aerospace	8.6
	Automobiles/Trucks	8.6
	Chemicals	14.3
	Electronics	14.3
	Electrotechnology	2.9
	Energy and fuel	8.6
	Food	5.7
	Manufactured metal goods	14.3
	Packaged goods	11.3
	Textile, clothing, shoes	5.7
	Wood products	5.7
2.	Company's year of incorporation	
	1900 or before	11.4
	Between 1901 and 1960	40.0
	Between 1961 and 1980	37.1
	1981 or later	11.4
3.	Year the subject joined the firm	
	1960 or before	8.6
	Between 1961 and 1980	40.0
	1981 or later	51.4
4.	Total number of employees at the plant	
	100 or less	20.0
	Between 101 and 300	37.1
	Between 301 and 1000	25.7
	1001 or more	17.1
5.	Position of respondent plant manager	
	Upper management	45.7
	Middle management	54.3
6.	Highest degree of respondent plant manager	
	High school diploma	8.6
	College degree	57.1
	Master's	28.6
	Ph.D.	5.7
7.	Planning department at the plant	
	Yes	40.0
	No	60.0
8.	Research and development (R&D) department at the plant	
	Yes	25.7
	No	74.3

[a] All figures are percentages, which exclude responses with missing data.
[b] This reduced sample and the statistical analysis exclude responses with missing data.

tions of similar items in a simultaneous comparison (Saaty, 1977). Generally, meaningful qualitative distinctions require precision when the items compared are close with regard to the property used for comparison. If this condition holds—the items differ slightly—then, the psychological limit of 7 ± 2 items in a simultaneous comparison suggests using nine-point scales (Miller, 1956).

Cronbach's alpha coefficient and item-to-total scale correlations assessed the internal consistency of response (Nunnally, 1978). Cronbach's alpha was 0.9025 for administrative innovations, 0.8898 for technical innovations, and 0.9737 for performance improvements. Also, all item-to-total correlations were positive and significant with probabilities better than 0.01.

Analysis

The data allowed deriving the production managers' proximity perceptions of production innovations and their effects on performance improvements. Subsequently, the ordinary Euclidean distance-based proximity among the twenty-eight production innovations, and among their effects on the thirty performance improvements, allowed generating a spatial representation of production proximity perceptions in a derived low-dimensional space. The Proximity and Alscal algorithms of SPSS[X] on a VAX-11/780 series obtained the proximity, the multidimensional scaling (MDS), and the multidimensional unfolding (MDU) solutions.

It is beyond the scope of this chapter to provide a detailed exposition of either the proximity or the MDS and MDU methodology (Davison, 1983; Kruskal, 1964; Schiffman, Reynolds, & Young, 1981; Shepard, 1962). Briefly, however, multidimensional scaling is a mathematical tool for spatially representing the proximity among objects of interest, as in a map. MDS procedures provide information on perceived relationships among objects when the underlying dimensions of evaluation are unknown. The objective of applying MDS and MDU on the study's data was to unearth production managers' underlying perceptual dimensions of organizational innovation and its effects on manufacturing performance improvements.

The ordinal nature of the questionnaire data dictated the use of nonmetric MDS procedure, where the computational criterion of Kruskal's (1964) least squares monotonic transformation maintains the initial rank order of data in derived proximity values. Applying this criterion to the questionnaire data transformed the production managers proximity perceptions of production innovations and their effects on performance improvements into two proximity symmetric matrices.

Subsequently, the two matrices of proximity values produced two two-dimensional MDS solutions, one for the twenty-eight production innovations and one for the thirty performance improvements. These initial solutions produced a rectangular joint-distance matrix, which contained the perceived distances among synchronous innovation techniques and manufacturing performance improvements. In two dimensions, the joint Euclidean distance is

$$d_{ij} = \sqrt{\sum_{k-1}^{2} (Y_{ik} - X_{jk})^2} \, , \tag{1}$$

where Y_{ik} is the coordinate of manufacturing performance improvement i, and X_{jk} is the coordinate of innovation technique j on dimension k.

Lastly, the rectangular matrix derived from (1) produced a classical multidimensional unfolding (MDU) solution. This solution allowed positioning both the administrative and technical production innovations and the manufacturing performance improvements in a single two-dimensional space.

RESULTS

The Alscal Euclidean algorithm of SPSS[X] derived MDS and MDU solutions in $T = 1$, 2, and 3 dimensions. The nonmetric option of Alscal attained the initial rank order of production manager perceptions in the derived proximity matrices. Kruskal's (1964) stress formula (Stress), the proportion of the weighted-variance-accounted-for (RSQ) and subsequent interpretation of coordinate plots converged on the parsimonious solutions derived in $T = 2$ dimensions.

Table 12.2 shows the Stress and RSQ criteria associated with the solutions derived in $T = 1$, 2, and 3 dimensions, respectively. Both the MDS solutions for performance improvements, and the MDU solutions for performance improvements and production innovations, provide the best fit with the data in $T = 3$ dimensions. Both three-dimensional solutions yield the lowest Stress—0.204 and 0.070, respectively—and the highest RSQ—0.960 and 0.995, respectively. However, the multidimensional scaling solutions for production innovations provide the best fit in $T = 2$ dimensions. In Table 12.2, the two-dimensional MDS solution for production innovations provides both the lowest Stress = 0.119, and the highest RSQ = 0.986.

Generally, more dimensions provide a better fit with the data. This does not mean that solutions with more dimensions solutions are necessarily better in a substantive sense. High dimensionality may produce "degenerate" solutions, which involve coordinates clumped together when plotted along the first and third dimensions, or along the second and third dimensions.

In Table 12.2, the lowest Stress and highest RSQ corresponding to the three-dimensional MDS of performance improvements and to the three-dimensional MDU solutions do not necessarily yield a better fit in a substantive sense. Specifically, the three-dimensional MDS solution for performance improvements raises RSQ by 0.017

Table 12.2
Statistical Results Derived in $T = 1$, 2, and 3 Dimensions

	T	Kruskal's STRESS	RSQ
Multidimensional scaling (MDS) of production innovations	1	0.448	0.804
	2	0.119	0.986
	3	0.174	0.971
Multidimensional scaling (MDS) of performance improvements	1	0.314	0.903
	2	0.242	0.943
	3	0.204	0.960
Multidimensional unfolding (MDU) of performance improvements and production innovations	1	0.433	0.819
	2	0.184	0.968
	3	0.070	0.995

only, or 1.7 percent over the solution derived in $T = 2$. Similarly, the three-dimensional MDU solution for both performance improvements and production innovations increases RSQ by 0.027 only, or 2.7 percent over the solution derived in $T = 2$. Together, these negligible improvements in the proportion of the weighted-variance-accounted-for (RSQ)—the "textbook" result of the two-dimensional MDS solution for production innovations and the subsequent interpretation of coordinate plots along the first and third—and the second and third dimensions converge on the parsimonious solutions derived in $T = 2$ dimensions.

Figure 12.1 shows the MDS solution for production innovations derived in $T = 2$ dimensions. Positioning the coordinates of the 28 production innovations along these two dimensions resembles a map in two dimensions. The map reveals the dimensions underlying production manager perceptions of administrative and technical innovations.

The first dimension (dim-1) of Figure 12.1 is congruent with existing dichotomy between the technical and administrative perspectives of production innovations. The tail's neighborhood of the arrow representing dim-1 contains computer-intensive (both hardware and software) or technical innovations such as robots (u), artificial intelligence (h), manufacturing resource planning (t), and automated storage and retrieval systems (j). The head's neighborhood of the arrow representing dim-1 contains administration intensive or administrative innovations such as flat-plant structure (6), JIT production and purchasing (7), new job titles and reporting positions (8), and productivity teams (9).

The second dimension (dim-2) of Figure 12.1 reflects the resources required for innovation adoption. Production innovations require both tangible and intangible resources. In addition to financial backing, tangible resources include facilities, staff, and the number of employees involved. Intangible resources include the time production managers, and other senior-level line and staff managers, spend on the adoption of production innovations (Georgantzas & Shapiro, 1991).

The tail's neighborhood of the arrow representing dim-2 contains innovations with low-capital, discretionary, and consequential resource requirements such as broad job descriptions (2), engineering blue-collar teams (4), group technology (k), engineering generalists (5), and autonomous work groups (1). Often at the discretion of a plant manager, these innovations may require both intangible resources—that is time and tangible expenses for employee training and development but little or no capital investment. Also, they may lower a plant's overhead, typically a consequence of self-coordinating teams (Hessel, 1986; Zeleny, 1987).

Conversely, the head's neighborhood of the arrow representing dim-2 contains innovations with high-capital, discretionary, and consequential resource requirements such as robots (u), computer-aided process planning (o), total quality control (g), flexible manufacturing systems (s), and technology agreements (e). Typically, automation investments require capital or leasing expenses beyond and above a plant manager's budgetary discretion. Consequently, the innovations near the top of Figure 12.1 require both tangible and intangible resources, allocated directly from top management. Without top-management involvement, total quality control (TQC) or management (TQM) both waste time and may have dire consequences.

Figure 12.2 maps the managers' proximity perceptions of the twenty-eight production innovations and their effects on the thirty performance improvements, in two dimensions. Multidimensional unfolding (MDU) allowed placing both production innovations and performance improvements jointly in this single low-dimensional Euclidean space. Alscal did not attain the initial coordinates of administrative and technological innovations. The MDU solution for both production innovations and performance improvements compressed the average proximity among production inno-

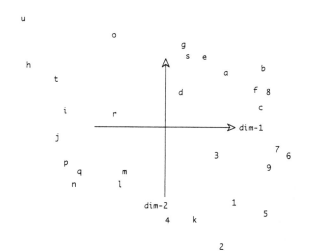

1 - autonomous work groups
2 - broad job descriptions
3 - contingent compensation schemes
4 - engineering blue-collar teams
5 - engineering generalists
6 - flat plant structure
7 - just-in-time (JIT) production & purchasing
8 - new job titles and reporting positions
9 - productivity teams
a - quality control circles (QCCs)
b - quality of work life (QWL) programs
c - research and development (R&D) teams
d - statistical quality control (SQC)
e - technology agreements
f - total preventive maintenance (TPM)

g - total quality control (TQC)
h - artificial intelligence (AI)
i - automated assembly
j - automated storage & retrieval systems (AS/RS)
k - group technology (GT)
l - computer-aided design (CAD)
m - computer-aided engineering (CAE)
n - computer-aided manufacturing (CAM)
o - computer-aided process planning (CAPP)
p - computer integrated manufacturing (CIM)
q - computer or direct numerical control (CNC/DNC)
r - design for manufacturing (DFM)
s - flexible manufacturing systems (FMS)
t - manufacturing resource planning (MRP-II)
u - robots

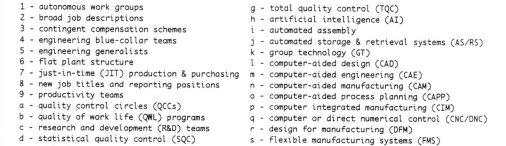

FIGURE 12.1   Initial Two-Dimensional Configuration of Production Innovations

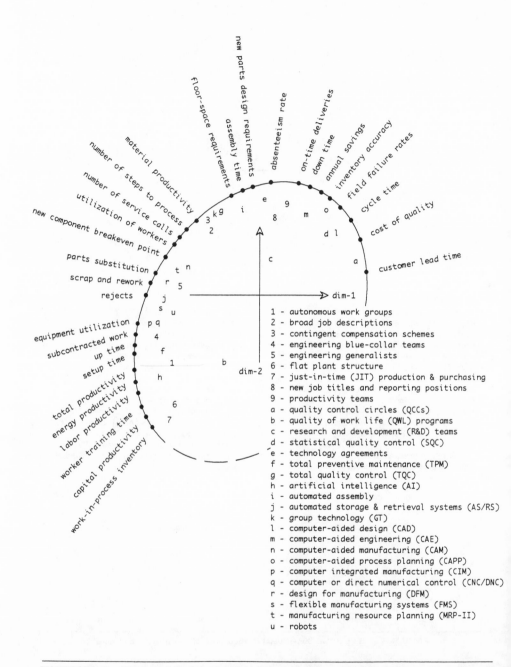

FIGURE 12.2 Two-Dimensional Configuration Linking Production Innovations with Performance Improvements

vations. Therefore, the dimensions in Figure 12.2 are not identical with those in Figure 12.1.

More important in Figure 12.2 is the smooth contour connecting the thirty performance improvements. Running clockwise from the lower-left to the upper-right corner of the figure, this smooth contour captures the transition from improvements concerning a company internal facets of production to improvements immediately transparent to, or concerning, its customers. For example, improvements in work-in-process inventory (WIP), capital productivity, and worker training time affect a company production performance directly, but constitute internal facets of production performance not immediately transparent to its customers. Conversely, customer lead time, cost of quality, cycle time, and field failure rates involve the company customers directly. Given that approximately 75 percent of the total cost of quality in the United States is a consequence of internal and external failures (Deming, 1985; Feigenbaum, 1980), production managers correctly place cost of quality among the facets of performance improvements closest to a company customers.

Also important in Figure 12.2 is the average proximity among production innovations and performance improvements. The smaller the average distance of a particular performance improvement from a set of production innovations, the more likely production managers are to associate that set with the particular performance improvement. Conversely, the larger the average distance of a particular performance improvement from a set of production innovations, the less likely production managers are to associate that set with the particular performance improvement.

For example, the small average distance between equipment utilization and the set of computer-related innovations—such as computer-integrated manufacturing (p), computer or direct numerical control (q), flexible manufacturing systems (s), and robots (u)—shows that production managers are likely to associate this set of innovations with improvements in equipment utilization. Conversely, the large distance between quality control circles (a) and work-in-process inventory (WIP) shows that production managers are not likely to associate QCCs with improvements in WIP inventory. Production managers are more likely to associate JIT production and purchasing (7) with WIP inventory reductions.

Validation

Given the well-known rotational and centering indeterminacy of two-way multidimensional unfolding, canonical correlation had to validate the stability of the MDU solution for performance improvements and production innovations in $T = 2$. The two-dimensional solution for twenty-nine of the thirty performance improvements, one of them randomly selected as a hold-out case, produced the following statistics: Stress = 0.216; variance-accounted-for RSQ = 0.956. The approximate configuration matching procedure involves canonical correlation analysis performed on each pair of two dimensions. The first pair includes dim-1 of the MDU solution for thirty performance improvements and dim-1 of the MDU solution for twenty-nine performance improvements. The second pair includes dim-2 of the MDU solution for thirty performance improvements and dim-2 of the MDU solution for twenty-nine performance improvements. The two canonical correlations for each pair configuration were 0.923 and 0.861, respectively. These canonical correlations show that these two sets of dimensions can be rotated to an almost perfect match, thereby suggesting that the MDU solution of Figure 12.2 is objectively valid and a stable one.

DISCUSSION AND CONCLUSION

This exploratory study is among a few that incorporate administrative innovation, technical innovation, production performance, and their relationships. To examine production manager perceptions of these relationships, the study combined the administrative and technical perspectives of organizational innovation. Yet the study is not free of limitations. First, both the multidimensional scaling and the unfolding solutions are static. Both the pertinent production innovations and the manufacturing performance improvements change over time. This leads to the second limitation: not all production managers of U.S. manufacturing plants are represented in the sample. If their entire population or a larger portion of it had been sampled, different relationships might have been derived. Lastly, the derived two-dimensional space depends on the study's sample. Accordingly, care must be taken in generalizing the results of this study to the economy's manufacturing sector.

Despite their limitations, the multidimensional scaling and multidimensional unfolding solutions produced results that can provide a base for better understanding of the relationships underlying the synergistic effects of synchronous production innovation on manufacturing performance improvements. The maps of Figure 12.1 and Figure 12.2 reveal production manager perceptions of administrative and technical innovations, and of their effects on manufacturing performance improvements. It is desirable to transform these perceptions into a low-dimensional space to visualize how they may affect adoption choices of administrative and technical innovations. However, are the study's transformations reasonable?

Assuredly, the ranking of production innovations attained in their MDS solution along dim-1 of Figure 12.1 is congruent with the existing dichotomy between the administrative and technical perspectives of organizational innovation (Damanpour, 1991; Ettlie, 1986; Hage, 1986; Hull & Hage, 1982; Kimberly & Evanisko, 1981; Landau, 1982; Solberg et al., 1985; Tornatsky et al., 1983). Also straightforward in Figure 12.2 is the smooth contour representing the transition from internal to external facets of performance improvements. Indeed, customers may be immediately concerned with delivery lead time, cycle time, and field failure rates, but less interested in worker training time, capital productivity, and WIP inventory.

It is reasonable, for example, that production managers expect quality of work life programs (b) to cause internal or worker-related performance improvements, and R&D teams (c) to cause performance improvements immediately concerning customers. Similarly, it makes perfect sense for total preventive maintenance (f) to improve production setup and up time simultaneously, and for statistical quality control (d) to reduce both field failure rates and cost of quality.

In Figure 12.2, the distances among JIT production and purchasing (7) and WIP inventory improvements, design for manufacturing (r) and parts substitution, and technology agreements (e) and new parts design requirements show how administrative along with technical innovations can improve performance independently. However, the coordinates of administrative innovations in Figure 12.2 are interspersed within the coordinates of technical innovations, and vise versa. This coordinate interspersion supports the necessity of adopting administrative and technical innovations simultaneously. Performance improvements may be negligible if companies emphasize either administrative or technical innovations.

For example, the interspersed coordinates of autonomous work groups (1), engineering blue-collar teams (4), total preventive maintenance (f) and artificial intelligence (h) suggest that these production innovations may have synergistic effects on total productivity. Similarly, the interspersed coordinates of broad job descriptions (2), contingent compensation schemes (3), total quality control (g), automated assembly (i), and group technology (k) suggest possible synergistic effects of these administrative and technical innovations on assembly time, floor-space requirements, material productivity, and number of steps to process. Also supportive of the synchronous production innovation and synergistic effects arguments are the interspersed coordinates in Figure 12.2 of productivity teams (9), statistical quality control (d), computer-aided design (l), computer-aided engineering (m) and computer-aided process planning (o), positioned next to on-time deliveries, down time, annual savings, inventory accuracy, field failure rates, and cycle time.

Overall, production manager proximity perceptions support Ettlie's (1988) position on the synergistic effects of congruous administrative and technical innovations, which can produce substantial improvements through small changes in administrative and technical systems. This intriguing result implies that a high potential for production improvements lies in the congruent interaction of administrative and technical innovations, rather than only within a specific administrative or technical innovation. Without synchronous innovation, performance improvements may be negligible. Neither can a company improve its performance significantly through emphasis only on either administrative or technical innovations.

In terms of production practice, a systemic perspective should enable companies to learn from the synchronous adoption of administrative and technical innovations. Yet it is crucial first to understand how organizational components interact with administrative and technical innovations, and subsequently to predict how a company's complex system might respond in its entirety as sacred past practices change.

Proponents of both the administrative and the technical perspectives treat production as a segmented division, with little awareness of how production innovations affect other departments or divisions of an organization. Accordingly, when managers push for change in one direction, they often end up with a totally different result than the one intended. When a production process or an employee involvement pattern changes, the structure of the entire company may shift. For example, JIT production and purchasing requires different accounting practices and changes customer-supplier relations (Monden, 1989). Our data show the close proximity between JIT production and purchasing and flat plant structure, thereby suggesting that, to understand the effects of production innovation on performance, production managers and researchers must scrutinize the effects of administrative innovation when predicting the effects of technical innovation, and vice versa.

In addition to their practical relevance, production manager perceptions of the relationships underlying administrative innovation, technical innovation, and manufacturing performance improvements are relevant to theory building and research. The study's results could guide future research toward the generation and use of a multivariate index of synchronous production innovation, which should combine the conceptually distinct but empirically related perspectives of administrative and technical innovation.

The specific effects of administrative and technical innovations on performance improvements may vary, depending on the particular industry in which a company competes (Bourgeois & Eisenhardt, 1988). Companies may function well with various degrees or forms of synchronous production innovation, along several performance dimensions. There is no indication in the data of a general form that synchronous innovation should cut across all companies and industries. In fact, there is little theoretical support for a standard model when researchers use organizational innovations to predict performance (Collins et al., 1988; Hull & Hage, 1982). The MDS-MDU procedures cannot deal with simultaneous adoption in real time; that should be the topic of a future study. Yet this study's data highlight the importance of integrating administrative and technical perspectives in models of production innovation.

Another implication for future research is the need for more longitudinal, fine-grained studies on the connections among administrative innovation, technical innovation, and performance improvement. It might be useful to identify and examine processes that facilitate the synchronous introduction of administrative and technical innovations in production. Future studies should identify effective adoption patterns over unstructured processes, test the advantages of planned adoption over incremental innovation, and thereby isolate the arbitrary or chance coincidence of effects. Production researchers should identify which adoption patterns work best over time, and in what organizational settings.

Also, future studies should reassess the relative effects of the administrative and technical innovations on performance improvements using a multivariate index of manufacturing performance. Lastly, future research should move toward a confirmatory, as opposed to this study's exploratory, mode of analysis. Confirming the effects of administrative innovations interspersed within technical innovations, and vice versa, should make a good start.

In conclusion, this preliminary attempt to conceptualize and test the effects of synchronous innovation on manufacturing performance improvements produced results relevant to both research and practice. The study supports the necessity of adopting a fine-grained approach to production innovation research and practice. To understand the synergistic effects of synchronous production innovation on manufacturing performance improvements, production managers and researchers should scrutinize the effects of administrative innovation when predicting the effects of technical innovation, and vice versa. Future studies addressing production innovation in specific organizational settings should acknowledge both the integrative nature of human systems, and the interdependence of administrative and technical innovations. Learning to manage the simultaneous adoption of administrative and technical innovations in manufacturing may significantly improve our national competitiveness and balance of trade.

REFERENCES

Abernathy, J. M., and P. Townsend. "Technology, Productivity, and Process Change." *Technological Forecasting and Social Change* 7 (1975): 379-96.

Abernathy, J. M., and K. Wayne. "Limits of the Learning Curve." *Harvard Business Review* 52 (2) (1974): 109-19.

Bourgeois, L. J., and K. M. Eisenhardt. "Strategic Decision Processes in High-Velocity Environments: Four Cases in the Micro-Computer Industry." *Management Science* 34 (1988): 816-35.

Clark, K., and T. Fujimoto. "Overlapping Problem-Solving in Product Development." Working paper, Harvard Business School, 1987.

Cohen, S. S., and J. Zysman. *Manufacturing Matters: The Myth of the Post-Industrial Economy.* New York: Basic Books, 1987.

———. "Manufacturing Innovation and American Industrial Competitiveness." *Science* 239 (March 1988): 1110-15.

Collins, P. D., J. Hage, and F. M. Hull. "Organizational and Technological Predictors of Change in Automaticity." *Academy of Management Journal* 31 (3) (1988): 512-43.

Daft, R. L. "A Dual-Core Model of Organizational Innovation." *Academy of Management Journal* 21 (2) (1978): 193-210.

Damanpour, F. "Organizational Innovation: A Meta-Analysis of Effects of Determinants and Moderators." *Academy of Management Journal* 34 (3) (1991): 555-90.

Davison, M. L. *Multidimensional Scaling.* New York: John Wiley, 1983.

Deming, E. W. *Quality, Productivity and Competitive Position.* Boston: MIT Press, 1985.

Drucker, P. F. *The New Realities.* New York: Harper & Row, 1989.

Dutton, J. M., and A. Thomas. "Treating Process Functions as a Managerial Opportunity." *Academy of Management Review* 9 (1984): 235-47.

Ettlie, J. E. "Manufacturing Technology Policy and Deployment of Processing Innovations." In *Flexible Manufacturing Systems,* edited by K. Stecke & R. Suri. New York: Elsevier, 1986.

————. *Taking Charge of Manufacturing.* San Francisco: Jossey-Bass, 1988.

Ettlie, J. E., and A. H. Rubenstein. "Social Learning Theory and the Implementation of Production Innovation." *Decision Sciences* 11 (4) (1980): 648-68.

Feigenbaum, A. V. "USA's Hidden Plant." *Quality Progress* 13 (6) (1980): 23-28.

Fennell, M. L. "Synergy, Influence, and Information in the Adoption of Administrative Innovations." *Academy of Management Journal* 27 (1) (1984): 113-29.

Gaedeke, R. M., and D. H. Tootelian. "The Fortune 500 List: An Endangered Species for Academic Research." *Journal of Business Research* 4 (1976): 283-88.

Georgantzas, N. C. "Learning to Manage the Deployment of Integrated Manufacturing Technology." *Proceedings of the Annual Midwest Decision Sciences Institute* (May 2-4, 1988), Louisville, KY: pp. 192-94.

Georgantzas, N. C., and H. J. Shapiro. "Viable Structural Forms of Synchronous Production Innovation." Working paper, New York: Fordham University at Lincoln Center, 1991.

Gerwin, D. "A Theory of Innovation Processes for Computer-Aided Manufacturing Technology." *IEEE Transactions on Engineering Management* 35 (2) (1988): 90-100.

Hage, J. "Responding to Technological and Competitive Change: Organization and Industry Factors." In *Managing Technological Innovation,* edited by D.D. Davis & Associates. San Francisco: Jossey-Bass, 1986, pp. 44-71.

Hayden, G. "IBM: CIM 18 Percent of GNP, Big Blue Wants a Share." *Automation News,* November 10, 1986, p. 38.

Hayes, R. H., and W. J. Abernathy. "Managing Our Way to Economic Decline." *Harvard Business Review* 58 (4) (1980): 67-77.

Hayes, R. H., and S. C. Wheelwright. *Restoring Our Competitive Edge: Competing Through Manufacturing.* New York: John Wiley, 1984.

Hessel, M. P. "On the Transformation of American Management: Towards System Integration." *Proceedings of the Annual Decision Sciences Meeting* Honolulu, Hawaii (1986): 113-15.

Hirsch, P. M., Friedman, R., and M. P. Koza. "Collaboration or Paradigm Shift? Caveat Emptor and the Risk of Romance with Economic Models for Strategy and Policy Research." *Organization Science* 1 (1) (1990): 87-97.

Hull, F., and J. Hage. "Organizing for Innovation: Beyond Burns and Stalker's Organic Type." *Sociology* 16 (1982): 546-77.

Jaikumar, M. "Post-Industrial Manufacturing." *Harvard Business Review* 64 (1986): 67-77.

Kimberly, J. R. "Managerial Innovation." In *Handbook of Organizational Design,* edited by W. Starbuck and P. Nystrom. New York: Oxford University Press, 1981, pp. 84-104.

Kimberly, J. R., and M. J. Evanisko. "Organizational Innovation: The Influence of Individual, Organizational, and Contextual Factors on Hospital Adoption of Technical and Administrative Innovations." *Academy of Management Journal* 24 (4) (1981): 689-713.

Kochan, T. A. "Adaptability of the U.S. Industrial Relations System." *Science* 240 (April 15, 1988): 287-92.

Kruskal, J. B. "Non-metric Multi-dimensional Scaling." *Psychometrica* 29 (1964): 115-29.

Landau, R. "The Innovative Milieu." In *Managing Innovation: The Social Dimensions of Creativity, Invention and Technology*, edited by S. B. Lundstedt and E. W. Colglazier. New York: Pergamon Press, 1982, pp. 53-92.

Miller, G. A. "The Magical Number Seven plus or Minus Two: Some Limits on Our Capacity for Processing Information." *Psychological Review* 63 (2) (1956): 81-97.

Monden, Y. "Cost Accounting and Control in the Just-in-Time Production Systems: The Daihatsu Kogyo Experience." In *Japanese Management Accounting—A World Class Approach to Profit Management,* edited by Y. Monden and M. Sakurai. Cambridge, MA: Productivity Press, 1989, pp. 35-48.

Nunnally, J. C. *Psychometric Theory.* New York: McGraw-Hill, 1978.

Perrow, C. "A Framework for the Comparative Analysis of Organizations." *American Sociological Review* 32 (1967): 194-208.

Saaty, T. L. "A Scaling Method for Priorities in Hierarchical Structures." *Journal of Mathematical Psychology* 15 (3) (1977): 234-81.

Sahal, D. *Patterns of Technological Innovation.* Reading, MA: Addison-Wesley, 1981.

Schiffman, S. S., Raynolds, M. L., and F. W. Young. *Introduction to Multi-dimensional Scaling.* New York: Academic Press, 1981.

Schonberger, R. J. *World Class Manufacturing.* New York: The Free Press, 1986.

Scott, W. R. *Organizations: Rational, Natural and Open Systems,* 2nd Edition. Englewood Cliffs, NJ: Prentice-Hall, 1987.

Shapiro, H. J., and T. Cosenza. *Reviving Industry in America.* Cambridge, MA: Ballinger, 1987.

Shepard, R. N. "The Analysis of Proximities: Multi-dimensional Scaling with an Unknown Distance Function." *Psychometrica* 27 (1962): 125-40.

Solberg, J. J., D. C. Anderson, M. M. Barash, and R. P. Paul. *Factories of the Future: Defining the Target.* West Lafayette, IN: Computer Integrated Design Manufacturing and Automation Center, Purdue University, 1985.

Tornatsky, L. D., et al. *The Process of Technical Innovation: Reviewing the Literature.* Washington, DC: National Science Foundation, 1983.

Utterback, J. M. "The Process of Technological Innovation within the Company." *Academy of Management Journal* 14 (1971): 75-88.

Utterback, J. M., and W. J. Abernathy. "A Dynamic Model of Process and Product Innovation." *OMEGA* 6 (1975): 639-56.

Woodward, J. *Industrial Organization: Theory and Practice.* London: Oxford University Press, 1965.

Zeleny, M. "Management Support Systems: Towards Integrated Knowledge Management." *Human Systems Management* 7 (1) (1987): 59-70.

―――. "Knowledge as Capital: Integrated Quality Management." *Prometheus* 9 (1) (1991): 93-101.

Chapter 13

Strategic Information System Planning in the Health Care Industry—A Case Study

Michael J. Corrigan and Chu-hua Kuei

Industries, and particularly those in manufacturing, have seen the integration of information systems for decades (Jones, 1989). Systems in these industries have automated the assembly processes, easily allowing the introduction and improvement of inventory handling, most notably the use of JIT, and lent true meaning to decision support systems (DSS) and executive information systems (EIS).

Hospitals, on the other hand, as a rule, have led an entirely different life until very recently. The advent of prospective payment—(that is, the diagnostic related groups (DRG) system)—has forced them to adopt an entirely different strategy, one that would position them to concentrate on containing costs, based on what was happening in both their external and internal environments. Drucker (1988) also indicated that the hospital is a typical example of an information-based organization, composed largely of specialists who direct or discipline their own performance through organized feedback from colleagues, customers, and headquarters. In other words, all specialists take individual responsibility while working toward a collective goal. To do this they must "take information responsibility"—be concerned with the purposeful use of information as a resource (Silk, 1991). Thus, information as a commodity, and an information system or information technology (IS/IT) as an investment, will be more important and will require a strategic response by management (Silk, 1991).

In this type of information-based organization, other than that patients walk out the door physically better than when they arrive, the only tangible product delivered by a hospital is the information generated in the process of making patients well. For example, information must be provided as fast and as accurately as possible to the correct location so the physician can treat the patient, and timely and accurate financial reports can be delivered to administration, so that the decisions and forecasting can be done that affect the financial health of the institution.

Recently, top-level managers in many organizations have increasingly been directing their attention toward the use of information systems for strategic purposes (Frenzel, 1992). There appear to be five major reasons for this: (1) transaction processing has matured, (2) information technology budgets continue to rise, (3) information technology offers great opportunity for innovation, (4) the technology is pervasive, and (5) precedents are becoming widespread (Frenzel, 1992). For these reasons, we feel there is a need for hospitals also to take a strategic approach to using information technology for competitive advantage.

In this chapter, we present as our example a major hospital in New Jersey, which is ahead of its time on managing information systems and technology. This institution already has in place an information network capable of meeting all the information needs listed earlier. It may not have fulfilled all the requirements just yet, but it certainly has positioned itself as a leader among health care providers.

We try to answer three strategic questions: (1) Where are we now (i.e., internal and external environment analysis)? (2) Where do we want to be (i.e., organization vision)? and (3) How will we get there (i.e., competitive strategy and IS/IT strategy)? Thus, we first examine the internal environment, focusing on the MIS evolution and organizational structure at Monmouth Medical Center. Second, we scan the external environment, focusing on competition in the health care industry. Third, we discuss organizational vision, competitive strategy, and IS/IT, focusing on creating and maintaining a competitive advantage.

THE EVOLUTION OF MIS AT MONMOUTH MEDICAL CENTER

Monmouth Medical Center, located in Long Branch, New Jersey, is a 526-bed teaching hospital affiliated with the University of Pennsylvania and Hahnemann medical schools in Philadelphia. More than 120 graduate physicians enroll annually in nine fully accredited residency programs. Monmouth Medical also serves as a major residency source for the University of Medicine and Dentistry of New Jersey School of Dentistry.

According to the annual report of Monmouth Medical Center, there were 20,398 total admissions in 1990, resulting in:
- 9,852,000 lab procedures
- 71,075 radiology procedures
- 9,280 major surgical cases

There were 256,782 total outpatient services provided:
- 114,985 visits to over 50 specialized clinics
- 94,554 private physician referrals
- 38,739 emergency room visits

Not the largest nor the busiest hospital in the nation to be sure, but Monmouth still requires that information generated from these services be delivered as expeditiously as possible. How does Monmouth Medical ensure this service? It began positioning itself in the early 1960s without realizing it.

Monmouth Medical was one of three New Jersey hospitals to utilize computers to any degree in its routine business functions. In 1965, the hospital purchased an IBM Model 360 mainframe for the sole purpose of batch processing the billing functions of the institution. Compared to today's standards, this model was truly a pterodactyl. In 1967-1968, the first step toward true implement of a network was launched. At that time, a programmer was hired to develop an order entry application to also run on the 360. This very rudimentary system allowed nursing stations to request laboratory tests, pharmacy orders, and radiology procedures directly from those departments.

In 1969, a first major strategic decision was made by the hospital. Digital Equipment Corporation (DEC) had entered the mainframe market, positioning itself directly against the giant, IBM. Digital's own industry competitive analysis told it that the company's strength was in integrating hardware and software via LAN technology. Providing the connectivity needed for true integration was an opportunity it could take advantage of. The company's weakness was having to go up against IBM with a new, and not fully proven, product. Based on price, Digital's performance to date, its commitment to providing the service needed, and the relative inability of IBM to guarantee a "connective" product, Monmouth Medical signed a contract with Digital to convert the existing system to DEC protocol, utilizing DEC hardware and LAN software—a marriage which has matured and grown through the years.

The use of DEC hardware and LAN capabilities expanded when, in 1970, the hospital hired a systems analyst to develop the first mainframe laboratory information system (LIS) in New Jersey. The applications were written completely in house and supported on a DEC model PDP 11/45. The overall planning, trial runs, checking for effects (including refinements and reworks), and final implementation took three years. This first attempt at a large-scale—in those days—LAN in a hospital followed almost exactly the system development life cycle (SDLC) approach, and it has remained the method for implementing all technology changes to date.

In 1978, the order entry system first designed to run on the IBM 360 was rewritten and implemented on a series of DEC PDP 11/70s. In 1984 and 1985, the 11/70s were upgraded, owing to a performance decision, to four PDP 11/84s, which are still used to support the order entry system. Also, a limited inventory management system was designed and implemented during this period. After installation of the 11/70s, the only application running on the original IBM 360 was a limited financial package, consisting only of accounts receivable, accounts payable, the general ledger, and billing cycle.

In 1988 and 1989, the hospital undertook the next major step in developing its Information System: implementation of a new lab system, a new patient management system (including medical records), and an expanded financial package. The technology literally took a light-year jump with placement of these applications; VAX clustering is used in both mainframe locations, while volume shadowing is used as a facet of "disaster planning." Perhaps the greatest advantage was just being realized: the true "transparency" of real, total connectivity (VAX clustering, and shadowing are discussed more fully in the section on Technical Perspective). At this time, the hospital severed all remaining ties with IBM by removing the 360. Introduction of the new financial package, which was integrated with the new patient management database, enabled the administration to make its first use of a true decision support system (DSS) in its budgeting and forecasting endeavors (further discussed in the Management Perspective section).

What will be happening in 1991 and throughout the 1990s? The hospital is implementing a JIT materials management system in December 1991—one of the first attempts at such a system in a hospital in New Jersey. In 1992, a separate yet integrated PC LAN will be completed, involving approximately 220 compatibles located at each nursing station and administrative office, and at remote locations, providing a user-friendly menu system for application of the user's choice. After 1992, the sky is apparently the limit: DEC's Relational Database system utilizing reduced instruction set commands (RISC) technology, a true executive information system (EIS) with real-time data retrieval, use of fiber distributed data interface (FDDI), or fiber optics, bedside computing, and remote reporting. As the character in the commercial says, "Master the possibilities!"

THE ORGANIZATIONAL STRUCTURE

How did Monmouth Medical manage the growth in both technology and support necessary to maintain the systems? Up to about 1978, the organizational chart expanded in small steps, with both main areas reporting to the COO (see Figure 13.1). There were

Figure 13.1

" The Formative Years "

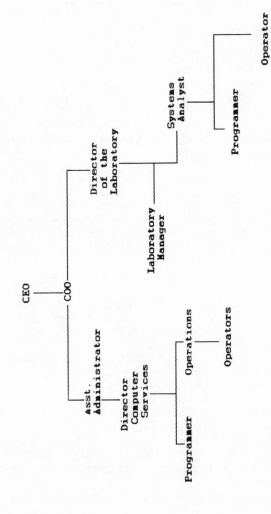

limited programming and analysis resources, mostly because of the newness of the technology involved, and the inability of a hospital to pay data processing wages competitive with other industries. The bulk of personnel devoted to the actual data processing was concentrated in operations, with redundancy in both areas; each mainframe had its own set of operators because of different processing needs. By utilizing Mintzberg's Organizations Configurations model (Mintzberg & Quinn, 1991), we can see that the hospital exhibited a relatively small strategic apex and middle line, a small technostructure, a smaller support staff, and a relatively large operating core (see Figure 13.2).

Since 1978, the structure has undergone an amazing metamorphosis, yet it was a natural one considering the expansive use of technology and systems. There are still two main divisions, but each with expanded resources in the areas of analysis and support (see Figure 13.3). The CIO, director of computer services, and chairman of pathology concern themselves solely with strategic issues and coordination of activities from an MIS view. There are expanded analysis and programming resources, and a much larger operating core, yet the redundancy of data processing operators in the two areas was eliminated when standardized hardware was implemented (e.g., VAX clustering). If Mintzberg's Organizations Configurations model were to be drawn now, it would look like that in Figure 13.4. The apex has expanded slightly, as has the middle line. There is a much larger technostructure, the support area has exploded (e.g., the expansion of the network allowed departments like Personnel, Payroll, Public Relations, and Management Services to access data unavailable to them previously), and the operating core has expanded in line with demands on the expanded systems.

Drucker (1988), among others, points out the tendency for levels of middle management to decrease and for an organization to become flatter in the information-based orientation. We have no doubt that the structure will change again as MIS at Monmouth Medical progresses through the 1990s, and into the twenty-first century. How much will change, and what Mintzberg's chart would look like, depends on how well Monmouth utilizes the available technology and resources, preparing itself to meet competitive forces as they change.

A HEALTH CARE INDUSTRY COMPETITIVE ANALYSIS

Hospitals never had to "compete" with each other, as have other industries, until recent years. Introduction of reimbursement systems (i.e., prospective payment systems) has refocused many hospitals' attentions on cost containment. Now hospitals must rethink and utilize some basic marketing strategies, in order to survive; they must attract "customers" to their services rather than "that other institution" down the road. They must differentiate themselves somehow.

There are three ways in which Monmouth finds itself in competition with other area hospitals:

1. Hospitals within the same geographic area compete for the same patient population.
2. Within this same geographic area, many physicians are on the same staff at the same hospitals.
3. There are many like services at each hospital.

The MIS Organizational Matrix at Monmouth

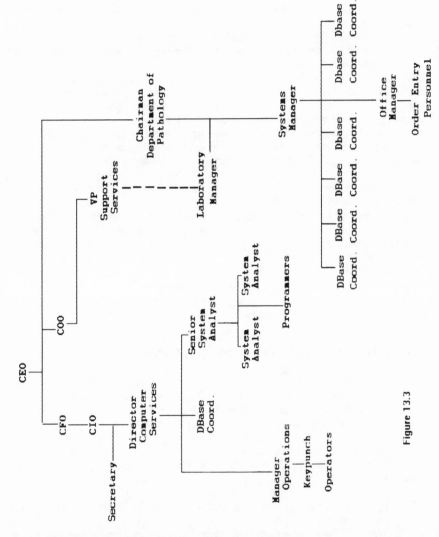

Figure 13.3

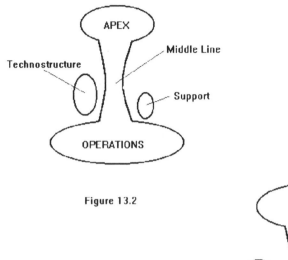

Figure 13.2

APEX

Middle Line

Technostructure

Support

OPERATIONS

APEX

Middle Line

TECHNO-
STRUCTURE

SUPPORT

OPERATIONS

Figure 13.4

Hospitals do not term their operating at a profit as a "profit." Any monies above operating expenses are reallocated to capital needed to maintain technology, expand facilities, pay salary and wages and so on. The strategic and capable use of this capital reinvestment can mean that a patient or a physician chooses to use a particular hospital over another because of a technological or service advantage.

Figure 13.5 illustrates Monmouth's (or any other hospital's) situation if Porter's Five Competitive Forces model is adapted to the industry (Porter & Millar, 1985). In Monmouth's case, there are seven competitors within its two-county service area, two of which share the same physician and patient population. There is a threat of substitution for some services: from physician office laboratories, reference laboratories, and "immediate" or STAT medical services (which strategically locate in shopping malls).

To further put this in perspective and formulate a competitive strategy, we apply the concept of a value chain (Porter & Millar, 1985). The primary activities of value chain (i.e., inbound logistics, operations, outbound logistics, marketing and sales, and service) are all fundamental to a hospital, just as any other industry. Where Monmouth has positioned itself for differentiation is in support activities such as human resource management (HRM), technology development, and procurement. For example, Monmouth Medical has made an effort to recruit and retain the best personnel (e.g., most experienced and innovative) in the hospital industry. It has also developed two key links: Digital Equipment Corporation has become the sole supplier of maintenance and most hardware for the information technology, and the new materials management system has enabled direct coordination between suppliers and the hospital for materials and services.

Today, Monmouth Medical has fully positioned itself for a solid differentiation strategy. It:

1. Provides better quality service for patients and physicians.
2. Has helped suppliers improve their services through a rapid dealer network.
3. Has toughened competition by highlighting Monmouth's unique features.
4. Has unique and well-differentiated services to complicate "new entrant decisions."
5. Provides many of the features that substitutes may offer in the future.

Hospitals that are most successful in following this strategy are those that can use IS/IT to assist in the delivery of services perceived as unique or special. Monmouth Medical Center is at the front of the pack.

CREATING AND MAINTAINING THE COMPETITIVE ADVANTAGE

As just stated, hospitals that have positioned themselves with strong IS/IT services have an advantage in differentiating themselves. Monmouth Medical, with its decision to implement an Ethernet-based LAN in 1969-1970, did that. Technologically, the hardware and software is state of the art, representing no small part of the annual capital and operating budgets. From a management perspective, availability of data previously not readily accessible lends crucial support to business decisions. We will now further explore both aspects.

Technological Perspective

Monmouth's total IS/IT services are currently divided into two main areas:

Perspective: Five Competitive Forces in
Healthcare

Figure 13.5

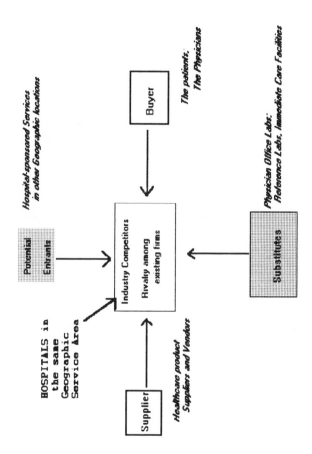

hospital information systems (HIS) and laboratory information systems (LIS), with separate computer rooms for each. The hardware is physically separated because, historically, each area uses distinctly different applications tailored to the department's specific needs, which is third-party vendor supported. Each area:

•Combined, supports over 500 terminals and 350 printers in the total network, yet recent measurements show only between 5 percent and 10 percent of capacity is being used.

•Uses clustering and disk shadowing as a contingency against down time. Minimal down time planning is in place, utilizing the clustering and shadowing capabilities in a DEC VAX system.

Clustering utilizes a piece of hardware called a STAR Coupler into which all CPUs and disk controllers (i.e., HSCs) are cabled. This produces a "transparency" effect: should one CPU or HSC fail, all processing automatically faults over to an available member of the cluster. Shadowing is a disk I/O software application that makes the system think two distinct disk drives are actually one, so that what is written to one is automatically written to the other. Should one drive fail, the system faults over to the remaining member of the shadow set.

All disk drives are dual-ported—that is, each drive is cabled to each HSC—to provide redundancy. All input stations (CRTs, bar code readers, lab instruments) are cabled using twisted pair, which is relatively inexpensive, flexible, and easy to connect. Each connection is made into an intermediate device called a terminal server, and each distinct work area's devices are spread out over several servers so that if a server should fail, the entire work area is not left in a state of non function. And finally, each terminal server is connected directly to the backbone (Ethernet cable) through a network device called a Delni.

Since there are two distinct service areas, and therefore two distinct Ethernet LANs, they are connected via a LAN bridge. Because the entire network is DEC hardware, utilizing Digital's DECnet protocol, there are no protocol conversion boxes necessary anywhere on the network, greatly simplifying maintenance and network support concerns. This would not have been the case if the hospital still ran an IBM network as well; then, a system network architecture (SNA) gateway protocol converter would have had to been added to the mixture. Figure 13.6 shows a simplified version of the laboratory LAN at Monmouth Medical two years ago. Figure 13.7 shows it as it existed after the addition of personal computers. And Figure 13.8 illustrates the complexity of the hospital information systems (HIS) LAN as it exists today.

How is Monmouth expecting to utilize technological advances in hardware and software? The following are examples of what is available that will most likely be implemented within the next two years:

VAX to FAX Machines or to PCs. Currently available, this application will automatically send laboratory test reports, radiology reports, and so on via telephone lines directly to either a FAX machine in a physician's office or to a file on a PC, which the physician could then print at his or her leisure (see Figure 13.9). This could be controlled either as a batch process, with distributions printing at specified times of the day, or on a real-time basis if needed. Reference laboratories already make use of this concept by placing printers in hospital labs that serve as report devices from the remote lab.

Distributed Bedside Reporting. A pilot project has been underway to study the feasibility and capabilities of this function. Departments such as the lab or radiology would send results over the network directly to a database located on a PC-based file server at the nursing station. From there it would be routed directly to a smaller monitor located at the patient bedside, so that nurses and physicians would have access to real-

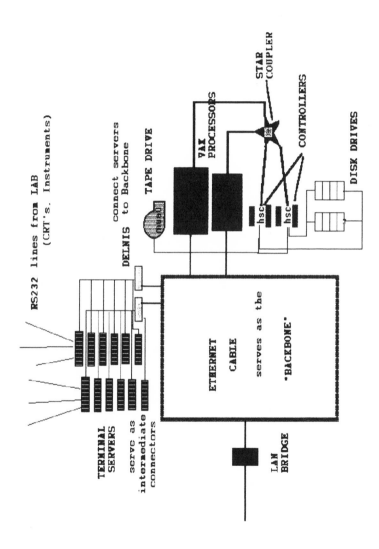

Figure 13.6
Ethernet Cable, Vax Processors, and STAR Coupler

The Network at Monmouth Medical Center for Pathology

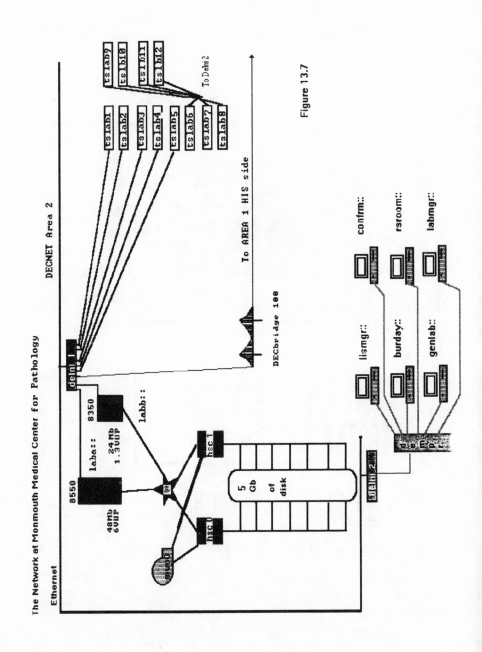

Figure 13.7

The Network at Monmouth Medical Center

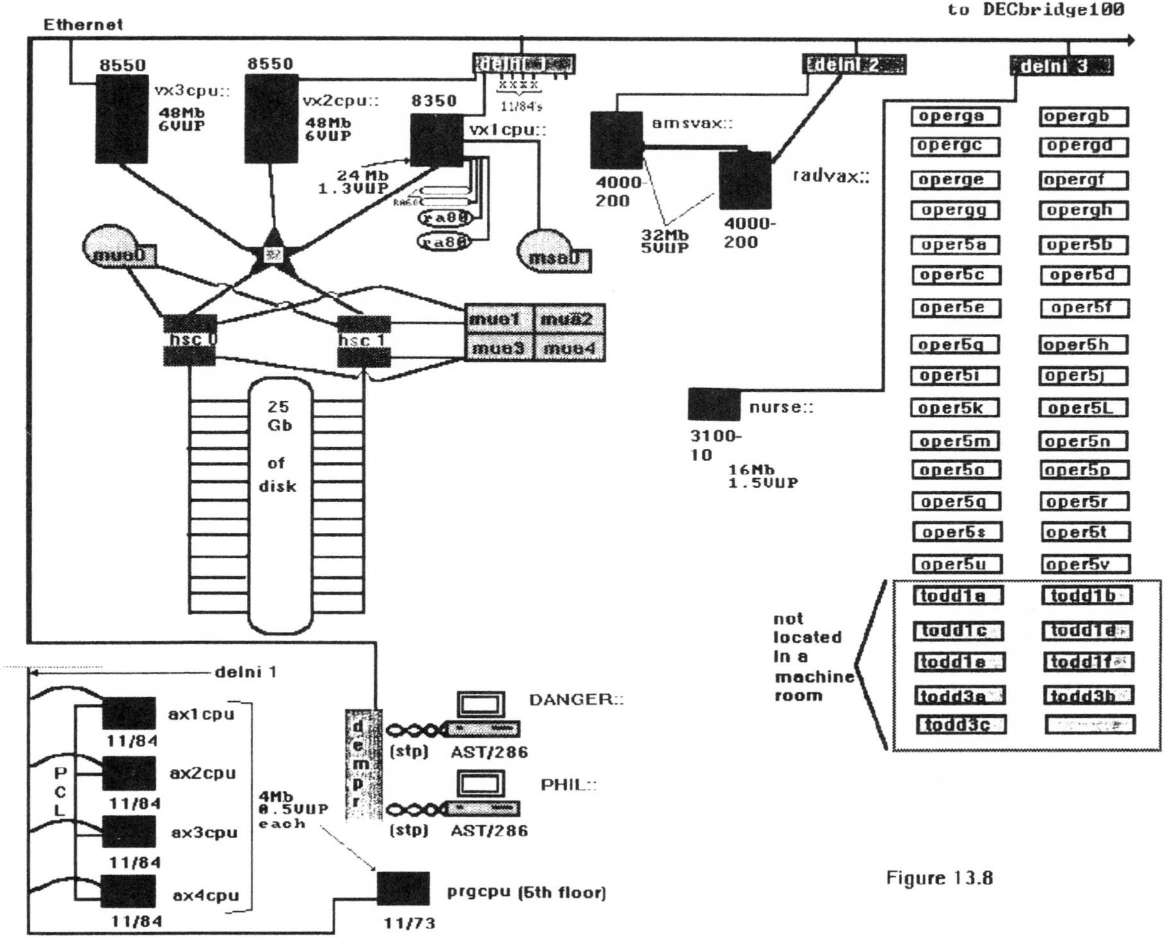

Figure 13.8

Figure 13.9

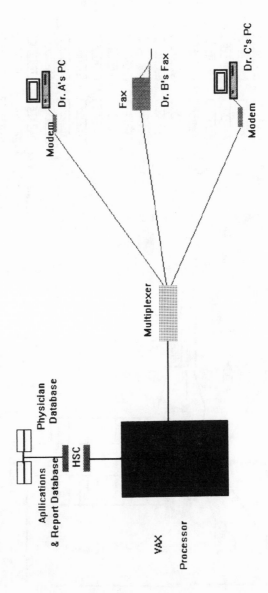

Integrating DIGITAL's VAX to Fax into Clinical Reporting

Figure 13.10

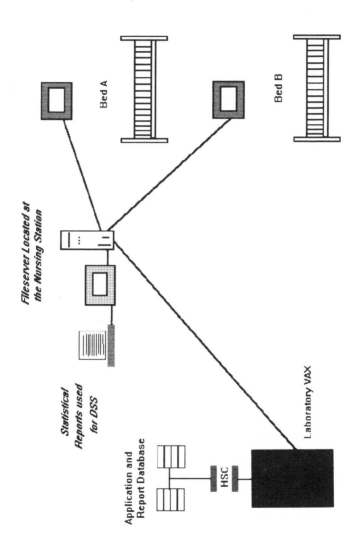

Bed A

Bed B

Fileserver Located at
the Nursing Station

Statistical
Reports used
for DSS

Application and
Report Database

HSC

Laboratory VAX

Distributed Bedside Reporting
via VAX - PC LAN

time data (see Figure 13.10). This would be most helpful in the critical care areas, where close monitoring is vital to patient care. A side benefit would be the ability to generate statistical reports directly from the database to provide decision support for therapy or longer term care.

Remote Clustering. Already a proven way to minimize down time within a given LAN area, remote clustering would enable true disaster planning. By upgrading the processors to support the "possibility," and connecting the areas remotely as a "cluster" via fiber distributed data interface (FDDI), which would enable enhanced transmission capabilities, each separate area would "think" it belonged with the other, so that if one entire area were to suffer some catastrophic event, the other side of the cluster would automatically continue the processing (see Figure 13.11). The cost of support and maintenance would be greatly reduced, while the level of LAN support would drastically increase.

Where will Monmouth go in the coming years? From a technology viewpoint, as far as is needed to have the soundest foundation to serve its customers' needs.

Management Perspective

As we stated earlier in this chapter, hospitals have been thrust into a different environment with the introduction of the prospective payment (i.e., diagnostic related groups, or DRG) system in 1983. Focus has shifted to decreasing costs in areas associated with inpatient care by trying to increase efficiency and productivity through any means possible, while trying to attract more customers for outpatient services, which do not fall under the DRG umbrella.

The prospective payment system sets reimbursement fees and schedules for expenses incurred by hospitals in caring for inpatient customers. Prior to 1983, hospitals could charge patients for actual expenses incurred for their care: hospital room and board; all lab, radiology, or electrocardiogram testing; all medications dispensed from the pharmacy; any rehabilitative physical therapy prescribed by the physician, and so on. You may have had the displeasure of seeing the enormous hospital bills resulting from these expenses. Pressure mounted from the public as the cost of health insurance started to skyrocket, especially during the high inflation in the mid- to late 1970s. The New Jersey legislature responded by formulating a standard method of charging a patient for his or her care—the diagnostic related group that the patient was treated for. Diseases, injuries, any conceivable ailment for which a patient may be treated were divided into over 400 groups, and the expenses for treating patients for these treatment groups were averaged, fixed to their appropriate DRG, and became the maximum amount a hospital could expect to be reimbursed, from either the insurance company or the patient directly. Irregardless of how long a patient had to stay in the hospital (and of course, the longer the stay, the greater the cost of care), hospital rates were fixed.

In theory, implementation of prospective payment should have greatly aided the cost of health care, and it did initially. But what happened was disastrous for many hospitals, causing the collapse and closure of several, forcing patients to seek treatment at hospitals perhaps not as close to their home, or to go to centers that specialized and therefore had higher reimbursement schedules. Hospitals found themselves in severe financial situations because reimbursement rates were based on average costs of several years earlier. For example, rates for 1983 were based on costs in 1978. Rates were not always adjusted accordingly, either. The reimbursement rates were always at least two

Figure 13.11

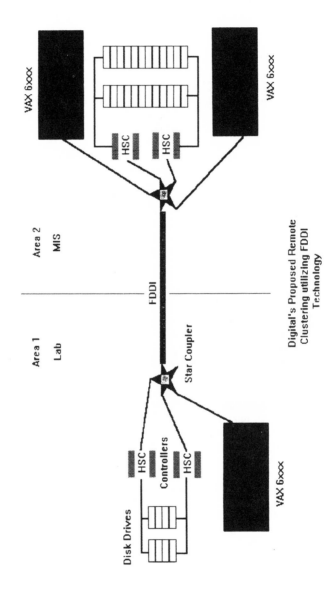

Digital's Proposed Remote
Clustering utilizing FDDI
Technology

years behind actual costs. Therefore, hospitals began turning to IS/IT to do what other industries have been doing for years:

1. Provide an "early warning signal" analysis, whether originating internally or externally.
2. Try to achieve efficiency and economy of scale through automation wherever possible, such as with routine clerical operations.
3. Provide managers with tools to make routine (i.e., structured) decisions.
4. Give top management the information to make strategic (i.e., unstructured) decisions.

The emphasis is still on quality patient care, but it has been refocused to be at a cost that would be nondetrimental to both the patient and the hospital. Hospitals with well-designed information systems have positioned themselves to meet this challenge, based on the following characteristics:

The System Must Focus a Manager's Attention on Critical Success Factors. Hospital administrators use the sophisticated information systems available today to retrieve valuable statistics from patient management applications. These applications can provide information on the case mix of a particular hospital and its population (i.e., patient and physician). Case mix statistics also tell administrators what the most frequent DRGs are associated with admissions and treatments, average length of stay for patients, associated costs by service and department, and so on. They then use this information to forecast expected reimbursement rates, and therefore what the hospital's capital and operating expenses are most likely to be. Knowing this information is critical to the survival of a hospital.

The System Must Present Information that is Accurate and of High Quality. With the connectivity associated with today's LAN technology, data even from disseminated databases can be pulled together to give the most accurate and up-to-date information available. A particular piece of information does not even have to reside locally—that is, within the walls of the hospital.

The System Must Provide the Necessary Information when it is Needed to Those Who Need it Most. A key concern of hospitals is keeping the length of stay as short as possible without compromising patient care. Laboratory information systems (LIS) offer a rapid means of providing vital results directly to the patient areas. In all lab systems, there is a results-reporting mechanism that routes data to the nursing station so that patient-care decisions can be made on a timely basis. Applications available in hospital financial packages can provide extremely timely and accurate exception reports for management to use in tracking costs of patient care. Materials management systems specifically designed for a hospital are beginning to utilize the JIT concept, so that inventory costs can be controlled as never before.

The System Must Process Raw Data so that it can be Presented in a Manner Useful to the Manager. The applications available for hospitals have become more specific to their needs and more user-friendly. If the particular system doesn't have some type of ad-hoc reporting capability included (which is infrequent nowadays), the raw data can almost always be extracted and downloaded into a popular spreadsheet package such as Lotus or Excel. Lotus has just released a version of 1-2-3 that can run on Digital's VAX systems, which would make it available to any user with just a CRT.

CONCLUSION

Monmouth Medical Center has indeed positioned itself for the challenge of surviving the 1990s and beyond. It has in place the technology to differentiate itself by (1) services provided when needed for the customer, whether he or she be patient or physician; and (2) information provided for management in a timely and accurate manner.

REFERENCES

Drucker, P. F. "The Coming of the New Organization." *Harvard Business Review* (66) (1) (January-February 1988): 45-53.

Frenzel, C. W. *Management of Information Technology.* Boston: Boyd & Fraser, 1992.

Jones, C. "Healthcare Information Systems Provide Strategic Business Planning." *Industrial Engineering* (21) (3) (March 1989): 23-25.

Mintzberg H., and J. B. Quinn. *The Strategy Process—Concepts, Contexts, Cases,* 2nd Edition. Englewood Cliffs, NJ: Prentice-Hall, 1991.

Porter, M. E., and V. E. Millar. "How Information Gives You Competitive Advantage." *Harvard Business Review* (63) (4) (July-August 1985): 149-60.

Silk, D. J. *Planning IT—Creating an Information Management Strategy.* Jordan Hill, Oxford: Butterworth-Heinemann, 1991.

Chapter 14

Scenario-Driven Technological Development Planning: A Process View·

Nicholas C. Georgantzas and William Acar

Technological innovations can improve human living conditions and create opportunities for cultural, sociopolitical, and economic progress. Desires for greater economic growth, more diversified employment opportunities, better societal infrastructure, and more equitable income distribution motivate technology transfer (Raines, 1987). Yet changes in technology do not always improve a nation's economic, sociopolitical, and cultural status. Vexing problems often arise in less-developed countries (LDCs) when there is fast and uneven industrialization. Poor countries—those with an annual per capita gross domestic product (GDP) of less than US$265—also have low productivity rates. Implicitly assumed is that the economies of poor countries have a marginal effect on the rich ones. Yet recent developments in international trade, commodity prices and the global environment, i.e., the greenhouse effect, render this assumption vulnerable (Two-Way Street, 1988).

One obstacle to technological development is inadequate planning for technology transfer. Generally, the location, market entry, and ownership patterns, and the intracompany link of multinational corporations (MNCs), foster technology transfer, typically welcomed by LDCs, yet a lack of foresight and adaptability may hinder the flow of information in two ways. One is the diffusion—the primary transmission of innovation from inventor to primary user (Utterback, 1974); the other is technology transfer—the use of innovation by a secondary user. There are more than 2,000 published studies on various aspects of technology (Rogers & Shoemaker, 1971), but technology development and transfer remain problematic in the social sciences (Sahal, 1981).

The planning processes LDCs and MNCs both use for technology development and transfer often lead to a paradoxical interplay between conservatism and radical change. Under the supposition that a paradox marks the beginning of an idea, this chapter presents a scenario-driven technological development planning framework. It also presents a comprehensive situation mapping (CSM) method, that can enhance organizational learning and facilitate negotiation between LDCs and MNCs, the principal agents in the technology transfer process. Such computed decision scenarios can sensitize managers and technology planners to the dynamic implications of technology transfer.

·A Fordham University Faculty of Business Research Grant partly supported this research.

The following section gives a brief account of the rapidly expanding technology development and transfer literature. Subsequently, the chapter presents the scenario-driven framework, which links CSM with the process of dialectical inquiry (DI), aimed at unearthing the critical assumptions and prominent cognitive biases underlying technology development and transfer decisions. Lastly, the chapter illustrates the use of CSM via Myrdal's (1957) "vicious circle" of technology development and transfer.

TECHNOLOGY DEVELOPMENT AND TRANSFER

Derakhshani (1983) defines *technology transfer* as the acquisition, development, and utilization of knowledge by a country other than its place of origin. This definition stems from the work of Schumpeter (1934) in economics, and Gilfillan (1952) and Ogburn (1922) in sociology. Both fields view innovation as an essentially autonomous phenomenon—an exogenous construct, yet central to socioeconomic development. LDCs rarely consider technological change within their national planning process (Technology Atlas Team, 1987c). Thus, with technology a given constant, it is impossible to assess the current technological capabilities of their economies.

Neither can industrial indicators answer the crucial question of how well a given or a desired macroeconomic structure fits national socioeconomic goals (Haustein & Maier, 1985). Technological development policies change direction depending on the priority given to a country's industrial policy objectives (Scholz, 1977). For example, the adoption of manufacturing automation in one country can increase profit through reduced wages, reduced processing time, and increased production flexibility. In a different country, with a different socioeconomic system, automation can close societal gaps and cut shortages of labor, energy, and raw material.

Goal Incompatibility

Differing priorities lead to goal incompatibility between MNCs and LDCs, causing technology transfer failures. MNCs transfer technology because they need a market presence in their rivals' home courts or profit sanctuaries (Kim & Mauborgne, 1988; Paul & Barbato, 1985; Prahalad & Doz, 1987). Yet what they transfer may not meet LDC needs or objectives, and may not use existing capabilities and resources (Doz & Prahalad, 1980; Komoda, 1986; Madu, 1988; Madu and Jacob, 1989; Prasad, 1986; Todd & Simpson, 1983; Tsurumi, 1979; Vernon, 1980). Moreover, legal provisions reduce an LDC's willingness to innovate and produce indigenous technology (Coughlin, 1983; Das, 1987; Ferdows & Rosenbloom, 1981; Mytelka, 1979).

Ignoring the incompatibility of goals is dangerous. This was clear in the Bhopal, India, disaster, where the interplay of tight coupling—in which errors in a subsystem quickly affect the whole system—and social isolation—the plant was cut off from the corporate system—led to the crisis (Shrivastava, 1988). System failures such as Bhopal, the *Challenger* disaster, or Chernobyl will continue unless stakeholder groups improve their ability to change. These groups need to learn to negotiate and expand their worldviews though "productive conflict" (Litterer, 1966; van de Vilert, 1985). Conflict resolution opens bargaining windows that make innovation acceptable (Robinson, 1988). With its sources and intensity understood, a conflict can motivate those involved to develop effective technology strategies. Indeed, conflict is necessary for a system to progress (Cosier & Rose, 1977). It fosters understanding of system limitations and leads to improvements in overall system performance over time.

Balancing Order and Disorder

Heller (1985) describes the tension that exists between order and disorder as technology and the environment in which it operates become inseparable: half the success factors in technology transfer pull in one direction; the other half tug the other way. Inasmuch as society is a product of its technology, its dominant economic, social, cultural, psychological, and political forces guide the direction of innovation. Their interface is a symbiotic relationship between order and disorder, or "negentropy" and "entropy" exchange. Increased entropy causes societal decay, the result of technology transfer driven by incompatible LDC-MNC goals, environmental pollution, and poor planning and implementation. Increased negentropy maintains social structure and order (Madu and Jacob, 1989). A country's ability to manage change between these two directions determines its "transilience" (Clark, 1987, p. 61).

Adaptive systems keep their transilience broad enough to absorb the consequences of innovation (Holling & Goldberg, 1971), and to achieve long-term benefits from technology transfer (van Gigch, 1978). This effort can lead to innovation through development of indigenous technology. For example, China, Japan, and the former U.S.S.R. matched the progressive transfer of foreign technology—that is, from material to design to innovative capability—with a progressively greater contribution of their indigenous technological resources (Hanson, 1976).

Naturally, these synergistic benefits can be reversed if an LDC's socioeconomic structure cannot sustain innovation. Even technologically advanced countries face declining productivity when their industrial systems cannot accommodate technological innovation (Summary of Sixth Annual Productivity Survey, 1986; Kochan, 1988). Technology planners should consider all the social, political, cultural, and economic factors of an LDC as well as its current capabilities and "technological innovation potential" (Boulding, 1977, p. 302) before beginning any joint ventures with MNCs or neighboring countries (Madu, 1988).

Neither does technology last forever. A technology's life span undergoes changes (Technology Atlas Team, 1987b). Emergent technologies are capable of modifying a competitive posture. Once they become key technologies, the company or country that controls them acquires a competitive edge. As key technologies mature they become basic technologies. The phases of introduction, growth, and maturity are not intrinsically bound to given technology but, rather, to the use made of them by companies, industries, and countries. Manufacturing automation, for example, while currently a key technology in the automobile and electronics assemblies, is now emerging in job shops, but has been basic technology in continuous oil and sugar refineries (Godet, 1987). Similarly, Stacey (1984) defines the basic, key, and emerging technologies used for automobile tire production, using S-shaped curves which assess the technology's life cycle in terms of market-share sales.

Theoretical Paradoxes

The technology development and transfer literature exhibits inconsistencies similar to those rendering the transmissibility of technology as difficult. Some authors argue that LDCs must make their citizens understand the role of technology in improving their living conditions (Ito, 1986). Others show that local participation increases when there is less central planning and control over technology transfer (Cole & Mogab, 1987). A third school of thought holds MNCs responsible for the identification and transfer of technology to LDCs. According to Meleka (1985), for example, if an MNC can fully comprehend and adjust its goals to match the industrial structure of an LDC, it should be able to safeguard and expand its markets globally. Yet MNC managers and LDC planners need to control not only production and the work force but change itself (Cohen, 1988).

The very notion of change clashes with mainstream research. Alarez, Smiley and Rohrmann (1985), Ito (1986), Kim and Kim (1985), Komoda (1986), Meleka (1985), Rodrigues (1985), and Singh (1983) advocate proper planning as the means for evaluating technology, so that MNCs and LDCs develop and transfer "appropriate" technology. They all stress the necessity of preserving the existing LDC culture and value systems while realizing that the socioeconomic needs and objectives of LDCs will change.

The Technology Atlas Team (1987b) attributes this paradoxical interplay of conservatism and radical change to the fact that, ordinarily, technology is considered as something physical (hardware). Zeleny agrees that, for purposes of technological development planning, it is quite useless to talk about "applications of science" (1986, p. 110). The classifications of both the Technology Atlas Team (1987b) and Zeleny (1986) include three components of technology, such as hardware or technoware, brainware or humanware, and inforware or software, but their concept of orgaware or support net is what separates—at least temporarily—the equipment from its embedding. This separation gives rise to a variety of phenomena, which should interest technology planners. The notion of misplaced technology—that is a car half-buried in the desert sand or packed on wooden stumps in a Siberian village—serves as a useful metaphor for a technology embedded in the wrong support net or in extreme separation from the orgaware. The support-net concept can bring the distinctions among high technology, technology, and appropriate technology into sharper operational focus (Georgantzas & Madu, 1990).

SCENARIO-DRIVEN PLANNING

The technology development and transfer literature supports the necessity of integrating productive conflict with dialectical inquiry (DI) (Madu and Jacob, 1989). The integration should help LDC and MNC decision makers understand the long-term ramifications of their decisions, expand their worldviews, and enhance their inquiry and problem-solving abilities. Typically, the planning processes LDCs and MNCs use for technology development and transfer lead to the paradoxical interplay between conservatism and change. Under the supposition that paradox marks the beginning of new ideas, Figure 14.1 presents a framework that can guide decision makers through the process of scenario-driven technological development planning.

To deal effectively with technology development and transfer decisions, this framework describes a process that allows creating new information by computing the combined effects of environmental and decision scenarios. New information creation allows acknowledging most of the dimensions relevant to a decision situation (Nonaka, 1988). In the process of new information creation, decision makers unearth the critical assumptions and cognitive biases (CBs) underlying their mental or cognitive models of the decision situation (Ackoff, 1981; Mason & Mitroff, 1981). Consequently, LDC and MNC decision-making teams can improve the quality of their decisions and reduce the

Figure 14.1 Scenario-Driven Technological Development
Planning Process

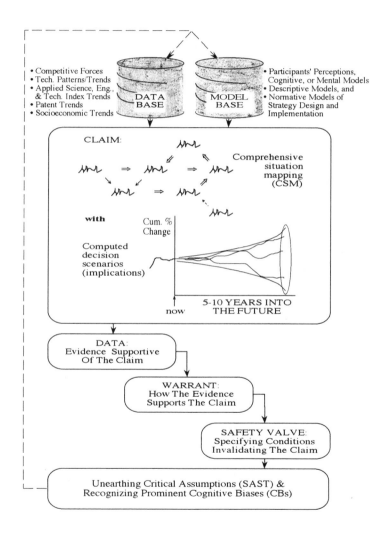

• Competitive Forces
• Tech. Patterns/Trends
• Applied Science, Eng.,
  & Tech. Index Trends
• Patent Trends
• Socioeconomic Trends

DATA BASE

MODEL BASE

• Participants' Perceptions,
  Cognitive, or Mental Models
• Descriptive Models, and
• Normative Models of
  Strategy Design and
  Implementation

CLAIM:

Comprehensive
situation
mapping
(CSM)

with

Computed
decision
scenarios
(implications)

Cum. %
Change

now

5-10 YEARS INTO
THE FUTURE

DATA:
Evidence Supportive
Of The Claim

WARRANT:
How The Evidence
Supports The Claim

SAFETY VALVE:
Specifying Conditions
Invalidating The Claim

Unearthing Critical Assumptions (SAST) &
Recognizing Prominent Cognitive Biases (CBs)

risk involved in technology development and transfer.

The principle of strategic variety dictates that LDCs and MNCs balance their short-term needs and long-term objectives (Prahalad & Doz, 1987). Accordingly, the process in Figure 14.1 helps LDC and MNC teams expose the opportunities and risks of technology development and transfer. In the process, participants discover and share multiple perspectives and conflicting worldviews. Though the need for new technology is overwhelming, even in the absence of compatible goals, eventually the participants' mental models become the source of conflict. Through conflict resolution, enriched by dialectical inquiry (DI), LDCs can work with MNCs toward a negotiated perception of the nature and structure of a situation. Sharing such negotiated perceptions may eventually lead to an increasingly integrated global socio-technico-economic system.

Shapiro and Chanin (1987) support the necessity of enhancing planning with dialectical inquiry (DI). DI aims at capturing worldview diversity in decision situations, and thereby rationalizes the inherent conflict between stability and change. By viewing rationality as the synthesis of perception and analysis, DI splits planning into two loops—one that extends the past and another that periodically attempts to break with it.

Rooted in Hegelian dialectics, where the search for truth leads to direct confrontation between thesis and antithesis from which a synthesis emanates, DI allows for the explicit consideration of pertinent decision variables and conflicting worldviews. This makes it pertinent for use in ill-structured decision situations, such as technology development and transfer. Mason and Mitroff (1981) stress the necessity of using DI in planning, and view the participation by decision-making teams as a prerequisite for its success. Ultimately, the success of planning for technology development and transfer depends on the participants' ability to identify and understand the interconnections in a country's internal and external environment (Madu, 1992).

In Figure 14.1, the input database includes changing forces of global competition; technology performance trends of participant LDCs and MNCs; applied science, engineering, and technology index trends; patent trends; and socioeconomic trends. Typically, the modelbase incorporates participant perceptions of, or mental or cognitive models of, the decision situation; existing descriptive models of; and even normative models of strategy design and implementation. Both the database and the modelbase are required inputs to scenario-driven planning, which begins with construction of participant claims about the nature and structure of a decision. Participants build such claims using comprehensive situation mapping (Acar, 1983; Acar, Chaganti, & Joglekar, 1985).

Figure 14.1 outlines the cascading inquiry of this cyclical process, which invites LDC and MNC participants to present their claim about the nature and structure of the technology development and transfer situation, along with implications—that is computed environmental and decision scenarios—suggesting action recommendations; to combine data and normative models of strategy to warrant their claim; and to specify conditions rendering the claim and its implications invalid.

Participants examine the situation in subgroups first. Then each subgroup presents its work to another, without discussion during these round-robin presentations. After the opening presentations, each with a claim and implications, data, warrant, and invalidating conditions, each subgroup presents another's claim to its designer(s) to the satisfaction of the latter. This divergence-convergence cycle of information creation continues until all participants acknowledge and understand opposing worldviews (Rapoport, 1967)—ingredients most critical to a DI interchange aimed at unearthing critical assumptions and prominent cognitive biases (CBs). The process enables participants to shift attention from CBs to understanding the structure and implications of the situation.

Specifying the conditions that invalidate the claim and its implications helps participants unearth critical assumptions—for example assumptions about events, environmental trends, and stakeholder goals or values—and to recognize CBs prominent in a claim. Specifying conditions that render each claim and its implications invalid is an extension of SAST (strategic assumption surfacing and testing), which can accommodate multiple strategic options; forces of continuity, tradition, and cognitive inertia; and in-depth analyses, so that decision teams are less vulnerable to nonpenetrating thinking and do not fall victim to implicit critical assumptions (Mason & Mitroff, 1981).

Comprehensive Situation Mapping (CSM)

Decision tools using diagrams to cope with complexity are not new. Precedence diagrams such as PERT (program evaluation and review technique) and CPM (critical path method) are well-known planning tools. A range of mapping techniques, somewhat imprecisely referred to as causal mapping, is well established and benefits from a growing literature. Acar's (1983) CSM is closely linked to the development of *signal flowgraph analysis* (Hall, 1962; Huggins & Entwisle, 1968; Lorens, 1964). Yet, CSM also belongs to the *cognitive mapping* (Eden, 1988) family of diagramming representations. More specifically, it is a sophisticated extension of influence diagramming (Diffenbach, 1982; Maruyama, 1963; Weick, 1979) that overcomes its limitations without introducing undue complexity.

The basic premise underlying all forms of mapping is that some order can be extracted from situations that may at first appear totally unstructured. Whether the order is inherent, as some MS/OR positivists believe, or in the eye of the beholder, according to pragmatists, has been debated (Churchman, 1968). What matters here is that causal mapping provides a way to transform the "doodling" that most planners do into a modeling device (Roberts, Andersen, Deal, Garet & Shaffer, 1983).

Cognitive mapping originated in the works of Kelly (1955) and Bannister and Fransella (1971) in psychology. Most varieties of cognitive mapping seek an understanding of the manner in which people actually associate concepts in their minds. Applications of cognitive mapping are associated with research aimed at uncovering people's perceptions or mental models. In the original spirit of MS/OR, a model of a situation is not meant to be an accurate representation of it, but simply an acceptable approximation for analysis (Ackoff, 1962).

Cognitive mapping authors have revived a sociometric notion developed in the 1950s and early 1960s. The idea is that there is significant interpretation in what sociometrists called the indegree and outdegree of a node in a directed graph of digraph (Harary, Norman, & Cartwright, 1965). The indegree of a node is the number of lines or vectors leading into the node; the outdegree of a node is the number of lines emanating from it. Cognitive mappers use the outdegree as a measure of the effect a particular variable has on other variables in a causal network of a directed graph. This notion is intuitively appealing, but there is no theoretical basis for construing the outdegree as either a measure or even a correlate of the importance of a variable.

Maruyama (1963) rightly acknowledges that a deviation-amplifying process may result in stabilization or oscillation, depending on the time lags involved and the size of amplification. Further, he contends that a qualitative assessment of the structure of a graphed situation can be obtained by mere inspection, but he also states that the system's behavior depends on the relative strengths of its loops. Weick concurs with this, but he mistakenly states that "positive cycles amplify whatever deviations may occur" (1979,

p. 76).

Diffenbach (1982) and Ramaprasad and Poon (1985) also propose a variation on another sociometric concept, that of the total influence obtained by summing up the number of direct and indirect *n*-order relationships (Harary et al., 1965). While more acceptable, this treatment also presents problems. First, it ascribes positivism or a "real" interpretation to the link. Second, it assumes that all elementary links are of equal importance, which places the burden of weighing the links primarily on the *n*-step aggregation procedure. Because our present concern is to explore the analytical advantage gained by certain modes of representation, we do not ascribe a positivist interpretation to cognitive diagramming, but view, in the spirit of MS/OR, a causal map as a temporary model of a situation. Our device for accomplishing this modeling is CSM, which we borrow from Acar (1983). CSM allows diagramming the web of interrelationships bearing on technology development and transfer decision situations. CSM can make the dynamics of the interrelationships more visible, more explicit, and, hence, more comprehensible. CSM is a desktop tool that LDC and MNC planners can use individually or collectively. In addition to providing a graphic representation of the network of causal effects, CSM allows tracing interrelationships quantitatively. Thus, CSM:

• Allows propagating multiwave change scenarios. Analyzing possible alternative futures under conditions of change yields a much deeper understanding of the structure of a problem than performing only structural analysis of an ID. Because CSM captures causal effects and changes from the status quo position, statements of purpose can be directly linked to LDC- and MNC- specific goals.

• Allows combining changes propagated through a particular channel of causal influence—a pure scenario—with changes propagated through other channels of causal influence—a mixed scenario. The analysis of causal linkages is a complex business. Ideally, it requires modeling and simulation (Forrester, 1968; Roberts et al., 1983; Watson, 1981). However, an approximation can be realized by the proper form of causal mapping such as CSM. The method captures the critical dimension of causality—namely, whether one or several drivers are necessary to produce the desired effect (Ackoff & Emery, 1972). Thus CSM's pure and mixed scenarios allow capturing the causalities involved in the transmission of change.

In CSM, a short name represents each variable that may cause change in itself and in other variables, or may prevent the transmission of change. Three types of arrows connect variables in CSM: a double-line arrow { ⇑ } connects a sender and a receiver of change, if the sender is sufficient, by itself, to transmit a change to its receiver; single-line arrows { ↑ } connect two or more senders to a receiver of change, if two or more senders must vary to coproduce a change in the receiver; lastly, a broken-line arrow { ⬚ } connects a sender and a receiver, if the sender can prevent the transmission of change to the receiver. If change is transmitted with a time lag, or if the change induced in a receiver is not comparable in sign or proportion to the change in the sender, then the time lag and a change transmittance coefficient written next to an arrow capture these quantitative relations. CSM's change transmittance coefficients express the ratio of the induced percentage change to the one generating it (Acar, 1983).

This technical summary of CSM is very sketchy. The following example using CSM with a classic technological development planning model should offer some clarification. A complete treatment of CSM and the derivation from its antecedents are given in Acar (1983). CSM is used here because it possesses modeling flexibility allied with computational capability that can assist LDC planners and MNC managers in technological development planning and technology transfer decisions.

CSM EXAMPLE

The Technology Atlas Team recently made a novel contribution by showing how useful cognitive mapping can be in understanding the "vicious circles of lack of technology and underdevelopment" (1987a, p. 7). Its pioneering work does not distinguish between cognitive mapping and influence diagramming. Yet there is a difference: cognitive mapping can take many forms (Eden, 1988; Montazemi & Conrath, 1986), while influence diagramming is a well-defined technique (Diffenbach, 1982; Maruyama, 1963; Weick, 1979). ID does have operational value, especially for representing perceptions or psychological relationships, but it could also lead to oversimplification of decision-making situations.

Figure 14.2 provides the ID and CSM of a technological development planning situation. One may assume that these maps have been developed through a consensual process that captured the opinions of LDC planners responsible for upgrading their country's current level of technological development. Actually, the ID is a modified version of Meier and Baldwin's (1976) view of Myrdal's (1957) vicious circle of underdevelopment. It was Myrdal's doubt about the capability of traditional economic theory to study underdeveloped societies that made him one of the paladins of a new methodology for economics. He derived this circular causation vision from two very simple hypotheses: first, the positive closed loop of growth with a low stationary point; second, the multiple effects of sociological variables in the process of economic development. The self-sustained characteristics of growth implied at higher levels of income agree with the general ideas about modern economic growth (Kuznets, 1966).

The maps in Figure 14.2 have nodes that represent variables relevant to technological development planning. Influence diagramming is the first step toward transforming cognitive mapping into a standard systematic analysis technique. In ID, the vectors are given a sign to clearly specify the mechanism of influence, but in order to lighten the diagrams the "+" sign is omitted. Hence, in Figure 14.2a, an increase in productivity would be expected to trigger an increase in real income, which in turn would increase savings. In ID, the influences are not vague conceptual relationships, but are interpreted each as the effect of the change in a variable over the change in a subsequent variable (Diffenbach, 1982; Maruyama, 1963; Weick, 1979). Yet ID remains a simple procedure using only one kind of linkage.

CSM is a more sophisticated system, which uses three kinds of linking relationships, time lags, and change transmittance coefficients that determine the magnitude of change. Hence, the CSM causal map (Figure 14.2b) indicates that, under a pure scenario of change transfer, a 10 percent increase in productivity would cause a relative 20 percent increase in real income, lagged three years. This one change would be immediately reflected as a relative one-fifth or 4 percent rise in savings, and a relative four-fifths or 16 percent increase in demand.

The ID merely indicates that a rising level of productivity would result in some increase in real income. CSM provides much more specific information, such as the fact that a 10 percent increase in productivity would, three years later, show up as a 16 percent increase in demand and as a 4 percent increase in savings (with respect to the initial levels of these variables). CSM allows capturing the causalities involved in the transmission of change and presenting them to higher authorities (Acar, Chaganti, and Joglekar, 1985).

A basic premise of planning is the generation of scenarios (Amara & Lipinski, 1983; Godet, 1987); a basic premise of the generation of scenarios is modeling and computer simulation (Watson, 1981); and a basic premise of modeling is an understand-

Figure 14.2 ID and CSM of Technological Development Planning

(a) **Influence Diagram (ID)**

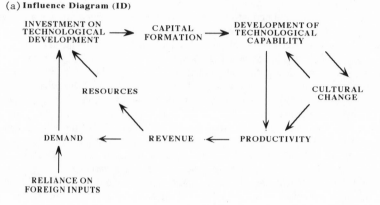

(b) **Comprehensive Situation Map (CSM)**

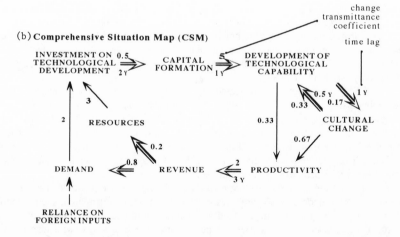

ing of causal effects (Roberts et al., 1983). The effects LDC and MNC planners must understand to trigger chains of events that lead to possible alternative futures are the ones pertaining to transmission of change (Tushman & Anderson, 1986). CSM embodies this feature.

Moreover, it allows expressing qualitative conditions in addition to capturing qualitative restrictions: the broken-line arrow indicates that a change in reliance on foreign inputs—a qualitative restriction—may qualitatively change the country's current demand. There would be no way to differentiate such conjunctive effects from qualitative restrictions into an influence diagram of the variety Diffenbach (1982), Maruyama (1963), and Weick (1979) describe.

CSM is a useful model because it is amenable to formal analysis, can become part of the institutional memory, and allows for future monitoring and control. CSM can help LDC and MNC planners capture and retain "the space and time memories that systems display and which increase the risk of bringing about unanticipated consequences far away and a long time after the change agents have been applied and removed" (Holling & Goldberg, 1971, p. 225). The process entailed in dialectically mapping a situation enhances participant understanding of decision scenarios, as abundantly discussed in the planning and dialectical inquiry literature (Ackoff, 1981; Chanin & Shapiro, 1985; Mason & Mitroff, 1981; Shapiro & Chanin, 1987).

In the CSM construction process, individually-owned maps become the grounded data (Chanin & Shapiro, 1985) for construction of an aggregate map that becomes a device for facilitating negotiation. As a facilitative device, CSM creates a dialectic by encouraging a group of decision makers to formulate their situation and envision their reference scenarios (Ackoff, 1981; Ozbekhan, 1971; Godet, 1987). This helps them uncover implicit assumptions about a situation (Mason & Mitroff, 1981) and lets them build simulation models that force counter-intuitive outcomes (Richmond et al., 1991; Roberts et al., 1983). A "natural dialectic" (Eden, 1988, p. 7) evolves because team members contribute their own views of a situation. Grounded to the team itself in a way that does not demand development of face-saving strategies, this dialectic increases the possibility of individual ownership, creativity, and interest in the implementation of recommended action.

In Figure 14.2, notice that the influence diagram fails to resolve whether demand or savings will be more influential on investment in technological development. There is no way of telling from an ID which path will dominate. This lack of guidance could mislead LDC planners and MNC managers into a naive and even incorrect determination of those variables in a decision scenario most critical to technology development and transfer. Conversely, CSM possesses computer-simulationlike capabilities that can handle both hard and soft as well as both external and internal variables, and represents a good first step toward computer modeling and simulation (Acar, 1983). Based on the CSM in Figure 14.2b, specific scenarios can be tested to explore possible alternative futures.

Assume that the rate of investment on technological development (ITD) increases by 75 percent, at time $t=0$. Call this pure scenario A. Similarly, a pure scenario B can be triggered by a 5 percent decrease in the rate of ITD, at time $t=3$. Each of these changes causes ripple effects through the causal network that CSM can capture quantitatively. Parts a and b of Figure 14.3 show the corresponding behavior of rate of investment on technological development (ITD), productivity (P), and real income (RI) for pure scenario A and pure scenario B. A comparison of the two simulation runs clearly shows that Myrdal's positive loop model is not equally sensitive to positive and negative changes in the rate of ITD.

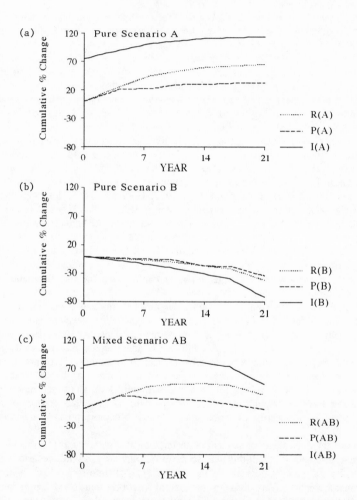

Figure 14.3 Behavioral Patterns of Investment (I), Productivity (P) and Revenue (R)

During the first seven years of pure scenario A, ITD and RI increase rapidly, while P does so only during the first three years. After three years in the same scenario, productivity almost becomes constant, while after seven years investment on technological development and real income increase at a declining rate. Conversely, during the first seventeen years of pure scenario B, ITD, P, and RI follow a fairly smooth downward trend, but their decline accelerates thereafter. In other words, the CSM representation of Myrdal's positive loop model of technological development verifies the paladin's motivation to call it a vicious circle.

Furthermore, CSM allows combining the changes propagated through multiple channels of causal effect through its mixed scenarios. Figure 14.3c shows the corresponding behavior of ITD, P, and RI for mixed scenario AB in terms of their cumulative percentage change over twenty-one years. During the first seven years of this scenario, ITD and RI follow an upward trend with RI increasing more rapidly, while P does so only during the first three years. After three years in the same scenario, productivity faces downward, while after seven years the rate of investment on technological development declines and real income rises at a declining rate. After the first seventeen years of mixed scenario AB, ITD, P, and RI all follow a smooth downward trend, their decline accelerating at different rates. Again, the vicious circle of Myrdal's positive loop of technological development holds.

Mixed scenario AB shows that an LDC's performance against real income and productivity objectives falls rapidly as the rate of investment on technological development is eroded by a mere 5 percent. This slight erosion makes it progressively more difficult to repeat the "virtuous" performance of RI and P under pure scenario A of Figure 14.3a, thereby creating the potential for poverty and lowered productivity. Even slight reductions in the rate of ITD exacerbate economic problems. It is difficult to attain not only productivity goals but also disposable income objectives. Poor performance on both measures leads to a decline in motivation, a decline in living standards, and a further decline in a country's cultural and sociopolitical capabilities.

This illustration shows that CSM is able to resolve the net effect of multiple paths of influence on various variables, when there are both positive and negative net paths of intervening effects. Although dealing with relative changes, hence preempting the difficulty of dealing with different units, CSM operates as a linearly additive and transitive model of the transmission of change. These features—of direct interest to LDC planners and MNC managers responsible for technological development and technology transfer—will be of use to both researchers and practitioners willing to integrate tangible and intangible variables in model formulations that incorporate some of the structural first- and higher-order effects of technological development planning and technology transfer.

CONCLUSION

The integration of process-based models complements the content-based technology development and transfer literature, and provides decision support to LDC and MNC planning teams. CSM offers a step-by-step approach to the technological development decision-making process. It can also integrate some of the well-known decision-making models of conflict resolution and idea analysis. An example presented the case of the vicious circle of technological development. The present study does not attempt to generate an ultimate solution to technological development and technology transfer issues, and in no way exhausts these issues. The purpose here is simply to show

how existing models can be integrated and applied by practitioners in their technological development decision-making process.

Comprehensive situation mapping greatly extends the power of the cognitive mapping approach. When time lags and transmission coefficients among pairs of variables are estimated from a database as required by CSM, subsequent what-if analyses of the map provide the correct evaluations of various variables. However, the key to effective planning support is not simply having a formal model of the problematic but using it in dialogue and discussion with LDC planners and MNC managers responsible for technology transfer. To be effective, CSM and computer-based simulation modeling must be used interactively to support and challenge intuition. In this dialectic role, CSM and computer simulation are removed from the pedestal of the infallible "black box" to occupy a more modest and appropriate position as complements to the powers of deductive thinking and reasoning.

It must, of course, be noted that the scenarios emitting from a CSM are only as good and as challenging as the map itself. Key variables must not be omitted from consideration, and the change-transmittance coefficients and time-lag estimates should not be fanciful; as in any modeling-based approach, they have to be gradually improvable (Eden, 1988). Processes for obtaining them, such as the nominal group and the Delphi techniques, ensure neither accuracy nor consistency; their contribution has been refuted in the literature (Mason, 1969; Linstone & Turoff, 1975). Dialectical inquiry has been proposed as a superior alternative (Ackoff, 1981; Georgantzas & Madu, 1990; Madu & Jacob, 1989; Shapiro & Chanin, 1987), and this chapter's process framework shows how CSM, or computer simulation modeling, can be integrated in a dialectical inquiry system to facilitate negotiation.

Scenario-driven technological development planning can enhance organizational learning and facilitate negotiation between LDCs and MNCs. Computing environmental and decision scenarios can sensitize LDC and MNC managers and technology planners to the dynamic implications of technology development and transfer, and allows creating new information. Without new information, a decision process may lead nowhere (Nonaka, 1988), unless there is a guide with a "superior vision over the maze" of organizational problems in transition (Churchman, 1971, p. 176).

Even if the quantitative information necessary to draw a full causal diagram might prove elusive in some cases, LDC and MNC managers and planners will still benefit indirectly from confronting the categories of available information, and with the relative importance of intangible and second-order effects of technological innovation. Undertaken within scenario-driven planning, CSM is a good first step toward modeling and quantitative analysis; it also becomes a methodologically defensible approach to uncovering critical assumptions, prominent CB recognition, and the appraisal of action alternatives in technology development and transfer decisions. CSM allows a welcome new kind of planning calculus and cost-benefit accounting, the kind that does not disregard indirect effects and intangible variables.

REFERENCES

Acar, W. *Toward a Theory of Problem Formulation and the Planning of Change: Causal Mapping and Dialectical Debate in Situation Formulation.* Ann Arbor, MI: UMI, 1983.

Acar, W., R. Chaganti, and P. Joglekar. "Models of Strategy Formulation: The Content-Focused and Process-Focused Modes Can and Must Meet!" *American*

Business Review 2 (2) (1985): 1-9.

Ackoff, R. L. *Scientific Method*. New York: John Wiley, 1962.

———. *Creating the Corporate Future*. New York: John Wiley, 1981.

Ackoff, R. L., and F. E. Emery. *On Purposeful Systems*. Chicago: Aldine-Atherton, 1972.

Alarez, J., S. M. Smiley, and F. Rohrmann. "Informatics and Small Computers in Latin America." *Journal of the American Society of Information Science* 36 (4) (1985): 259-67.

Amara, R., and A. J. Lipinski. *Business Planning for an Uncertain Future: Scenarios and Strategies*. New York: Pergamon Press, 1983.

Bannister, D., and F. Fransella. *Inquiring Man: The Theory of Personal Constructs*. London, UK: Penguin, 1971.

Boulding, K. E. "The Universe as a General System." *Behavioral Science* 22 (1977): 299-306.

Chanin, M. N., and H. J. Shapiro. "Dialectical Inquiry in Strategic Planning: Extending the Boundaries." *Academy of Management Review* 10 (4) (1985): 663-75.

Churchman, C. W. *Challenge to Reason*. New York: McGraw-Hill, 1968.

———. *The Design of Inquiring Systems: Basic Concepts of Systems and Organizations*. New York: Basic Books, 1971.

Clark, K. "Investment in New Technology and Competitive Advantage." In *The Competitive Challenge*, edited by D. J. Teece. Cambridge, MA: Ballinger, 1987.

Cohen, B. *Global Perspectives: The Total Culture System in the Modern World*. Hertfordshire, UK: Codek Publications, 1988.

Cole, W. E., and J. W. Mogab. "The Transfer of Soft Technologies to Less-Developed Countries: Some Implications for the Technology Transfer/Ceremony Dichotomy." *Journal of Economic Issues* 21 (2) (1987): 309-20.

Coughlin, C. C. "An Economic Analysis of Yugoslav Joint Ventures." *Journal of World Trade Law* 17 (1) (1983): 12-33.

Cosier, R. A., and G. L. Rose. "Cognitive Conflict and Goal Conflict Effects on Task Performance." *Organizational Behavior and Human Performance* 19 (1977): 378-91.

Das, S. "Externalities, and Technology Transfer Through Multinational Corporations: A Theoretical Analysis." *Journal of International Economics* 22 (2) (1987): 171-82.

Derakhshani, S. "Factors Affecting Success in International Transfers of Technology: A Synthesis and a Test of a New Contingency Model." *Developing Economies* 21 (1983): 27-45.

Diffenbach, J. "Influence Diagrams for Complex Strategic Issues." *Strategic Management Journal* 3 (2) (1982): 133-46.

Doz, Y. L., and C. K. Prahalad. "How MNCs Cope with Host Government Intervention." *Harvard Business Review* (58) (2) (March-April 1980): 149-57.

Eden, C. "Cognitive Mapping." *European Journal of Operational Research* 36 (1) (1988): 1-13.

Ferdows, K., and R. S. Rosenbloom. "Technology Policy and Economic Development: Perspective for Asia in the 1980s." *Columbia Journal of World Business* 16 (2) (1981): 36-46.

Forrester, J. W. *Principles of Systems*. Cambridge, MA: Wright-Allen, 1968.

Gee, S. *Technology Transfer, Innovation and International Competitiveness*. New York: John Wiley, 1981.

Georgantzas, N. C., and C. N. Madu. "Cognitive Processes in Technology Management and Transfer." *Technological Forecasting and Social Change* 38 (1) (1990): 81-95.

Gilfillan, S. C. "Prediction of Technical Change." *Review of Economics and Statistics* 34 (1952): 368-85.

Godet, M. *Scenarios and Strategic Management.* London, UK: Butterworths, 1987.

Hall, A. D. *A Methodology for Systems Engineering.* Princeton, NJ: Van Nostrand, 1962.

Hanson, P. "International Technology Transfer from the West to the USSR." In *Soviet Economy in a New Perspective.* Washington, DC: U.S. Government Printing Office, 1976, pp. 786-812.

Harary, F., R. Z. Norman, and D. Cartwright. *Structural Models: An Introduction to the Theory of Directed Graphs.* New York: John Wiley, 1965.

Haustein, H.-D., and H. Maier. *Innovation and Efficiency: Strategies for a Turbulent World.* Oxford, UK: Pergamon Press, 1985.

Heller, P. B. *Technology Transfer and Human Values.* New York: University Press of America, 1985.

Holling, C. S., and M. A. Goldberg. "Ecology and Planning." *Journal of the American Institute of Planners* 37 (4) (1971): 224-29.

Huggins, W. H., and D. R. Entwisle. *Introductory Systems and Design.* Waltham, MA: Blaisdell, 1968.

Ito, S. "Modifying Imported Technology by Local Engineers: Hypotheses and Case Study of India." *Developing Economies* 24 (4) (1986): 334-48.

Kelly, G. A. *The Psychology of Personal Constructs*, Volumes 1 & 2. New York: Norton, 1955.

Kim, L., and Y. Kim. "Innovation in a Newly Industrializing Country: A Multiple Discriminant Analysis." *Management Science* 31 (3) (1985): 312-23.

Kim, W. C., and R. A. Mauborgne. "Becoming an Effective Global Competitor." *Journal of Business Strategy* 9 (1) (1988): 33-37.

Kochan, T. A. "Adaptability of the U.S. Industrial Relations System." *Science* 240 (April 15, 1988): 287-92.

Komoda, F. "Japanese Studies on Technology Transfer to Developing Countries: A Survey." *Developing Economies* 24 (4) (1986): 405-20.

Kuznets, S. *Modern Economic Growth: Rate, Structure and Spread.* New Haven, CT: Yale University Press, 1966.

Linstone, H., and M. Turoff (eds). *The Delphi Method.* Reading, MA: Addison-Wesley, 1975.

Litterer, J. A. "Conflict in Organizations: A Reexamination." *Academy of Management Journal* 9 (1966): 178-86.

Lorens, C. S. *Flowgraphs for the Modelling and Analysis of Linear Systems.* New York: McGraw-Hill, 1964.

Madu, C. N. "An Economic Decision Model for Technology Transfer." *Engineering Management International* 5 (1988): 53-62.

Madu, C. N. *Strategic Planning in Technology Transfer to Less Developed Countries.* Westport, CT: Quorum Books, 1992.

Madu, C. N. and R. Jacob. "Strategic Planning in Technology Transfer: A Dialectical Approach." *Technological Forecasting and Social Change* 35 (4) (1989): 327-338.

Maruyama, M. "The Second Cybernetics: Deviation-Amplifying Mutual Causal Processes." *American Scientist* 51 (1963): 164-79, and 250-56.

Mason, R. O. "A Dialectical Approach to Strategic Planning." *Management Science*

15 (8) (1969): B403-14.

Mason, R. O., and I. I. Mitroff. *Challenging Strategic Assumptions*. New York: John Wiley, 1981.

Meier, G. M., and J. Baldwin. *Economic Development: Theory, History, Policy*, 2nd Edition. New York: Krieger, 1976.

Meleka, A. H. "The Changing Role of Multinational Corporations." *Management International Review* 25 (4) (1985): 36-45.

Montazemi, A. R., and D. W. Conrath. "The Use of Cognitive Mapping in Information Requirements Analysis." *MIS Quarterly* 10 (1) (1986): 27-38.

Myrdal, G. *Economic Theory and Under-developed Regions*. London, UK: Duckworth, 1957.

Mytelka, L. K. *Regional Development in a Global Economy: The Multinational Corporation, Technology and Andean Integration*. New Haven, CT: Yale University Press, 1979.

Nonaka, I. "Toward Middle-Up-Down Management: Accelerating Information Creation." *Sloan Management Review* 29 (3) (1988): 9-18.

Ogburn, W. F. *Social Change*. New York: Viking Press, 1922.

Ozbekhan, H. "Planning and Human Action." In *Hierarchically Organized Systems in Theory and Practice*, edited by P. A. Weiss. New York: Hafner, 1971.

Paul, K., and R. Barbato. "The Multinational Corporation in the Less Developed Country: The Economic Development Model Versus the North-South Model." *Academy of Management Review* 10 (1) (1985): 8-14.

Prahalad, C. K., and Y. L. Doz. *The Multinational Mission: Balancing Local Demands and Global Vision*. New York: Free Press, 1987.

Prasad, B. S. "Technology Transfer: The Approach of a Dutch Multinational." *Technovation* 4 (1) (1986): 3-15.

Raines, H. "Nobel in Economics to M.I.T. Professor. "*New York Times*, October 22, 1987), pp. D1, D6.

Ramaprasad, A., and E. Poon. "A Computerized Interactive Technique for Mapping Influence Diagrams (MIND)." *Strategic Management Journal* 6 (4) (1985): 377-92.

Rapoport, A. "Escape From Paradox." *Scientific American*, 217 (1) (1967): 50-56.

Richmond, B. et al. *ithink User's Guide*. Hanover, NH: High Performance Systems, Inc., 1991.

Roberts, N., D. F. Andersen, R. M. Deal, M. S. Garet, and W. A. Shaffer. *Introduction to Computer Simulation: A System Dynamics Modeling Approach*. Reading, MA: Addison-Wesley, 1983.

Robinson, R. D. *The International Transfer of Technology*. Cambridge, MA: Ballinger, 1988.

Rodrigues, C. A. "A Process for Innovators in Developing Countries to Implement New Technology." *Columbia Journal of World Business* 20 (3) (1985): 21-28.

Rogers, E. M., and F. Shoemaker. *Communication of Innovation: A Cross-cultural Approach*. New York: Free Press, 1971.

Sahal, D. *Patterns of Technological Innovation*. Reading, MA: Addison-Wesley, 1981.

Scholz, L. *Causes and Dimensions of Sectoral Structural Changes in the Manufacturing Industry until 1985*. Munich, FRG: IFO-Schnelldienst, 1977.

Schumpeter, J. *The Theory of Economic Development*. Cambridge, MA: Harvard University Press, 1934.

Shapiro, H. J., and M. N. Chanin. "Dialectical Materialism Inquiry System: A New Approach to Decision Making." In *The Idea of Psychology: Conceptual and*

Methodological Issues, edited by J. D. Greenwood. Singapore: Singapore University Press, 1987.

Shrivastava, P. *Bhopal: Anatomy of a Crisis*. Cambridge, MA: Ballinger, 1988.

Singh, Z. N. *Technology Transfer and Economic Development: Models and Practices for the Developing Countries*. Jersey City, NJ: UNZ & Co., 1983.

Stacey, G. S. *Tech Forecasting and the Tech-Risk Array: Linking R&D and Strategic Business Decisions*. Review No. 14. Columbus, OH: Battelle Memorial Institute, 1984.

Summary of the Sixth Annual Productivity Survey: Productivity Today. Norcross, GA: Institute of Industrial Engineers (IIE), 1986.

Technology Atlas Team. "A Framework for Technology Based National Planning." *Technological Forecasting and Social Change* 32 (1) (1987a): 5-18.

———. "Components of Technology for Resources Transformation." *Technological Forecasting and Social Change* 32 (1) (1987b): 19-36.

———. "Evaluation of National Technological Capabilities." *Technological Forecasting and Social Change* 32 (1) (1987c): 69-84.

"The Two-Way Street between North and South." *Economist*, October 1, 1988, p. 75.

Todd, D., and J. A. Simpson. "The Appropriate-technology Question in a Regional Context." *Growth and Change* 14 (4) (1983): 46-52.

Tsurumi, Y. "Two Models of Corporation and International Transfer of Technology." *Columbia Business of World Business* 14 (2) (1979): 43-50.

Tushman, M. L., and P. Anderson. "Technological Discontinuities and Organizational Environments." *Administrative Science Quarterly* 31 (1986): 439-65.

Utterback, J. M. "Innovation in Industry and the Diffusion of Technology." *Science* 183 (February 15, 1974): 620-26.

van de Vilert, E. "Escalative Intervention in Small-Group Conflicts." *Journal of Applied Behavioral Science* 21 (1985): 19-36.

van Gigch, J. P. *Applied General Systems Theory*. New York: Harper & Row, 1978.

Vernon, R. "Gone are the Cash Cows of Yesteryear." *Harvard Business Review* (58) (6) (November-December 1980): 150-55.

Watson, H. J. *Computer Simulation in Business*. New York: John Wiley, 1981.

Weick, K. *The Social Psychology of Organizing,* 2nd Edition. Reading, MA: Addison-Wesley, 1979.

Zeleny, M. "High Technology Management." *Human Systems Management* 6 (1986): 109-20.

Chapter 15

Managing Innovative Technologies

Chimezie A. B. Osigweh, Yg., and Michael Segalla

Consider the following: Last month our office received a fax machine. The supplier's telecommunication service set it up and left a simple three-page set of instructions about how to dial a number and change the paper. The fax machine has almost two dozen multifunction buttons on it with cryptic labels. But none of us knows how to use all of its advanced, and expensive features because the manual is kept in the telecomm office. The telecomm technicians do not think we can understand the manual, and have neither the time nor talent to provide a simplified set of instructions for all of the features. What is odd is that all of us have college degrees!

This situation reflects the sentiments of the typical office worker in the 1990s. If only the problems of adapting new workplace technologies to people's needs could be solved as easily as supplying a simplified manual!

If companies are unable to get the small things right, how can they be expected to do the big jobs? Assuming that the big job in this decade is becoming globally competitive, companies around the world are searching for technologies that will help them prosper. Help will come from both production and managerial technologies. In this chapter some of the problems of selecting and integrating new technologies into the daily work life of employees is examined. Some of the critical issues are presented with examples. Additionally, an often overlooked area of new technology adoption—the resulting changes in employee and employer responsibilities and rights—is discussed.

DEFINING THE NEW TECHNOLOGY

New technology includes not only new production or office equipment such as computers, telecommunication devices, and automated or computer-controlled gadgets but new managerial tools as well. Stoneman (1983) argues that the introduction of a new technology is a process of economic change regarding the goods and services produced and/or the methods used to create those products. While most observers focus on the physical machinery or electronic devices of technological change, it is important to remember that changes in managerial techniques and the organization of work are also subject to technological improvement (Bamber & Lansbury, 1989). In fact, changes in the management or organization of a company are often necessary for successful introduction of a new production technology (Majchrzak & Davis, 1990).

The two parts of the change process—namely, adoption of new production or

mechanical technology and modification of managerial or organizational technology—are
the focus of this chapter. Both have a long history of interdependence in industry.

For example, the ability to generate massive amounts of power, such as provided
by the steam engine and later by electricity, fueled the growth of large-scale, twenty-
four-hour-a-day mass assembly and manufacturing operations. But without the
organizational theories of Max Weber (who outlined the control value of the bureaucratic
structure) or Frederick Taylor and Henry Ford (who increased productivity with training,
division of labor, and standardized assembly lines), the value of those new power-based
production technologies could not have been maximized.

THE LINK BETWEEN PRODUCTION
AND MANAGERIAL TECHNOLOGIES

From a historical perspective, companies are constantly under pressure to increase
productivity, and have tended to do so by developing both new production and new
managerial technologies (Braverman, 1974). The introduction of new production
technology often goes hand-in-hand with new managerial technology. For example,
Corning's expanding use of automated plant technology has increased its reliance on
self-managing production teams, which require extensive on-the-job training and
decision-making autonomy (Hoerr, 1990). However, the link between the two is unclear.

One way to conceive this link between production and managerial technology is
to realize that the introduction of any new production technology will force organizational
change (Spacapan & Oskamp, 1990). The connection is unidirectional—that is,
organizations and people adapt to new technology rather than that the adoption of new
technology is dependent on changes in the organization or people. The pioneering
development of standardized assemble lines and rigid subdivision of labor by Henry
Ford, founder of the Ford Motor Company, helped decrease the skill requirements of
the labor force while simultaneously increasing the feasible span of management,
resulting in depersonalization of the supervisor-subordinate relationship.

A second, more compelling view of the link between new production technology
and progress in managerial technology opposes the technological determinism just
described. According to this second view, new production technology is only one of
several factors that influence the managerial technology of a company or industry
(Bamber & Lansbury, 1989). Other influences are markets for labor and raw material,
product markets, workplace traditions, and government policies. At Volvo Car
Company's innovative assembly plant in Uddevalla, Sweden, intensively trained
autonomous work teams of seven to ten employees assemble four cars per shift without
the use of a production line. But this innovation was not forced on the workers merely
for the sake of improved productivity (Kapstein & Hoerr, 1989). Indeed, Sweden has
a highly educated labor force that finds factory work unattractive. Because taxes are
high, additional income has a low marginal value, and given Sweden's extremely low
unemployment rate, there is little compulsion to accept undesirable jobs. Therefore
Volvo's new managerial technology was intended to make the work environment
rewarding enough to offset the negative aspects of factory work. Giving workers
responsibility for managing themselves, establishing schedules, maintaining quality
control, hiring new team members, and performing other duties normally reserved for
managers improves the job's desirability and work-force morale. As a direct measure
of such improvements, Volvo reveals that absenteeism at the Uddevalla plant is only 8
percent rather than the 17 to 20 percent at other Volvo plants (Kapstein & Hoerr, 1989).

In the United States, many companies have adopted flexible working arrangements owing to the changes in the composition of the labor force and the expectations of workers. Arrangements such as flextime, job sharing, telecommuting, or employee leasing can benefit both company and employee. But the impetus for these programs has often been an employee need, not the one-way technological determinism suggested by the first view.

Keen observation of contemporary business environments reveals that an admixture of myriad social, technical, and economic conditions have directly or indirectly influenced employers to experiment with new forms of work and organizational technology. Among the influences are:

1. The growing number of women employees in the work force who want a career and motherhood simultaneously.
2. The increased skill level of some occupations allowing workers to demand conditions better suited to their needs.
3. The large pool of underutilized skilled workers, created by the widespread corporate restructuring and downsizing of the 1980s, who are willing to accept less than optimal working conditions.
4. The continuing movement from a manufacturing economy requiring highly coordinated work schedules to a service economy where work schedules can be more flexible.
5. The development of inexpensive computers, facsimile machines, cellular telephones, and high-speed data networks.
6. The growth of temporary employment agencies and leased employee firms.

Stackel's (1987) look at the flexible modern organization provides a good analysis of the dynamics these social, technical, and economic factors bring about. Illustrating the dynamic nature of these factors, SmithKline Beckman introduced a flex-time program over ten years ago at its Philadelphia operations. According to Mitchell Abramson, director of personnel, the program has been successful in improving employee morale. But Abramson cautions against its adoption in every organization. Indeed, the system may not be well suited for companies whose reward systems are not robust enough to allow for a separate class of "haves," since it is unlikely that a flex-time program could be extended across every operation of a company (Stackel, 1987).

Organizational and human needs can be the driving force behind adoption of a new production technology. In France, where school children have no classes on Wednesday, Groupe AXA Assurance (the country's largest private insurance company) offers workers the option of telecommuting on this day using company-supplied terminals and modems. This increases the company's attractiveness, especially to working mothers; lowers wage demands to cover the cost of daycare; and reduces Wednesday absenteeism (Michel & Kocinski, 1991).

Aside from issues of technological adoption, *not* adopting new production technology has also been attributed to economic, social, and cultural factors. For example, productivity growth in the U.S. service sector has long lagged behind the growth in some European countries. While U.S. productivity growth averaged only .06 percent from 1972 to 1984, in France and Germany productivity grew at 2 percent and 2.1 percent, respectively. The difference has been attributed to higher capital spending in Europe, where the labor supply of office workers is restricted by minimum-wage laws and strong union influence (Bernstein, 1989). The companies, lacking a cheap supply of labor, are forced to search for technological improvements through new equipment.

In contrast, the U.S. labor supply surged during that period as increasing numbers of older women and baby-boomers flooded the labor market, making it cheaper to hire unskilled workers than to purchase productivity improvements through training or equipment.

Fortunately, to effectively integrate the new technologies with the work force, human resource management (HRM) does not need to dwell on the technological source of the new methods. The major focus should be on what effect the new technology has on factors most important to employers and employees. Four areas of basic human issues, are addressed in this regard—namely, the human resource practices inherent in managing people, organizational structure and culture, employment and displacement, and the implementation process (Majohrzak & Davis, 1990).

We view these four areas broadly in terms of organizational implications. To enhance our understanding of these basic human issues in adoption of new technology, the factors exogenous to the company, particularly environmental influences such as cultural, political, and legal constraints, are briefly considered.

ENVIRONMENTAL FACTORS CONSTRAINING
THE ADOPTION OF NEW TECHNOLOGY

There are several types of constraints or problems that affect the adoption of new technology. First are economic constraints, with questions such as, Does the cost of introduction have a positive, measurable payoff? A simplified economic measure could be the cost per client served, such as in operating a bank teller machine versus a human bank teller. More elaborate measures might measure overall productivity increases, product quality improvements, or product marketability. But direct economic constraints are only part of the picture. There are also cultural and organizational constraints that exert powerful influences over the adoption process. For example, in the banking industry, installation of automated teller machines (ATM) in many countries lags considerably behind the technical possibilities, because of a lack of customer acceptance (Rajan, 1985). Either through inertia, discomfort with new technology, or the desire to maintain a human relationship with the employees of the bank, many consumers refrain from using an ATM.

Other examples of user reluctance to accept a new technology are available. In the 1980s the introduction of new office and telecommunications technology was often slowed by weak consumer acceptance. Probably everyone knows of one or more secretaries who continued using a typewriter long after a personal computer with word processing software was made available. The same might be said of some managers. In telecommunications, new telephone features such as call forwarding, automatic callback, and three-person calling are common, but are rarely used by the majority of deskbound workers and managers. One might argue that among the most important recent technological improvements for the average phone user are voice mail and automatic redial. Yet a keen observer will see that far, from helping callers reach the person or information they want, voice mail systems may irritate callers with excessive menus. Extant legal and political constraints also slow the introduction of new technology. In some countries, telecommuting has been condemned by unions. Indeed, unions want the telecommuting technology restrained by law in countries that prohibit or regulate work at home (Goodrich, 1990; Greve, 1989). In countries such as France, Germany, and the United States, the worrisome but unknown effects of video display terminals (VDT) and other new technologies have led to introduction or extension of regulations that limit the time spent in front of VDTs. Sometimes laws (e.g., in the United States) influence the design of the workstation itself, including placement of VDTs and radiation emission levels. In addition, shopfloor production or managerial changes are often limited by union agreements, or are subject to union bargaining.

Political constraints, such as in Europe, where many companies are government owned, include restrictions on the introduction of new technology that threatens jobs. However, governments need not be part-owners of a company to influence the adoption of new production technology. The government's role can also take the form of tax-saving investment incentives that promote expenditures on new technology and thus bring long-range economic and social benefits. Therefore, it is not surprising that some observers (e.g., Lansbury, 1989) argue that governments must become more proactive, encouraging the introduction of new technology so as to improve productivity, which over the long run results in lower deficits, better trade balances, and higher value-added employment. The implication here is that the adoption of new technologies has not been politicized enough, and that governments have not done enough to promote their use.

ORGANIZATIONAL IMPLICATIONS
OF ADOPTING NEW TECHNOLOGY

Managing People

Perhaps the most important constraints on the adoption of new production and managerial technology are inside the company itself. One such constraint is organizational and human resource management attitude (Majchrzak & Davis, 1990). Because humans manage and use new technologies, the quality of implementation depends on the quality of the human, managerial, and organizational infrastructures. This sentiment is shared by executives and other persons in the world of organizational practice. For example, Paul O'Neill, chairman of Alcoa, began a major reorganization of the company by flattening the hierarchy, increasing the decision-making authority of managers, and increasing accountability throughout. Midway he realized there was a risk: previously untested line executives may not have the managerial skill and expertise to handle their new responsibilities (Schroeder, 1991).

To limit the risk encountered by O'Neill requires a spectrum of strategies such as initiating training and reward policies that reinforce the motivation of newly empowered managers. But in doing so, there is a need to modify many of Alcoa's existing human resource practices. Pay, training, selection, promotion, collective bargaining, and other employment practices would need to be reviewed and, if need be, redesigned for a more dynamic environment.

The need to match HRM practices to new technology is vital. For example, with regard to Corning's or Volvo's autonomous work teams, it soon becomes apparent that a pay system rewarding individual performance is unlikely to enhance morale or motivate a production team. Similarly, asking workers to take more responsibility for new managerial or production systems, such as total quality management (TQM), without providing a strong, visible commitment from management is unlikely to modify worker behavior. Not surprisingly, Arden Sims, president and CEO of Glode Metallurgical, (and the 1988 winners of the prestigious Baldridge Award for innovation in management), demonstrated his commitment to TQM in several ways. He developed a company-wide profit-sharing plan, eliminated time clocks, started a no-layoff policy, and held small group meetings with all employees to review the company's financial performance (Harvard Business Review, 1992). In other words, Sims set out essentially to shorten the worker-manager continuum reinforced by old-style HRM practices. Compare his approach to what happens in a typical (French) company, where salary increments are fixed to seniority and annual cost-of-living raises; workers are seldom consulted; and companies maintain rigid, multilevel hierarchies with little likelihood of deflating any time soon!

Like the executive Sims, researchers Joshua Hammond and Gilbert Papaille have sought to identify human factors in the workplace that inhibit the adoption of TQM programs. They have found that Americans do not seem to have an unconscious need to strive for perfection, and therefore, they feel guilty when a company insists on it (Carey, 1991). Furthermore, many companies still reward their employees with either salary increases or prestige awards on a fixed yearly schedule rather than providing immediate feedback. Perhaps neither of these practices is conducive to optimal motivation, and therefore must be modified to make introduction of TQM and other emerging technologies more successful.

Organizational Structure and Culture

An organization's structure supports a complex web of units and reporting relationships that constitute the organization. Organizational culture is the unique set of values, norms, and symbols manifested in the distinctive formal and informal interactions that characterize the organization (Osigweh, 1985, p. 180). To the extent that the sum total of units, and formal and informal practices, in organizations both define and are defined by people, organizational structure and culture provide an area from which important basic human issues can be addressed. Consider the practice of computer-integrated manufacturing (CIM). As a work-place technological innovation, CIM strives to link computerized information regarding company strategy, marketing, and production to control the manufacturing process. This allows a higher degree of manufacturing variability and integration than fixed-machine assembly lines. But the necessary tight integration of information and equipment is difficult to achieve in a traditional organizational design and culture developed to manage unskilled, mass-production assembly lines. With automated equipment producing hundreds of products a minute, a flawed batch of component parts can cause havoc very quickly, as workers monitoring the equipment need to locate a supervisor for permission to shut down the production line. In this environment, old concepts of organizational structure and management roles, such as Max Weber's strictly structured bureaucracy or Rensis Likert's linch-pin theory (each of which describes the manager as the central link among work groups) have to be modified or discarded. Information networks that bypass traditional managers will force a new concept of the organization's design and the manager's role.

Consider also the adoption of computer numerical control (CNC) machines. These machines can easily be reprogrammed to allow companies to move to short production runs. Therefore the use of CNCs is in itself an innovation in manufacturing management, which symbolizes a move from mass-production technology to small-batch production. Such a move requires organizations to more evenly distribute authority, increase the quality of the work force, spend more time on worker training, and modify reward systems. Corporate efforts to harmonize various aspects of CNC underscore the interrelationship of production technology, organizational design, and performance management (see Hirschhorn, 1984; Woodward, 1965).

The use of CNC raises certain core human issues in the workplace. Consider that installation of new production technology can change the nature of work; innovative technologies not only can create new, skilled jobs but also potentially eliminate jobs, particularly unskilled ones. Quite simply, the tasks accompanying new production techniques require a very skilled work force. Consequently, there must be increased emphasis on the appropriate initial selection and training of workers, and on means to relieve the boredom associated with repetitive production jobs, where the new technology requires routine or simplified tasks. Further, pay systems (including additional compensation for poor, sterile, or boring working conditions, or for more sophisticated tasks) may have to be redesigned. On-going training may be needed for workers in areas requiring frequent use of conceptual skills—for example, in order to continually update skills and prepare for emergency situations when automated systems fail. One can immediately think of pilots or nuclear power station operators receiving continuous training in simulators, so as to respond appropriately to occasional failures of complex technical systems. However, the same principle applies elsewhere in the work force, given that increased professionalization of the modern organization is transforming employees into a corps of knowledge workers (Osigweh, 1987). Even machine or process operators must have the knowledge and authority to bring emergencies under control. An organizational structure and culture that continue to view workers merely as subordinates, rather than as fellow professionals, is unlikely to be unsuccessful in adopting new technologies that contribute to competitiveness.

Employment and Job Skill Changes

The influence of new technology on employment opportunities, in both the quantity and quality of jobs, opens up another core area of human issues in the work place. There are two relevant themes in this area. The first is the "labor process theory" (Braverman, 1974); its central thesis is that all new work technologies are designed to reduce the amount and skill of labor required. The consequences are job loss and work deskilling, leading to increased managerial control over the work process and ultimately producing a dependant, poorly paid labor force. The second theme is "flexible specialization" (Hirshhorn, 1984; Piore & Sable, 1984); its main premise is that new technology changes jobs for the better by increasing the skill content and, consequently, making labor more rewarding.

While there is considerable debate concerning the consequences and determinism of new technology (Sorge & Streeck, 1988), companies must be cognizant that new technology will psychologically threaten workers. The psychological threat to clerical workers is based on the knowledge that new technology can lead to fewer jobs and a change in the level or type of skills required. As a result, alarmed observers might even suspect that some companies may systematically "deskill" workers (retrain) as a means to control, retain, or extract surplus value. Even employment forecasts associated with new technologies are often so gloomy that workers who occasionally peruse them can become depressed. For example, Ayres and Miller (1983) predict that perhaps 38 percent of American production workers will be replaced by robots before the year 2002. Hunt and Hunt (1983) depict how mercilessly entire classes of jobs, such as spot welders and spray painters, are losing their occupation as robots take over these difficult but highly repetitive tasks. Even popular managerial innovations sometimes have employment repercussions that are psychologically threatening. Installation of the new quality management technology, at Wallace Company provides a case in point. Wallace, the 1990 Baldridge Award winner, fired 25 percent of its work force and bought new computers. The company used principles of scientific management to teach drivers new ways of loading their trucks (Ivey & Carey, 1991). Ironically, by the following year Wallace had lost nearly $700,000, had its credit line cut off, and was perilously close to bankruptcy. Similarly, Sikorsky Aircraft, a division of United Technologies, attributes a 1,350 blue- and white-collar payroll reduction in 1990 to its recently implemented quality program (Driscoll & LaMonica, 1990).

Disheartening predictions and experiences, such as these, do little to relieve fears. Yet evidence suggests that such predictions and facts apply not only in the United States or in lower organizational cadres but also in Europe, and for supervisors and managers as well. In a European study of human resource strategies to deal with rapidly changing technology in the banking and insurance sectors, Bertrand and Noyelle (1988) found that net employment changes are generally difficult to summarize. Some companies gain while others lose employment; more significant differences are summarized in Table 15.1. The table reveals that changes in skill requirements and working conditions are distributed throughout the organization. Some jobs require intensified skills while others require broader skills, however all jobs share some common new competencies such as adaptability, abstract reasoning, decision making, teamwork, and company- or market-wide (national or international) understanding. If these examples apply to other sectors, companies will need to design training and/or recruitment strategies to satisfy both organizational and individual needs.

The threat to supervisors and managers must be recognized. Layoffs once were uniquely associated with production workers. Managers decided how many workers, and for how long, would be idled. With modern data networks that allow a manager to be in several places at once, and global competition providing the raison d'être for corporate downsizing, managers at all levels are experiencing unemployment. Kanter (1990) argues that if companies can no longer guarantee managers employment, they must offer them the opportunity to increase their reputation and skill portfolio to ease reintegration into the labor force.

Supervisors may fear for their relevancy as worker autonomy increases or as the factory automates. Mid-level managers are often unhappy with the heightened pressure that comes from a new managerial technology that requires more human relations skills. A study of large U.S. companies thought to be on the vanguard of managerial technology found that middle managers felt that the human relations approach to worker supervision often put excessive demands on their time, since employee problems usually need to be dealt with individually rather than a by-the-book approach common among unionized work groups (Foulkes, 1980).

In short, if the skills of production workers increase and companies integrate these workers into total quality management, or other high-commitment programs, there will need to be more sophisticated and sensitive management as well. This new breed of manager may have to upgrade his or her human-resource management skills and attitudes.

ISSUES OF IMPLEMENTATION

Short of firing all current workers, implementing a new technology may require an extensive training program, depending on the function, responsibility, initial skill level, and skills required of workers. Three training strategies can be used to upgrade the skills of current employees: (1) outside trainers; (2) training in-house by the HRM

Table 15.1
The Changing Nature of Skills in Banks and Insurance Companies

Common Emerging Competencies	
Old Competencies	**New Competencies**
1. Ability to operate in well-defined and stable environment	Ability to operate in ill-defined and ever-changing environment
2. Capacity to deal with repetitive, straightforward and concrete work process.	Capacity to deal with non-routine and abstract work process
3. Ability to operate in a supervised work environment	Ability to handle decisions and responsibilities
4. Isolate work	Group work; interactive work
5. Ability to operate within narrow geographical and time horizons	System-wide understanding; ability to operate within expanding geographical and time horizons

Specific Emerging Competencies Among Upper-Tier Workers

1. Generalist Competencies. Broad, largely unspecialized knowledge; focus on operating managerial skills	The New Expertise. Growing need for high-level specialized knowledge in well-defined areas needed to develop and distribute complex products
2. Administrative Competencies. Old leadership skills; routine administration; top-down, carrot-and-stick personnel management approach; ability to carry out orders from senior management	The New Entrepreneurship. Capacity to not only manage but also set strategic goals; to share information with subordinates and to listen to them; to motivate individuals to develop new business opportunities

Among Middle-Tier Workers

1. Procedural Competencies. Specialized skills focused on applying established clerical procedural techniques assuming a capacity to receive and execute orders	Customer Assistance and Sales Competencies. Broader and less specialized skills focused on assisting customers and selling capacity to define and solve problems.

Among Lower-Tier Workers

1. Specialized Skills focused on data entry and data processing	Disappearance of low skill jobs

Source: Bertrand, O. and T. Noyelle, (1988).

department; or (3) training by the line manager. Each method has certain strengths and weaknesses.

Training programs run by outside trainers under contract (or purchased from consulting firms or local business, technical, or trade schools) can provide both general and specific technical training. Groups of workers can be large or small; include production, clerical, technical, or unskilled workers; and cover nonmanagerial levels as well as executive and management cadres. Sometimes, these programs fall short of expectations unless their sponsors (e.g., organizations, managers) work closely with the contractor to ensure proper content, level, and quality of the program.

Many companies send lower and mid-level managers to both accelerated MBA and nondegree programs offered by HEC-ISA, INSEAD, or IMD in Europe, or any number of business schools in North America. Annual revenues from such programs range from under $2 million for small U.S. programs to over $20 million for larger programs offered by INSEAD in France, IMD in Switzerland, and Harvard in the United States. Unfortunately the general-purpose courses do not always meet the immediate needs of companies that require quick results to survive current market conditions. Not surprisingly, observers have found that corporate training managers are unhappy with outdated, irrelevant, overpriced educational programs at many schools (Byrne, 1991). On the other hand, companies such as Ford Motor Company, Johnson & Johnson, and Banque Nationale de Paris, which have worked closely with schools to design custom training courses that have had an immediate effect on job performance, tend to be pleased with what they purchase. Such courses often include exercises that reflect the current problems the company is facing. As is to be expected, these programs are growing at the rate of 25 percent per year (Byrne, 1991), although many larger schools avoid them because of their commercial overtones.

Most companies probably try to do as much in-house training as they can. In-house programs range from informal training by older workers, to elaborate on-the-job training, to established training divisions, such as McDonald's Hamburger University. GE's in-house program in New York trains 6,000 managers annually. Procter & Gamble in France has a four-level in-house training program, starting with basic managerial skills and finishing with an executive leadership program open only to top managers. The program consists of sixteen courses lasting from one to five days. Well-organized in-house programs, while very costly to operate, can be more directly controlled.

A trend among many large firms, notably IBM, is to encourage HRM departments to become aggressive marketers of their skills to other units of the company. In a discussion of this idea, Collins and Payne (1991) use market segmentation to illustrate how a company can plan its training programs. Based on our understanding of marketing segmentation and internal training, the market segmentation approach to training is depicted in Figure 15.1.

The in-house training process can be visualized as a model with four segmentation quadrants. Typical market segments are delineated by two dimensions—namely, the importance of training to the organization's unit, its objectives, and the degree of customization required. Quadrant 1 (HIHC) presents a scenario in which the company or unit provides some important training to a specialized client group within the company: For example, a strategic management seminar using company and industry data delivered to senior management by a small team of highly rated university professors. Quadrant 2 (HILC) presents a situation in which a company or its unit needs a high-quality standard training program: for example, a change in some technical system, perhaps the introduction of a new off-the-shelf computerized accounting system. Needed here is a smooth, low-cost transition achieved by a standard training program for

Figure 15.1
Market Segmentation Approach to Training Needs

	2. HILC	1. HIHC
HIGH Importance of organizational objectives met by training	Standardize material Off-the-shelf program Contracted or in-house classes	Sensitive information Highly targeted Customized program Outside expertise
	3. LILC	4. LIHC
LOW	Standardize material Off-the-shelf program Contracted classes	Sensitive information Standard problems Tailored to dept. In-house expertise

Amount of customization
required to implement
training program

LOW   HIGH

1. *HIHC*: High importance, high customization
2. *HILC*: High importance, low customization
3. *LILC*: Low importance, low customization
4. *LIHC*: Low importance, high customization

all the accounting clerks, purchased from a consulting agency. Quadrant 3 (LILC) presents a situation that might be quite common in Europe. An increasing number of corporations and organizations are encouraging their employees to improve their fluency in English. This is central to the company's immediate goals and requires little customization; the training is easily purchased with no company input other than scheduling personnel and monitoring quality. The final quadrant (LIHC) illustrates a situation in which a client group within the company may want to develop an employee satisfaction questionnaire, exit interview procedures, or an affirmative action plan. Sensitive company-specific information is needed, so the program is best designed and offered by in-house staff.

Once training activities have been segmented, the next step is to involve managers directly in the human-resource management implications of adopting the new technology. With current worldwide emphasis on corporate downsizing, managers who survive "early retirement" offers will find themselves carrying more responsibility for their business units. They will likely demand more from other members of the company and from themselves, including an important role as facilitator of technology adoption by subordinates.

Part of the push to develop internal and segmented training strategies derives from renewed emphasis on corporate members working together to achieve globally competitive companies. While all function areas in an organization can benefit from internal marketing principles, the HRM function can be a prime benefactor.

In many U.S. companies, the HRM department focuses on administrative and control functions, although by European Standards they are well equipped with technical tools for evaluating, developing, and compensating employees. Over the past two decades, U.S. companies have been particularly influenced by affirmative action issues. In France, HRM departments have seldom ventured beyond the administrative and control stage. Firing employees is difficult, and companies historically have based salary increments on seniority. Therefore, French HRM departments are more of record keepers, far removed from the strategic elements of a company mission (Besseyre des Horts, 1988). HRM professionals need to understand that the new emphasis on global competition requires their restructuring their departments to provide services to line managers, rather than acting as watchdogs over the hiring, promoting, salary, and retiring process.

Line managers who are being given much more responsibility are unlikely to allow HRM departments to rule unfettered over the work force. Advanced computer and information technology, fewer layers of bureaucracy, and decentralization are already extending the managerial reach of line managers, who do not want a doctrinaire HRM department. But these line managers will need advice, since they will no longer be delegating the responsibility for technological adaptation to the HRM department. They will find it necessary to take an active part in the adaptation process, visibly supporting and utilizing the new technology. Actually, this is nothing new to observers of the change process. Rojot (1989) points out that managers have always been dealing with new production and managerial technologies. And Drucker (1954) wrote long ago that managers must provide unambiguous indications of their commitment to an objective before they can seriously expect their subordinates to commit themselves.

ON WORKPLACE RESPONSIBILITIES
AND RIGHTS: A FINAL CONSIDERATION

We have considered the relationships among types of technologies, the constraints on adopting new technological forms, and the direct impact of technology on organizational structures, functions, management style, and individual employees. The indirect impact of technological change remains to be addressed. We explore two important indirect results related to the human-resource management function—namely, new employee responsibilities and rights.

Indeed, issues of responsibilities and rights—of both employees and employers—are being raised as technology progresses into more facets of the workplace. It enters through traditional and untraditional work processes such as communications, computerized meter scanning, drug testing, computer credit checks, and polygraph exams (Osigweh, 1988, 1991). This is so because, among other means, historically organizations have sought to advance their business interests through technological innovations, which are then justified by the necessity for business efficiency (Fortado, 1991). Because rights and responsibilities are inwined—in the sense that rights for one party ordinarily evokes responsibilities for the other party, owing to the reciprocal nature of workplace relationships (Osigweh, 1987, 1988)—the following discussion examines employee rights (and management responsibilities) and employee responsibilities (and management rights).

Employee Rights and Management Responsibilities

In the area of innovative communications technology, fondly known as HiComTech, the scramble by organizations to avoid being caught tomorrow in yesterday's technology is finding more and more workers enmeshed in new communication technologies (Goldhaber & DiSalvo, 1987). Such emersion not only affects employees directly, through interaction with electronic devices, but also indirectly, as work behavior, patterns, and requirements are altered to suit the new tools and new management processes. One issue is whether organizations have the right to exploit the unlimited opportunities ushered in by technological innovation in communications for the purpose of improving organizational effectiveness. Workers have a right to be safeguarded from unwelcome HiComTech innovations. Therefore, employers have a responsibility to investigate how the HiComTech changes they are promoting will affect their workers, and to minimize their unfair consequences for the employee.

Other, more specific workplace responsibilities and rights can be identified within and beyond the general area of HiComTech. Innovations in computer, word processing, facsimile (fax) machines, telephone technology, and other mechanized information and production systems make it possible for secretaries, journalists, research and development personnel, and typists to work at home. Historically, workplace rights have been won in small and seemingly harmless precedents or concessions. The increasing practice of allowing people to work at home can be viewed as conferring on such employees the right to work and maintain an office at home, while management bears the responsibility of assuring fulfillment of such rights. Likewise, video technology, television monitors, drug testing, computerized meter scanning, and infrared badges are some of the intrusive innovations by which the employer can keep an eye on just about anything an employee does. These technologies raise the question of invasion of employee privacy rights. For example, computerized meter scanners are devices originally developed and popularized in the home utility industry. They possess internal clocks that can chart a worker's exact movements. Similarly, infrared badges continuously transmit the wearer's (employee's) position to readers attached to walls and doors. Implied, of course, is that the organization has a responsibility to refrain from intrusive employer practices.

Technological changes necessitate specialized skills and training, as argued earlier. Consequently, employees have a right to receive training for such skill, as well as a right to training and promotion selection decisions based on skills and other job-related criteria; the organization has responsibility to make these objective decisions.

Sometimes, new technologies create a safety or health hazard in the workplace. For example, the Occupational Safety and Health Administration in the United States has recommended that workers not be exposed to 95 to 100 decibels of noise for more than four hours. Between 95 and 100 decibels is about the level of noise generated by a room full of computer printers (Goldhaber & DiSalvo, 1987). Employees reserve the right to refuse to work in an environment where technology creates an objectively dangerous condition. On their part, organizations have the responsibility of providing a healthful and safe setting in which to work.

Employee Responsibilities and Management Rights

As noted, rights and responsibilities mandated by advances in technology for one party underscore corresponding responsibilities and rights for the other party. Following are illustrations of some rights and responsibilities for employees and employers discussed earlier, this time considering employee responsibilities.

When technological progress wins for the employee the right to work or keep an office at home, that same right confers on the worker the responsibility of devoting a full effort to the employer's work. The employer is credited the right to expect a 100 percent effort from the employee working at home.

Issues that suggest organizational intrusions (or "espionage") into the personal work lives of employees continue to generate polemics. Regardless of controversy, advances in such technology (drug testing, computerized meter scanning, and video monitors) gain acceptance in the workplace and, consequently, create responsibilities and rights. The new technology that makes possible polygraphs or drug testing also mandates for employees the responsibility to submit to such tests. The employer has the right to conduct only valid inquiries or tests that are job related. Quite possibly, the employee's responsibility to devote a full effort while working at home might be argued as conferring on the employer the right to monitor that employee's work via "whatever means." Such monitoring might include other innovative but intrusive devices, creating the perception that the employer has the right to spy on the worker's home life as well.

When new technologies necessitate additional training or specialized skills, workers have the responsibility of accepting management's selection decisions (who is chosen for promotion based on skill, or who is selected for further training). Management has the right to make selections consistent with organizational objectives, based on standards of law, fairness, and job relatedness.

In the area of health and safety, workers have the responsibility to do their jobs when protected from adverse safety and health conditions. Employers have the right to expect workers to be at work when jobs are safe and work environments are free of technology-induced hazards. A more detailed but general treatment of these and other employee-employer-rights and responsibilities, can be found in a recent compilation by Osigweh and Miceli (1991, pp. 5-8).

CONCLUSION

We have presented a simple framework of human-resource issues to be addressed when considering the adoption of new production and/or managerial technologies. The consequences of each technique for various facets of the organization, and the effects of the organization has on the efficacy of the new technology, have to be considered. Of particular importance are the roles of organizational structure, employee attitudes, skills, responsibilities, and rights, as well as the manger's personal style and position. Human resource departments must also adapt to the new reality of global competitiveness. This requires full consideration of the strategic consequences of new technology; delivering services to line managers; viewing restrictive and orthodox sets of policies more cautiously than ever; and more carefully balancing their role as provider versus advisor for the traditional services offered by most HRM departments.

REFERENCES

Ayres, L., and S. Miller. *Robotics: Applications and Social Applications.* Cambridge, MA: Harper & Row, 1983.

Bamber, G., and R. Lansbury. *New Technology: International Perspectives on Human Resources and Industrial Relations.* London: Unwin Hyman, 1989.

Bernstein, A. "What's Dragging Productivity Down? Women's Low Wages." *Business Week*, November 27, 1989, p. 171.

Bertrand, O., and T. Noyelle. "Human Resources and Corporate Strategy." Paris: OECD, Besseyre des Horts, C. H. Vers une gestion strategique des ressources humaines. Paris: Editions d'Organisation, 1988.

Braverman, H. *Labor and Monopoly Capital: The Degradation of Work in the Twentieth Century.* New York: Monthly Review Press, 1974.

Byrne, J. "Back to School." *International Business Week*, October 28, 1991, pp. 34-39.

Carey, J. "Think Tanks Have Their Thinking Caps On." *International Business Week*, December 2, 1991, pp. 72-79.

Collins, B., and A. Payne. "Internal Marketing: A New Perspective for HRM." *European Management Journal* 9 (3) (September 1991): 261-70.

Driscoll, L., and M. LaMonica. "It'll Take More than Saddam for Sikorsky to Soar Again." *Business Week*, October 1, 1990, p. 37.

Drucker, P. "Management by Objectives and Self-Control." In *The Practice of Management*, by P. Drucker. New York: Harper & Row, 1954, pp. 121-36.

Fortado, B. "Management Rights: A Topological Survey of the Terrain." *Employee Responsibilities and Rights Journal* 4 (4) (December 1991): 293-310.

Foulkes, F. *Personnel Policies in Large Non Union Companies.* New York: Prentice-Hall, 1980, p. 180.

Greve, R. M. "Technological Change and Women Workers." In *New Technology: International Perspectives on Human Resources and Industrial Relations*, edited by G. Bamber and R. Lansbury. London: Unwin Hyman, 1989, pp. 199-211.

Goldhaber, G. M., and V. S. DiSalvo. "The Communication Revolution: Will Cold Plastic Replace Warm Flesh?" In *Communicating Employee Responsibilities and Rights: A modern Management Mandate*, edited by C. A. B. Osigweh, Yg. NY: Quorum Books, 1987, pp. 119-33.

Goodrich, J. "Telecommuting in America." *Business Horizons*, July-August 1990, pp. 31-37.

Harvard Business Review. "Debate: Does the Baldridge Award Really Work?" January-February, pp. 126-47.

Hirshhorn, L. *Beyond Mechanization.* Cambridge, MA: MIT Press, 1984.

Hoerr, J. "Sharpening Minds for a Competitive Edge." *Business Week*, December 17, 1990, pp. 72-78.

Hunt, H., and T. Hunt. *Human Resource Implications of Robotics*. Kalamazoo, MI: Upjohn Institute, 1983.

Ivey, M., and J. Carey. "The Ecstasy and the Agony." *International Business Week*, October 21, 1991, p. 41.

Kanter, R. *When Giants Learn to Dance*. New York: Touchstone Books, 1990.

Kapstein, J., and J. Hoerr. "*Volvo's Radical New Plant: The Death of the Assembly Line?*" *Business Week*, August 28, 1989, pp. 92-93.

Lansbury, R. "Technological Change and Labour Relations: Introduction." In *Current Issues in Labour Relations*, edited by A. Gladstone, with R. Lansbury, J. Stieber, T. Treau, and M. Weiss. Berlin: Walter de Gruyter, 1989, pp. 11-17.

Majchrzak, A., and D. Davis. "The Human Side of Flexible Factory Automation: Research and Management Practices." In *People's Reaction to Technology*, edited by S. Oskamp and S. Spacapan. Newbury Park, CA: Sage, 1990, pp. 33-66.

Michel, D., and A. Kocinski. "La revolution des horaires de travail. Jamais le dimanche?" *L'Enterprise/A Pour Affaires Economique* 70 (July 1991): 42-51.

Osigweh, C. A. B. *Professional Management*. Dubuque: W.C. Brown Co., Kendall/Hunt Division, 1985.

———. "Communication, Responsibilities and Pro-Rights Revolution in the Industrial Workplace." In *Communicating Employee Responsibilities and Rights*, edited by C. A. B. Osigweh, Yg. NY: Quorum Books, 1987, pp. 3-40.

———. "The Challenge of Responsibilities: Confronting the Revolution in Workplace Rights in Modern Organizations." *Employee Responsibilities and Rights Journal* 1 (1) (March 1988): 5-24.

———. "Toward an Employee Responsibilities and Rights Paradigm." *Human Relations* 43 (12) (1991): 1277-1309.

Osigweh, C. A. B., and M. P. Miceli. "The Challenge of Employee Rights and Responsibilities in Organizations." In *Managing Employee Rights and Responsibilities*, edited by C. A. B. Osigweh, Yg. Quorum Books, 1991, pp. 3-20.

Piore, M., and C. Sable. *The Second Industrial Divide*. New York: Basic Books, 1984.

Rajan, A. *New Technology and Employment in Insurance, Banking and Building Societies: Recent Experience and Future Impact*. Hants, England: Gower Publishing Company, 1985.

Rojot, J. "Employers' Response to Technical Change." In *Current Issues in Labour Relations: An International Perspective*, edited by A. Gladstone, R. Lansbury, J. Stieber, T. Treu, and M. Weiss. Berlin: Walter de Gruyter, 1989, pp. 29-42.

Schroeder, M. "The Recasting of Alcoa." *International Business Week*, September 9, 1991, pp. 38-39.

Sorge, A., and W. Streeck. "Industrial Relations and Technical Change: The Case for An Extended Perspective." In *New Technology and Industrial Relations*, edited by R. Hyman and W. Streeck. Oxford: Basil Blackwell, 1988, pp. 19-47.

Spacapan, S., and S. Oskamp. "People's Reaction to Technology." In *People's Reaction to Technology*, edited by S. Oskamp and S. Spacapan. Newbury Park, CA: Sage, 1990, pp. 9-32.

Stackel, L. "The Flexible Work Place." *Employment Relations Today* (14) (2) (Summer 1987): 189-97.

Stoneman, P. *The Economic Analysis of Technological Change*. Oxford: Oxford

University Press, 1983.
Woodward, J. *Industrial Organization: Theory and Practice.* London: Oxford University Press, 1965.

Chapter 16

Setting Priorities for the Information Technology Industry in Taiwan—A Delphi Study

Christian N. Madu, Chu-hua Kuei, and Assumpta N. Madu

The information systems industry (ISI) is one of the fastest growing. Worldwide sales exceed US$250 billion annually, and this trend is expected to continue with sales to reach US$900 billion by the year 2000 (Arthur Little, 1989). This exponential growth has attracted the interest of policymakers attempting to forge a new direction for their countries. Several years ago, the Institute for Information Industry (III)—an agency of the government of Taiwan—commissioned a study to identify opportunities in the information systems industry for Taiwan. The III also prepared a configuration map of information industry resources (Institute for Information Industry, 1989). This map identifies five major areas of ISI: software, components, communications, systems, and equipment. Figure 16.1 shows what products are in each of these five groups. The III also classified industries as "strategic," including electrical and nonelectrical machinery, information systems, and allied industries (Study on Regulations, 1987; Taiwan Republic, 1988). The strategic industries are characterized by a high interdependence with other industries, a high-technology orientation, greater marketing opportunities, and, possibly, a lower rate of pollution (Study on Regulations, 1987).

A study conducted for the government singled out the information systems industry as one of the future (Arthur Little, 1989). The government also developed incentive programs through the Industrial Development Bureau (IDB) to assist entrepreneurs in one of the strategic industries (Study on Regulations, 1987). The program included low-interest loans, tax deductions, and management and technical support. Since December 1981, when the IDB identified 199 products from the strategic industries, the government has disbursed about US$1.6 billion in low-interest loans and has spent about US$4.8 million on developing appropriate management and technical support for these strategic industries. Between 1984 and 1988, US$34 million was allocated to assist private companies in developing new products that fall within the definition of a strategic industry. Among these industries, information systems seems to attract the greatest attention.

The objective of this chapter is, therefore, to identify the government's priorities for the five areas of information technology it has identified. Businesses are likely to improve their chances of receiving government support and incentives if they invest in areas with high government priority. These priorities can also assist the government in allocating resources (Liberatore, 1987; Saaty & Mariano, 1979). Thus, this chapter offers a systematic approach to the analysis of government policy. We introduce a strategic framework, then recount our interviews with two information systems industry

Figure 16.1
The Information Systems Industry in Taiwan

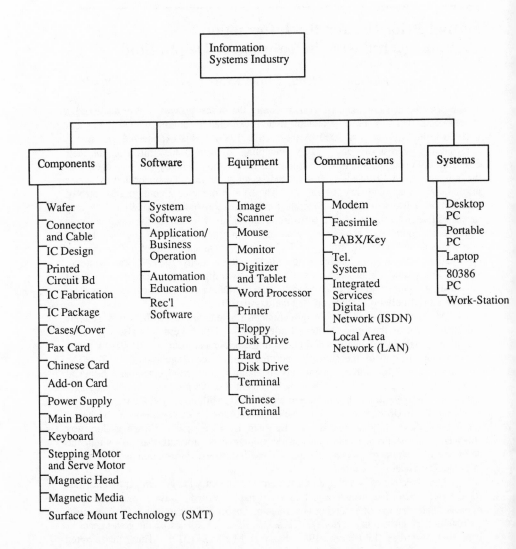

experts and use their views to interpret the priority indices.

THE STRATEGIC FRAMEWORK

The first step in the strategic framework, as shown in Figure 16.2, is a definition of national goals and objectives. These goals have to be realistic and achievable, given the country's strengths and weaknesses. The overall goal for Taiwan is to develop its information systems technology. In this study we identify those factors that will significantly influence development of the ISI, evaluated in relation to the country's capabilities and limitations. A team of experts sets the objectives and identifies and evaluates the critical factors. Each of the information technology areas is evaluated on the basis of these factors or with the aim of ensuring that development of the ISI will maximize the country's social welfare. In light of the multiple variables and constraints involved, some areas of information systems technology may better satisfy the government's goal and needs, and thus may be given higher preference. It should be stated, however, that technology areas are not independent of one another. Rather, they are interdependent among the different areas of information technology.

A strategic analysis of this prioritization also enables the government to identify the factors that ultimately will bring about the successful development of the ISI. International and local competitiveness, ease of market penetration, quality of products, and environmental effects play a major part in achieving the government's goal. In some of these areas, the government may be able to assist businesses, either through some form of trade protection for local manufacturers, subsidized waste clean up, or an international commerce agency to help market products abroad.

Once a national goal has been formulated, it needs to be operationalized. Stakeholders are identified to satisfy these needs, and they participate in the decision-making process. Radford (1980) refers to this group as the active participants. In this chapter, the stakeholders are the information technology experts affiliated with the information industry in Taipei, Taiwan. These experts independently identified the decision alternatives, or different areas of the information systems industry, that Taiwan may wish to develop. As mentioned, the III developed a configuration of information industry resources in Taiwan. Where these choices did not exist, brainstorming generated them. In fact, this approach was also applicable in the next step, identification of the criteria.

Each of the information technologies identified was evaluated using specific guidelines on *output* and *criteria*. The criteria were those elements that can bring about successful development of information technology, or that may be the result of developments in information technology. For example, information technology may lead to better data management; applications of computer technology in manufacturing (flexible computer-integrated manufacturing, inventory control and planning) have been shown to increase productivity. However, highly automated systems may also lead to psychological problems for workers, who may have to relinquish some of their skilled operations to the newly automated system. These problems have to be anticipated, and steps such as job enrichment, training, and job redesign, can limit the negative impact. Problems may also arise if information is not well protected. Unauthorized access to a data base may create social problems that are difficult to assess. Thus, the impact of information technology on a society should be fully considered, and strategies that will lead to its effective development adopted. The cost of a technology may also make it difficult to select it for development.

Figure 16.2
A Strategic Framework for the Transfer of Technology

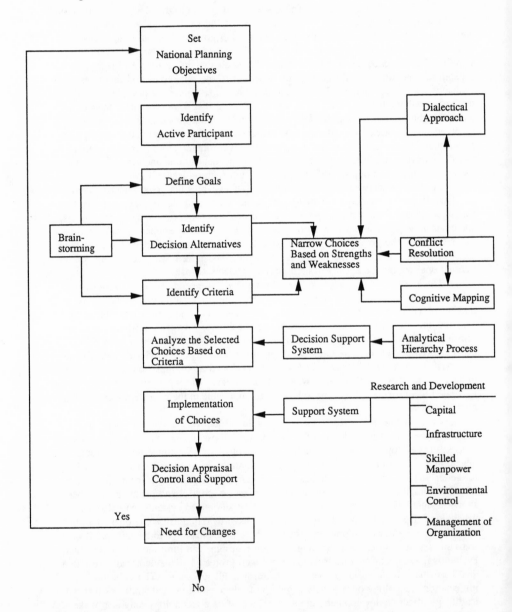

Several criteria and alternative choices were identified. The criteria were narrowed down so that only very significant factors were considered. The essence of this was to avoid information overload. March and Simon (1958) note that an individual's mind is limited, with "bounds of rationality." As the number of alternatives and criteria grows, it becomes difficult to comprehend and compare all the choices at one time. Even with only a few alternatives, there are doubts concerning the rationality of an individual's choice.

An inability to achieve rationality is expected when decision making involves subjective judgment. In our case study, conflicts of this nature were resolved via a dialectical approach. The participants presented arguments in favor of each criterion (thesis); a critique of the criterion (antithesis) followed, until a synthesis was achieved. A dialectical approach is instrumental in resolving conflict. Madu and Jacob (1989) developed a strategic planning framework to use a dialectical approach in the transfer of technology from multinational corporations to less developed countries. This model applies in the present situation as well. The exchange of information among team members also helps resolve some of the conflicts. Cognitive maps, if constructed, may encourage understanding of different perceptions regarding a particular problem. Eden (1988) defines the purpose of cognitive mapping:

> to guide careful problem construction whereby each member of the team can gently "change their mind" and do so creatively. By seeing others' concept in the context of their own concepts the meaning of them changes, this process coupled with sensitively managed social dynamics leads to new insights (team elaboration) created by the synergy stimulated by the team map.

Thus, cognitive maps were used in this study to elicit differing perceptions of the factors that may significantly influence development of information systems technology. Cause-and-effect relationships were developed via signed digraphs, leading to a critical evaluation of the relationships between the different factors as feedback loops.

A comparison was made of decision alternatives with respect to each criterion. This analysis ranked the alternatives with respect to each criterion and also ranked the alternatives with respect to all the criteria. The rankings offered decision support and helped policymakers decide what priority to give to each information technology area.

To assure the successful development of a particular information technology, the capability to operate it should already exist. Society has to be prepared for the new technology through training, mass education, and public-awareness programs. These serve to limit the "rejective reflex" (Legasto, 1979). For example, computer technology leads to changes in life style that as society becomes dependent on that technology. Information technology also brings change. It's important to emphasize the positive side of information technology in improving the quality of life and enhancing sociocultural values. Management of change is, therefore, critical to the new technologies.

Implementation of new technology also requires an adequate support system. For example, in order to profitably operate in a market with short-term product life cycles, as in the information technology industry, there needs to be a highly flexible production and distribution system (Madu & Georgantzas, 1991).

The new technology should be responsive to this dynamic environment. A strategy adopted today may not be suitable for the future. New information and knowledge may revolutionize the way things are done. There is, therefore, a need to monitor and provide feedback to the ISI development process. Objectives and goals set today may need to be changed when present needs and demands are satisfied. This evolving process must continue to grant long-term benefits.   Thus, the strategic framework shown in Figure 16.2 was applied in a real-life setting, as our case study illustrates.

THE EXPERIMENTAL ANALYSIS

This study was conducted in the summer of 1989, at the Institute for Information Industry (III), Taipei, Taiwan.   The goal was to determine Taiwan's focus for information technology through the year 2000.   Decision were to be based on the present level of information technology development, present expectations for the future, and present and foreseeable limitations.

The III provided four information technology experts to participate in the Study. The four participants had five basic qualities: (1) they were enthusiastic about participating, (2) they were committed to the experiment, (3) they had prior experience with decisions on information systems development (4) they had extensive knowledge of the information technology industry, and (5) they knew the industry both in Taiwan and abroad.   Before the study was started, the participants were lectured on the use of the analytic hierarchy process (AHP) and the meaning of the scales.   The work was conducted in Mandarin, Taiwan's national language.

The participants defined the goal, criteria, and decision alternatives as presented in Figure 16.3.   The decision alternatives, in fact, existed prior to the start of our study (Institute for Information Industry, 1989).   The goal was also obvious to the participants. However, the difficulty was in defining the criteria.   Several factors were generated, as suggested in Figure 16.3.   Through negotiation, these factors were narrowed down to seven.   This avoided an information overload, as well as duplication and overlap of factors, since subsequent experiments would require comparison of factors identified as significant.   The seven major factors and the overall goal are presented in a cognitive map shown in Figure 16.4.

Our cognitive map was based on group discussion.   Hart (1976) has shown how such maps can be created using the documentation of actual decision makers.   Roberts (1976) follows a Delphi-type approach.   Signed digraphs were used in this map to show the cause-and-effect relationships between criteria.   It was easy to create an adjacency matrix; from this matrix, the links between variables were established, and the cognitive map could easily be constructed.

From the map, information was derived on cause-and-effect.   For example, the map shows that development of information technology will increase problems, such as environmental pollution, migration of workers to industrial sites, and urban congestion. The demand on the environment may also lead to low acceptance of the technology.   The policy on development of information technology might need to be reconsidered.   More important, policymakers would be able to anticipate the consequences of this decision and develop strategies to handle these problems before they become serious.   Thus, the plus (+) shows a positive influence while the minus (-) shows a negative influence.   The small size of this map makes it possible to analyze feedback through signed digraphs and loops.

As shown in the map, environmental problems were just one of seven criteria that will affect the goal of developing the country's information technology.   On the map, a plus and minus *(±)* is used to link improved socioeconomic conditions (7) and development of information technology (3).   This implies that there are both positive and negative influences in both directions.   For example, development of information tech-

Figure 16.3
Generation of Criteria

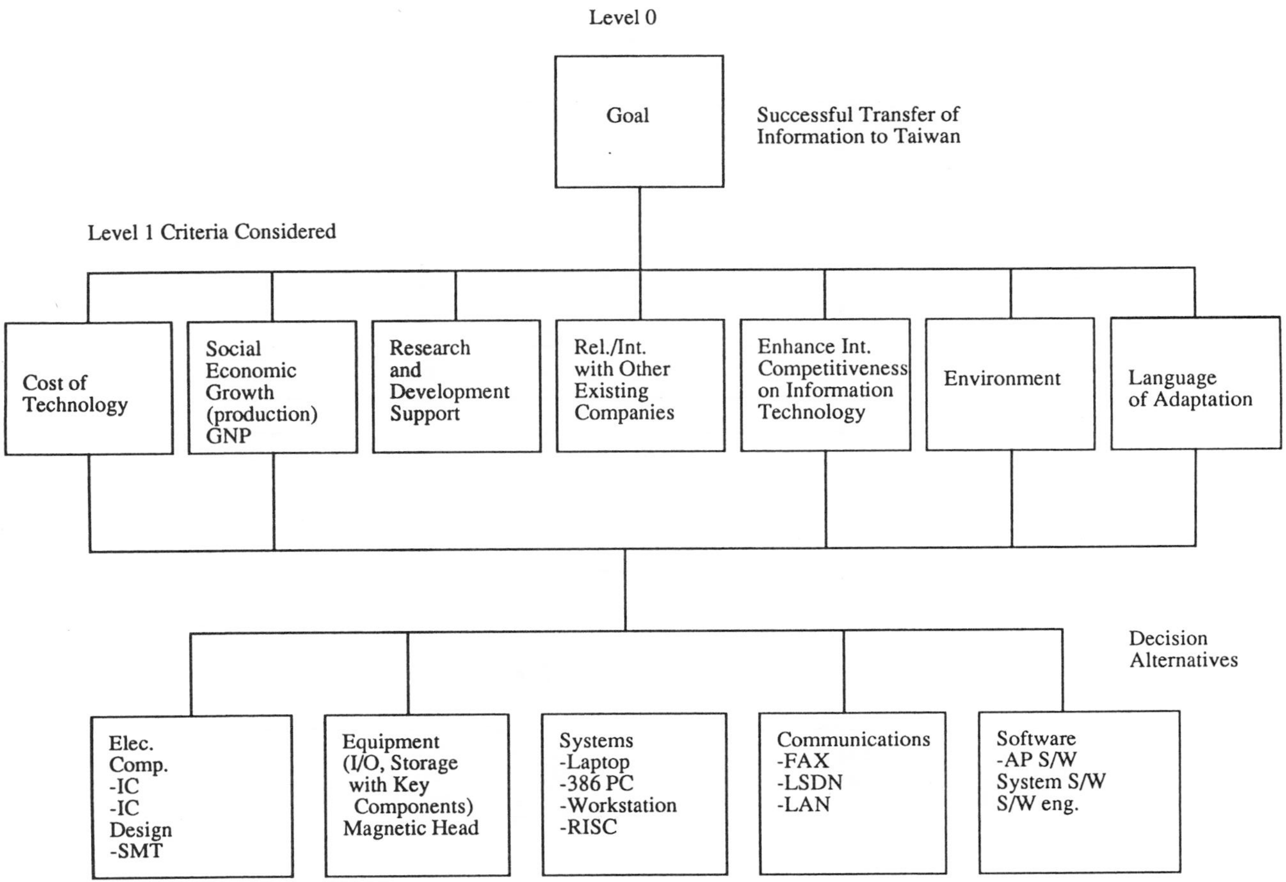

Figure 16.4
Cognitive Map

Cause-effect Relationships Between Different Factors

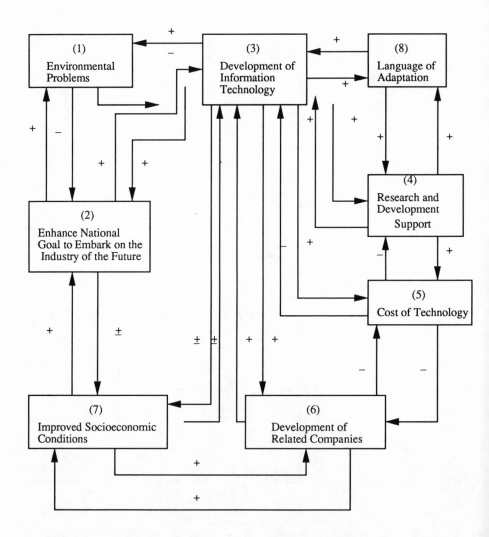

nology may lead to increased employment opportunities, higher standards of living, and improved quality of life. However, these cannot be achieved without development of related industries that may benefit from their interdependence with the information industry. For example, most manufacturing and service sectors depend on the information industry for increased efficiency. Flexible computer-integrated manufacturing relies heavily on the information industry, as does database management in an expanding service sector. But development of these related industries will reduce dependence on the information industry for employment. The country stands to face increased socioeconomic problems if the interdependence is not achieved.

Signed digraphs helped the experts evaluate the consequences of each criterion on the overall goal. Further interpretation of cognitive maps with signed digraphs are presented in Axelord (1976). Linstone (1984) presents a slightly different form of cognitive map, considering technical, organizational, and personal perspectives. Roberts (1976) has argued that cognitive maps are "context sensitive"; in other words, the signed digraphs may change as the context in which the map is derived changes. Nevertheless, the map conveys useful feedback on cause-and-effect relationships. The map also presents a structured way to narrow down the factors, and view their perceived relationships. Thus, the cognitive maps lead to a logical analysis of the problem.

The consistency of decision makers is often difficult to conceptualize and measure. Hart (1976) presents one such analysis in his study of the politics of international control of the oceans. To carry out our own analysis, we introduced weights on these signed digraphs. Forrester's (1971) well-known urban dynamic models can, in fact, be viewed as weighted signed digraphs. In our study, we used the analytic hierarchy process (1980) to analyze our map.

The signs between these factors are presented in what is known as an adjacency matrix (see Table 16.1). This matrix can also help examine the cause-and-effects the

Table 16.1
Cognitive Mapping—Exploring Linkages

Factor No.	1	2	3	4	5	6	7	8
1	O	-	+	O	O	O	O	O
2	+	O	+	O	O	O	±	O
3	+	+	O	+	O	+	±	+
4	O	O	+	O	+	O	O	+
5	O	O	O	-	O	-	O	O
6	O	O	+	O	-	O	+	O
7	O	+	±	O	O	+	O	O
8	O	O	+	+	O	O	O	O

O = no direct link between the pair; + = positive influence of one factor over the other; - = negative influence of one factor over the other; ± = both positive and negative influence of one factor over the other.

group perceives as important. An entry of circle (O) is used in those cells where no direct links are established from the map. The analytic hierarchy process further explores these relationships and priority indices can be developed for the factors. The adjacency matrix in our example showed that out of the fifty-six possible links in the map, only twenty-four were perceived by the experts to exist (42.8%).

Signed digraphs also have an additional utility in analyzing complex decisions. Keeney and Von Winterfeld (1989) point out that experts often worry that the use of numbers as a quantitative expression of their judgment "may reflect more precision and knowledge than they really have." Thus, many experts prefer verbal qualifications since they reflect vagueness. Our map created from the discussion sessions may reflect such vagueness if not weighted. However, the use of qualitative judgment introduces fuzziness. Quantification of expert judgments helps reduce such ambiguity. Although the AHP used here tended to be too precise in its assignment of weights and generation of priority indices, recent studies demonstrate the need to establish ranges in estimating expert judgment (Keeney & von Winterfeldt, 1989; Yoon, 1989). Fuzzy set theory explicitly considers the imprecision in human judgment by analyzing ill-structured and complex decision situations (Kangari & Riggs, 1989; Zadeh et al., 1975).

The Decision Support System

A decision support system (DSS) was built for this case study using the Expert Choice cell (1983). Saaty (1980) developed the methodology underlying Expert Choice, which he refers to as the analytic hierarchy process (AHP). The AHP is defined as "a multi-criteria method that uses hierarchic or network structures to represent a decision problem and then develops priorities for the alternatives based on the decision makers' judgments throughout the system" (1987, p. 157).

The AHP uses a nine-point scale to show judgments or preferences of one factor over another. The judgment may be based on experience, intuition, or available quantitative data. Through the AHP, policymakers reach a decision by applying their judgment systematically. The factors to be considered are organized in a hierarchic structure with three main levels. The highest level denotes the goal, the middle level denotes the criteria, and the bottom level the decision alternatives.

In our study, in order to implement AHP, a comparison was made of each pair of criteria with respect to meeting the overall goal. For example, competition and R&D were compared with respect to successfully developing an appropriate information technology. These comparisons went on until all pairs of criteria were compared with respect to the overall goal. The nine-point scale utilized by AHP is presented in Table 16.2.

The AHP also measures the consistency of the decision makers' judgments by computing what is called an "inconsistency index." If this index is less than 0.1, then the decisions are consistent; otherwise, they are inconsistent. Although consistency does not guarantee quality decisions, all quality decisions are consistent (1983).

Since it is so easy to use AHP, it can consider both quantitative and qualitative information, and it can measure the consistency of judgments, AHP has been applied in a wide range of studies (Liberatore, 1987; Madu & Madu, 1988; Saaty & Mariano, 1979; Madu & Georgantzas, 1991; Madu, 1989; Saaty, 1987, 1977; Alexander & Saaty, 1987, 1990; Ramanujam & Saaty, 1981; Saaty & Rogers, 1976; Saaty & Khouja, 1976; Saaty & Alexander, 1981.) An excellent review of AHP and its applications is provided by Zahedi (1986).

The generation module of the DSS starts with establishment of objectives and

Table 16.2
Expert Choice—The Hierarchy of Preferences

Numerical Assignment	Natural Language
1	The two alternatives are of equal importance
3	One alternative has a weak importance over the other
5	An alternative has an essential or strong importance over the other
7	There is demonstrated importance on one factor over the other
9	One factor is absolutely more important than the other
2, 4, 6, 8	Shows intermediate values between the two adjacent judgments
Reciprocals	For any activity A that has one of the above values assigned to it when compared to activity B, then B has a reciprocal value assigned to it when compared to activity A

identification of criteria, as shown in Figure 16.3. In executing this module, the different worldviews of the experts, stemming from their cognitive differences and experiences, were captured via brainstorming, while a dialectical approach helped understand and analyze the differences in their premises. This process eliminated duplication and overlap of factors, thus reducing the number of factors to be compared. The second phase is the analysis module. This was performed using cognitive maps as described above and the Expert Choice cell. Here, we used a real-life problem and experts who frequently participate in decision situations involving information technology development. The third phase is the evaluation module, and this was executed using the inconsistency index to measure the consistency of the judgments. Thus, the quality of the decisions were evaluated before implementation.

The small size of the group encouraged active participation in discussions. After these discussions, participants were asked to assign their judgments in a pairwise format. They were given a form with matrices to show which items to compare. A sample of this form is shown in Figure 16.5.

The group identified the cost of technology, socioeconomic growth, R&D support, relatedness or interdependence to existing businesses, competitiveness, environment, and language of adoption, as factors that influence successful development of information technology. The language of adoption factor applied especially when the technology would come from a foreign source. Specifically, the major areas of information technology of interest in this study were: computer components, systems (8088, 80286, 80386), equipment, software, and communications. Figure 16.1 outlines the different products in each of these areas.

Each subject was asked to assign a judgment on each pair of alternatives under consideration. Before assignment, these pairs were discussed. To avoid group effect or domination of the process by one member of the team, participants were asked not to voice their judgments on the alternatives.

The group judgment was derived by computing the geometric mean of the individual judgments (Expert Choice, 1983). These averages were inputed to an IBM-PC

Figure 16.5
Pairwise Comparisons

(A) Pairwise Comparisons

	Cost of Techn.	Soc-Eco Growth	R&D Support	Relat./ Interd.	Compet- ition	Envir.	Language
Cost of Techn.							
Soc-Eco Growth							
R&D Support							
Relat./ Interd.							
Compet.							
Environ.							
Language							

(B) Pairwise Comparison of the Decision Alternatives
for any given Criterion

	Electr. Compon.	Equip.	Systems	Comm's	Software
Electr. Compon.					
Equip.					
Systems					
Comm's					
Software					

loaded with Expert Choice to generate the results. The team was to regroup, should inconsistent decisions be reached; this, however, was not the case in this experiment.

The Results

The group judgment obtained by computing the geometric mean of the individual judgments was analyzed using the Expert Choice cell. These results are presented in Table 16.3.

The results gave an inconsistency index of 0.02, implying that consistent judgments were made. Note that this value has to be greater than 0.1 for decisions to be inconsistent. Of the seven criteria, international competitiveness was seen as the most important factor in deciding which information technology the government should emphasize. Participants perceived that Taiwan would enhance its competitiveness if software development was emphasized. A priority index of 0.247 was assigned to competitiveness. The emphasis on international competitiveness is not surprising, since Taiwan would expect to face industrial giants from the United States, Japan, and Europe. Furthermore, emphasis on software development may be directly related to local conditions. There may be a need for Taiwan to develop suitable software owing to language barriers and legal differences in banking and accounting practices.

The results further showed that the relatedness or interdependence of the information technology to existing technological conditions was important. This factor got a priority index of 0.198. It was also used in defining strategic industries. A further breakdown showed that computer components are high when relatedness is emphasized. For example, computer components such as connector cables or printed circuit boards may be needed in computer systems or devices. Some of these products are well developed in Taiwan. R&D was also high on the priority scale, with an index of 0.157. To effectively compete in the development of computer systems and components, Taiwan needs to develop an effective R&D program. The other results were similarly interpreted. Cost of technology was seen as of least importance. Priorities for these five alternatives are given in Table 16.4.

The results showed that, for Taiwan, the most important area of the information systems industry to develop is software. However, by observing the generated results, it can be seen that software, components, systems, and communications ranked very close to each other and also demand attention. The results also showed that equipment did not rank very high. These results provide guidelines for developing Taiwan's information technology, however the views expressed here may reflect the conditions and aspirations of government, and may not necessarily be the consensus in industry.

The next phase of the experiment will be to implement the decisions via resource allocation. Clearly, the alternatives are mutually dependent. However, at the time of this study, adequate budgetary data did not exist to carry out this phase of the study.

Our study showed that the experts were consistent in their judgment and that the consensus was also consistent. However, further analysis suggests that consistency may not be as important in group decision making as in individual decision making. Of ultimate importance is identifying and analyzing the sources of disagreement in group decision making. Even when consistent judgments are made, disagreements may not be adequately resolved. Further analysis, such as graphic displays of each expert's priority indices with respect to the group, may help identify major disagreement points. Further discussion of the procedure may be required to bridge such disagreements (Madu, 1989). Owing to time constraints, we were not able to investigate this issue.

Table 16.3
Expert Choice—the Group Judgment

International competitiveness =0.247
Software	0.078
Systems	0.055
Components	0.041
Communications	0.038
Equipment	0.035

Interdependence with existing technology =0.198
Software	0.044
Systems	0.035
Components	0.070
Communications	0.037
Equipment	0.013

Research and development support =0.157
Software	0.026
Systems	0.051
Components	0.049
Communications	0.019
Equipment	0.013

Socio-economic growth =0.146
Software	0.035
Systems	0.029
Components	0.039
Communications	0.033
Equipment	0.010

Environment =0.122
Software	0.041
Systems	0.020
Components	0.010
Communications	0.041
Equipment	0.010

Cost of technology =0.085
Software	0.017
Systems	0.017
Components	0.015
Communications	0.035
Equipment	0.015

Language of adoption =0.044
Software	0.016
Systems	0.006
Components	0.03
Communications	0.014
Equipment	0.005

Table 16.4
Overall Priorities for IT Policy

1. Software	0.255
2. Systems	0.213
3. Components	0.226
4. Communications	0.204
5. Equipment	0.101

After the study the consensus was that the procedure was useful in expanding participants' worldviews and knowledge. The process exposed them to alternative paradigms and helped transform some of their views. It may also have strengthened some of their positions. If there is repeated discussion, this transformation will be evident in the priority indices generated.

Interpretation of Results

Further interpretations of the priority indices were obtained by consulting two industry experts. he context under which the priorities were generated was explained and they were asked to interpret the results. Although these interpretations may be biased by individual perceptions of what the government ought to focus on, nevertheless they offer useful insights.

Software. The experts noted that custom-designed computer packages are popular in Taiwan. In addition, there is adequate skilled labor to develop such packages. Presently, many companies in Taiwan, such as Third Wave or KUO CHIAU, develop application software. One of the most popular word-processing packages, known as KSII, was developed by KUO CHIAU. Although these companies have made remarkable progress, they have not achieved the same level of success in developing systems software, systems development tools, network software, multiuser application software, and parallel processing software. These areas are perceived as important to developing a strong information systems industry. They concur with the government on giving software development high priority. They also note that, with the exception of systems software, there are many opportunities in software for parallel processing, multiuser Chinese language application software, computer-aided software engineering (CASE) tools, and fourth-generation languages. They argued that, on a relative basis, hardware development is strong in Taiwan. The weakness in software development is in part due to the inability to enforce software copyright laws, and in part to the considerable time, skill, and resources required to develop software. These difficulties lead to a lower rate of return and make software development unattractive to many businesses. In fact, they pointed out that many companies in Taiwan have pulled out of software development.

One of the exceptions is ETEN, a software development company. One of its products—also called ETEN Chinese system—provides a Chinese operating environment within MS-DOS. ETEN is priced very low, making it affordable to a wide range of users. Its low cost also makes it unattractive to copy. When this product received market acceptance, the company introduced Chinese Interface Cards, which permit printing near letter-quality Chinese characters. These more expensive cards are designed for a wide range of users including government and schools. Thus, while its software is cheap, the cards needed to improve its printing quality are not. This way the company is able to recover some of its software development costs.

While the experts saw the need for a strong software development program in order to develop the information technology industry, they also suggested steps that will encourage software development. For example, they pointed out the need for government incentives for software developers, grants to academic institutions to facilitate software development, strategic planning, and strict enforcement of copyright laws.

Systems and Components. The personal computer systems market is difficult to penetrate. Producers have to contend with patent laws, since patents to computer hardware systems belong mostly to foreign companies like IBM. Only a few companies in Taiwan, such as ACER, ARC, or PLUS & PLUS, are able to produce an entire computer hardware system (8088, 80286, 80386) and market it abroad. For smaller companies, getting into this market is not attractive. One of the ways it may be achieved is through licensing agreements with foreign manufacturers who hold the patents. Smaller companies can also combine their resources and negotiate from a position of strength; otherwise, ·their option is to concentrate on development of computer components.

Computer components development has a wide market both locally and internationally. The dependence of computers on components such as keyboards, main boards, magnetic heads, and CRTs partly explains this surge in demand. Moreover, many entrepreneurs have the basic technology to support development of new components at very low cost. Consequently, any new product development would have a related effect on existing industries through higher R&D support, greater economic growth, lower pollution, and lower cost. The results in Table 16.3 are evidence of this. Since component development offers potential benefits, it is not surprising that the III experts chose it as second in their priority scale.

Communications. Communications ranked fourth in the priority index. This may be partly due to the fact that some products in this area are in the embryonic stage, even in the United States—for example, the integrated service digital network (ISDN), a physical telecommunications network that extends over wide geographical areas (continents) and integrates a broad variety of voice and nonvoice telecommunications traffic (Arthur Little, 1989). In Taiwan, many of the underlying technologies are not yet developed; furthermore, this area is currently under government monopoly. Some of the government's services and research have not been introduced to a wide range of users. For example, local area networking (LAN) is popular only among research institutions and universities. In time, the importance of the communications sector and its many applications may push the government toward privatization. Increasing interest in Taiwan's stock market is one area where this need may become manifest.

Equipment. This area given the lowest priority was perceived by the experts in Taiwan perceive as the most developed among the five areas. There are many large corporations that produce computer equipment in Taiwan. Technological skills in this area are quite matured and the market is stable. For example, TATUNG one of the big corporations, manufactures computer monitors for IBM. Emphasis, therefore, should be on areas not adequately developed.

CONCLUSION

We have described a strategic framework that will assist in Taiwan's development of its information systems technology. The strategic framework was based on decision making by a group of experts. Brainstorming generated the different factors involved, and conflicts were resolved via dialectical methods. These conflicts were often a result of differences in worldview and were necessary to stimulate thinking and understanding of the situation. The causal relationships among the factors were explored via a cognitive map derived from the experts' discussion sessions. The map exhibited feedback loops and was used in the logical analysis of cause-and-effect relationships. This map also focused discussion so as to expand the knowledge and understanding of the team members. The conceptual framework was tested by building a decision support system based on the Expert Choice cell.

Information technology experts from the Institute for Information Industry, Taipei, were the subjects in this case study. Their role was to (1) determine the criteria that will influence successful development of information technology in Taiwan, (2) narrow down the criteria to a list of seven significant ones, (3) identify possible decision alternatives, and (4) compare the decision alternatives, given the identified criteria and the strengths and weaknesses of Taiwan.

A priority ranking for both the criteria and the decision alternatives was derived, with the results reflecting the views of participants on the direction Taiwan's information industry should take. The priority indices might also be used to allocate government resources to the development of the ISI. Lastly, the results are of value to businesses wanting to take advantage of the government's incentive programs.

An integrated approach to the development of the appropriate information technology has been described. The study shows how a multicriteria model can help make decisions about information technology, allowing for equal treatment of qualitative and quantitative factors. Thus, this method presents a decision support system (DSS) for policymakers, especially in solving ill-structured problems.

The following lessons can be drawn from the strategic framework proposed in this study:

1. The strategic framework offers a step-by-step approach to a complex decision-making situation.
2. The discussions expanded the worldviews and understanding of the team about the problem and the methodology. However, this was achieved easily, since all members were information technology experts who have participated in similar decisions. Also, the methodology was well understood by the team members.
3. Using a homogeneous group speeded up the decision-making process. The experts were consistent in their initial assignments, and there was no need for regrouping. With a heterogeneous group, this process could have taken longer (Madu & Georgantzas, 1991).
4. A facilitator directed the discussions. The facilitator also explained the nine-point scale used in AHP and how the matrix could be completed.
5. Consistency in group decision making does not imply that all conflicts have been resolved. In fact, wide divergence in opinion remained even after consistency in judgment was achieved. These lingering conflicts may be resolved through negotiations on those factors, however this problem demands further attention.
6. It is easier to control a smaller group. Also, the small size of the group helps ensure active participation.

The information technology experts in the study are actively involved in Taiwan's information systems industry. Their opinions and judgments, as analyzed via AHP, show that Taiwan needs to emphasize software development foremost. Following software in importance, are components, systems, and communications, while computer equipment is last in preference.

An interpretation of these results has also been given. The analysis shows that international competitiveness is the major criterion to determine the future of Taiwan's information systems industry. Environment and cost ranked low in terms of priority.

These decisions reflect the experts' worldviews, life experiences, cognitive feelings, and perceptions, thus, the results are subjective assessments that may have been influenced by data. Decision making in itself is subjective, however the use of experts in a systematic manner can yield a satisfactory solution to sociotechnical problems. The objective has never been to achieve an optimal solution, but the implications here, to both government and business, are evident.

REFERENCES

Alexander, J. M., and T. L. Saaty. "The Forward and Backward Processes of Conflict Analysis." *Behavioral Sciences.* 22 (1987): 87-98.

———. "Stability Analysis of the Forward-Backward Process: Northern Ireland Case Study. *Behavioral Sciences* 22 (1990): 375-82.

Arthur D. Little. "Taiwan 2000: Industry Opportunities Information Systems." Report prepared for Council for Economic Planning and Development, Industrial Development Bureau, MOEA, March 1989.

Axelord, R. *Structure of Decisions—The Cognitive Maps of Political Elites.* Princeton, NJ: Princeton University Press, 1976.

Eden, C. *Cognitive Mapping. European Journal of Operational Research* 36 (1) (1988): 1-13.

Expert Choice. McLean, VA, Decision Support Software Inc., 1983.

Forrester, J. W. *World Dynamics.* Cambridge, MA: Wright-Allen, 1971.

Hart, J. "Comparative Cognition: Politics of International Control of the Oceans." In *Structure of Decisions—The Cognitive Maps of Political Elites*, by R. Axelord Princeton, NJ: Princeton University Press, 1976, pp. 180-217.

Institute for Information Industry. "Configuration Map of Information Industry Resources in the Republic of China." January 1989.

Kangari, R., and L. S. Riggs. "Construction Risk Assessment by Linguistics." *IEEE Transactions on Engineering Management* EM-36 (2) (1989): 126-31.

Keeney, R. L., and D. von Winterfeldt. "On the Uses of Expert Judgment on Complex Technical Problems." *IEEE Transactions on Engineering Management* EM-36 (2) (1989): 83-86.

Legasto Jr., A. "Towards a Calculus of Development Analysis." *Technological Forecasting and Social Change* 14 (1979): 217-30.

Liberatore, M. J. "An Extension of the Analytic Hierarchy Process for Industrial R&D Project Selection and Resource Allocation." *IEEE Transactions on Engineering Management* EM-34 (1) (1987): 12-18.

Linstone, H. A. *Multiple Perspectives for Decision Making.* New York: Elsevier North-Holland, 1984.

Madu, C. N. "A Quality Control Framework for GDSS Application on Multicriteria Decision Making." *IIE Transactions* (forthcoming).

Madu, C. N., and N. C. Georgantzas. "Strategic Thrust of Manufacturing Automation Decisions." *IIE Transactions* 23 (2) (1991): 138-48.

Madu, C. N., and R. Jacob. "Strategic Planning in Technology Transfer: A Dialectical Approach." *Technological Forecasting and Social Change* 35 (4) (1989): 327-38.

Madu, C. N., and A. N. Madu. "A Systems Approach to the Transfer of Mutually Dependent Technologies." Working Paper, Pace University, 1988.

March, J. G., and H. A. Simon. *Organizations.* New York: John Wiley, 1958.

Radford, K. J. *Strategic Planning: An Analytical Approach.* Reston, VA: Reston Publishing Co., 1980.

Ramanujam, V., and T. L. Saaty. "Technological Choices in the Less Developed Countries: An Analytic Hierarchy Approach." *Technological Forecasting and Social Change* 19 (1981): 81-98.

Roberts, F. S. "Strategy for the Energy Crisis: The Case of Commuter Transportation Policy." In *Structure of Decisions—The Cognitive Maps of Political Elites*, by R. Axelord Princeton, NJ: Princeton University Press, 1976, pp. 142-79.

Saaty, T. L. "The Sudan Transport Study." *Interfaces* 8 (1) (1977): 37-57.

———. *The Analytic Hierarchy Process.* New York: McGraw-Hill, 1980.

———. "Rank Generation, Preservation, and Reversal in the Analytic Hierarchy Decision Process." *Decision Sciences* 18 (2) (1987): 157-77.

Saaty, T. L., and J. M. Alexander. *Thinking With Models.* Oxford: Pergamon Press, 1981.

Saaty, T. L., and M. Khouja. "A Measure of World Influence." *Journal of Peace Science* 2 (1) (1976): 31-47.

Saaty, T. L., and R. S. Mariano. "Rationing Energy to Industries: Priorities and Input-Output Dependence." *Energy Systems and Policy* 8 (1979): 85-111.

Saaty, T. L., and P. C. Rogers. "Higher Education in the United States (1985-2000)." *Socio-Economic Planning Sciences* 10 (1976): 251-63.

"Study on Regulations of the Strategic Industries in ROC." Executive Yuan, Taiwan (translated from Chinese), 1987.

Taiwan Republic of China. "Economic Development." Report for Council for Economic Planning and Development, Taipei, Taiwan, 1988.

Yoon, K. "The Propagation of Errors in Multiple-Attribute Decision Analysis: A Practical Approach." *Journal of Operational Research Society* 40 (1989): 681-86.

Zadeh, L. A., et al. *Fuzzy Sets and Their Application to Cognitive and Decision Processes.* New York: Academic Press, 1975.

Zahedi, F. "The Analytic Hierarchy Process—A Survey of the Method and its Applications." *Interfaces* 16 (1986): 96-108.

IV

Knowledge-Based Techniques

Chapter 17

The Role of Artificial Intelligence and Expert Systems in New Technologies

Adedeji B. Badiru

Artificial intelligence (AI) is defined as the ability of a machine to use simulated knowledge in solving problems. There has been a significant increase in research and applications of artificial intelligence over the past few years. It is expected that the high level of interest in AI will continue for many years into the future. New, innovative applications of artificial intelligence continue to surface. Expert systems (ES) represent the most successful branch of artificial intelligence to date. By definition, an *expert system* is a computer program that simulates the thought process of a human expert to solve complex problems in a specific area. An expert system operates as an interactive process that responds to questions, asks for clarification, makes recommendations, and generally aids decision making. Expert systems provide "expert" advice and guidance in a wide variety of activities, from computer diagnosis to delicate medical surgery. The role that artificial intelligence and expert systems can play in new manufacturing technology cannot be overemphasized (Badiru 1990a). Any technology problem dealing with data interpretation, identification, diagnosis, design, monitoring, and control can benefit from the techniques of AI and ES (Weitz, 1990).

THE DESIGN OF AN EXPERT SYSTEM

An expert system can be viewed as a computer simulation of a human expert. Complex decisions involve intricate combinations of factual and heuristic knowledge. In order for the computer to retrieve and effectively use heuristic knowledge, the knowledge must be organized in an accessible and compatible format that distinguishes among data, knowledge, and control structures. To facilitate this distinction, expert systems are organized into three major components, each with unique operations:

1. *Knowledge base.* This consists of problem-solving rules, procedures, and intrinsic data relevant to the problem area.
2. *Data structure.* This refers to task-specific data for the problem under consideration.
3. *Inference engine.* This is a generic-control mechanism that applies the axiomatic knowledge in the knowledge base to the task-specific data to arrive at some solution or conclusion.

The knowledge base is the nucleus of the expert system. It is not a data base.

The conventional data base typically represents a static relationship among the elements in the subject area. A knowledge base, by contrast, contains the knowledge of human experts, expressed in terms of dynamic rules and solution strategies. These rules and strategies can change, depending on the prevailing problem scenario. The modularity of an expert system is an important distinguishing characteristic compared to a conventional computer program. The knowledge base constitutes the problem-solving rules, facts, or intuition that a human expert might use in solving problems, with information usually stored in terms of if-then rules. The working memory represents relevant data for the current problem. The inference engine is the control mechanism that organizes the problem data and searches the knowledge base for applicable rules. Figure 17.1 presents the integrated structure of the three components.

REPRESENTATION OF TECHNOLOGY KNOWLEDGE

An important aspect of artificial intelligence and expert systems is the model for representing human knowledge in a computer code. Human experts use heuristic reasoning in solving problems. This reasoning approach, commonly called rules of thumb or expert heuristics, allows the expert to quickly and efficiently arrive at a good solution. Expert systems base their reasoning process on symbolic manipulation and heuristic inference procedures that closely match the human thinking process. The common models for representing this knowledge include:

Rules
Frames
Semantic networks
Predicate calculus
Object-attribute-value triplets
Scripts

The model used for a particular technology problem depends on the nature of the problem to be solved. Rules are the most frequent method. The process of developing a knowledge base involves developing the cause-and-effect relationships associated with the problem domain, as shown in Figure 17.2.

DATA ANALYSIS REQUIREMENTS

A good problem for an expert system is one in which there is general agreement on the facts of a situation and in which clear boundaries exist for the problem and data sets can be determined. Just like human experts, expert systems don't always arrive at the best possible solutions at all times. An expert system will sometimes generate better solutions than a real expert and will sometimes generate inferior ones based on prevailing data. A problem selected for an expert system should be such that the user is willing to accept an imperfect solution based on whatever imperfection is associated with the available data. This is particularly important in technology-based applications. A careful analysis of technology data requirements (Badiru 1990b) is essential in implementing artificial intelligence techniques. Manufacturing technology often involves different measurement scales depending on the problem being considered. The problem analysis and solution approach are influenced by the type of data and measurement scale to be

Figure 17.1
Expert Systems Structure

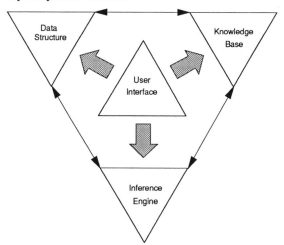

Figure 17.2
Technology Condition and Action Relationships

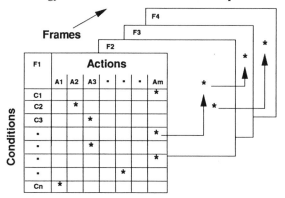

used. The symbolic processing approach of expert systems requires understanding the different types of data.

A *nominal scale* is the lowest level of measurement scale, grouping items into categories. The categories are mutually exclusive and collectively exhaustive; that is, they do not overlap and they cover all possible characteristics. Examples of data using the nominal scale are product quality classification, technology type, employee gender, job classification, color, and name.

An *ordinal scale* is distinguished from a nominal scale by the property of order among the categories. An example is the process of assigning hierarchical classification codes to product quality based on a measured characteristic. A code of A may be known to be better than a code of B, but there is no indication of how much better it is. Similarly, first is ahead of second which is ahead of third, but there is no indication of the relative spacings between the categories. Other examples of data on an ordinal scale are high, medium, and low; thick and thin, hot and cold, and good and bad.

An *interval scale* is distinguished from an ordinal scale by having equal intervals between the units of measure. The assignment of weights to technology capability on a scale of 1 to 10 is an example of such a measurement. A weight of 1 does not imply that the technology has no capability at all. For example, temperature is measured on an interval scale. Even though there is a zero point on the temperature scale, it is an arbitrary relative measure. It cannot be determined that an item is zero degrees cold simply by touching it, because different people have different levels of sensitivity to temperature. Other examples of an interval scale are IQ measurements and aptitude ratings.

A *ratio scale* has the same properties of an interval scale, but with a true zero point. For example, an estimate of zero processing time for a machining operation is a ratio scale measurement. Other examples of items measured on a ratio scale are volume, length, height, weight, and inventory level.

In addition to the measurement scale, a data set can be classified based on its inherent nature. Examples of the relevant classifications are transient data, recurring data, static data, and dynamic data. *Transient data* is defined as a volatile set of data encountered once during a problem and not needed again. The data need not be stored in a permanent data base unless they may be needed for future analysis or uses. *Recurring data* refers to data that is encountered frequently enough to necessitate permanent storage. Recurring data may be further categorized as *static* and *dynamic data*. Recurring data that are static retain their original parameters and values each time they are encountered during a problem. Recurring data that are dynamic have the potential for taking on different parameters and values each time they are encountered. In an expert system designed to solve technology-based problems, a mixture of data scales is needed for effective heuristics to arrive at a practical solution.

TECHNOLOGY SEARCH STRATEGIES

In making use of the encoded knowledge, an expert system must use an efficient search strategy. It must search for the piece of knowledge that best matches the current problem data. In this process, it can use either forward or backward chaining.

Forward Chaining

Commonly referred to as data-driven reasoning, this reasoning approach involves checking the condition part of a rule to determine whether it is true or false. If the condition is true, then the action part of the rule is also true. The procedure continues until a solution to the current problem is found or a deadend is reached. An example of forward chaining in technology adoption is to first acquire a technology and then attempt to find suitable uses of the technology.

Backward Chaining

Also called goal-driven reasoning, backward chaining is used to backtrack from a goal to the paths that lead to the goal. It is the reverse of forward chaining, and very good when all outcomes are known and the number of possible outcomes is not large. In this case, a goal is specified and the expert system tries to determine what conditions are needed to arrive at the specified goal. An example of backward chaining in technology adoption is to first specify the goal of the organization and then backtrack to find the right technology to accomplish the goal.

Technology implementation often involves a search for alternate means of satisfying a specified goal. Artificial intelligence techniques can play a significant role in the search and selection processes. These processes typically involve the following steps:

Problem identification
Problem analysis
Search for alternate solutions
Selection of the preferred solution
Presentation and implementation of the selected solution

There is always a need to improve the search strategies used in artificial intelligence techniques. An expert system must search for a solution to a given problem in an efficient manner. In the search process, the expert system faces a number of potentially conflicting solutions; the solution that best fits the scenario must be identified quickly. Forward and backward chaining are the two most common strategies presently used. However, several enhancements to the basic search process have been proposed in recent years. Pearl (1984) presents various heuristic search strategies for artificial intelligence. Badiru (1992) offers a new search methodology based on the mathematical theory of Cantor Sets.

PROBLEM PARTITION AND ORGANIZATION

It is often necessary to organize a problem into a form that will facilitate an efficient solution procedure. Problem partitioning is an important approach to problem organization. A large problem can be broken into smaller subproblems or subsets, which can be better handled by AI. Similarly, the knowledge base for a problem can be partitioned into smaller integrated subknowledge bases. Thus, a true subset of a knowledge base should solve a subproblem corresponding to a subgoal. The partitions or subsets of a knowledge base can be used to construct subframes for specific subgoals of the main goal. In other words, let A and B be two knowledge bases. If every rule element of A is a rule element of B, then A is a subset of B and B is a superset of A, as presented graphically in Figure 17.3.

TECHNOLOGY RELATIONS AND SOLUTION DOMAINS

For the search process, it is helpful to determine the range of elements to be searched in one knowledge subset relative to another. Let A and B be two technology options. If R is a relation from technology A to technology B, then the domain of R is the set of all technology attribute a belonging to A such that aRb for some attribute b belonging to B.

As an example, consider the two knowledge sets in Figure 17.4. Let set A contain the subgoals $a1$, $a2$, $a3$, $a4$, and $a5$ while set B contains the subgoals $b1$, $b2$, $b3$, $b4$, $b5$, $b6$, $b7$, and $b8$. Define a relation Z from A to B such that an element a belonging to A has a link (i.e., is related) to an element b belonging to B, if and only if there is a rule in B that has a as a premise and b as a conclusion.

Now suppose only the following rules exist in set B:

If $a1$,	then $b2$.
If $a2$,	then $b5$.
If $a3$,	then $b6$.

The domain of Z is then given by the set:

$$\text{Dom}(Z) = \{a1, a2, a3\},$$

since the elements $a1$, $a2$, and $a3$ are the only elements of A that can successfully trigger rules in B. The image of the relation, R, is defined as:

$$\text{Im}(R) = \{b \in B \mid (a, b) \in R \text{ for some } \alpha \in A \}.$$

Thus, the image of the relation Z is:

$$\text{Im}(Z) = \{b2, b5, b6\},$$

which corresponds to the set of rules that are fired in set B. With the above relations, a decision maker can use AI/ES techniques to evaluate alternate technologies and identify complementary attributes. Both technologies that can coexist and those that are mutually exclusive can be identified in the technology adoption process.

UNCERTAINTIES REGARDING NEW TECHNOLOGIES

Uncertainty is one of the major concerns in·the adoption and implementation of new technology, but artificial intelligence can be helpful in evaluating risk. Some techniques for handling uncertainty in expert systems applications are:

Certainty factors
Fuzzy sets
Classical probability
Dempster-Shafer theory

Owing to limited space, only the Dempster-Shafer theory is discussed here, and that only briefly. Dempster-Shafer attempts to distinguish between ignorance and uncer-

Figure 17.3
Formation of a Subset of a Knowledge Base

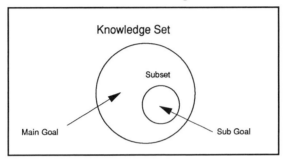

Figure 17.4
Technology Relations on Knowledge-Base Sets

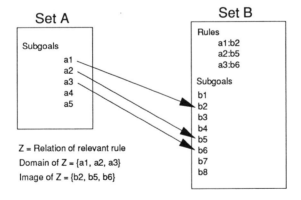

tainty. Not knowing the specific value of a variable does not necessarily imply that the variable is subject to uncertainty. With classic probability theory, we are required to consider belief and disbelief as functional opposites. That is, if A, B, and C are the only three events in a sample space S, and we know that $P(A) = 0.3$ and $P(B) = 0.6$, then classic probability theory yields 0.1 as the probability for the event C, since $P(S) = 1.0$ and $P(A) + P(B) + P(C) = P(S)$. Unfortunately, this may not represent human reasoning because it is possible for a person to believe or disbelieve three different items with the same level of assurance. The assurance of C may actually have nothing to do with uncertainty or probability; the fact may be that we are ignorant of the assurance level of C. Thus, knowing the probabilities of A and B does not necessarily imply that we can infer the probability of C.

In an attempt to overcome the shortcomings of classical probability in representing human reasoning, Dempster (1968) proposed a general theory of uncertainty versus ignorance. The theory, later extended by Shafer (1979), has come to be known as the Dempster-Shafer (D-S) theory of evidence. It is based on the notion that separate probability masses may be assigned to all subsets of a universe of discourse, rather than just to indivisible single members as required in traditional probability theory. As a result, D-S theory permits the following inequality:

$$P(A) + P(B) \leq 1.0$$

To illustrate the application of D-S theory, let us assume a universe of discourse representation X and a set corresponding to n propositions. We will assume that one and only one of the propositions is true. The propositions are assumed to be exhaustive and mutually exclusive. Define all the subsets of X as follows:

$$H = \{A\} \ni A \subseteq X$$

Set H contains 2^n elements including the null set and X itself. Let the set function f, called the basic probability assignment, defined on H be a mapping to the interval [0, 1]. That is:

$$f: H \to [0, 1] \ni \forall A \subseteq X, f (\Phi) = 0 \qquad and \sum_{A \subseteq X} f (A) = 1$$

The function f defines a probability distribution on H as well as X. This is in contrast to classic probability theory, where probability distribution is defined only on the individual elements of the sample space X. The function f represents the measure of belief committed exactly to A. A belief function, Bel, corresponding to a specific f for the set A, is defined as the sum of beliefs committed to every subset of A by f. In other words, Bel(A) is a measure of the total support or belief committed to the set A and establishes a minimum value for its likelihood. The belief function is defined in terms of all belief assigned to A as well as to all proper subsets of A. That is:

$$Bel (A) = \sum_{B \subseteq A} f (B)$$

For example, if X contains the mutually exclusive technologies P, Q, U, V, and W, and we are interested in the particular subset $A = \{P, Q, W\}$, then we would have:
$Bel(\{P,Q,W\}) = f(\{P,Q,W\}) + f(\{P,Q\}) + f(\{Q,W\}) + f(\{P,W\}) + f(\{P\}) + f(\{Q\}) + f(\{W\})$

Some important definitions related to D-S theory are:

SUPPORT FUNCTION: The support function of the subset A is defined as Bel(A).

PLAUSIBILITY: The plausibility of A is defined as PL(A) = 1 - Bel(A^c).

UNCERTAINTY OF A: The uncertainty of a subset A of X is defined as $U(A)$ = PL(A) - Bel(A).

BELIEF INTERVAL: The belief interval for a subset A (i.e., the confidence in A) is defined as the subinterval [Bel(A), PL(A)] of the interval [0, 1].

FOCAL ELEMENTS: The subsets A of X are called focal elements of the support function Bel when $f(A) > 0$.

Bel() = 0 indicates that no belief should be assigned to the null set.

Bel(X) = 1 indicates that the "truth" is contained within X.

DOUBT FUNCTION: This is defined as $D(A)$ = Bel(A^c), which is a measure of the extent to which one believes in the complement of A. That is, the level of doubt associated with A.

Suppose we define a proposition that states: TECHNOLOGY X IS CAPABLE OF MEETING STATED PRODUCTION GOALS. Some examples of belief intervals and their explanations relevant to the proposition are:

[Bel(A), PL(A)] = [0, 0]	Denotes belief that the proposition is false.
[Bel(A), PL(A)] = [1, 1]	Denotes belief that the proposition is true.
[Bel(A), PL(A)] = [0, 1]	Denotes no belief that supports the proposition.
[Bel(A), PL(A)] = [.5, 1]	Denotes belief that supports the proposition.
[Bel(A), PL(A)] = [0, .9]	Denotes partial disbelief in the proposition.
[Bel(A), PL(A)] = [.4, 1]	Denotes partial belief in the proposition.
[Bel(A), PL(A)] = [.4, .8]	Denotes partial belief and partial disbelief in the proposition.

To reduce uncertainty, a consolidation function is used in D-S theory to combine evidence available from multiple knowledge sources. The combining function is defined as $Bel_1 Bel_2$. Given two probability assignment functions, f_1 and f_2 corresponding to the belief functions Bel_1 and Bel_2, let $A_1, \ldots, A_k$ be the focal elements for Bel_1 and let $B_1, \ldots, B_p$ be the focal elements for Bel_2. Then $f_1(A_i)$ and $f_2(B_j)$ each assigns probability masses on the unit interval [0, 1]. The probability masses are then combined orthogonally to draw inferences about the problem. Readers interested in further details should refer to Pearl (1988).

The preceding concepts can be implemented in expert systems designed to address the issues in new technology adoption and implementation. The following sections present two examples of expert systems designed for technology justification and implementation. The first concerns the justification of any advanced manufacturing technology (AMT). The second deals with implementation of robots in manufacturing.

CASE 1: EXPERT SYSTEM FOR TECHNOLOGY JUSTIFICATION

Justifying technology both from technical and economic standpoints is not easy. The task involves a search of the best alternative based on several important factors. Justification calls for specialized search strategies similar to those presented in the preceding section of this paper. Sundaram and Badiru (1991) present the Justex (Justification Expert) expert system, which can serve as a decision aid for managers and engineers. The system provides a synergistic approach by incorporating tactical, strategic, and economic methods in the justification process. Justex combines these strategies and presents one of the following recommendations: Go, Defer, or No Go. Its knowledge base is structured in production rules, with four different knowledge bases linked together. The sources of the knowledge include experts from industry, and published materials. For purposes of Justex, advanced manufacturing technology includes the following:

1. Design Ventures
2. Specialized Manufacturing Ventures
3. Miscellaneous Ventures

Under each of these headings are subheadings that narrow the types of technology. For example, under Design Ventures, are subheadings for computer-aided design (CAD), computer-aided engineering (CAE), Simulation, and numerical control (NC), computer-aided manufacturing/design (CAM)/CAD. Categories under Specialized Manufacturing Ventures are Material Handling, flexible manufacturing system (FMS), and Robotics. Categories under Miscellaneous Ventures are Total Quality Control and Group Technology. The categories are illustrated in Figure 17.5.

Justex adopts a comprehensive search, taking into account the interactions among strategic components for justification. Justex takes a tactical approach first, enabling the user to decide specific areas of technology to explore. This is short term, but the decisions are based on a match between the company's objectives and the exact nature of the technology. If these do not match, then Justex displays an appropriate decision on whether to implement the technology. Next, Justex takes a strategic approach that is more long term and considers several organizational aspects. Lastly, Justex's economic approach considers the quantitative economic aspects of the technology investment. Thus, the expert system combines the three approaches so that a comprehensive decision can be reached.

Justex uses a backward chaining search strategy, developed with the VP-Expert shell. The knowledge base consists of four separate knowledge bases linked together. In addition to this, the expert system has two BASIC programs linked from within the VP-Expert shell: The tactical module of Justex has about 200 rules; it is linked to the tactical module by using the backward chain clause. The strategic module addresses six issues vital to a manufacturing technology decision:

1. Effective management of high-technology options
2. Match between technology and business plans
3. Ideal accounting system
4. Uncertainty in the industrial environment
5. Benefits arising as a result of implementation
6. Present worth of the investment

With regard to the first issue, many strategic investment decisions can be temporarily postponed to give the decision maker time to explore the uncertainty involved. The second issue, the match between technology and business plans, assures that the long-range business plan is consistent with the company's technological resources. To have viable investment alternatives, the company's technological and busi-

Figure 17.5
Decision Flow Diagram for Justex

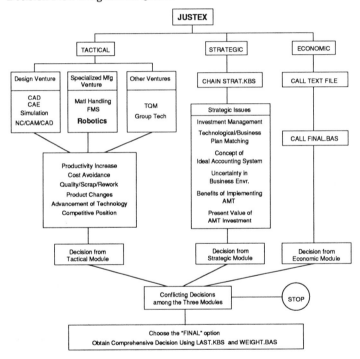

ness portfolios must be integrated into the company's business policies. The third issue considers what is an ideal accounting system. Companies seeking to compete must devise cost-accounting systems that reflect their investment decisions and cost structures. Thus, internal accounting practices should be guided by corporate strategies. The fourth issue is the uncertainty inherent in the industrial environment. The fifth issue, the benefits to be derived from implementation, attempts to capture the key benefits of AMT.

The sixth issue is the present worth of the investment, helping to combine monetary and nonmonetary aspects of the justification process. The discounted cash flow (DCF) method is used since it is the most common means of economic justification. It takes into account the time value of money and factors such as inflation. The model is as follows:

$$PW = \sum_{j=0}^{j=N} P_j$$
$$= \sum_{j=0}^{j=N} C_j \left(\frac{1}{1+i}\right)^j$$
$$= \sum_{j=0}^{j=N} C'_j \left(\frac{1}{1+\theta}\right)^j \left(\frac{1}{1+i}\right)^j$$
$$= I + \sum_{j=1}^{j=N} S(1+k_1)^j + M(1+k_2)^j \left(\frac{1}{1+\theta}\right)^j \left(\frac{1}{1+i}\right)^j$$

I = Initial cash flow
S = Annual savings in present dollars
M = Annual cash flow in present dollars
k_1 = Annual rate of increase in the relative value of annual savings owing to price differentials
k_2 = Annual rate of increase in the relative cost of Operation and Maintenance (O&M) owing to price differentials
θ = Annual rate of general inflation
i = Inflation-free discount rate
C'_j = Cash flow in period j in current (then) dollars
and C_j = Equivalent cash flow in period j in present dollars.

Savings are classified as direct and indirect. The program starts with a display of selected text files, which give the user an introduction to the system and its capabilities. The economic module was written in Basic and is run from within the VP-Expert shell. The user is asked to input numerical values for the capital, amount of savings, inflation rate, and so on.

The final knowledge base enables the user to arrive at a comprehensive decision when there are conflicting decisions from the three modules. This knowledge base also invokes a Basic program from within the VP-Expert environment. Selected screen displays from a Justex consultation are presented in Figures 17.6 through 17.9.

CASE 2: EXPERT SYSTEM FOR ROBOT IMPLEMENTATION

Robotics is one of the more popular ways to automate. As a branch of AI, it has been widely applied. Though largely an American invention, robots are not as prevalent

Figure 17.6
Justex Consultation Screen 1

```
Which justification methodology would you like to try first?
The ideal path recommended by the system is, TACTICAL, ECONOMIC
and STRATEGIC.
  TACTICAL              *              *
  STRATEGIC             *              *
  ECONOMIC              *              *
  FINAL                 *              *
```

Figure 17.7
Justex Consultation Screen 2

```
  Specialized Mfg       *              *
  Misc Applications     *              *

  The following list shows some of the possible ventures. Please
  select the most appropriate application that best fits your
  choice.
  CAD                   *              *
  CAE                   *              *
  Simulation            *              *
  NC\CAM\CAD            *              *
```

Figure 17.8
Justex Consultation Screen 3

```
The following list shows some of the areas which have scope for
improvement. Please identify the areas where you seek improvement
or change. Limit your choices to TWO (2). Press <End> after confirming
selection.
  Production Increase       *                        *
  Cost Avoidance            *                        *
  Quality Scrap Rework      *                        *
  React to Prod Change      *                        *
  Advancement of Tech       *                        *
  Competitive Position      *                        *
```

Figure 17.9
Justex Conclusion Screen

```
        **********DECISION FROM THE TACTICAL MODULE**********
        ------------------------------------
        Your responses have been recorded. The system recommends a

        DEFER CNF 100 at this time. Please try to justify your venture

        strategically and economically.

        **********************************************************
                        Press any key to continue
```

in U.S. industry as they are abroad. This is mainly due to poor implementation strategies. Many companies have been reluctant to make the necessary investment, particularly when faced with surplus capacity and labor, and with no pressure to hold down prices. However, increased competition in many industries previously believed to be secure from foreign encroachment has led to more aggressive pursuit of robotics. In the past few years, robotics has been used in many phases of manufacturing. In many instances, discouraging results have been caused by improper planning and misplaced implementation. Many people think that robots can do everything, but that is not true. A careful analysis of what robots can and cannot do is essential.

Sunku and Badiru (1990) present an expert system named ROBEX (Robot Expert), which serves as a consultant to engineers and managers involved in planning and installing robots. The system was developed with a VP-Expert inference engine. ROBEX is an extension of Robcon (Robot Consultant) developed by Datar (1989). Robcon, developed with Texas Instrument's Personal Consultant Plus inference engine, deals with robots as an individual item, not as a system. Robex goes further than Robcon by finding out whether there is a suitable environment to implement robots, then preparing a comprehensive specification sheet and an implementation schedule. It also conducts a system safety review. Ralph Heinze, a manufacturing automation manager at Seagate Corporation in Oklahoma City, served as the primary domain expert for both Robcon and Robex.

Robex consists of fifteen knowledge bases chained together to facilitate the sequential execution of consultation without exiting the system. It contains 521 rules and 369 variables, which can be instantiated with 989 different values. The rules are written in ARL (Abbreviated Rule Language), and are executed in a backward chaining search process. Output can be generated to the screen or directly to a printer. Figure 17.10 shows the personnel, hardware, and software organization for development and implementation of Robex. Figure 17.11 shows Robex consultation interaction. The knowledge bases are chained in the same sequence of the tasks that would constitute any robot system implementation project.

The overall capabilities of Robex are:

- Evaluates the manufacturing environment (users, processes, management, etc.) for potential robot applications.
- Develops a workstation information sheet to identify potential applications.
- Reviews the concept design and provides recommendations.
- Develops an application sheet with a general description, unique considerations, and justification.
- Aids the user in developing a specification sheet to get quotations from vendors.
- Provides guidance on some preimplementation tasks.
- Generates an implementation involvement sheet to help determine involvement needed from the implementation team.
- Helps the user develop a robot implementation schedule.
- Reviews the safety measures and provides recommendations to ensure safe operation.

Robex was validated by an industry expert. Engineers have found it helpful in learning about the capabilities of robots. Future enhancements to the system include the addition of an economic module to perform an economic analysis based on the specification sheet, an interface to a CAD system in order to conduct a work-area design, and a Gantt chart for the implementation process.

Figure 17.10
Development and Implementation of Robex

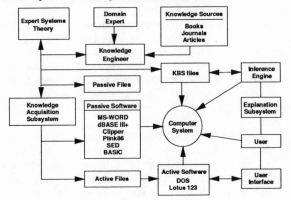

Figure 17.11
Consultation Interface for Robex

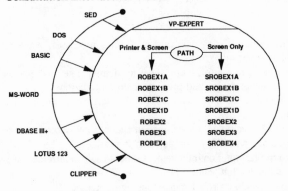

CONCLUSION

As more advanced technologies are introduced, there will be a greater need to use more efficient techniques for their design, adoption, implementation, and management strategies. Artificial intelligence and expert systems offer such efficient techniques. This chapter presented the basic concepts of AI/ES with specific emphasis on technology applications. The chapter also presented two examples of expert systems designed for the justification and implementation of new manufacturing technology.

REFERENCES

Badiru, A. B. "Artificial Intelligence Applications in Manufacturing." In *The Automated Factory Handbook: Technology and Management,* edited by D. I. Cleland and B. Bidanda. New York: TAB Books, 1990a, pp. 496-526.

———. "Analysis of Data Requirements for FMS Implementation is Crucial to Success." *Industrial Engineering* 22 (10) (October 1990b): 29-32.

———. *Expert Systems Applications in Engineering and Manufacturing.* Englewood Cliffs, NJ: Prentice-Hall, 1992.

Datar, N. N. "A Prototype Knowledge Based Expert System for Robot Consultancy— ROBCON." Master's thesis, School of Industrial Engineering, University of Oklahoma, 1989.

Dempster, A. P. "A Generalization of Bayesian Inference." *Journal of the Royal Statistical Society* (Series B) 30 (2) (1968).

Pearl, J. *Heuristics: Intelligent Search Strategies for Computer Problem Solving.* Reading, MA: Addison-Wesley, 1984.

———. *Probabilistic Reasoning in Intelligent Systems: Network of Plausible Inference.* San Mateo, CA: Morgan Kaufmann, 1988.

Shafer, G. A. *Mathematical Theory of Evidence.* Princeton: Princeton University Press, 1979.

Sundaram, D., and A. B. Badiru. "JUSTEX: An Expert System for the Justification of Advanced Manufacturing Technology." In *Knowledge-Based Systems and Neural Networks: Techniques and Applications*, edited by Ramesh Sharda, et al., New York: Elsevier Science Publishing Co., 1991, pp. 89-98.

Sunku, R., and A. B. Badiru. "ROBEX (Robot Expert): An Expert System for Manufacturing Robot System Implementation." *Computers & Industrial Engineering.* 19 (1-4) (1990): 481-83.

Weitz, R. "Technology, Work, and the Organization: The Impact of Expert Systems." *AI Magazine* 11 (2) (1990): 50-60.

Wilhelm, M. R., and H. R. Parsaei. "A Fuzzy Linguistic Approach to Implementing A Strategy for Computer Integrated Manufacturing." *Fuzzy Sets and Systems* 42 (1991): 191-204.

Chapter 18

Knowledge-Based Techniques for Management of New Technologies

Bay Arinze

For many managers in both the industrial and service sectors, the cost of intellectual expertise has stubbornly refused to follow the same downward trend as have costs for other resources. While technological and methodological advancements have brought greater efficiencies in the production of goods and services, the cost of well-trained managers has, if anything, increased over the years (Gallagher, 1988). The heightened competitiveness of today's marketplace has, therefore, made quality decision making crucial for companies intent on gaining an edge over their rivals.

In the manufacturing sector, pressures for greater productivity and quality have generated activity in the areas of total quality control (TQC), data communications in the form of electronic data interchange (EDI), just-in-time (JIT) processes, flexible manufacturing systems (FMS), and computer-integrated manufacturing (CIM). Other important advances in operations management have occurred in such areas as forecasting, setup reduction, project management, facilities location and layout, and production planning.

The emergence of so many new, vital areas of technology and methodology has brought about a need for a more varied skills from the contemporary operations manager (Turban, 1987; Schonberger & Knod, 1988). The expertise to manage these technologies is evolving as a costly but necessary item (Gallagher, 1988). Furthermore, applying computer technology to these tasks has not proved to be as straightforward as those automated earlier, such as MRP and inventory management. Reasons for this include subjective aspects, the combinatorial explosion phenomenon, qualitative parameters, and data variability—all of which call for human expertise in the decision process (Turban, 1987; Badiru 1988; O'Keefe, 1988).

The knowledge-based system (KBS), which replicates the functionality of human specialists, was developed and applied in research environments up until the early 1980s. Recently, however, there has been large-scale transfer of this technology and methodology to commercial (Rauch-Hindin, 1988; Gallagher, 1988) and industrial (Turban, 1987; Kusiak, 1990) areas. The major reason is that KBSs, unlike procedurally developed programs, can successfully model captured knowledge or expertise in many more advanced areas and solve tough problems. KBSs use a unique declarative paradigm to represent and manipulate knowledge in different domains to arrive at solutions.

It is important for organizations of all types to be keenly aware of the capabilities and potential of KBSs, a technology that promises to become a $6 billion industry by the mid-1990s (Ignizio, 1991). KBSs provide the capacity not just to improve decision making accuracy and consistency but also to provide the greater efficiencies to cope with shortages of expertise and its growing costs. The preservation of human expertise and training capabilities inherent in KBSs also offers additional opportunities. Thus, this chapter presents the opportunities that exist for KBS use in both manufacturing and service organizations, and discusses the relevant knowledge-based approaches and issues, both old and new.

The chapter is organized as follows: the first section examines knowledge-based systems—their development life cycle and their suitability for operations management. A discussion of KBS uses in management of both manufacturing and service activities follows, with a description of specific knowledge-based applications. Next, new knowledge-based techniques, approaches, and trends are outlined. Following that are highlighted new knowledge areas in operations management, as well as possible uses of the new knowledge techniques in these areas. The concluding section presents a summary and guidelines for companies seeking to deploy KBSs.

CURRENT KNOWLEDGE-BASED SYSTEMS AND APPLICATIONS

A knowledge-based system (KBS) is a computer-based information system that models the behavior of human experts to solve problems in a narrow problem domain. These problems require clearly identifiable human expertise. Amenable problems possess considerable complexity, rules of thumb (or heuristics), incomplete descriptions, and qualitative or symbolic problem aspects. KBSs have emerged from the wider area of artificial intelligence (AI), which is concerned with replicating human problem-solving capabilities such as machine vision, speech processing, robotics, and game playing (Barr and Feigenbaum, 1981; Parsaye and Chignell, 1988).

KBSs that map broadly onto a human expert's overall range of activity are generally referred to as expert systems (ESs). When only part of the expert's functions are handled, or the system's knowledge is extracted primarily from documentation (i.e., fundamental or causal knowledge), the system is referred to as a KBS. Both systems represent a declarative problem-solving paradigm, in which knowledge is separated from the means of processing it. This frees the developer to focus on the structure and content of the knowledge used to solve problems.

A KBS consists of several components. At minimum, these include a knowledge base, an inference engine, and a user interface. Additionally, an explanation component, data base, and sensors may also be incorporated, as illustrated in Figure 18.1. The knowledge base is the repository of modeled expertise extracted from human experts. Any of several knowledge representation schemes may be used to model the facts and heuristics pertaining to the knowledge domain. Examples of such schemes include semantic nets, production rules, logic, and frames (see Barr and Feigenbaum, 1981; Parsaye and Chignell, 1988).

Knowledge acquisition—that is, the extraction of knowledge from experts—has long been regarded as the KBS development bottleneck (Barr & Feigenbaum, 1981), owing to the difficulty and cost of the process. The unavailability of experts, their inability to properly articulate their decision making, the time and effort required to document and transcribe the protocols, and the perception of KBS as a threat to job security are all factors contributing to this difficulty.

The KBS's inferencing mechanism represents the reasoning model or means by which new knowledge is generated from existing and user-entered knowledge. With a rule-based system, for example, backward chaining (testing and proving facts from hypo-

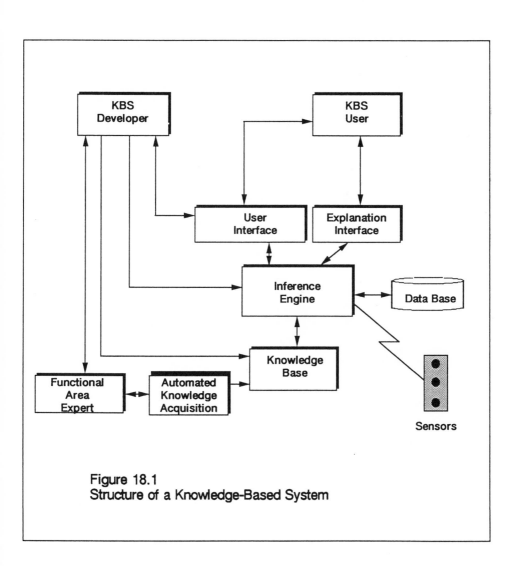

Figure 18.1
Structure of a Knowledge-Based System

thesized goals) might be used, as might the converse, forward chaining. In representing knowledge using logic, however, resolution is used to prove the truth or falsehood of an assertion. Furthermore, KBSs can perform inexact reasoning using certainty factors or Bayesian probabilities, as well as cope with unknown or incomplete knowledge pertaining to problems.

The capabilities of the inference engine and knowledge base are made available to the KBS user through the user interface. At minimum, this interface allows the user to supply facts required by the KBS to pursue lines of reasoning. Additionally, the KBS may possess an explanatory capability (see Figure 18.1) that enables the user to ascertain the reasons for a particular KBS conclusion.

In service and manufacturing sectors, the practice has been to apply a wide range of models and their associated algorithms to activities or functions performed at all levels of operations management. These typically quantitative models have proved themselves remarkably efficient in automating such structured tasks as capacity planning, scheduling, inventory management, and process control (O'Keefe, 1988). Even in higher-level operations management, there has been a relentless application of modeling techniques for functions such as facilities deployment, forecasting, and technology selection (Schonberger & Knod, 1988). However, the use of quantitative operational research (OR) techniques at all these levels have shown several significant limitations:

1. The inability of many quantitative OR techniques to incorporate qualitative or symbolic information. Qualitative terms such as *high, low,* or *competitive,* or other symbolic concepts, cannot easily be represented or meaningfully manipulated using quantitative approaches.

2. Quantitative techniques by and large, cannot adequately handle uncertainty or incomplete data—features which characterize many operations management problems (O'Keefe, 1988).

3. The combinatorial explosion phenomenon, found in such problems as facilities location, layout, and product distribution, requires an inordinate amount of computing power (Brandeau & Chiu, 1989). Even with heuristic models, CPU requirements may be excessive.

4. Many operations require monitoring and interpreting a large number of inputs from sensors or other sources. In general, pattern matching and recognition functions are not available from quantitative models.

5. A large number of quantitative models require expertise in their selection and use. For example, it is well known that forecasting model selection is context dependent (Makridakis et al., 1982). Such expertise is not easily modeled using these techniques.

6. Other tasks of operations management primarily require human expertise. Domain-dependent knowledge, such as heuristics, when extracted as available knowledge representations, does not lend itself to quantitative formulation and processing.

The benefits of KBSs, therefore, are more apparent when dealing with knowledge-rich (vs. numerically rich) applications. The need for expertise in many operations management functions thus favors a knowledge-based solution.

The approach taken in developing expert systems or KBSs is referred to as the expert systems development life cycle, or ESDLC. It consists of the following stages: (1) feasibility analysis to determine the suitability of KBS for the problem; (2) knowledge acquisition form identified experts or other sources; (3) knowledge representation of the extracted knowledge using KBS formalisms; (4) testing and validation of the KBS against a range of expectations; (5) KBS deployment; and (6) maintenance and evolution to handle future changes.

Two major classes of KBS development tools are languages and shells. Historically, most KBS development was carried out using such languages as Prolog, a logic programming language popular in Europe and Japan, and Lisp, a list-processing language used mainly in the United States. Other languages include OPS5, a general-purpose, rule-based language, and such conventional third-generation languages as C and Pascal. Development may also use KBS shells, which contain a built-in inferencing mechanism, user interface, knowledge representation scheme, and empty rule base. The KBS developer benefits from these preconstructed KBS components, but may lose out with the shell's inflexibility. However, the power and sophistication of contemporary KBS shells make them the preferred tool for most KBS development (Rao & Lingaraj, 1988), with the exception of those requiring complex mathematical or statistical functions, or convoluted knowledge representations.

RATIONALE FOR AND USES OF KBS IN MANUFACTURING AND SERVICE INDUSTRIES

The focus of investment in the manufacturing and service industries has traditionally been on improving the efficiency of basic production technology. There has not been the same attention on technologies that sustain and improve the productivity of managers and users of that basic technology. Rauch-Hindin (1988) describes how the cost of white-collar labor often exceeds 50 percent of total labor costs, underscoring the importance of productivity aids for this kind of worker. Another compelling argument is the high cost of operational management errors—for example, erroneous quality control procedures, leading to discarding whole batches of manufactured goods. Developing the requisite levels of expertise in managers is time consuming and costly. One major motivation for deploying KBSs, then, is to make vital expertise available to these managers, as a tool for both formulating as well as validating decisions.

In manufacturing, total quality control (TQC) may be viewed as a consequence of the realization that activities in the manufacturing cycle are interdependent. These interdependencies—such as those between marketing and product design, and design and production—increase the amount of cross-disciplinary knowledge required. This comes at a time when shortages of skilled managers are being reported in many sectors of the economy (Ignizio, 1991). Many companies now realize that it is those wielding not just information but also knowledge who are likely to achieve both strategic and tactical advantage in the marketplace (Gallagher, 1988).

The technology, too, has matured. Once seen as a "blue sky" concept, KBSs are now a proven technology, used profitably by a·large number of organizations and for diverse applications. The technology factor has proved crucial in driving the adoption of expert systems. Even as powerful workstations have become more affordable, their capabilities have increased by orders of magnitude. Networking abilities, improved user interfaces, and sophisticated KBS development tools have stimulated more and varied development. Some of these tools permit the representation and use of larger knowledge bases—and even automated knowledge acquisition. The ability to integrate them with other, more conventional development tools and languages (e.g., third-generation languages) has been an important means of incorporating mathematical and statistical capabilities within KBSs.

Modes of KBS Use

There are three major modes of KBS used in the manufacturing and service industries. The discussion of these modes is a useful framework for assessing not just their usage patterns but also their future direction. These three usage modes are: (1) selecting a quantitative model for a problem best suited to an algorithmic solution; (2) using the KBS's knowledge and inferencing capabilities to solve the problem directly; and (3) a combination of both methods.

In the first case, it may be clear to the expert system designer that a quantitative or OR model is best suited to the problem at hand. However, determining the appropriate model to use may be complex and context dependent. Examples of this include facilities layout, with over fifty possible models (Brandeau & Chiu, 1989) or forecasting, with well over thirty available models (Makridakis et al., 1982). Using a KBS may prove effective in narrowing the number of suitable quantitative models.

The second mode of KBS use, which is more widespread, is using the KBS to provide a wholly knowledge-based solution to the problem at hand. The range of problems include:

- *Diagnosis applications.* Diagnosing a condition based on exhibited problem characteristics, involving pattern recognition and interpretation, and usually accompanied by recommendations or prescriptions.
- *Configuration applications.* The design of complex entities, based on a knowledge of parts, interactions, and constraints.
- *Planning applications.* The development of plans within given constraints to achieve determined goals.
- *Monitoring applications.* For monitoring some phenomenon, often accompanied by interpretation of sensor data, phenomena recognition, and controlling actions taken in response to these.

The third, hybrid mode of KBS use involves a combination of the above for different parts of the problem. For example, particularly with frame-based systems, algorithmic models may be invoked, with the results part of an overall knowledge-based solution.

Examples of KBS Use

There are literally thousands of KBSs deployed in practically all types of manufacturing and service companies. These systems handle process control, financial, medical, insurance, and many other areas. One useful view of the range and type of contemporary KBSs is against a background of operational, tactical, and strategic managerial decision making, as shown in Figure 18.2. This shows a sample of actual KBSs used at the different organizational levels (for fuller details, see Turban, 1987; Rauch-Hindin, 1988; Turban, 1990; Gallagher, 1988; and Kusiak, 1990). These KBSs are as follows:

1. *ExMarine.* A KBS used for insurance underwriting at Coopers and Lybrand. Developed using the Goldworks KBS development shell, ExMarine suggests premiums for insurance applicants, using stored knowledge of insurance policies and entered applicant knowledge. ExMarine is a frame-based system, represent-

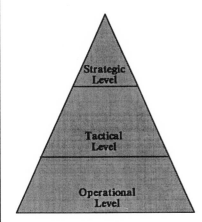

Strategic Management of Technology - Authur D. Little

FADES - Facility Layout, Equipment Selection

ExperTAX - Corporate Tax Planning,

FMSCS - Forecasting

ISIS - Job Shop Scheduling

CALLISTO - Project Management

XCON - Equipment Configuration

CATS-1 - Equipment Fault Selection

ExMarine - Insurance Underwriting

Figure 18.2
Commercial Examples of Knowledge-Based Systems

ing an operational use of KBSs.

2. *Cats-1.* A KBS used to diagnose and recommend solutions to problems in diesel-electric locomotives. Developed using the Forth language by GE, Cats-1 is a rule-based system deployed in minor repair shops handling locomotives made by General Electric.

3. *Xcon.* A well-known KBS developed and used by Digital Equipment Corporation for equipment configuration. It uses acquired knowledge of computer components, their interactions, and user-entered requirements in the form of expert heuristics to configure DEC minicomputers for their customers.

4. *Callisto.* A rule-based KBS used for project management at Digital Equipment Corporation. This KBS incorporates project manager heuristics as well as knowledge of PERT and CPM techniques. It models the interactions among tasks, resources, and entities such as suppliers to derive the consequences of changes in a project.

5. *Isis.* A frame-based KBS developed at Carnegie-Mellon University for scheduling in large-scale job shops. It possesses knowledge of the manufacturing environment (resources, activities, costs, etc.) and applies its encoded heuristics to develop schedules for manufacturing operations.

6. *Fmscs.* This forecasting KBS uses production rules and incorporates the heuristics of an expert forecaster. It is used to select the best forecasting method in a specific context from among time series, causal, and judgmental forecasting methods (Kwong & Cheng, 1989).

7. *ExperTax.* Located even higher in the hierarchy of management activity, this KBS is designed to support corporate tax planning. Developed by Coopers and Lybrand, it is a frame-based system for use by accounting staff to analyze tax data and identify important issues for tax planners.

8. *Fades.* Used for facilities layout. It employs first-order predicate logic (via a Prolog interpreter) to represent knowledge of equipment, facilities, product characteristics, and algorithmic models. Fades selects the appropriate algorithmic facilities layout model in various contexts, using resident heuristics and supplied knowledge of the manufacturing setting.

9. *Strategic Management of Technology.* Developed by Arthur D. Little, Inc., this is a KBS used at the level of strategic planning to develop R&D investment plans for corporations.

These applications illustrate KBS use at all levels of the organizational hierarchy. The scope of applications is wide, ranging from operations to strategy, and includes both manufacturing and service functions.

NEW KNOWLEDGE-BASED TOOLS AND APPROACHES

Knowledge-based techniques and systems are poised as a primary competitive weapon for a large number of companies today. These systems have allowed companies to capture expertise and profitably deploy it. For example, Xcon is reported as producing savings of $15 million yearly (Turban, 1990). Consequently, industry must be aware not only of the promise these current systems offer but also the opportunities emerging from research in KBSs. Recent advancements that hold much promise include machine learning, hardware and software improvements, improved understanding of the technology, hybrid systems, and the frame-based, object-oriented approach.

As mentioned earlier, a pressing problem has been the knowledge bottleneck, or the extensive time and effort required to acquire knowledge from experts. Approaches to machine learning have made it possible to automatically acquire knowledge of problems and knowledge domains. While several machine-learning methods exist, the most popular ones are based on case learning—specifically, neural network and rule induction-based KBSs.

Artificial Neural Networks

Massive parallel-problem-solving models predicated on the physical characteristics of the human brain, these are composed of large numbers of interconnected cells (analogous to human neurons) that collect, then propagate signals through the network. Figure 18.3 illustrates a neural network. Input cells are primary inputs or problem characteristics inputed to the system. Intermediate cells, also referred to as "hidden units," receive inputs from preceding cells and pass on outputs to subsequent cell layers. Output cells present the results or outputs of the network as a whole (see Gallant, 1988; Knight, 1990, for further details). In a KBS, these outputs constitute the recommendations of the system, with different outputs for different input combinations (i.e., problem features).

The knowledge base of a neural network comprises the weights on the interconnections between nodes, which affect the propagation of signals through the network. Various algorithms (backward propagation, Boltzmann machines) are used to develop these weights. Each algorithm involves training the neural network using a set of examples and incremental adjustment of the weights, as expected results are compared with the output of the neural network (Knight, 1990). A trained network, in effect, represents a causal model for explaining the examples and thus predicting the outputs or solutions to new inputs. Developing neural networks has been made much easier with the introduction of powerful shells.

Rule-Based Induction

A large number of KBS-building tools, such as the first class KBS shell, incorporate rule-based induction as a means for automatically acquiring knowledge. Messier and Hansen (1988) describe induction as "a process of going from specific observations about objects and an initial hypothesis to an inductive assertion that accounts for the observations." With a set of examples, an inductive algorithm, such as ID3 is used to produce a meta rule consistent with the initial set of examples. This meta rule explains the initial rule set, but is essentially a superset capable of producing outputs or solutions to rules not explicitly described. In effect, both induction and neural networks extract underlying logic from the examples to implement machine learning (see also Michalski et al., 1983, 1986).

Other developments affecting the proliferation of KBS have been in the areas of hardware and software. Historically, KBS development was associated with powerful workstations such as special-purpose LISP machines, which are optimized toward efficiently executing Lisp (or in some cases, Prolog) code. Sun workstations, for example, are typical, possessing exceptional storage, graphics, and CPU (in recent times, incorporating reduced instruction set, or RISC) capabilities. These systems are mostly single-user configurations.

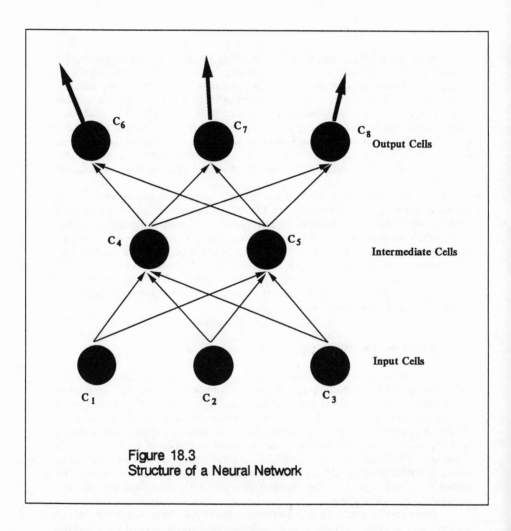

Figure 18.3
Structure of a Neural Network

In recent times, however, many software developers have ported both Prolog and Lisp to mainstream personal computers. They have also developed PC shells in C or Pascal, and utilized dedicated hardware coprocessors to run both expert system development languages and packages. In the first case, current microprocessor technology (such as the Intel 80486 chip) provides computing power almost comparable to workstations. The use of C and Pascal, portable languages, has enabled researchers to develop ever more sophisticated KBS shells on a greater number of platforms. Specialized processor cards, such as the i860 card (on IBM compatibles), provide co-processor or even parallel processing capability. This is particularly important for situations involving neural networks or large numbers of rules.

Hybrid systems, particularly those of the frame-based variety, have provided greatly improved knowledge representation and processing capabilities. Frame-based systems offer contemporary "object-oriented" capabilities such as inheritance and encapsulation, enabling representation of knowledge with greater economy and power. Furthermore, this class of system in particular (but not exclusively) now easily integrates algorithmic models within the KBS declarative framework. The statistical and operations research models that may be invoked broaden the scope and complexity of problems that can be successfully tackled using KBSs.

FUTURE CHALLENGES, ISSUES AND APPLICATIONS OF KBSs

The pressures on manufacturers and providers of services in the United States are arguably greater than they have ever been. Manufacturers have to deal not only with challenges from the Japanese but also from emerging Asian and European manufacturers. They have to respond with more effective and efficient manufacturing strategies at a time when tools and techniques have greatly multiplied, with new areas of specialization. The same phenomenon has occurred in services, with new opportunities characterized by heightened competitiveness, more sophisticated and demanding consumers, and a proliferation of technologies. How will existing and new knowledge-based techniques enable companies to respond to these challenges? This section examines current issues and approaches in both service and manufacturing, and assesses the possible contributions KBSs can make.

Five Contemporary Operations Management Issues

If globalization is the theme for current manufacturing and service strategies, then data communications is the glue. In fact, globalization has been accompanied, and usually preceded by, interconnectedness at local and regional levels. A contemporary approach facilitating this interconnectedness is electronic data interchange (EDI); related to EDI is the just-in-time, or JIT, manufacturing concept.

EDI represents the use of data communications and computer technology to link customers, suppliers, and their agents—for example, banks, or shippers. It facilitates faster, computerized inventory reordering, as well as lower inventories and reordering costs, as reorders and payments are carried out with minimum human intervention through value-added or other networks. Furthermore, EDI is considered by many as critical to JIT success in facilitating the rapid procurement of materials. In fact, effective use of JIT was an important contributor to Japan's success in manufacturing.

Two other critical areas are computer-integrated manufacturing (CIM) and flexible manufacturing systems (FMS). CIM is the use of computers in all parts of the manufacturing cycle for activities ranging from product and process design through scheduling, to control of production processes and materials handling. The ability of manufacturers, particularly those producing high-technology items with considerable added value, to successfully use CIM is vital to their success (Hsu & Skevington, 1987). FMS, the approach for implementing computerized control of work cells, is used as the process control component of CIM. FMS, which involves combining work cells with robots, offers benefits such as reduced setup times and the potential for increased variety of manufactured items.

A further area of focus within practically all areas of industry is the quality issue—specifically, total quality control (TQC). TQC is best seen not as a single method or technique, but as a methodology designed to eradicate poor quality goods and services, with the producer taking responsibility for quality at the source (Ishikawa, 1985).

Opportunities for KBS Use

KBSs will play a major role in meeting the challenge of global competitiveness, through both current and future technologies and techniques. Some of the major opportunities that exist for these are:

New Applications. Sophisticated new tools, such as neural network and ES shells, and improved hardware will spur development of an even greater set of KBS applications. While it is true that not every activity is suited to KBS application, many areas remain virtually unexplored. Examples include model selection in areas such as forecasting (especially for JIT and CIM), and quality management methods. Emerging tools will change this picture in future years.

"Networked" KBSs. A stark fact of KBS usage is that, by and large, most existing systems are standalone. It is not too difficult to envision a move to networks or to integrate these KBS islands, such that information is communicated within these systems at various organizational levels. For example, ES-designed strategic plans could be used by other KBSs to plan and schedule specific projects, with another ES for monitoring and control. Also, a quality-control KBS may be used in concert with another KBS for CIM-based production processes.

Database Mining. This KBS ability (using machine learning) facilitates pattern identification and extraction of heuristics from current organizational data bases. These often huge data bases represent a considerable untapped store of knowledge. They thus offer an opportunity to capture and deploy knowledge "hidden" in data bases of transactions and decision making.

Intelligent Data Communications Management. As mentioned earlier, EDI has been made feasible by the proliferation of various inter- and intracompany networking options. Using KBSs to manage these networks is already being advanced as a way to apply expert heuristics to this complex and dynamic problem. Network analysis, intelligent routing, EDI transaction decisions, and distributed computer performance management are attractive areas for application of KBSs.

Machine Learning. This represents the area of possibly greatest promise for KBS use. Machine-learning developments appear set to pervade almost every area of KBS use for which examples are available. For computer-automated process planning (CAPP), instruction (CAI), design (CAD), manufacturing (CAM), and forecasting, quality control, facilities design, and other applications, machine learning will likely characterize the next wave of widespread deployment of KBSs.

While some of these applications have been advanced in prior years, usage is not yet widespread. Their impact will be fully felt in future years, however, as methods and technologies improve. Companies will find it increasingly necessary to grasp more fully the nature of knowledge-based technologies in order to unlock their potential. They must do this in an increasingly globalized and competitive economy, where the management and effective deployment of knowledge will separate winners from losers.

SUMMARY AND CONCLUSIONS

This chapter has examined some of the key issues of knowledge-based technology. In particular, it has focused on knowledge resources, and the need for their management and deployment. KBSs are penetrating the operational, tactical, and strategic decision making, capturing human expertise to improve decisions.

Future KBS advances will have a significant impact on operations management issues, such as TQC, EDI, and CIM, including improvements in the underlying technologies. The advances are spearheaded by machine-learning methodologies, which will significantly reduce knowledge bottleneck.

KBSs, which embody symbolic computation and have emerged from AI, will see increasing use in practically all industrial and commercial sectors. Just as the past three decades have been called Information Age, the coming decade will be the Knowledge Age, where KBSs and allied technologies provide the next significant computing paradigm.

REFERENCES

Badiru, A. B. "Expert Systems and Industrial Engineers: A Practical Guide to a Successful Partnership" *Computers and Industrial Engineering* 14 (1) (1988): 1-13.

Barr, A., and E. A. Feigenbaum. *The Handbook of Artificial Intelligence*, Vols. 1 and 2; Los Altos, CA: William Kaufman, 1981.

Brandeau M. L., and S. S. Chiu. "An Overview of Representative Problems in Location Research." *Management Science* 35 (6) (June 1989): 645-74.

Gallagher, P. J. *Knowledge Systems for Business.* Englewood Cliffs, NJ: Prentice-Hall, 1988.

Gallant, S. I. "Connectionist Expert Systems." *Communications of the ACM* 31 (2) (1988): 152-69.

Hsu, C., and C. Skevington. "Integrating of Data and Knowledge in Manufacturing Enterprises: A Conceptual Framework." *Journal of Manufacturing Systems* 6 (4) (1987): 277-84.

Ignizio, J. P. *Introduction to Expert Systems: The Development and Implementation of Expert Systems.* New York: McGraw-Hill, 1991.

Ishikawa, K. "What is Total Quality Control? The Japanese Way." Englewood Cliffs, NJ: Prentice-Hall, 1985.

Knight, K. K. "Connectionist Ideas and Algorithms." *Communications of the ACM* 33 (11) (1990): 59-74.

Kwong, K. K., and D. Cheng. "A Prototype Microcomputer Forecasting Expert System." *Journal of Business Forecasting* 7 (1988): 21-27.

Kusiak, A. *Intelligent Manufacturing Systems.* Englewood Cliffs, NJ: Prentice-Hall,

1990.

Makridakis, S., A. Andersen, R. Carbone, R. Fildes, M. Hibon, R. Lewandowski, J. Newton, E. Parzen, and R. Winkler. "The Accuracy of Extrapolation (Time Series) Methods: Results of a Forecasting Competition." *Journal of Forecasting* 1 (1982): 111-53.

Messier, W. F. and J. V. Hansen. "Inducing Rules for Expert System Development: An Example Using Default And Bankruptcy Data." *Management Science* 34 (12) (December 1988): 1403-15.

Michalski R. S., J. G. Carbonell, and T. M. Mitchell, eds. *Machine Learning: An Artificial Intelligence Approach*, Vol. I. Palo Alto, CA: Tioga Publishing Co., 1983.

————. *Machine Learning: An Artificial Intelligence Approach*, Vol. II. Los Altos, CA: Morgan Kaufman Publishers, 1986.

O'Keefe, R. M. "Artificial Intelligence and the Management Science Practitioner: Expert Systems and MS/OR Methodology (Good News and Bad)." *Interfaces* 18 (6) (November-December 1988): 105-13.

O'Leary, D. E. "Validation of Expert Systems with Applications to Auditing and Accounting Expert Systems." *Decision Sciences* 18 (1987): 468-85.

Parsaye, K., and M. Chignell. *Expert Systems for Experts*. New York: John Wiley, 1988.

Rao, H. R., and B. P. Lingaraj. "Expert Systems in Production and Operations Management: Classification and Prospects." *Interfaces* 18 (6) (November-December 1988): 80-91.

Rauch-Hindin, W. B. *A Guide to Commercial Artificial Intelligence*. Englewood Cliffs, NJ: Prentice-Hall, 1988.

Schonberger, R. J., and E. M. Knod. *Operations Management*, 3rd Ed. Plano, TX: Business Publications, 1988.

Turban, E. "Expert Systems—Another Frontier for Industrial Engineering." *Computers and Industrial Engineering* 10 (3) (1987): 227-35.

————. Turban, E. *Decision Support and Expert Systems*. New York: Macmillan Publishers, 1990.

V

**Product Design
and Inventory Management**

Chapter 19

Product Design: The Next Source of Competitive Advantage

Vasanthakumar Bhat

Product design in the 1990s is going to be what cost reduction was in the 1960s, or flexibility in the 1970s, or quality in the 1980s. A good product design projects a pleasant corporate image, delivers excellent brand identity, and maximizes customer satisfaction. Design may soon be the only element that differentiates one product from another (Business Week, March 25, 1991). Design activity consumes only a very small fraction of the development budget, consequently it does not receive as much attention as it should from finance-oriented top management. However, design locks in more than 60 to 80 percent of total product costs. In addition, product design influences input materials, processing and assembly strategies, distribution methods, and a product's overall competitiveness. In short, product design is a strategic activity. Product design may very well make or break a company.

Several companies have come to realize that product design can be a significant offensive weapon, from improving manufacturing performance to boosting customer satisfaction. Traditionally, the product design focused on function; therefore, it may not have been optimal for manufacturability, assembly, reliability, environmental effects, or distribution.   Recently, however, design engineers have developed a variety of approaches to develop superior designs. For example:

1. By reducing the number of components for a normal watch from about 150 to 51, using a new product structure, and providing a large number of variants, Swatch introduced a successful designer watch for about $25 (Andreasen et al., 1988).
2. By using new design guidelines, IBM Corp., reduced parts of its new printer by 40 percent, and manufacturing costs by 14 percent (Venkatachalam, 1992).
3. By redesigning cash register terminals, NCR reduced purchased parts from 110 to 15, eliminated screws by introducing push-and-snap assembly, reduced assembly time by 75 percent, and cut down on subcontractors by 65 percent. The new product can even be assembled blindfolded (Business Week, May 8, 1989).

WHAT IS GOOD DESIGN?

It is hard to come up with criteria to evaluate a design. A product is poorly designed if it fails to function properly, is impractical, and costs too much to manufacture. A good design has high reliability, long useful life, low maintenance cost, low cost, and high quality. Since customers are the final judges of a design, the design obviously should be evaluated with criteria employed by customers.

A product obviously should satisfy customer requirements. It should fulfill its purpose. It should work under the worst conditions. It should be easy to install, operate, and maintain. Designs that lead to a family of products are preferred. Novelty, ergonomic tractability, quality, cost, pleasant impression, and other factors can make a design effective. Hauser and Clausing (1988) have developed ways to communicate customer needs to design engineers. Parsons (1989) has a checklist for evaluating product designs using customer-specific factors grouped under value analysis and firm-specific factors grouped under suitability analysis. Design evaluation factors include usability, ergonomic tractability, technical and economic viability, aesthetic sensibility, and image projectability.

In this chapter we discuss some approaches for achieving good designs.

DESIGN FOR MANUFACTURABILITY

Product range proliferation, increased need for manufacturing flexibility, and stiff international competition are forcing companies to review their design and manufacturing strategies. The effect of product design on the manufacturing process, and thereby on the product cost, has contributed to the design-for-manufacturing philosophy. Manufacturability in design is a critical factor for competitive advantage. Worldwide competition has made it imperative that a design lead to low-cost production. A design should conserve materials, maximize production, and minimize costs. Modern manufacturing methods by themselves do not minimize costs; an older product must be redesigned to take advantage of new manufacturing methods.

Even though there are no sure-fire approaches to design for manufacturability, there are design strategies that promise the most effective results. One of them is to design products for maximum simplicity, physically and functionally. Simplicity in design is achieved by eliminating or combining parts so that joining or assembly can be eliminated. Another approach is to break complex assemblies and parts into simpler parts. Selection of proper materials and treatments can also improve producibility and reduce costs. Tolerances and surface finishes have a dramatic effect on the choice of manufacturing methods and costs. Therefore, design should specify the widest possible tolerances; likewise, using standard parts can reduce in-house manufacture of parts. Tailoring new products to existing production methods can boost manufacturing efficiency, just as eliminating manufacturing steps can improve production efficiency. Choosing raw material dimensions close to the finished design can cut processing time and generation of scrap materials. Combinatorial methods produce designs for parts, subassemblies, and assemblies to satisfy product variations with the least possible number of basic parts. Jigless production improves material handling, fabrication, and assembly processes and eliminates obsolescence of jigs. Therefore, the design aim should be to develop parts with common jigging features. In-house development of products should be encouraged to maintain process secrecy, reduce costs by eliminating vendor markups, and improve productivity through learning effects (Whitney, 1989). A summary of goals for designing for manufacturability is shown in Figure 19.1.

DESIGN FOR AUTOMATION

Good design is essential to reap the full advantages of automation. High design costs and low labor costs in some parts of the world make automation elsewhere an

Figure 19.1
Design for Manufacturability

Consider the entire product.

Incorporate maximum simplicity in physical and functional attributes.

Choose materials for their suitability and low cost.

Use the maximum possible tolerances and finishes.

Use standard parts and products.

Design to suit the existing production methods.

Reduce production steps.

Design for improved setup, feeding, holding, and transferring parts; eliminate handling.

Try jigless, fixtureless manufacturing.

Encourage in-house manufacturing.

Select raw material dimensions close to the finished design.

Utilize unique process characteristics.

Specify the product characteristics and not the process to be used.

Source: Bralla, 1986; Stillwell, 1989; Whitney, (1989).

attractive manufacturing strategy. However, products must be designed for automation. Automating existing products without any design changes is usually costly and difficult to carry out.

Even though there are no hard-and-fast rules to design products for automation, there are guidelines a designer can follow to improve the efficiency of automated manufacturing. For instance, reducing parts in subassemblies is an effective method of improving automated manufacturing. This way the number of parts in a manufacturing line manufactured, inspected, and stocked is reduced. Every attempt should be made to use common parts, subassemblies, and covers. This reduces work-in-process, material handling, and inventory costs. By adopting a modular design for all models in a product family, products can be manufactured and assembled using a common process. By making components, subassemblies, and assemblies physically similar, automated manufacturing and assembly become economically viable. Redford and Lo (1986) recommend consideration of shapes and functions of parts; reduction in the number of parts; use of symmetrical or widely asymmetrical parts; avoidance of parts that can jumble; standardization of internal and external radii, hole diameters, and screw threads; and machining from a minimum of datums and only surfaces of functional importance.

For a company to take full advantage of automation, Bolz (1985) suggests eliminating slow processes, machining, impossible combinations of operations, parts hard to assemble automatically, and useless operations and handling. His design ideas for flexible manufacturing systems are shown in Figure 19.2.

Quality is the name of the game in automated manufacturing. A defective part not only can stop an automated manufacturing line but can damage production equipment. In a manual process, a defective part can be isolated through visual inspection. In a manual assembly, if a defective part passes through an inspection, then it is discarded during the next operation. However, this is not so in an automated manufacturing process. In addition, automated manufacturing requires narrower tolerances.

Figure 19.2
Design for Flexible Manufacturing Systems

Consider product functionality, simplicity, utility, durability, quality, and cost.

Minimize critical dimensions.

Evaluate fixtures, handling lugs, bosses, and surfaces.

Castings should be closed to final finished product.

Avoid hard to process alloys or materials.

Standardize hole patterns and sizes.

Provide liberal screw clearance in screw holes.

Evaluate mating parts and assembly problems.

Minimize setups.

Facilitate inspection while processing.

Evaluate rework options.

Reduce fasteners.

Avoid compound angles.

Design so as to allow production to choose manufacturing process.

Provide redundant information on blueprints.

Proper choice of material is essential for successful automated manufacturing. Plastics are superior to metals, since plastics have better insulation properties, greater electrical and wear resistance, better mechanical damping, lower cost, and so on. Plastics are easy to manufacture into complex shapes, and to higher dimensional accuracy.

DESIGN FOR ASSEMBLY

The purpose of design for assembly (Andreasen et al., 1983) is to rationalize assembly to maximize productivity, quality, profitability, working conditions, and so forth. Technological developments in production have dramatically reduced the proportion of labor in manufacturing operations and have increased them in assembly operations. Most product designs involve some assembly, consequently most companies are using assembly lines, specialized labor, and time and motion studies. However, the productivity improvements that can be achieved by proper design of products are far more significant than those using traditional industrial engineering techniques. See Figure 19.3 for guidelines on design for assembly.

Significant automation has already taken place in manufacturing operations, and future automation will be in the assembly sector. However, unlike automating, the manufacturing process, automating assembly involves more than programming. Assembly operations must be considered when the product is designed, not after the design has been completed. Assembly cost is proportional to the number of parts; therefore, reducing the number of parts in an assembly will reduce costs. Redesigning existing products, eliminating components by combining with other components, and changing joining methods are some ways to reduce the number of parts.

Product redesign can reduce the labor content in any product. To design for assembly, a company should:

- Focus its product designs.
- Reduce assembly steps or stages.
- Simplify the design and assembly sequence.
- Coordinate all assembly facilities.
- Reorganize design and manufacturing activities to realize automated assembly goals.

Rapid advances in adhesive bonding, ultrasonic welding, heat sealing, electron beam, and laser welding have considerably increased options for economical assembly. The purpose of assembly is to join components, subassemblies, and formless materials to make products. An assembly consists of handling, composing, and checking. Assembly is hard to eliminate, since it is required for degrees of freedom, material differentiation, production considerations, replacibility, function differentiation, functional requirements, and design considerations.

There are basically two-design-for-assembly philosophies. Boothroyd and Dewhust (1983) concentrate on components, whereas Andreasen et al. (1983) focus on product assortment, product structure, and component shapes. There are also a number of computer programs to improve design for assembly (Swift, 1982; Jakiela & Papalambros, 1986)). A product can be assembled manually, using special-purpose equipment or robots. Manual assembly is economical when production volume is low. When volume of production is high, automatic assembly is more economical. However,

Figure 19.3
Design for Assembly

Design multifunctional parts.

Standardize quality and tolerances.

Design parts to perform production processing on the assembly machine on demand.

Plan parts and assemblies so that they can be handled without damage.

Select proper materials.

Reduce number of parts.

Standardize a product's function and style.

Standardize components.

Make parts easy to insert by providing location features.

Improve ease of handling in parts.

Design parts for fewest possible directions of insertion.

Group parts into subassemblies.

Design parts for rapid orientation.

Improve stability of parts during assembly.

Reduce product weight.

robotic assembly may be economical for intermediate volumes. Design requirements for manual, automatic, and robotic assemblies are widely different. A product designed for manual assembly may be difficult if not impossible to assemble using a robot or special-purpose equipment.

A product may be assembled using a combination of methods. Manual assembly involves simple and inexpensive tools, mostly consists of variable costs, exhibits no economies of scale other than due to learning effect, and is flexible and adaptable. Manual assembly is preferred when tasks change frequently and products are complex. Automated assembly involves high fixed costs and very small variable costs, requires considerable engineering preparation, and is inflexible to volume changes. Robotic assembly is extremely adaptable to volume, design changes, and product styles.

Design-for-assembly strategies focus on two fronts. The first concentrates on tools for constructive rationalization of assembly. Every component is examined to improve ease of assembly and design suitability for assembly (Boothroyd and Dewhurst, 1983). The second strategy concentrates on the design degrees of freedom (Andreasen, 1983). Boothroyd and Dewhurst (1983) provide charts to decide approximate economical assembly methods for single and multiple-style products. They select the method using estimated costs based on annual production volume, number of parts in the assembly, and total number of parts. They present a systematic procedure for method study to improve manual assembly. The procedure consists broadly of the following steps:

1. Collect information.
2. Assign identification numbers to parts as they are taken apart.
3. Estimate time and cost of assembly of each part, using charts.
4. Determine whether a part can be eliminated.
5. Estimate total assembly time and cost.
6. Calculate the efficiency of manual assembly.

A part cannot be eliminated or combined with another if:

* The component needs to move relative to other components during operation or service.
* The component needs to be of different material or be isolated from other components.
* The component needs to be separate to facilitate assembly or disassembly.

For automatic and robotic assembly, the systematic procedure to estimate time and cost is similar to that of manual assembly. However, cost of assembly using these methods can increase as the number of parts increases. Therefore, a significant reduction in assembly costs can be realized by eliminating even an insignificant part, such as fasteners. For instance, Apple uses snap-in plastic subassemblies to improve robotic assembly.

Andreasen et al. (1983) suggest the use of product design to improve assembly productivity. They suggest three levels of strategies: first, adaption of design to the assembly system; second, incorporating flexibility in the assembly system; and third, redesign for CIM. Adaption of design at the assembly level involves rationalization of assembly at the product assortment, the product structure, and the components used in the product. At product assortment level, in addition to other principles, they suggest avoiding variants, making variants uniform in assembly, and avoiding dangerous assembly principles. To rationalize product structure, they recommend simple and clear designs and use of frames, modules, stacked construction, base, building blocks, and standardization. On the component level, they advise eliminating assembly operations; avoiding orientation using magazines; facilitating orientation, transportation, and insertion; and selecting correct joining methods. The potential for productivity improvement is high in product assortment and product structure levels. However, quantification of design based on assembly considerations is one of the factors of design optimization. Product rationalization can also be achieved via new production processes, simplified handling, automation, and group technology.

Design for flexibility represents adaptability of design to changes or new developments. It considers all variations of the product, existing and future equipment, and product structures and components. Andreasen et al. (1983) recommend using a high proportion of preassemblies, variants creation as late in assembly stage as possible, and checkable assembly units. Design for CIM involves integration of goals, and activities, procedures and choice of solutions; and use of computers for flexibility and control.

For automatic assembly, Whitney (1989) suggests eliminating or reducing the rotation of parts while assembling, eliminating the drifting of parts with a view toward avoiding expensive sensors to identify parts, providing space for tools and grippers for making automatic assembly or testing, and preventing subassemblies from falling apart during reorientation, handling, or transport.

DESIGN FOR RELIABILITY

Increasing capital costs for equipment make even a minor problem a financial debacle. One of the goals of design, therefore, is to have the longest mean wearout life and mean time between failures as compatible with other design constraints. By designing simple system configurations, the number of failure modes can be reduced. Using fewer parts fabrication, with reduced number of operations, can increase reliability and reduce costs. One approach to simplifying design is to use multifunction parts. If proven components and configurations are used as much as possible, it is possible to design reliable systems in the least possible time. The choice of most reliable components can also improve product reliability. Probabilistic design approaches should be preferred over ones using safety factors to account for uncertainties in design. Redundancy can also improve reliability. By protecting parts from environmental conditions such as shock, vibration, and corrosion, higher reliability from design can be achieved. Identifying and eliminating critical failure modes, using techniques such as fault tree analysis and failure modes, effects and criticality analysis, or sneak analysis, can enhance reliability. Incorporating failure-detecting methods and devices can signal impending failures, thus diverting disasters.

Personnel changes and the unreliability of human memories make it essential for a company to devise a system to make information about past design successes and failures available to the designers. Companies without practical procedures to record what worked and what did not work are bound to repeat mistakes and waste time and money. Expert systems, cross-functional teams, and systematic maintenance of design "memory" are some ways of making sure that design experience is not lost (Ealey & Soderberg, 1990).

DESIGN FOR GREENNESS

Pollution reduction may be one of the critical issues confronting designers in the 1990s. Recent polls indicate that consumers are likely to avoid polluting products, consequently market share for polluting products will erode. According to a conservative estimate, American companies are producing five times as much pollution per dollar of revenue as their Japanese counterparts and twice as much as comparable German companies (Wall Street Journal, December 24, 1990). Therefore, more and more companies are redesigning their products into what are dubbed "green" items.

Reducing the amount of material entering the waste stream, using recycled materials, and designing for disassembly are major strategies to design greener products. Consumer-product companies are directing their efforts toward packaging and concentration. Eliminating excess packaging; developing returnable, reusable, or refillable packaging; and using recyclable packaging are some ways to reduce waste from packaging. A concentration strategy has been implemented by a number of detergent manufacturers to cut down on packaging. Other waste-reduction design strategies are reducing the thickness of components, increasing usable product life, and recycling.

Increasing the recoverability of materials with which products are made is another strategy. Metals are easier to recycle than plastics. Even though a designer can design products that are easily recyclable, an effective waste and scrap industry is essential to complete the process. Logistics, cost, mill capacity all contribute to waste gluts that can kill recycling (Wall Street Journal, January 17, 1992). Since impure materials yield less price than pure materials, a product should be designed so as to reduce or eliminate contamination of reclaimable metals. One way to do that is to concentrate them in a few areas of a product and make them easy to segregate. Another is to eliminate use of coated or composite materials. Coated material as far as possible should not be detrimental for recycling. In addition, metal parts should not be coated with plastic, which can be removed only by burning. Designers should specify the lowest grade of metal possible to satisfy design requirements. To reduce mixing of high-value materials with low-value ones, there should be identification methods. Every material should be examined for ultimate disposal. Materials that can be incinerated without producing hazardous fumes should be preferred.

Unlike metals, plastics are hard to recover economically for identical application. Incompatibility among plastics makes it essential they be separated before recovery. In addition, plastics deteriorate in properties on successive recycling. As a result, they can be used only to manufacture products such as garbage pails and fence posts.

To improve recyclability, products must be designed to disassemble. Snap fits are, therefore, preferred to screws or glues; however, snap fits require closer tolerances and therefore more expensive tooling. Fewer parts also promote faster disassembly. Reducing the number of materials in the design can promote disassembly. Using materials that can be recycled together can eliminate need for disassembly. Thus, proper selection of fasteners is important for successful disassembly. For example, adhesives used in the installation of windshield glass are considered responsible for its low recycling. Some guidelines for design for disassembly are (Design for Disassembly, 1991):

1. Design all product components for ease of separation, handling, and cleaning.
2. Incorporate two-way snap fits or break points on snap fits.
3. Indicate separation points and materials.
4. Have tight tolerance to consolidate parts and reduce fasteners.
5. Minimize energy usage.

Figure 19.4 summarizes the guidelines for designing for recyclability.

DESIGN FOR UNIVERSAL USE

Products must be designed to be comfortable to use. Since some devices need to be manipulated, controls must be placed at convenient locations, identified clearly with the function they perform. Design must also consider human limitations of speed and accuracy, force and work. Products should also be designed to avoid errors and minimize operator learning time. Syntex's Rumen Injector design (Abler, 1986) and

Figure 19.4
Design for Recyclability

Improve material identification at scrap-yard level to avoid mixing.

Consider effects on industries of secondary materials before one material is replaced by another.

Evaluate all materials for ultimate disposal.

Eliminate materials that produce pollution when incinerated.

Introduce formalized collection system for low-value discards containing materials of strategic importance.

Consider possible effects of coated or composite material.

Evaluate substances for their hazards in service.

Consider recyclability aspect during design.

Source: Henstock, 1988.

personal computer design (Dickinson, 1984) are examples of designing to make a product usable.

Individuals with physical and visual handicaps are not able to use all products. Design engineers should consider ways to eliminate built-in obstacles in appliances, tools, and household devices using universal design approaches. These approaches are based on the simple principle that "products designed to be easily used by disabled individuals also work better for the rest of us" (Business Week, 1992). The growing proportion of older people and specifically the Americans with Disabilities Act (ADA) are providing impetus to universal design. A knob, button, switch, dial, or other design feature can be a hurdle for a physically handicapped person. But, a design engineer, by simple modification, can make a product easily usable. For example, microwave ovens have attributes that make them easy to use by handicapped individuals. They can be placed anywhere there is an outlet. Since their doors open to the side, not down, they can be used by persons in wheelchairs. However, people with low dexterity or strength find it hard to use their door-latch mechanism. By modifying the latch mechanism so that the door opens and latches by some gross movement, like pushing on it, microwave ovens can be made operable by persons with disabilities. Designing products to be usable by special-needs consumers is neither impractical nor costly. Larger knobs, plastic braille labels on controls, voice controls, and so forth can make a product operable by more people.

LOGISTICALLY FRIENDLY DESIGNS

Design engineers traditionally have believed that a design is good if it performs the desired function at the targeted cost and is aesthetically pleasing. According to Mather (1990), to be logistically friendly a design should provide maximum product availability with least inventory and maximum flexibility to respond to market shifts. To make a design logistically friendly, Mather (1990) recommends:

- Development of accurate market needs.
- Consideration of all design objectives.
- Development of multifunctional designs.
- Selection of standard, common, short lead-time components.
- Selection of short procurement and production time designs.
- Incorporation of variability as late as possible in the manufacturing and assembly stages.

Physical requirements of a product must be defined to make distribution and marketing easier (Witt, 1986). A design engineer should consider physical dimensions, product variations, options, and so forth. Special conditions in the distribution process, such as fragility, stability in transportation, shelf life, store-display factors, and so forth, should also be considered. Oakley (1984) and Witt (1986) suggest considering factors relating to sourcing, production, service, logistics, and regulations when considering physical design.

DESIGN ORGANIZATION AND METHODS

According to Kotler and Rath (1984), many companies mismanage their design capabilities because of design illiteracy, cost constraints, tradition-bound behavior, and company politics. They suggest that every company periodically review its design function. For this purpose, they have developed a design-sensitivity audit that reviews factors relating to role of design in marketing decisions, product development, environmental design, information design, and corporate identity. They also have developed a design management effectiveness checklist to help companies evaluate how well management uses design.

In many large companies, the design function is a bureaucratic nightmare. According to Whitney (1989), the design of a single part at an automobile company requires 350 workups requiring 350 signatures. Therefore, organizing multifunctional teams is the most effective way to good design. The design team should involve (Whitney, 1989):

1. Determination of product character, design, and production methods.
2. Product function analysis.
3. Improved producibility and usability.
4. An assembly process.
5. A factory system to optimally involve workers and reduce costs.

Concurrent Engineering

The traditional product-development function is characterized by independent work groups called chimneys, because the organization consists of side-by-side vertical structures that don't communicate. Each of these groups works on its own ideas, sequentially, with no priority for particular attribute and meeting tolerances instead of targets. Typically, the products are developed in a series of steps starting with design and engineering; the letting of contracts for various materials, parts, and services; then production. Each step is performed independently and any changes made after design cause major breakdowns. In addition, the late fixes result in rework. Therefore, traditional product development often causes delays and increases costs dramatically. Concurrent engineering, on the other hand, is characterized by multifunctional teams working concurrently with an identical focus on customer needs and desires, with an explicit operating target.

Concurrent engineering has helped Boeing, John Deere, AT&T, and several other companies bring out products in less time and at lower cost. Concurrent engineering stands for teamwork. People from several departments collaborate over the life of a product to ensure that products satisfy customer needs and desires. Marketing, engineering, manufacturing, purchasing, and finance work together to foresee problems and bottlenecks, and to overcome them early on. Since most products involve parts bought from suppliers, vendors are also involved in concurrent engineering. This way a company can avoid delays and reduce costs.

Concurrent engineering involves much more than teamwork, however. Computer-aided design, engineering, and manufacturing play a major role. Integrating designs for manufacturing, automation, assembly, continuous process improvement, total quality control, recyclability, and other features, concurrent engineering tries to develop successful new products of high quality and low cost by bringing together the company's resources and experience. Concurrent engineering reduces overall product-development time by performing steps at the same time instead of in a series. By reducing product-development time, a company can retire a product from the market at close to its optimum profitability. It can be more responsive to customer demands and can produce the product at the lowest possible cost using advanced technology. Sequential development of a product inevitably leads to manufacturing rework, disparity between field performance and advertised specifications, and customer dissatisfaction. Concurrent engineering shortens the product introduction cycle, improves quality, reduces design iterations, shortens production time, and raises quality.

In order to implement concurrent engineering, a company should:

1. Evaluate the strengths and weaknesses of its current manufacturing process with structured analysis and data flow diagrams.
2. Review parts for manufacturability, serviceability, testability, and repairability.
3. Develop an integrated system to transfer computer-aided design and engineering representations to manufacturing equipment, thus eliminating transfer errors in tooling up fabrication and assembly.

Design Axiomatics

The design axiomatics proposed by Suh (1990) provide general principles to guide a designer's thinking and creativity toward product requirements. These principles are in the form of axioms such as "Maintain the independence of functional requirements (FRs)" and "Minimize the information content." Together, these two axioms mean that an optimal design has the minimum information content. In other words, each part should perform one and only one function.

Design Science

Design science, in addition to teaching creativity, proposes design catalogs of methods to achieve familiar functions. A typical design project may proceed with identification of product functions, determination of various methods to perform functions from design catalogs, and so on. (Roth, 1987). The German Standards Institute has published elaborate catalogs and standardized procedures for many industries.

New Manufacturing Methods

Computers are being used to reduce product development times. Computer-aided design (CAD) (Groover, 1987) helps an engineer try different designs and test their performance. Computer-aided engineering (CAE) helps in initial logical design processes such as analyzing design functions. Both CAD and CAE improve product quality, shorten development time, and lower costs of design. Computer-aided manufacturing (CAM) involves the use of computer in process control, cost estimation, work standards, and input media for numerically controlled machines. CAD/CAM, an integration of CAD and·CAM, takes design directly into the manufacturing stage. It helped IBM develop its laser printer by simplifying design, shortening product development time, and allowing cheaper assembly by hand (Fortune, May 21, 1990). Rapid prototyping helps companies produce models, patterns, and prototypes in a matter of hours. A computer evaluates a CAD file that defines the product and creates cross sections of that product; the cross sections are then methodically produced using solidifications of liquids, powders, or solids combined to form a 3-D object.

Quality Function Deployment

Quality function deployment (QFD) (Hauser & Clausing, 1988) is a quality assurance system that pays special attention to customer needs and desires. Since QFD helps a designer respond effectively to the customer's voice, products can achieve faster market penetration and larger market share. Preservation of customer needs and desires, cross-functional teams, concurrent engineering, and concise graphical displays help QFD develop a product right the first time. QFD helps focus on the few characteristics that are most strongly linked to customer satisfaction. Product specifications are based on customer needs rather than supplier availability. House of Quality is a graphic representation used in QFD. It consists of areas for customer needs (whats), customer priority ratings, functional characteristics (hows), relationships between needs and characteristics (the whats and the hows), target values, technical importance of each how, and interaction among the hows.

Robust Design

Taguchi and Wu (1979) provide a novel approach to achieving product quality. According to Kackar (1986), Taguchi's ideas include quality as the total loss generated by a product to society, emphasis on continuous improvement and cost reduction, focus on reducing variations in product performance, ultimate quality and cost of a product determined by the engineering design, and determination of design parameters so as to reduce performance variations. Taguchi emphasizes focus on a target value rather than operating within tolerance limits. He proposes a quadratic loss function to express the customer's loss from a variation in product performance. With a view to establishing design parameters that reduce performance variations, Taguchi proposes statistically planned experiments. His methods have contributed to Japanese design superiority in several industries.

Competitive Benchmarking

Competitive benchmarking is a technique to improve a company's products and services by comparing them against their best performers (Camp, 1989). It involves selecting a function to benchmark, identifying the best in class for that function, choosing key performance variables, analyzing and comparing the data, predicting future performance by the benchmarked company, setting functional goals and developing action plans, and implementing and recalibrating of benchmarks.

CONCLUSION

The 1990s are going to be the Design Decade. To be successful in the 1990s, a company must accord the design function the same importance it gives finance, marketing, and other functions. A number of experts believe that Japanese design excellence is the principal reason for their worldwide success in manufacturing. In this chapter, we have summarized some of the new approaches being taken to improve the design function.

REFERENCES

Abler, R. A. "The Value Added of Design." *Business Marketing* (September 1986): 96-103.

Andreasen, M. M., S. Kahler, T. Lund. *Design for Assembly.* New York: IFS Publications and Springer-Verlag, 1983.

Andreasen, M. M., and T. Ahm. *Flexible Assembly Systems.* IFS Ltd., 1988.

Bolz, R. W. *Production Processes: The Productivity Handbook,* 5th Edition. New York: Industrial Press, 1981.

———. *Manufacturing Automation Management: A Productivity Handbook.* New York: Chapman and Hall, 1985.

Boothroyd, G., and P. Dewhurst. *Product Design for Assembly.* Wakefield, RI: Boothroyd Dewhurst, 1983.

Bralla, J. G., Ed. *Handbook of Product Design and Manufacturing.* New York: McGraw-Hill, 1986.

Business Week. Statement attributed to Norio Ohga, president of Sony, March 25, 1991, p. 52.

Business Week. April 20, 1992, p. 112.

———. May 8, 1989, p. 150.

Camp, R. C. "Benchmarking: The Search for Industry Best Practices That Lead to Superior Performance." Milwaukee: ASQC Quality Press, 1989.

"Design for Disassembly." *Industry Week,* June 17, 1991, pp. 44-46.

Dickinson, J. "Straining to See the Screen." *PC 3,* October 2, 1984, pp. 127-36.

Ealey, L., and L. G. Soderberg. "How Honda Cures 'Design Amnesia'". *McKinsey*

Quarterly Spring 1990.

Groover, M. P. *Automation, Production Systems and Computer Integrated Manufacturing*. Prentice-Hall International, 1987.

Hauser, J. R., and D. Clausing. "The House of Quality." *Harvard Business Review* (May-June 1988): 63-73.

Henstock, M. E. *Design for Recyclability*. London: Institute of Metals, 1988.

Holbrook, A. E. K., and P. J. Sackett. "Design for Assembly—Guidelines for Product Design." In *Developments in Assembly Automation*, edited by A. Pugh. New York: IFS Publications/Springer-Verlag, 1988, pp. 201-12.

Howard, W. "Bio Tech Add-Ons." *PC 3*, October 2, pp. 139-48.

"IBM Discovers a Simple Pleasure." *Fortune*, May 21, 1990, p. 64.

Jakiela, M. J., and P. Y. Papalambros. "A Design for Assembly Optimal Suggestion Expert Systems." *ICAA* (1986).

Kackar, R. N. "Taguchi's Quality Philosophy: Analysis and Commentary." *Quality Progress* (December 1986): 21-29.

Kotler, P., and G. A. Rath, "Design: A Powerful but Neglected Strategic Tool." *Journal of Business Strategy* 5 (2) (Fall 1984).

Mather, H. "Strategic Logistics—A Total Company Focus." In *Strategic Manufacturing*, edited by P. E. Moody. Homewood, IL: Dow Jones-Irwin, 1990.

Nevins, J. L., and D. E. Whitney, Eds. *Concurrent Design of Products and Processes*. New York: McGraw-Hill, 1989.

Oakley, M. *Managing Product Design*. New York: John Wiley, 1984.

Parsons, L. J. "Product Design." In *New Product Development and Testing*, edited by W. Henry, M. Menasco, and H. Takada. Lexington, MA: Lexington Books-D. C. Heath, 1989.

Redford, A. A., and E. Lo. *Robots in Assembly*. Open University Press, 1986.

Roth, K. "Design Models and Design Catalogs." Proceedings of 1987 International Conference on Engineering Design, ASME, Boston, pp. 60-67.

Stillwell, H. R. *Electronic Product Design for Automated Manufacturing*. New York: Marcel Dekker, 1989.

Suh, N. P. *The Principles of Design*. New York: Oxford University Press, 1990.

Swift, K. "Design for Optimum Assembly Costs." *Engineering* (August, 1982).

Taguchi, S., and Y. Wu. *Introduction to Off-line Quality Control*. Romulus, MI: American Supplier Institute, 1979.

Venkatachalam, A.R. "Design for Manufacturability, A Survival Strategy for the American Manufacturing Industry." *Industrial Management* (May/June, 1992): 7-10.

Wall Street Journal. Statement attributed to Joel Hirschhor, former official of Office of Technology Assessment, December 24, 1990, p. A1.

———. January 17, 1992, pp. A1, A6.

———. February 24, 1992, p. A11.

Whitney, D. E. *Manufacturing by Design in Managing Projects and Programs*. Boston, MA: Harvard Business School Press, 1989.

Witt, P. R. *Cost Competitive Products*. Reston, VA: Reston, 1986.

Chapter 20

Reducing Lot Sizes—Analytical Results and Techniques for Implementation

John F. Affisco, Farrokh Nasri, and M. Javad Paknejad

Flexibility is the keystone for effective competition in the 1990s and beyond. Global markets will demand an ever increasing variety of products whose life cycles are shorter than ever. To meet this challenge, manufacturers must reduce production and transportation time. Furthermore, setup time must be reduced so that batch sizes and inventory levels can be reduced as well.

To confirm the connection between lot size and flexibility, we turn to a set of examples. First, assume a machine processes five different parts, each of which requires a two-hour setup. The total run time is thirty hours, or six hours per part number. Assuming a forty-hour, five-day work week, we make one part per day with one daily setup. This means we carry, on average, one half-week's supply of each part. We are operating at capacity, which means any production problems require overtime or additional shifts. If we reduce setup time to three minutes, our operation will change correspondingly. If we were to follow the policy of a single setup per day with the same lot size, we would realize an additional capacity of 117 minutes but average inventory would remain the same. However, if we change the schedule so that each part is made daily, we achieve quite different results. This new schedule implies five setups per day of three minutes each and five smaller lots of one hour 12 minutes each. We still have available capacity of 105 minutes per day, but we carry only one half-day's supply of each part. We now have greater flexibility in what we produce and when we ship, since any combination lots of the five parts can be made on a given day—which was clearly not the case for the larger lots.

In this chapter we investigate the phenomenon of lot size reduction. First, we discuss some basic concepts related to setup cost reduction, and present some analytical results associated with setup cost reduction under deterministic conditions and conditions of variable lead time. Next, we do the same for the impact on lot sizes of lead time variability reduction. In the next two sections we discuss some basic techniques that reduce lot sizes and develop effective long-term suppliers. Finally, some concluding remarks are offered.

SETUP COST REDUCTION

Some Basic Concepts

Traditionally, the economic order quantity has been a major tool in production planning and inventory control. The classic economical order quantity (EOQ) may be expressed as

$$Q_o = \sqrt{\frac{2KD}{h}} \tag{1}$$

where

K = setup cost per setup

D = annual demand

h = holding cost per unit per unit of time

This relationship is obtained from the result that holding cost, h, and setup cost, K, are constant, and that total setup cost exactly equals total holding cost at the optimum. This is illustrated in Figure 20.1, where costs are plotted against order quantity. The straight line THC represents the annual total handling cost, the curve TSC1 represents the total annual setup cost, and the curve TIC1 represents the total annual inventory cost, which is simply the sum of THC and TSC1. The economical order quantity and the resulting optimal total inventory cost are represented by the points Qo1 and TICo1, respectively.

One clear implication of the use of the economical order quantity is that it causes trade-off thinking on the part of managers. Let us once again refer to Figure 20.1. If we were to operate at a lot size (order quantity) less than Qo1, total setup cost, TSC1, would increase faster than total holding cost, THC; THC would decline, resulting in an increased total inventory cost, TIC1. Managers who adhere to this model are unwilling to trade off smaller lot sizes for increased total costs. This position is compounded by cost systems that emphasize efficiency (standard earned hours vs. actual hours worked) and therefore dictate that equipment should be kept running as much as possible. Under this regime, since no parts are made while the equipment is being set up, the way to maximize standard hours earned, and thereby maximize efficiency, is to avoid setups and run as long as possible. This encourages supervisors to produce as much as possible before setting up again, even if it is not needed. It also encourages them to run as many as possible of the parts in which there is the highest contribution to efficiency, regardless of demand and timing of demand for these parts. Such policies clearly discourage setups, result in large manufacturing lot sizes, and severely limit manufacturing flexibility.

One major flaw in trade-off thinking is the assumption that setup cost is a constant. This may not be the case. For example, a basis for the Japanese just-in-time philosophy is that setup times and, thereby setup costs per setup, may be reduced. To determine the impact of reducing setup cost, we return to Figure 20.1. A reduction in setup cost per setup results in a downward shift in the total setup cost curve from TSC1 to TSC2, and an accompanying downward shift in the total inventory cost curve from TIC1 to TIC2. Further, the optimal order quantity is reduced from Qo1 to Qo2, and the corresponding optimal total inventory cost decreases from TICo1 to TICo2. Thus, reducing setup cost results in a smaller lot size, which, in turn, leads to improved flexibility and manufacturing performance.

Two questions remain. First, what magnitude of lot size reduction can be achieved through a program of setup cost reduction? Second, what level of investment is required to attain these reduced lot sizes? Various analytical studies aimed at answering these questions have been conducted in recent years.

Figure 20.1 EOQ and Inventory Costs

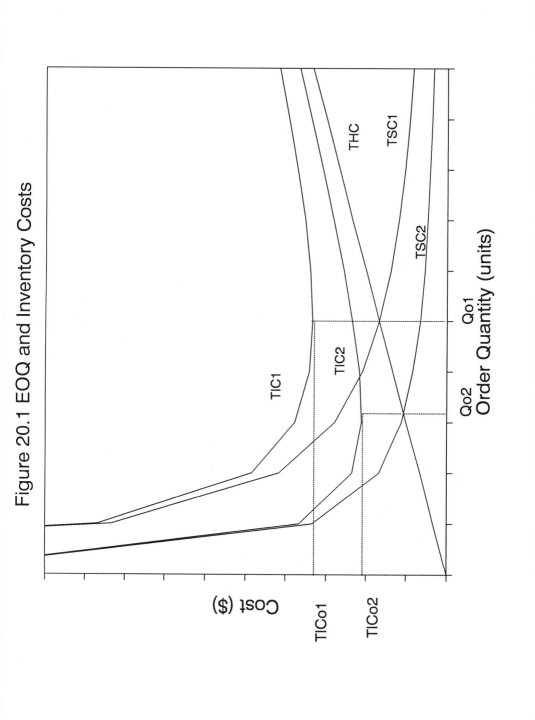

Some Analytical Results

The classic economical order quantity, which was presented as equation 1, is based on a series of assumptions about the nature of inventory systems. These include deterministic demand, constant lead time, instantaneous replenishment, and no stockouts or backorders, in addition to the constant setup and holding costs discussed previously. The analytical results that follow are based on more realistic models that result from relaxing one or more of these assumptions. A starting point for this research is the economical order quantity including backorders. This relationship may be expressed mathematically, where p is the backorder cost per unit per unit of time and all other variables are defined as before.

$$Q_o = \sqrt{\frac{2KD(h+p)}{hp}} \tag{2}$$

We can now consider investing in methods and/or technology to reduce the setup cost parameter, K, in this model. To accomplish this we must develop a mathematical representation of the dollar impact on setup cost of each dollar invested in methods or technology. Any such representation must follow the law of diminishing returns. That is, dollars spent early in a setup cost-reduction program should have a greater impact than those spent later. In fact, this property has been observed in many manufacturing situations, and it is reported as consistent with the Japanese experience in Hall (1983). A function that exhibits the required properties is the logarithmic function. Specifically, we assume investment occurs according to the following relationship:

$$K = K_o e^{-\delta a_K} \quad for \quad 0 \le a_K < \infty \tag{3}$$

where K_o is the original setup cost and δ is the percentage decrease in K per dollar increase in investment, a_K. When this is the case, the optimal setup cost and the optimal order quantity become:

$$K^* = \frac{2i^2b^2}{D}[\frac{h+p}{hp}] \tag{4}$$

where i is the cost of capital and $b=1/\delta$.

$$Q^* = 2ib[\frac{h+p}{hp}] \tag{5}$$

A numerical example will help us understand the impact of such an investment. Consider an example where the following parameters are known: $D=5,200$ units/year, $K_o=\$500$/setup, $h=\$10$/unit/year, $p=\$20$/unit/year, $i=0.10$, and $\delta=0.0002$. Table 20.1 presents the results of calculations for the economical order quantity including backorders, and the economical order quantity including backorders and investment in setup cost reduction (EOQ-INVEST). An annual investment of $1,773 results in an 83 percent decrease in order quantity with an accompanying 53 percent reduction in total inventory costs. Of course, additional savings will accrue owing to the increased flexibility occasioned by the smaller lot size. In any case we see that the impact of a setup cost-reduction program can be quite significant.

Table 20.1
Comparative Results for Setup Cost-Reduction Case

Variable	EOQ	EOQ-INVEST
Order quantity (units)	883.18	150.00
Setup cost ($)	500.00	14.42
Total inventory cost ($)	5887.84	2772.89
Percent decrease in order quantity	---	83.02
Percent total inventory cost savings over EOQ	---	52.90

$D=5,200$, $K_0=500$, $h=10$, $p=20$, $i=0.10$, $\delta=0.0002$

A more realistic case is one in which we relax the constant lead time assumption and allow for variability in lead time. *Lead time* is defined as the amount of time that elapses between the placement and receipt of an order. Variations in lead time can occur for both purchased items and those that are manufactured inhouse. These variations can result from a number of factors including transportation delays, internal quality problems causing lots to be shipped late, scheduling problems, and excessively large lot sizes. Such variability is introduced into the model by assigning a probability distribution to lead time. Sphicas and Nasri (1984) derive a relationship for EOQ with backorders when the range of the lead time distribution is finite. Specifically, the optimal order quantity Q^* is shown to be:

$$Q^* = \sqrt{\frac{2DK(h+p)+VD^2(h+p)^2}{hp}}$$

(6)

where V is the variance of the lead time distribution and all other variables are defined as before.

Typically, some type of buffering strategy is adopted to compensate for the uncertainty introduced into the inventory system by variable lead times. For statistical order point systems, this strategy involves holding a level of safety stock determined by the desired service level. For inventory planning systems, such as time phased order point and material requirements planning, either safety stock or safety lead time may be used. Regardless of which strategy is utilized, lot size is a major determinant of the level of additional inventory held. Therefore, in the case of lead time variability, the lot size not only has an impact on normal inventory costs but also is a major contributor to the additional inventory costs generated by the buffering strategy. As a general rule, the larger the lot size, the larger average inventory and the greater total inventory cost.

Consequently, an investigation of the impact of reducing setup cost on lot size and inventory costs under conditions of lead time uncertainty was warranted.

Nasri, Affisco, and Paknejad (1990) conducted such a study. Utilizing the logarithmic investment function previously presented as equation 3, they derive the following expression for optimal setup cost and optimal order quantity:

$$K^* = \frac{ib}{D}[\frac{h+p}{hp}][ib + \sqrt{i^2b^2 + hpD^2V}]. \tag{7}$$

$$Q^* = [\frac{h+p}{h}][ib + \sqrt{i^2b^2 + hpD^2V}]. \tag{8}$$

Table 20.2 presents the results of two numerical examples comparing the economical order quantity with variable lead time (EOQ-SLT) to the economical order quantity considering both the logarithmic investment function and variable lead time (EOQ-SLT-INVEST). All data are the same as for the example presented in Table 20.1 except, of course, for the addition of the lead time distribution parameters. First, we assume a uniformly distributed lead time over a one-week interval; this is equivalent to an average lead time of 0.5 week and a lead time variance of 0.0833 week (Heard & Plossl, 1984). For this case, investment in setup cost reduction results in a decrease of 80.59 percent in order quantity with an accompanying decrease in total inventory cost of 51.70 percent. In the second example we assume a normally distributed lead time over a one-week interval; this is equivalent to an average lead time of 0.5 week and a lead time variance of 0.0278 week (Heard & Plossl, 1984). Here the investment in setup cost reduction results in a decrease of 82.13 percent in order quantity and a decrease in total inventory cost of 52.48 percent. Note that a smaller lot size and greater savings in total cost are exhibited in the second case for which the lead time variance is smaller. This raises an interesting question: How does total cost change with increasing lead time variability?

Figure 20.2 is a plot of percent total cost savings achieved by investment in setup cost reduction versus lead time interval for both the uniform and normal cases. As lead time interval increases, which is equivalent to increasing lead time variability, percent total savings decreases at an increasing rate for both distributions. It is also evident that the rate of decrease is quicker for the uniform distribution than for the normal. This is to be expected, since equal lead time intervals imply greater lead time variability for the uniform case. An important implication of this result is that, when one invests in setup cost reduction to reduce lot size, there is also a significant incentive to reduce lead time variability so that the maximum relative total cost savings may be realized. In essence, then, one can see the logic of two major factors of the Japanese just-in-time philosophy: small lot sizes through engineering smaller setup times, and the co-maker concept to encourage vendors to reduce lead time variability through smaller and more frequent shipments. In fact, these two steps must be integrated to successfully achieve a true JIT system.

LEAD TIME VARIABILITY REDUCTION

The previous study points out the potential impact on lot size of lead time variability reduction. This potential is confirmed in practice. Heard and Plossl (1984) discuss the interaction between lead time variability and large lot sizes. They attribute

Figure 20.2   Percentage Total Cost
Savings Over EOQ-SLT

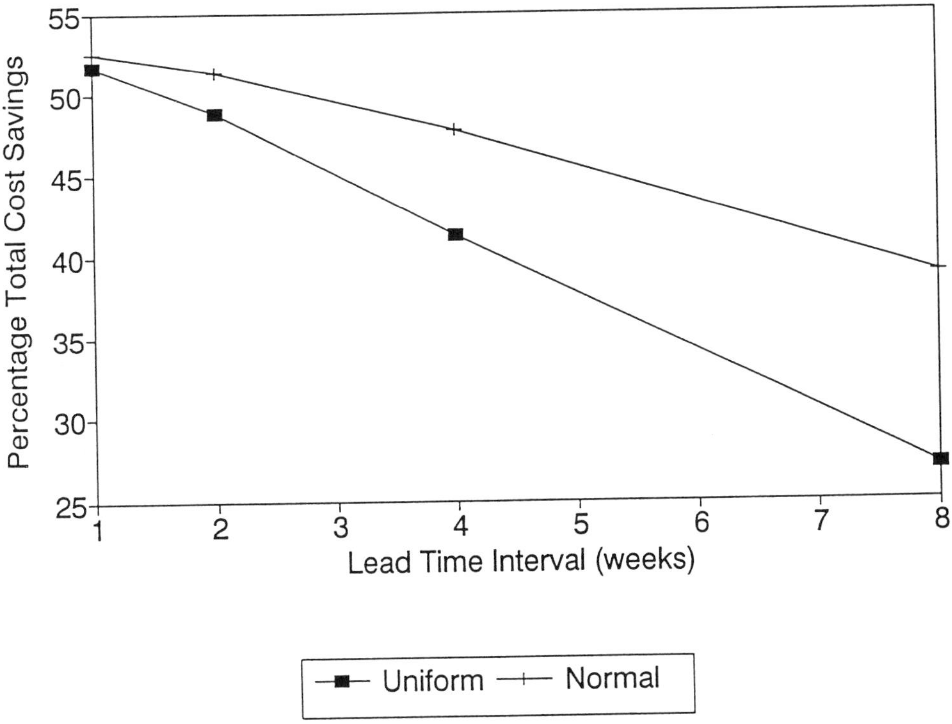

Table 20.2
Comparative Results for Uniform and Normal Lead Time

Variable	Uniform EOQ-SLT	EOQ-SLT INVEST	Normal EOQ-SLT	EOQ-SLT INVEST
Order quantity (units)	885.30	171.81	883.89	157.94
Setup cost ($)	500.00	16.52	500.00	15.19
Total inventory cost ($)	5901.97	2850.42	5892.57	2800.02
Percent decrease in order quantity	---	80.59	---	82.13
Percent total inventory cost savings over EOQ-SLT	---	51.70	---	52.48

$D=5,200$, $K_0=500$, $h=10$, $p=20$, $i=0.10$, $\delta=0.0002$

large lead time variability, in major part, to poor manufacturing engineering practices and large manufacturing run quantities. Specifically, manufacturing engineering creates high lead time variability through ineffective execution of its responsibilities for plant layout; processing methods selection; and setup, tool, fixture, and jig design. Large manufacturing lots (and long setup times), which are seen as spreading high setup costs and keeping unit processing costs down, contribute to high lead time variability by lengthening work order lead times and stores turnover times. Lead time variability also increases because large batches generally increase waiting times. It remains to determine the magnitude of the potential impact of investment in lead time variance reduction on order quantity. In the next section we discuss an analytical study that is directed at doing just that.

Some Analytical Results

Paknejad, Nasri, and Affisco (1992) derive relationships for optimal order quantity, optimal lead time variability, and so on for investment in reducing lead time variability and investment to simultaneously reduce lead time variability and setup cost.

In the first case they examine the issue of optimally determining the lead time variance. The lead time variance, V, is a decision variable. The cost per unit time of changing the lead time variance to V is $a_v(V)$. Once again a logarithmic investment function is used. This is justified based on the idea that lead time variability reduction should exhibit decreasing marginal returns. Further, since high lead time variability is inevitably related to poor manufacturing, it is conceivable that the steps taken to improve the manufacturing process through reduced setup time are analogous to that of lead time variability reduction.

In this case, lead time variance, V, declines exponentially as the investment amount a_v increases. That is:

$$V = V_0 e^{-\Gamma a_v} \quad for \quad 0 \le a_v < \infty \tag{9}$$

where V_0 is the original lead time variance and Γ is the percentage decrease in V per dollar increase in lead time variance reduction, a_v.

When this investment function is adopted, the optimal order quantity when investment in lead time variance reduction alone is allowed becomes:

$$Q^* = \frac{iB(h+p) + [(h+p)^2 i^2 B^2 + 2(h+p)hpDK]^{1/2}}{hp} \tag{10}$$

and the optimal lead time variance is:

$$V^* = \frac{2\{i^2 B^2 + [i^4 B^4 + (2i^2 B^2 hpDK)/(h+p)]^{1/2}\}}{hpD^2} \tag{11}$$

where $B = 1/\Gamma$ and all other parameters are defined as before.

In the second case, simultaneous investment in lead time variance reduction and setup cost reduction both follow exponential functions. Under these conditions the optimal order quantity is:

$$Q^* = [\frac{h+p}{hp}][2i(b+B)] \tag{12}$$

the optimal lead time variance is:

$$V^* = \frac{4i^2 B(b+B)}{hpD^2}, \tag{13}$$

and the optimal setup cost is:

$$K^* = [\frac{h+p}{hp}][\frac{2i^2 b(b+B)}{D}]. \tag{14}$$

A few numerical examples help us understand the comparative impact of each policy. Consider an example where the following parameters are known: $D = 2,600$ units/year, $K_0 = \$1,000/$setup, $h = \$5/$unit/year, $i = 0.10$, $\Gamma = 0.002$, and $\delta = 0.0002$. Table 20.3 presents the results of calculations for both the lead time variance reduction (LTV-INVEST) and the simultaneous (SIM-INVEST) models for a set of exponentially distributed lead times. The lead time distribution is truncated from above at twice the value of the mean to conform to the finite lead time assumption of the basic model presented previously as equation 5. For all three mean lead time values, both LTV-INVEST and SIM-INVEST result in optimal solutions to their respective problems. Regardless of the value of the initial lead time variance, the resulting optimal values of the lead time variance for each model are identical as are the optimal lot sizes; 3.371 weeks and 1264.09 units for LTV-INVEST, and 0.880 weeks and 330 units for SIM-INVEST (Heard & Plossl, 1984). For LTV-INVEST, this results in a 98.85 percent reduction in lead time variance for a mean lead time of 12.365, whereas a 6.57 percent reduction is realized for a mean lead time of 1.373 weeks. Similarly, in the case of

Table 20.3
Optimal Values for Lead Time Variance Reduction and Simultaneous Models

Variable	Mean Lead Time (weeks) LTV-INVEST			Mean Lead Time (weeks) SIM-INVEST		
	1.374	6.870	12.365	1.374	6.870	12.365
Order quantity (units)	1264.09	1264.09	1264.09	330.00	330.00	330.00
Initial lead time variance	3.608	90.201	292.251	3.608	90.201	292.251
Optimal lead time variance	3.371	3.371	3.371	0.880	0.880	0.880
Optimal setup cost ($)	1000.00	1000.00	1000.00	63.46	63.46	63.46
Percent reduction in lead time variance	6.57	96.26	98.85	75.61	99.02	99.70
Total inventory cost ($)	4217.03	4377.98	4436.75	2549.22	2710.15	2768.93

$D=2,600$, $K_0=1,000$, $h=5$, $p=10$, $i=0.10$, $\Gamma=0.002$, $\delta=0.0002$

SIM-INVEST, this yields a 99.70 percent reduction in lead time variance for a mean lead time of 12.365 weeks, whereas a 75.61 percent reduction is realized for a 1.374 mean lead time. This indicates that in both models there is a significant incentive for those faced with long lead times to invest to reduce them.

At this point, to determine the impact of these two models we compare their performance with that of the three models introduced previously—EOQ, EOQ-SLT, and EOQ-SLT-INVEST. Table 20.4 presents the results of this comparison. The EOQ-SLT-INVEST findings indicate that investment in setup cost reduction alone results in an order quantity of 1768.73 units, which represents a 13.26 percent reduction from EOQ-SLT but no reduction in lead time variance. The LTV-INVEST findings indicate that investment in lead time variance reduction alone results in an order quantity of 1264.09 units, which represents a 38.01 percent reduction from EOQ-SLT, and a lead time variance of 3.371 weeks (Heard & Flossl, 1984), which represents a 98.54 percent reduction. It is interesting to note that in this case there is some synergistic impact on lot size from the investment in lead time variance reduction. The most interesting and significant results are those for SIM-INVEST. These include a lot size of 330 units, which represents a 83.82 percent reduction from EOQ-SLT, and a lead time variance of 0.88 weeks (Heard & Plossl, 1984), which represents a 99.62 percent reduction. Thus, there is a meaningful interaction effect of simultaneous investment on both lot size and lead time variance. Simultaneous investment leads to a 81.34 percent reduction in order quantity when compared to investment in setup cost reduction alone and a 73.89 percent reduction in lead time variance when compared to investment in lead time variance reduction alone.

A major finding of this research is that there is significant synergistic impact of simultaneous investment in the reduction of setup cost and lead time variance. Therefore, setup cost reduction and measures to reduce lead time variability should be pursued concurrently. This result is consistent with suggested practice both in Japan and the United States.

REDUCING LOT SIZES IN PRACTICE

Now that we have presented research that indicates significant gains may be obtained from reducing lot sizes, we turn our attention to how this might be accomplished. While our discussion has, to this point, focused on reducing lot sizes via investing to reduce setup costs, actual efforts in manufacturing plants concentrate on reducing setup or changeover time. Since setup time accounts for the major portion of setup costs, they are essentially surrogates for each other. We may define *setup time* as the time that elapses between the production of the last good piece of the prior part to the production of the first good piece of the new part.

In general, setup time is distributed among four basic steps: (1) preparation, after process adjustment, checking of materials, tools, etc.; (2) mounting and removing blades, tools, parts, etc.; (3) measurements, settings, and calibrations; and (4) trial runs and adjustments.

The first step ensures that all parts and tools are where they should be and that they are functioning properly. Also included in this step is the period after processing when these items are removed and returned to storage, machinery is cleaned, and so on. This step typically accounts for 30 percent of the total setup time.

Step two includes the removal of parts and tools after completion of processing and attachment of the parts and tools for the next lot. This step usually accounts for just

Table 20.4
Comparative Results for Lead Time Variance Models (16-week mean lead time)

Variable	EOQ	EOQ-SLT	EOQ-SLT INVEST	LTV INVEST	SIM INVEST
Order quantity (units)	1249.00	2039.07	1768.73	1264.09	330.00
Optimal lead time variance	-	230.914	230.914	3.371	0.880
Optimal setup cost ($)	1000.00	1000.00	340.14	1000.00	63.46
Total inventory cost ($)	4163.33	6796.88	6434.96	4424.98	2710.15
Percent total cost savings over EOQ-SLT	-	-	5.30	34.90	59.44
Percent reduction in setup cost over EOQ-SLT	-	-	65.99	0.0	93.65
Percent reduction in lead time variance over EOQ-SLT	-	-	0.0	98.54	99.62
Percent reduction in order quantity over EOQ-SLT	-	-	13.26	38.01	83.82

$D = 2,600$, $K_0 = 1,000$, $h = 5$, $p = 10$, $i = 0.10$, $\Gamma = 0.002$, $\delta = 0.0002$

5 percent of the total setup time.

The third step refers to all the measurements and calibrations that must be made in order to perform a production operation, such as centering, dimensioning, and measuring temperature or pressure. In most cases this accounts for 15 percent of the total setup time.

During the last step, adjustments are made after a test piece is machined. The greater the accuracy of the measurements and calibrations in the previous step, the easier these adjustments will be. This step accounts for the remaining 50 percent of total setup time.

Setup operations may also be classified as internal (on-line) setup or external (off-line) setup. Internal setup can be performed only when a machine is shut down while external setup can be done while the machine is running. A new die can be attached to a press, for example, only when the press is stopped, but the bolts to attach the die can be assembled and sorted while the press is operating. Typical external setup tasks include preparation of dies, fixtures, and so on, and the transfer of dies. On the other hand, internal setup tasks include attachment and detachment; adjustment of location, height, pressure and so on, and test runs.

Various companies give slightly different accounts of what the key steps are in reducing setup times, but many of them have adopted the approach advocated by Dr. Shigeo Shingo, the noted Japanese manufacturing expert. The Shingo method (Shingo & Robinson, 1990), in part consists of four conceptual stages that must be included in any setup improvement program.

During the preliminary stage, internal and external setup conditions are not distinguished. This results in operations that could be done externally being done internally. Consequently, machines remain idle unnecessarily for extended periods of time. At this stage, actual setup operations must be studied in great detail. Techniques that have proved useful in the past for accomplishing this include stopwatch studies, work sampling studies, and worker interviews. Perhaps the best method available today is to videotape the entire setup operation. Best results are achieved if the videotape is shown to the workers immediately after the setup has been completed. This offers them the opportunity of analyzing the operation while it is fresh in their minds. Valuable insights about the process can result from this.

After the preliminary stage and during stage 1, we begin to separate internal and external setup. This is the most important stage in implementing a setup improvement program. Here we make a scientific effort to treat as much of the setup operation as possible as external setup, then the time required for internal setup can usually be cut from some 30 to 50 percent.

In stage 2 we convert internal to external setup. This stage involves two important notions. First, we reexamine operations to see whether any steps are wrongly assumed to be internal. Next, we find ways to convert these steps to external setup. Examples might include preheating elements that have previously been heated only after the setup has begun, and converting centering to an external procedure by doing it before production starts.

In stage 3, we attempt to streamline all aspects of setup operations. We focus here on individual tasks in internal and external setup, and attempt to simplify and streamline them. For example, we may reduce the time required for internal setup by eliminating adjustments, simplifying attachments and detachments, and adding a person for additional help. The last two stages need not be performed sequentially—in fact, they may be nearly simultaneous. But let us look at the last three of these stages in greater detail.

Three techniques useful in accomplishing the aims of stage 3 are using checklists, performing function checks, and improving transportation of dies and other parts. A checklist should be made of all the parts and steps required in a setup operation. This list is then used to double-check that there are no mistakes in operating conditions. By doing this before hand, you can avoid many time-consuming errors and test runs. A second check device is the check table. On a check table drawings are made of all the parts and tools required for a setup. The corresponding parts and tools are simply placed over the appropriate drawings before the internal setup is begun. Thus, the operator can save valuable operating time by visually determining whether any parts are missing prior to the beginning of internal setup. A specific checklist and table should be established for each machine.

While checklists are useful in determining whether all the required parts are available prior to internal setup, they do not assure that these parts are working properly. Consequently, it is necessary to perform function checks in the course of external setup. Parts and equipment found to be operating improperly must be repaired before internal setup is begun, so as not to interrupt production.

Parts have to be moved from storage to the machines, and then returned to storage once a lot is finished. This must be done as an external setup procedure in which either the operator moves the parts himself while the machine is running automatically, or another worker is assigned the task of transportation. Reduction in transportation time results from effective design of such procedures.

Two major steps are involved in converting internal to external setup. These are the advance preparation of operation conditions and function standardization. Let us look at two examples of the former from very different situations—a die casting plant and a fabric manufacturing plant—as presented in Shingo and Robinson (1990).

Trial shots are usually performed as part of the internal setup of die casting machines. Cold dies are attached to the machine and gradually heated to the appropriate temperature by injecting molten metal. The first casting is made. Since the material injected during the heating process will produce defective castings, items from the first casting must be remolded. If the die is preheated in some other fashion, however, good castings result from the first injections into the mold. Typically, gas or electric heat can be used for this purpose with a savings of one-half hour in internal setup time in addition to the improved quality of the initial casting. Another method is to use recycled heat from holding ovens to preheat the dies.

At a fabric manufacturing plant, dyeing operations had been conducted by immersing a rack holding a number of threads in a dyeing vat and then heating the vat with steam. This was a time-consuming internal setup because it took quite a while for the vat to reach the prescribed temperature. To solve this problem, a second vat filled with dye and preheated to the correct temperature was set up while the previous lot was being processed in the original vat. When the first lot was completed, a valve was opened in the second vat and the preheated dye was allowed to flow into the dyeing vat. Thus, by converting the heating operation to external setup, the internal setup time was reduced by eliminating the delay caused by heating the dye. This solution also had the effect of improving product quality by producing crisper colors.

Function standardization calls for standardizing only those parts whose functions are necessary from the standpoint of setup operations. To implement function standardization, individual functions are analyzed and then considered one by one. That is, general setup operations are broken down into their basic elements—for example, clamping, centering, dimensioning, expelling, grasping, and maintaining loads. The engineer must decide which of these operations, if any, need to be standardized. He must distinguish between parts that can be standardized and parts that necessitate setting changes. An excellent example of function standardization is the Volkswagen instrument panel. Although the exterior of the instrument panel for a new model was redesigned, the new instrument panel was attached in precisely the same way as the old one. Thus, neither the operation nor its required setup had changed.

In stage 3 we seek to improve all aspects of setup operations, external and internal. Workplace organization is the key to reducing external setup work. A review of the setup operation often reveals much time wasted in looking for tools, dies, and fixtures. Designating areas by color-coding shelves, and assigning addresses for each storage area are basic first steps. For example, Harley-Davidson, as part of its material-as-needed manufacturing improvement program, installed color-coded racks for storage of fixtures and dies on the shop floor, where it is easily accessible to the operator; in a second area, an existing shelving unit was enhanced with plastic tubs for the consolidation and storage of tools and gauges; and in a third area, fabricated small tool racks were added in which each compartment was labeled, so at a glance anyone could tell if a tool or gauge was missing.

Three techniques useful in decreasing internal setup time are the implementation of parallel operations, the use of functional clamps, and the elimination of adjustments. Operations on plastic molding machines, die-casting machines, and large presses invariably involve work at both the front and back of the machine. When a single person performs these operations, movement is continually being wasted as he or she walks around the machine. Assigning an additional operator to this task, so that one works the front of the machine while the other works the back, can significantly decrease the elapsed time required for the operation. The PERT technique can be useful in developing such operations by graphically displaying precedence relationships and those tasks which may be done in parallel. The PERT method also helps identify the critical path for internal setup and helps focus efforts to reduce it.

Clamping methods can be improved to reduce attachment and detachment time. The result of such improvement efforts is a functional clamp that is an attachment device serving to hold objects in place with minimal effort. For example, the number of bolts may be reduced, the bolt head may be standardized, or unnecessary threads may be eliminated so that only one turn is needed to accomplish attachment or detachment. Other functional clamps include pear-shaped holes, *u*-shaped washers, *u*-slots, and direct clamps.

Since adjustments account for 50 percent of setup time, clearly they are a major target for improvement. Test runs and adjustments are necessitated by inaccurate centering, or dimensioning earlier in the internal setup procedure. Therefore, to eliminate them we must improve the earlier internal setup tasks. One way to accomplish this is to substitute calibrations for intuitive judgments of the performance characteristics of machines. Calibration allows everyone to know what it means to "set the dial to three," and the same value can be set the next time. It eliminates imprecise intuitive judgments and replaces them with precise constant value settings. Graduated scales derived through calibration lead to significant improvements in setups involving a wide range of possible settings. In addition, installing modern, more accurate measurement devices for numerical settings may be a relatively simple way to achieve improvements.

Another problem is that when setup is actually being performed on a machine, no center lines or reference planes are visible. They must be found by trial and error, which can be a lengthy process. To compensate for this we may substitute visible center lines and reference planes for imaginary ones. A gear milling example comes, once again, from Harley-Davidson. The setup for the milling of pockets in the back side of gears involved changing one of the plates under the index unit to give the correct angle of cut. Each plate was slightly different in thickness and position. After changing the angle plate, the operator would then have to adjust the height and position of the table in relationship to the cutter. Besides the differences in the plates, a lift truck was required to do the changeover. This was unsafe, since it could lead to damage of the machine, the index unit, and the plates. To solve this problem a single plate with all the angles built in was fabricated. Now to do a setup the operator loosens one bolt, pulls the locating pin, and swivels the plate to the proper position. Lift trucks are no longer required and the potential damage to the equipment has been eliminated.

SUPPLIER DEVELOPMENT IN PRACTICE

Supplier development programs have a major impact in reducing lead time variance for purchased parts. A basic premise of JIT is that suppliers are part of a total manufacturing system. Essentially this means that supplier facilities are considered extensions of a manufacturer's own factory. To accomplish this, mutually beneficial long-term relationships with a limited number of suppliers must be established. Suzaki (1987) delineates the following important considerations when developing such supplier relationships:

1. From the supplier's point of view, manufacturers are customers. Suppliers should guarantee delivery, quality, and cost to the manufacturers. They should work closely to understand and incorporate the manufacturer's requirements in their services.
2. In the delivery area, frequent, small-lot, on-time deliveries should be targeted in order to make the manufacturer-supplier link tighter.
3. In the quality area, the idea of "quality at the source" should be practiced as much as possible.
4. In the cost area, improvement activities similar to those in the manufacturer's factory should take place.

An example of the successful implementation of a supplier development program is that of Harley-Davidson. Harley-Davidson's program is based on increasing business with a limited number of preferred suppliers on a long-term basis. To accomplish this, Harley-Davidson communicated the goals of its MAN program to supplier CEOs. Supplier MAN teams, made up of skilled individuals who had been deeply involved in improving Harley-Davidson's in-house manufacturing activities, were established. Once a commitment was obtained from a CEO, these teams trained people in JIT, statistical process control (SPC), and employee involvement (EI). Monthly sessions at each of the supplier's plants gave an overview of setup reduction, flow processing, lead time reduction, inventory reduction, stable schedules and consistent daily production, employee involvement, containerization, parts control, statistical process control, and preventive maintenance. These were supplemented by a two-day session on quality circle problem-solving techniques and three sessions on statistical process control techniques.

In addition to training the supplier, MAN teams have assisted suppliers in evaluating their operations. After the joint evaluation is developed, specific needs relating to JIT, SPC, and EI are defined and a joint development plan is agreed upon. From this plan flow all the activities that compose the development program for an individual supplier.

CONCLUSION

We have reviewed the area of lot size reduction, which is critical for any manufacturing improvement program. Specifically, we have investigated analytical results that illustrate the impact of setup cost reduction on lot size under deterministic and variable lead time conditions. In both cases the impact was shown to be significant with order quantity reduction—on the order of 80 percent. Further, reducing lead time variability simultaneously with setup cost reduction was shown to have a synergistic impact on lowering order quantity. Finally, we discussed techniques to accomplish these gains. The resulting reduction in setup times facilitates production changeovers, thereby making it possible to respond rapidly to changes in demand and substantially increase manufacturing flexibility.

REFERENCES

Hall, R. *Zero Inventories.* Homewood, IL: Dow Jones-Irwin, 1983.

Heard, E., and G. Plossl. "Lead Times Revisited." *Production and Inventory Management* 25 (3) (1984): 32-47.

Nasri, F., J. F. Affisco, and M. J. Paknejad. "Setup Cost Reduction in an Inventory Model With Finite-Range Stochastic Lead Times." *International Journal of Production Research* 28 (1) (1990): 199-212.

Paknejad, M. J., and J. F. Affisco. (1987). "Effect of Investment in New Technology on Optimal Batch Quantity." In *Northeast Decision Sciences Institute 1987 Proceedings*, edited by W. Naumes, Northeast Decision Sciences Institute, 1987, pp. 118-20.

———. "Lead Time Variability Reduction in Stochastic Inventory Models." *European Journal of Operational Research* 62 (3) (November 1992).

Shingo, S., and A. Robinson. *Modern Approaches to Manufacturing Improvement: The Shingo System.* Cambridge, MA: Productivity Press, 1990.

Sphicas, G., and F. Nasri. "An Inventory Model With Finite-Range Stochastic Lead Times." *Naval Research Logistics Quarterly* 31 (1984): 609-16.

Suzaki, K. *The New Manufacturing Challenge—Techniques for Continuous Improvement.* New York: Free Press, 1987.

Index

Contributors

WILLIAM ACAR is an Associate Professor at the Graduate School of Management of Kent State University. He received an MASc in MS/OR from the University of Waterloo, and a Ph.D. in systems sciences from the Wharton School of the University of Pennsylvania. He has published in various journals, including *Systems Research, INFOR, Public Finance, Journal of Enterprise Management, Commerce, Journal of Management, Behavioral Science, Journal of Applied Systems Analysis,* and *Decision Sciences.* Dr. Acar is the author of a causal mapping method for the analysis of complex business situations. This method is being used for developing an "intelligent" GDSS (group decision-support system).

JOHN F. AFFISCO is Associate Professor and Chairperson of the Department of Business Computer Information and Quantitative Methods at Hofstra University. He received his Ph.D. in business from the City University of New York Graduate School. Dr. Affisco's current research interests are total quality management and the application of decision support and expert systems to operations problems. His research has appeared in *International Journal of Production Research, European Journal of Operational Research, Quality Engineering,* and *Expert Systems with Applications,* among other journals. Dr. Affisco is a member and regional officer of the Decision Sciences Institute, and a certified member of APICS.

JOHN AHETO is an Associate Professor at Pace University. He has been teaching since 1973. He teaches accounting and finance and also coordinates the CPA Review Program at Pace University. He received his B.Sc. from the University of Ghana and his MBA and M.Ph. from New York University. Professor Aheto's research interests are in accounting, communication and technology transfers to foreign investments in less developed countries. Professionally, he is a CPA, CMA, and CIA. He is a member of the American Accounting Association (AAA); American Institute of Certified Public Accountants (AICPA); National Association of Black Accountants (NABA); Institute of Certified Management Accountants (ICMA), Colorado and Florida; State Society of CPAs; and American Finance Association.

BAY ARINZE is an Assistant Professor of Management Information Systems in the

Department of Management at Drexel University. He holds a B.Sc in computer science from the University of Lagos and an M.Sc. and Ph.D. in systems analysis from the London School of Economics and Political Science. His current research interests include DSS design methodologies and applications, and knowledge-based systems and their uses in operations management. He has published articles in *Journal of Management Information Systems, Decision Support Systems, IEEE Transactions in Engineering Management, International Journal of Man-Machine Studies, Computers and Industrial Engineering,* and *Computers and Operations Research.*

ADEDEJI B. BADIRU, P.E., is an Associate Professor of industrial engineering at the University of Oklahoma. He received his BS degree in industrial engineering, MS in mathematics, and MS in industrial engineering from Tennessee Technological University. He received his Ph.D. degree in Industrial Engineering from the University of Central Florida. His previous publications include Project Management in *Manufacturing and High Technology Operations* (John Wiley & Sons, 1988), *Computer Tools, Models, and Techniques for Project Management* (TAB Professional Reference Books, 1989), *Project Management Tools for Engineering and Manufacturing Professionals* (IIE Press, 1991), and *Expert Systems Applications in Engineering and Manufacturing* (Prentice-Hall, 1992). He is a member of IIE, SME, TIMS, ORSA, TIMS, PMI, and AAAI.

VASANTHAKUMAR BHAT is an Assistant Professor of Management Science at the Lubin Graduate School of Business, Pace University, New York. He has a Ph.D. in management science from Yale University; MS in industrial engineering from Asian Institute of Technology; and BS in mechanical engineering from the Indian Institute of Technology. His research interests include manufacturing systems, engineering design, and queueing theory.

MAHESH CHANDRA is an Associate Professor, Department of BCIS/QM, at Hofstra University, Hempstead, New York. He received his Ph.D. in operations research from George Washington University. His research interests are in the area of total quality management, expert systems, and telecommunications.

MICHAEL J. CORRIGAN is currently the Laboratory Systems Manager for the department of Pathology at Monmouth Medical Center, Long Branch, New Jersey.

NICHOLAS C. GEORGANTZAS is Associate Professor of Management Systems at the Martino Graduate School of Business, Fordham University at Lincoln Center, New York. He received his Ph.D. in management planning systems and M.Ph. in management science/operational research from the Graduate School and University Center/CUNY, an M.B.A. in production management from the Bernard M. Baruch College/CUNY; an M.B.A. in corporate and international finance from the University of Scranton, Scranton, Pennsylvania; and a B.A. in macroeconomic analysis and public accounting from the Graduate School of Industrial Studies, Piraeus, Greece. In 1987, his Ph.D. dissertation won the Oscar Lasdon Award for the Best Dissertation of the Year, Baruch College/CUNY. Primarily interdisciplinary, his research intermingles ideas from system dynamics, strategic management, and production management. Dr. Georgantzas has published and co-authored over thirty abstracts in refereed proceedings as well as numerous articles both in edited books and in refereed journals, including *Computers & Industrial Engineering, Computers & Operations Research, Decision Sciences, Engineering Management International, IIE Transactions, International Journal of*

Quality & Reliability Management, Journal of Education for Business, Management International Review, Managerial & Decision Economics, Mid-Atlantic Journal of Business, and *Technological Forecasting & Social Change.*

RUDOLPH A. JACOB is Professor and Chairman of the Accounting Department at Pace University. He holds a M.Ph. and Ph.D. in accounting from the Graduate School of Business, New York University. His articles have appeared in professional and academic journals. His teaching areas are managerial accounting and corporate financial policy.

CHU-HUA KUEI is Assistant Professor of Management at Monmouth College, New Jersey. He received his MBA in management information systems from the University of New Haven, and his Ph.D. in management planning systems from the City University of New York. He has contributed articles to *Computers and Operations Research, Long Range Planning, International Journal of Production Research,* and others. His current research interests include Total Quality Management, Strategic Information System, and Global Management.

CHINHO LIN is Associate Professor of Industrial Management Science at the National Cheng Kung University. He received his M.S. in industrial management from the National Cheng Kung University, his M.S. in operations research from Columbia University and his Ph.D. in business from the City University of New York. Dr. Lin's research interests include manufacturing strategy, total quality management, queueing network and FMS, and simulation metamodel. His recent paper has appeared in the *International Journal of Production Research.*

ASSUMPTA N. MADU is an resident at Montefiore Medical Center at Albert Einstein College of Medicine, Bronx, New York; she holds an MD from Albert Einstein College of Medicine; Doctor of Pharmacy degree from St. John's University and a B.S. in Pharmacy from SUNY at Buffalo. She also did a Fellowship in toxicology at New York City Poison Control Center. She is a registered pharmacist in the State of New York and previously worked as Clinical Coordinator of Pharmacokinetics and Research at Montefiore Medical Center, and as Poison Specialist at New York Poison Control Center. She has published articles in *Long Range Planning* and *Antimicrobial Agents and Chemotherapy.*

CHRISTIAN N. MADU is Professor and Program Chair of Management Science at the Lubin School of Business, Pace University. His articles on technology management have appeared in journals such as *Long Range Planning, IIE Transactions, Reliability Review, Technological Forecasting and Social Change, Futures, Journal of Technology Transfer,* and *Engineering Management International.* He is the author of *Strategic Planning in Technology Transfer to Less Developed Countries* (Quorum Books, 1992).

FARROKH NASRI is Assistant Professor of Business Computer Information Systems and Quantitative Methods at Hofstra University. He holds a Ph.D. from the City University of New York, M.B.A. from Baruch College, and another M.B.A. from St. John's University. He has publications in *Naval Research Logistics Quarterly, International Journal of Production Research, European Journal of Operational Research, ZOR Methods and Models of Operations Research,* and *OMEGA* (International Journal of Management Science). In addition, he has published numerous articles, including an award-winning paper in various proceedings. He is a member of the Institute of

Management Sciences, Decision Sciences Institute, the Production and Operations Management Society, Canadian Operations Research Society, and the Association for Computing Machinery.

ROY NERSESIAN is Associate Professor and Chair of the Management Department, Monmouth College, West Long Branch, New Jersey. He has an MBA from Harvard Business School. His research is mostly in computer simulation. He wrote three books on the application of computer simulation to business, (Quorum Press).

CHIMEZIE A. B. OSIGWEH, YG., is Distinguished Professor of Management at the Norfolk State University, Virginia. He holds a Ph.D. in human resources management, labor relations, and international relations from Ohio State University; an M.L.H.R. in human resources management and labor relations, and an M.A. in international relations, political science; and a B.Sc. in special education and political science from East Tennessee State University. His research interests include employee responsibilities and rights and concept formation in organizational science. He has published articles in *Academy of Management Review, Journal of Management, Journal of Management Development, Group & Organizational Studies, Policy Studies Review, Public Personnel Management Journal, Journal of Management Case Studies, Case Research Journal, Educational Evaluation and Policy Analysis, College Teaching, Journal of Business Education,* and *Journal of Education for Business*. He has also published several books.

M. JAVAD PAKNEJAD is Assistant Professor of Business Computer Information Systems and Quantitative Methods at Hofstra University. His publications have appeared (or will appear) in the *International Journal of Production Research, European Journal of Operational Research, ZOR Methods and Models of Operations Research, OMEGA* (International Journal of Management Science). In addition, he has published numerous papers, including an award winning paper in various proceedings. He is a member of the Institute of Management Science, Decision Sciences Institute, and the Production and Operations Management Society.

MICHAEL SEGALLA is Visiting Professor of Management at Hautes Etudes Commerciales (Groupe HEC), Jouy-en-Josas, France, and Assistant Professor of Management (on leave) at The City University of New York, Baruch College. His research interests center on the human resource management and industrial relations implications of the internationalization process. He has conducted research on European human resource management practices, managerial attitudes toward human resource management in Eastern Europe, and international labor conflict.

JACK SHAPIRO is Professor of Management and Director of the Center for Management at Bernard M. Baruch College of the City University of New York. Prior to assuming his present duties he was Chairman of the Department of Management for six years. Before joining the university sixteen years ago, he was President and Chief Executive Officer of Ogden Technology Laboratories, Inc., a subsidiary company of the Ogden Corporation. He was founder and associated with Ogden Technology Laboratories, Inc. and its predecessor company for twenty-five years. It was the second largest organization of its type in the country. Dr. Shapiro is a graduate professional engineer with several publications and a patent in the aerospace field. He has a BME cum laude from City College, CUNY, and MS in Management Engineering from Long Island University, an MBA from Baruch College, CUNY, and a Ph.D with distinction from the Graduate Center, CUNY. He is the co-author and co-editor of three books in the field of management and has had over fifty articles published in various journals such as *Management Science*, *Decision Science*, *Academy of Management Journal*, *Academy of Management Review*, and *Long Range Planning*. He has sat on several corporate boards of directors and is active in the field of strategic management as a researcher and consultant. He was a Governor of the Eastern Academy of Management.